Parting with Illusions

PARTING WITH ILLUSIONS

◄◆►

VLADIMIR POZNER

Introduction by Brian Kahn

THE ATLANTIC MONTHLY PRESS
NEW YORK
◆

Published simultaneously in Canada
Printed in the United States of America

Library of Congress Cataloging in Publication Data

Pozner, Vladimir
  Parting with illusions.
    1. Pozner, Vladimir   2. Journalists—
Soviet Union—Biography. I. Kahn, Brian. II. Title.
PN5276.P68A3 1990   070'.92   89-18224
ISBN 0-87113-287-7

Design by Laura Hough

The Atlantic Monthly Press
19 Union Square West
New York, NY 10003

FIRST PRINTING

‹◆›

Acknowledgments

This book took a long time to happen. I first attempted to write it some fifteen years ago, an attempt that failed. Over the years, I sat down with pen and paper, with a typewriter, and finally with a computer, all with the same result. For some reason, the brew would not come to a boil; some ingredient was missing. It turned out to be travel, the possibility of returning to my roots—to France, where I was born, and to America, where I grew up. But when that happened at last, I no longer had the time to sit down and write, for the demands of my work were overwhelming—at least so I thought. Had it not been for Brian Kahn, who came walking into my hotel room in Washington, D.C., during the Reagan-Gorbachev summit of December 1987; had he not, upon interviewing me for an article, suggested that I write a book; had he not then come to Moscow for several months to work for the *Moscow News* while simultaneously filing stories for the *Los Angeles Times;* had he not come barging into my apartment every morning to ask endless and sometimes brutal questions, taping my answers for hours on end; had he not then spent weeks and months typing up what he had taped, whipping my rambling thoughts into four draft chapters and spending more weeks trying to interest an agent in the United States—had Brian not done all of these things, thereby putting me under the moral obligation to write, I might still be thinking about writing it.

I must also thank Ann Godoff, whose amazing understanding of what I was attempting to say and unflagging support for what I was trying to do gave me strength and confidence when I most needed it. As my one-time mentor Samuel Marshak used to say, "Talented writers are rare, talented editors are unique." I have been unbelievably lucky.

❖

I dedicate this book
To the memory of Geraldine and Vladimir Pozner,
without whom I could not have been.
To the memory of Iosif Gordon,
without whom I could not have become.
To Kathrin,
without whom I could not be.

Contents

Introduction

I first met Vladimir Pozner because of an exquisitely beautiful bird that lives on the brink of extinction—*Grus grus*, the Siberian crane. After half a dozen trips to the Soviet Union, I had finished a television documentary depicting United States–Soviet cooperation to save this endangered species. The film parable about our collective choice between survival and extinction in the nuclear age was well received, and in the summer of 1987 the film was selected for screening at the Moscow International Film Festival. It was there, in the halls of the mammoth Rossiya Hotel, that I met Pozner.

I did not expect to like him. The few times I had seen him on television he had struck me like most of his American commentator peers—glib and lacking depth. But in our half-hour talk, Pozner surprised me. He was a good listener, and his comments about perestroika and environmental issues were thoughtful and sober.

Six months passed before our paths crossed again. In December, Mikhail Gorbachev came to Washington for a summit. Pozner was there. A quick interview, I thought, could surely net something quotable for the piece I was writing on the summit's long-term implications.

Because of his heavy interview and television schedule, it took a while to track him down. Finally, at eleven at night we met in his hotel room. Tired and drawn, Pozner sat in a stuffed chair, sipping a Coke, while I set up the tape recorder.

What I thought would be a few pithy answers to several questions turned into something very different. His responses were lengthy and thoughtful and reflected a highly unorthodox view of what was happening at the summit and, more importantly, in the world. His style of talking, of *thinking,* was informal and, well, *American.* After half an hour I turned off the recorder.

"Why don't you talk this way on television?"

There was a trace of a smile. "They don't ask me these kinds of questions."

I told him he ought to do a book about the issues we were discussing, the changes unfolding in the Soviet Union, in America, the world. "Except for Gorbachev, you're probably the only Soviet who can communicate effectively with Americans. You've lived in both societies. You see things other people don't."

He said that he had wanted to write a book for a long time. He'd hoped to write a novel—then shelved the idea but not abandoned it. A book on Soviet perestroika and America? He'd thought about it, he said, but with his Soviet and foreign television work, he just didn't have the time.

I told him how my father, the late author Albert E. Kahn, had written a book with Pablo Casals. He had interviewed Casals for many hours about his life, work, and views, then shaped the taped transcripts into chapter form. Casals had reviewed the chapters, making any changes he saw fit. The book (*Joys and Sorrows*) was truly Casals, written in the first person, the words his. But the time he spent working on it was immeasurably less than if he had written it himself. "You could do the same thing," I said.

"All right," he said. "Let's do it."

In fact our agreed-upon work method would not produce a book. Rather it would result in a skeletal framework that would require Vladimir to do precisely what he felt he lacked the time to do—sit down and write a book. But sitting in his hotel room, neither of us foresaw that.

Personally, I was as pleased as I was surprised that he agreed to undertake the project. Pleased, because with the United States and the Soviet Union in the midst of a historic realignment, I was to be part of a project that could shed some light on that process. Surprised, because the idea and the decision had come so unexpectedly, so quickly, so easily.

Why had Pozner decided to do it, I asked myself over the next few days. The only answer I could find was that he must see in the book the same potential that I did. I was soon to learn that I was only partially correct.

Six weeks later I arrived in Moscow, having assured myself a two-month stay by arranging to write a weekly column for both the *Los Angeles Times* and the *Moscow News*. Sixty days was not much time to complete interviews for a book, but Vladimir had agreed to make the project his first priority. Once I arrived, however, other obligations intervened. An unexpected overseas trip knocked out the first week. An important television special had to be done . . . "Sorry, I have to be at the office all day."

After two weeks we had taped only one or two hour-long sessions. I was worried. Was Vladimir getting cold feet?

And there was another problem. Pozner's views, as I had found in Washington, were both unorthodox and provocative. But it had become clear to me in contemplating the book that unless the reader understood who Pozner was as a person, what life experiences had shaped his views, the book would have limited appeal. I explained this to him and he immediately resisted.

"This is not going to be any autobiography," he said emphatically. "I want to say what I think about important issues. Period."

"Fine. But unless the reader learns through the book what personal events shaped your thinking, how you came to see things the way you do, they simply won't read it. People will want to know who is talking to them—what kind of human being? For example, Americans will take your views about America a lot more seriously if they know you grew up in New York, if they come to know how New York shaped you as a person."

Pozner reluctantly agreed to discuss personal issues—but only so long as he felt them relevant to the political or philosophical questions under discussion. The tug-of-war between political and personal focus continued for the full two months. Initially, I thought his reluctance to discuss personal experiences was simply a reflection of the traditional Soviet view that autobiographies are immodest. But over time it became clear that exploring the experiences that shaped Vladimir's most strongly felt views—his relationship with his father, his feelings about being Jewish, what he learned in his New York school, or his reaction to seeing Stalin's corpse lying in state—was forcing him to examine himself in ways with which he was not entirely comfortable.

His discomfort was displayed in various ways. Here we were, collaborating on a book we both wanted to see written. Yet Vladimir, a humorous and friendly person, was often cool and distant. Never once during my visits to his Moscow apartment did he offer me a cup of tea or even a glass of water. His tone and body language during interviews varied dramatically—from forward-leaning intensity and eager exploration of a controversial point to sitting back, voice reluctant and words flat, never refusing to answer but skirting the central issue. As time passed, I came to understand that Vladimir Pozner was involved in more than writing a book. Much like his country, he was wrestling with the innermost parts of himself, driven to search through his life, to reexamine the dark and the light, to come to grips with what he believed to be true. And simultaneously, he was repelled by the prospect.

I was not oblivious to the risks for him. His views on central issues—freedom of the press and conscience, the right to travel, the Soviet Communist Party's monopoly on political power—differed from the official positions of the party of which he was and remains a member. Each day I left his apartment with tapes of his voice saying things that only a year or so earlier would certainly have cost him his job, ended his career. And even though Gorbachev was in power and the winds of change were blowing, the consequences of Pozner's views being known were far from certain. The titanic struggle between Soviet reformers and reactionaries was (and remains) in full swing. Should Gorbachev fail, or his policies be reversed, the impact on Pozner would be swift and severe.

The issue surfaced one morning when I asked a particularly sensitive question. Vladimir paused. And the silence pushed me to say what had been on my mind.

"Look. I know you are taking all the risk in this. It's easy for me to ask the questions. I don't have to answer. But that is my job—to push as far as you will go. Only you can decide how far that is."

He looked at me for a few seconds. "I understand your role. I've thought about this a great deal. I have reached the point in my life where I have to say precisely what I feel, let the chips fall where they may. This may be my only chance."

In April I left Moscow with the tapes—more than thirty hours of them. Back home, I transcribed them, then worked some into several draft chapters. They were forceful and would be provocative. Still, in key areas, depth was missing. Angus Cameron, an old friend and a retired senior editor at Alfred A. Knopf, read the samples. "Tell him he has to be willing to reveal himself fully. There is no other way."

When Atlantic Monthly Press bought the rights to the book, Ann Godoff became Vladimir's editor. Her concise and forceful analysis paralleled Angus's.

Pozner took the draft chapters and the transcripts and began to write the book in earnest.

Vladimir Pozner has taken the final step. He has revealed himself fully. It is an act of courage—and not simply because of the political and personal risks. It is an act of courage because he has exposed to all of us, including those who are his deadly serious enemies, not only his acts of courage but his moments of weakness as well; not only his deepest convictions but his innermost doubts.

In his final chapter, Vladimir writes that the book is the story of one man's search for truth. It is that, but it is also more. It is the story of the search for truth of a man who was raised in the America of the Great Depression and World War II, adopting some of our finest democratic, egalitarian traditions; who grew up with romantic illusions about Soviet socialism and began a wrenching confrontation with Stalinist reality when, at age nineteen, he arrived in Moscow; who is, in fact, a "citizen" of two nations that for most of his life have been engaged in unceasing, merciless political warfare—a warfare that profoundly shaped his consciousness, and that of every reader of this book, as well.

Vladimir Pozner's personal search gives us a unique window through which to comprehend the searing questions being raised by Soviet perestroika. And he provides us with something else. Because he grew up "American," because he was with us in the depression and the war, because he lived through the quintessential shift from alliance to cold war, because, for reasons he did not comprehend, he stayed in touch with America for nearly four decades, finally being able to return to see firsthand what had changed and what had not—because of all these things, he provides us with a chance to take an honest look at ourselves. In the fifty-odd years about which he writes, where have we come from as a people, a nation, a world? Where do we now stand? And where, as we glimpse the horizon of the twenty-first century, do we want to go?

BRIAN KAHN
October 25, 1989

Parting with Illusions

1

⟨◆⟩

My America

I remember one afternoon of my childhood distinctly. I was upstairs in the country home of my mother's friends, playing with a little boat that had a string attached. I couldn't untie the string. Try as I could, the knot would not give way. It didn't take me long to conclude that the boat was the cause of my frustration. I slammed it down on the floor and began to kick it around. I was mad as a hornet. Then my mother appeared.

"Why don't you go downstairs?" she said. "There's a man down there who is very good at untying knots."

I went downstairs, and there was this man sitting on the sofa. My memory may be playing tricks on me, but I recall his eyes: yellow and flecked with green and distinctly laughing at me. Not that I really cared. All I wanted was that the string be untied. So I walked up to him and said hello and asked if he would please untie the knot. He said, "Well, I'll try," and he took the string and began to work on it. I was watching him very, very closely, and for some reason was struck by a kind of bump that he had on the ring finger of his left hand. He untied the knot easily, which somehow made me feel stupid, and handed me the boat. I said thank you. And my mother said, "This is your father."

He had come to America to take us back to France. I was five years old.

I don't recall being particularly impressed by that meeting. Nor do I recall having missed a father during the first five years of my life. I hadn't had a dad and now I did, it was as simple as that. And as I tunnel back through the years to that now distant day, there is no jolt, no hint of goose-flesh, no quickening of the heart, none of the telltale signs that your memory has jangled the wires of recognition.

And yet this was a fateful moment, for had my father not come for us, my entire life would, beyond a question of a doubt, have taken an entirely different course.

My mother was French, one of four girls and a boy born into a fine family, one of whose forebears had been awarded a barony by none other than Napoleon. Being of the nobility quickly became part of family legend and lore, a fact of enormous magnitude. I realized this fully in 1980, when my mother's cousin had me and my wife over to his Paris home for dinner. He ushered us into the presence of a painting of "Grand-grand-grand-grandpapa" and the framed baronial scroll as if this were nothing less than the Holy Grail.

My mother looked on the barony with irony and was far prouder of another ancestor, France's first great suffragette, Eugenie Niboyet. When a commemorative matchbox bearing that lady's semblance and a quote from her work of 1848, *La voix des femmes,* was issued in France in 1982, I know this thrilled my mother more than any aristocratic title ever could have.

But while the family heritage satisfied both its vainer and its more socially minded members, and in that sense had much to offer, it was sadly lacking in one area: money. Thus it came to pass that my maternal grandmother, a brilliant, beautiful, and highly educated woman who had inherited virtually nothing and was twice widowed before the age of thirty-five, had to shift for herself and her five children. This involved a variety of activities, from running a bed-and-board château in France to teaching aristocratic manners and French to rich brats in Peru. My mother never forgot her childhood trip to Lima over the Andes, hanging in a mule basket and looking down into a bottomless chasm. Perhaps that is when, at the age of three or four, she acquired her fear of heights, a fear she was never fully to overcome.

As the children moved with their mother, they were schooled here, there, and everywhere until, finally, they were put into boarding schools, my mother at a Catholic convent in Dumfries, Scotland. After finishing her studies there, she returned to Paris, where she got a job as an assistant cutter at the local Paramount film studio. Soon after that, she met my father.

To say that his background differed from hers is to say nothing. They were opposites in just about every imaginable respect. My father's ancestors, Spanish Jews, had fled the Inquisition and wound up in the Polish city of Poznań—hence the name Pozner. Centuries later, when that country found itself incorporated into the Russian Empire, one of the more enterprising Pozners must have come to the conclusion that in a country of centralized power and authority, the action was at the center, in the capital city of St. Petersburg. And so there he went. One of his no less enterprising, but certainly less principled, descendants, whose guiding rule must have been "If you can't beat 'em, join 'em," converted from Judaism to the Russian Orthodox church, thereby bestowing upon that particular strain of Pozners the privileges of being Russian and, even more specifically, freeing them from the discrimination practiced against the Jews.

My father and his two sisters attended one of St. Petersburg's finest gymnasiums, never having to think about the 5 percent quota for Jews—just as their father had been able to enroll at and graduate from the Institute of Road Engineers, the doors of which were closed to Jews, and had later even been sent by the imperial government to America to study the most modern techniques of bridge building. Somehow I feel that my paternal ancestors were glad to be relieved of their Jewishness. I know my father never expressed any sense of kinship with the Jewish community. Though fluent in many languages, he did not speak Yiddish, let alone Hebrew, and they showed no interest whatsoever in learning it or in Jewish culture in general. The Pozners were atheists (the one who converted to Russian Orthodoxy was presumably not motivated by religious considerations), but that did not stop them from dyeing eggs, baking kulich and making paskha on Russian Easter, or from enjoying gefilte fish at the appropriate time. This readiness to celebrate religious feasts in form but not in content is, it seems to me, quite characteristic of the Russian intelligentsia. Nowhere have I seen people gather together to celebrate Easter according to the Gregorian calendar (the one modern civilization lives by), Easter according to the Julian calendar (adhered to by the Russian Orthodox church and lagging thirteen days behind [symbolically?]), and Passover according to the Jewish calendar with greater enthusiasm than in the Soviet Union. The same applies to Christmas, celebrated both on December 25 and January 7. Needless to say, none of these are national holidays in a country with an atheistic philosophy, but neither are the vast majority of those who celebrate on such occasions believers.

On the other hand, New Year is a national holiday, at least the one feted on the night of December 31. But Old New Year is marked on January 13.

In short, my father was born into a typically Russian intellectual milieu, where open-mindedness, tolerance, and thought-provoking debate were no less a part of the daily diet than buckwheat kasha for breakfast. When the revolution of February 1917 that overthrew the czar was followed in November by the Bolshevik revolution, the Pozners, like most Russian intellectuals, applauded. My father, who was nine years old at that time, never forgot those heady days with their promise of brotherhood, liberty, and equality, with Alexander Blok's Jesus Christ wearing a crown of white roses and leading the revolutionary march, with the Baltic Sea sailors in their traditional black jackets and bells, caps rakishly pushed low over their eyes or perched on the back of their heads, cartridge belts crisscrossing their chests, rifles slung over their shoulders as they strode resolutely past to stop General Yudenich's drive on Red Petrograd. These were images and ideas my father carried with him to his last day; they had a lasting impression and profoundly affected his outlook. Certainly not a sentimental man or one to demonstrate his emotions, I saw him cry three times in my life. Once in 1940, as we were leaving Marseilles and he was parting, perhaps forever, from his sister; once in 1969, when he had been forced to retire and had seen his most cherished dreams destroyed by an all-powerful and indifferent bureaucracy; and once when we were watching a movie about the revolution that showed a company of sailors, soldiers, and workers tramping by and singing the words of the old Russian marching song: "Our wives are the loaded cannon."

When I saw tears streaming down his cheeks and asked what was wrong, he told me how that song took him back to his childhood, to Petrograd of 1918, to the men who were indeed married to cannons, who fought, first on the fronts of World War I, then during the revolution, then during the civil war, who never had the time to fall in love, marry, have children, and who sang this song as a kind of bittersweet joke about themselves, poor cannon fuckers whose babies brought only death and destruction, a song that had wrenched his heart as a boy.

In 1922, the Pozner family emigrated from Soviet Russia.

By that time, the civil war was over and it was clear that the Bolsheviks had come to stay. It was also clear that the revolution had not fulfilled everyone's expectations—at least not my grandfather's. And so, along with hundreds of thousands of others, my father found himself in the ranks of the Russian émigrés in Berlin. After three years there, during which time his parents separated, he moved to Paris with his mother and sisters. His father established residence in Kaunas, capital of Lithuania.

He completed his high-school education in Paris and then went to work doing all kinds of jobs to help support his ailing mother and younger sister (Lola, the elder, had married an American and gone to the United States). His closest friends were all former Russians who, like himself, had been forced by circumstances to leave their country. He met most of them while finishing his studies at the Russian-French Lycée, a school created specifically for Russian émigrés. The ties born there were further cemented when my father and a couple of his buddies founded the BBCR—Basketball Club Russe—a team of dedicated cagers who started out at rock bottom in the last league and went on to become French national champions. More than a ball club, it was a family. As I write these words, some of the original players are still around. Well into their late seventies and early eighties, they still meet on Sundays to pass the ball around and take shots—and they are still amazingly good.

My father found a job in the movie business thanks to Vova Barash, a Russian friend who worked for Paramount. True, Paramount had no openings at that moment, but MGM did. There my father met Iosif Gordon, another expatriate. These two men were his closest friends. They roomed together for several years, sharing wine, women, and wild escapades until 1936, when Iosif, more commonly called Yuz or Papashka, returned to the Soviet Union. My father would not see him again for nineteen years, this friend who was to play a major part in my life.

The Vova Barash story is worth telling separately. A kind, compassionate, loving, and hysterically funny man who had all of his neighborhood in stitches when he did a parody of Hitler from his apartment balcony, Barash was one of those who reported to the Gestapo in occupied Paris when all Jews were ordered to report. He put on the armband with the Star of David when the Gestapo ordered Jews to wear it. His French friends couldn't believe it. "Don't you understand," they would say, "the Germans live by *Ordnung,* for them *verboten* is sacred because the rules are sacred, if you refuse to play their game, they don't know what to do with you. If you play it, you are dead." Barash wouldn't believe them. One day two French gendarmes came to see him. They informed him that later that day they would come to pick him up and take him away. "Be ready," they said. They looked him deep in the eyes and left. Barash got their message but refused to believe that anything serious could happen, so he hid halfheartedly in his garden. That evening, the two gendarmes came back accompanied by a detachment of German soldiers. They looked through the house and, failing to find its owner, checked the garden, where they found Barash crouching behind a lilac bush. They took him away. The next day, one of the gendarmes came back to see Barash's wife. "We risked our lives for that prick," he said, "and if that is what Jews are about, they deserve what they get." Years later, my father learned that story and told it to me. For some reason, I have never forgotten it.

The movie business brought my mother and father together. That was in 1930 or 1931. I was born in Paris in 1934 and formally baptized in the Catholic faith Vladimir Gerald Dimitri Pozner—in honor of my father, Vladimir; my mother, Geraldine; and one of my father's closest friends who also acted as my godfather. Whether being born on my mother's birthday, April 1, was meant as a sign that there would always be a very special bond between us is anyone's guess. But the fact that I spent the first five years of my life without a father could not but have left its imprint on me. As my mother told me many years later, my father was not overjoyed at the prospect of being tied down with a baby. My mother, who in her own quiet way was an extremely strong and terribly proud woman, packed up, picked me up, and left France for America, where her mother and younger sister were living. We arrived in New York City when I was three months old. Not surprisingly, my first memories are American memories.

I hardly remember my mother during that period, probably because I really didn't see her all that much. She had to work to support the both of us as well as her mother, who was ailing and would die in a few years of bone cancer. One scene remains branded in my memory, I can close my eyes and let it roll in harsh black and white, clearer than in any screening room. A little boy of three or four comes running into a room. It must be evening because the room is dark, except for the lamp standing just behind the bed on which a woman lies, propped up on pillows. She is reading, and as the little boy comes running in, she raises her head and smiles. She has fine, noble features. The lines of suffering cannot deny the beauty of her face; in fact, they somehow underscore it. The little boy runs toward her, his entire being filled with joy at loving her so and being loved. He throws himself on the bed across her legs and is transfixed with horror as she lets out a piercing scream of pain and he realizes he has caused the pain by jumping on her sick leg, something he was told never to do but forgot about in the joy of seeing her. The boy is me, and that is the only memory I have of my maternal grandmother.

6

Other memories are far more incomplete, like pictures from a photo album with neither beginning nor end. My nanny Aegus. The time she would not let me leave the table until I had eaten my fish, a kind of mashed sole as I recall that I refused to eat because of the bones. To this day, I approach any fish dish with apprehension. Aegus's daughter Mary, who gave me a piece of candy and a hug to console me after I had been forced to swallow that last morsel of fish and, much worse and to this day leaving a bad taste in my mouth, my pride.

I can vaguely recall the apartment my mother shared with another couple, the Windrows, and their two daughters, Midge and Pat. Stellan Windrow must have embedded himself in my memory because he was huge and loved to crack jokes at which he laughed uproariously. The only time I remember laughing too was when he laughed so hard his dentures fell out. I was hysterical until Stellan whacked me on the backside with a pair of suspenders.

Most of all I remember my first friend, Steve Schneider, who lived in the same house one floor up. His bedroom was right over mine, and our favorite thing when we went to bed was to talk through the air shaft that connected all the rooms on that side of the building. No matter how long our whispered conversations went on, they always ended the same way. I would initiate the ritual: "Good night, Steven." "Good night, Vova," he would respond, and this exchange would float up and down that air shaft until one of us reluctantly dozed off—because the idea, of course, was to get to say the last good night, provided no one came storming into the bedroom telling us to shut up.

The only times neither of us had any desire to go through with this routine was when my mother would get home from work early enough to read me a story before putting out the light. I must have been five years old when she began reading me *The Adventures of Tom Sawyer.* To this day I remember my delight at the description of Aunt Polly looking for Tom under and over her spectacles but never looking through them for anything so unworthy as a mere boy. Another passage that I asked my mother to read over and over again, while Steve hugged the air shaft above, was the story of the cat Peter and the painkiller. I still have that volume, *The Favorite Works of Mark Twain,* published by the Garden City Publishing Company, Incorporated, in 1939.

During the summers, my mother couldn't take care of me. She continued to work for Paramount as a cutter. I stayed with the Schneider family at a place they rented somewhere in the country. My recollections of that place are faint. One has to do with getting into a fight and being hit on the head with a rake. But what does stand out in my mind are the weekends I waited for, knowing my mother would come. I must have lived for those Saturdays and Sundays.

My mother was a very attractive woman, and she could have had her choice of men. But she was one of those truly rare people who can love only once. I know for a fact that she not only never looked at another man, she didn't even have the slightest inclination to. She happened to love my father. That was it, period. And so she waited for him for those five years. I think she would have waited twenty-five. Meanwhile, my father, a very different kind of character, had sown his wild oats over the better part of France and had come to realize that my mother was the only woman he would really ever love (although this by no means would exclude the possibility of an affair here and there). And he came to get her.

We sailed on the *Normandie,* at that time the world's most luxurious ship. Steve Schneider and his parents, Saul and Nina, came to see us off and stood, waving from shore, as we sailed out of New York Harbor. It was spring 1939.

On September 1, 1939, Germany invaded Poland. Two days later, France and Great Britain declared war. World War II was on. I have no recollections of the fighting, most likely because there wasn't any for something like six months. During that time, there was not a single casualty on the Franco-German front—with the exception of a British soldier who accidentally shot himself while cleaning his rifle. The Germans called it the "Sitzkrieg," the French, "la drôle de guerre," while in England it became known as "the phoney war." As was later testified to by Wehrmacht chief of staff Halder, as well as by Marshal Keitel, the Germans made a calculated military gamble when they attacked Poland. France had a preponderance of divisions on the western front. Had she attacked, the Germans would have stood very little chance of holding the Ruhr, their industrial heartland, without which they could not have hoped to sustain any kind of military effort. Hitler could have been defeated then and there. But for the record, both Halder and Keitel were wrong when they spoke of a military gamble. The gamble was political, an astute assumption on Hitler's part that as long as he pushed eastward, the West would do very little, if anything, to stop him. Once finished with Poland and ready for his next campaign, Hitler attacked France in May 1940. It was over by June.

8

I don't remember the war. As a matter of fact, I don't think I noticed the absence of my father, to whose presence I had not yet become fully accustomed when he volunteered for service in the French army. He did not have to do that, for he was not a French citizen. Because of a variety of factors, not the least being his vivid memories of revolutionary Petrograd, he had matured into a staunch supporter of socialism and of the Soviet Union. Though not a member of the Communist party (nor would he ever become one), he was, most undoubtedly, a Red, a professed Marxist.

My father had what was called a Nansen passport, a document devised by Fridtjof Nansen, the famous Norwegian polar explorer, scientist, statesman, and humanitarian who was awarded the Nobel Peace Prize in 1922 for his service in the Russian famine and work in prisoner of war repatriation. The Nansen passport was designed to give displaced persons a degree of legitimacy and the right to enjoy the same privileges as citizens of the country they were living in. It was respected by most civilized governments—which naturally ruled out fascist Germany. As far as the Germans were concerned, my father was a perfect candidate for the gas chamber and cremation. First of all, he was a Jew, and please do not insult our intelligence with that talk of his ancestors having been converts; Jewishness is not just a state of mind, it's genetic, just like being black. Second, he was not just a Jew, but a Jew-commie, and never mind about the card carrying and non–card carrying business. He was card-carrying in his heart, and what could be worse than that? Third and last, he supported Bolshevik Russia and, in fact, made no secret of his intentions to return to that country as soon as conditions would allow. In addition to all this, my father promptly went to work for the Resistance, selling meat pasties where German troops were quartered. Thanks to his fluent German, picked up during his Berlin years, he could simply stand there and listen to the soldiers and officers talk, picking up information about what kind and how many units were there, and so on.

This was dangerous business, especially for someone like my father. As the Gestapo machine meticulously sucked in bits and scraps of information about his activities, it became obvious that my father had to get out—and that meant crossing over into the so-called Free Zone.

Of course these are things I learned much later, conclusions I drew from stories I was told. But in addition to that and well before it, there was a learning process, little vignettes that, taken separately, meant very little, but that added up constituted an education.

I see us strolling down the Champs Elysées, my mother and two German officers, both tall, both handsome, both with chiseled faces marked by dueling scars, both of them holding one of my hands and swinging me—upsa-daisy—off my feet and up in the air. I squeal with delight and my mother laughs. Hey, the Boches are OK, right?

A few days later, as I was leaving school, one of the German soldiers standing guard there—a precaution against the "misbehavior" of overly patriotic lycée seniors—patted me on the head and gave me a bag of marbles. My mother found me playing with them on the living-room rug when she got home. "Where did you get those marbles?" she asked. "A German soldier gave them to me," I replied. And for the first and last time in my life my mother, that gentlest of all women, slapped me in the face. "You will never accept any gift from a German," she said. But what about swinging from their arms in the middle of Paris?

My mother and I are in the metro in a second-class car (first class is for Aryans only). However, there is a German officer sitting next to us. At the next station a woman comes in. She is very, very pregnant, and the officer stands up and offers her his seat. She ignores him. "Please, sit down," he says. The woman looks right through him as if he were not there. "Please," he repeats, almost imploring. The woman is oblivious to his existence. At the next station, the officer dashes out of the car, cursing under his breath. The general sigh of satisfaction is louder than a chorus of triumphant hoorays, and my mother looks at me with shining eyes.

The summer of 1940. I have been sent to live in Biarritz, a town on the Bay of Biscay, with Marguerite, a friend of the family's, a person I adore and lovingly call Guiguite. The windows of her apartment look out onto a hospital where German soldiers are convalescing. One day I see a group of them playing soccer, a spectacle that rivets me to the open window and soon has me yelling encouragements to "my" team. Suddenly my ear is caught in a vice. A grim and foreign Guiguite literally drags me by the ear from the window, lets down the blinds, and informs me that for looking at German soldiers I will not get chicken or salad for dinner— my two favorite dishes. I was sent off to bed two hours earlier than usual only to be brusquely woken up at five in the morning and told to dress. It was still chilly outside as Guiguite marched me through the breaking dawn to the pier. It seemed to me that the whole town had assembled there, hundreds of people standing in total silence, waiting, watching, their eyes probing the dark waters. So there I stood, pressing up against Guigite, waiting for something, not knowing what, but knowing it would come, whatever it was. And then there was a stirring in the crowd, all heads turning to look in one direction, and IT came, carried in by the treacherous current that made swimming here terribly dangerous, something that all the local people knew but that the master race refused to acknowledge: first one, then a second, until finally the dead bodies of five drowned German soldiers slid past in the eerie silence. Guiguite turned me around and marched me back home. She gave me a mug of hot tea. "You can look at those Germans," she said.

I had learned my lesson.

We moved to Marseilles in what must have been the fall of 1940. At that time, France was still divided into two zones, one occupied by the Germans, the other, the so-called Free Zone, run by the pro-fascist Pétain-Laval government. Permission in the form of a special pass was required to move from one to the other, something my father could not apply for. Unlike his friend Barash, he knew he was safe as long as he did not become a digit in the German recording apparatus, a ponderously Teutonic piece of machinery that was relatively easy to avoid but deadly and inescapable once you were entered in its files.

Although I didn't know it at the time, my father's pass was forged. The work was amateur and sloppy, but in those early days of the occupation the Germans had not yet really clamped down. In Marseilles, we stayed at the Pension Mimosa, a less than luxurious hotel run by Barash's parents. Looking back on those times, I hear Madame Barash, usually referred to as Madame Rita, stridently summoning all the guests of the Mimosa to lunch, where the main dish would be snails cooked in garlic sauce and the main attraction would be to goad *le petit Vova,* meaning me, into talking back after having made a bet to sit through an entire meal without saying a word. The conditions were simple: if I won, I could pick whatever toy I wanted. If I lost, I would have to eat snails seven days a week. Of course I won. The toy I chose was a magnificent boat that ran on a battery. I sailed it in one of the hotel bathtubs with a little girl of my age, Marie, who was killed in an Allied air raid soon after we left.

Leaving presented certain difficulties, not so much for my mother and myself, since her passport was in perfect order and all she needed was a German stamp authorizing her departure. But my father needed a permit, and this time it had to be a real one. Luckily, the Gestapo could be bribed—provided you had the money. We didn't. As it turned out, a rich Jewish family agreed to provide us with the money in exchange for taking their adult daughter with us. So I was told by my parents that we would be leaving with my "nanny." Now I had never seen this person before, I had no idea what she looked like, I was just a little six-year-old being told to accept something I knew was not true. But I remember with absolute clarity that I had no problem with that at all: She is not my nanny, but she's supposed to be, and I am going to say that to everyone who asks. I knew exactly who that everyone might be, and I didn't have to be told what might happen to my nanny if they found out. The environment and conditions that a child finds itself in can make an adult of that child overnight. I didn't need any explanations as to why I was being told to call this girl my nanny, I knew exactly why I had to say that. No one had ever told me that the Germans shot Jews. But I *knew*.

We got the money and we got our papers. I met my nanny at the train station. I have completely forgotten what she looked like, whether she was tall or small, thin or fat, blond or dark. I remember just one thing: the number of rings she was wearing on her fingers.

We had no problems. We passed the Spanish frontier, spent a few days in Madrid and Barcelona, then traveled to Lisbon, boarded a steamer called the *Sibonee,* and sailed for America. The trip is a blank in my mind except for a couple of things. The first was when my mother lost one of her favorite belongings, a silk bow tie, blue with white polka dots encircled with red, that was found by a boy slightly older than myself; my heart skipped a beat when I saw the tie in his hand, and when he refused to give it to me, I flew at him with the righteous rage and fury of a Sir Lancelot fighting for the honor of his damsel. I have enjoyed more than a few pleasures in my life, but not many can compare with the surge of pure delight I felt as I handed my mother what I had won back for her and saw the pride in her eyes.

The second incident I remember was of a very different nature. Fearing a possible attack by German U-boats, the captain of our ship had chosen to sail a more southern route than was usual from Lisbon to New York. Not far from the Bermudas, we chanced upon the carcass of a whale. Although the stench was overpowering, the captain and the crew decided to haul it aboard in the hope of finding ambergris. The ship was stopped and the crew went to work. It took them a while to get a net around what was left of the rotting whale; twice the steel cables hanging from the derricks broke with the sound of a cannon shot. Finally they lifted the white mass from the water, and as they did, several sharks came leaping after it—a whole school had been in a feeding frenzy and were now suddenly deprived of their food. Once the carcass was safely lifted onto the lower deck, the sailors decided to have some fun and catch a shark. A hunk of pig fat was stuck on a big iron hook tied to a thick rope, which was then passed from hand to hand by the sailors who lined the railing. One of the sharks took the bait, and after much heave-hoing, the sailors pulled it aboard. I was standing on the middle deck immediately above it. The shark must have been about twelve feet long—not monstrous as far as sharks go, but certainly big enough to impress a boy of six. One of the sailors took a fire ax and began to hit the shark. The ax just bounced off its body, leaving no trace. After a few minutes, the shark stopped beating the deck with its tail. It lay there looking very dead, yet somehow very dangerous. Then a sailor walked up to it and stuck his thumb into its eye. The shark jerked its head and the man staggered back, a jet of blood spurting up at me from where his hand had once been. The shark had taken it off in one bite. Ever since then I have been afraid of sharks, the only animal I truly fear. And every time I fly across the Atlantic, my nightmare is not that the plane will crash, but that it will crash into the water and I will survive the crash only to be eaten alive by a great white.

When our ship docked in New York, Steve Schneider and his parents were there to meet us. I was surprised that we were the same height. When we had parted, a year and a half before, I had been much taller than Steve. Later I realized that because of the scarcity of good food in occupied France, my growth had been stunted. Back in the States, I immediately shot up again.

Our first apartment was on Bleecker Street, down in the Village. It was a great street. In fact, it even made its way into one of my favorite folk songs, "Freight Train": "When I die please bury me deep, / Down at the end of Bleecker Street." It was a small apartment, three rooms and a tiny kitchen. The rooms marched in a straight line, one after the other. My parents slept in the middle room, I slept in the back room, which gave access to the bathroom. The first room, if you stretched it, could be called a dining room.

One of my first memories there was of my father tacking a map of Europe and the Soviet Union to the closet door and drawing, in black pencil, the advance of the Germans, who had attacked the Soviets in June of 1941. And as he penciled in the Nazi advances, he explained to me that there was no way the fascists would ever win. "They will never take Leningrad," he would tell me, "they will never take Moscow." I remember the defiance in his voice when he repeated those words and how everyone else was saying, "Oh, those poor Russians, they don't stand a chance, it's only a matter of a few weeks, maximum a couple of months, before they are wiped out." The Germans could never win, my father insisted, because fascism could not triumph over socialism, the only truly fair system, one that brought all people together as brothers and made them invincible.

Then, in December 1941, came the first Soviet counteroffensive at the gates of Moscow. There, Hitler's Wehrmacht suffered its first defeat. As the Red Army advanced, my father drew that in with a red pencil, and I remember the pride in his voice when he said, "You see? I told you so." That was part of my initial political education, the first time I remember hearing the word *socialism*, the first time the notion of a system's being just or unjust ever crossed my mind. It was then that I actually registered in my mind the existence of a country called the Soviet Union, a country worthy of respect, gratitude, and love.

One of my first memories during the war in America is of anti-Semitism. One day when I was seven, I was walking up Eleventh Street when two kids stopped me. They were both bigger than I and, I found out later, Irish Catholics. One of them said, "Are you Jewish?" As I recall that particular moment, it seems to me that I had never thought about what I was. I had heard something about the Jews in occupied France, and I knew the Nazis persecuted Jews—a fact that automatically made all Jews good as far as I was concerned. I also had been taught by my father that all people were people and that prejudice of any kind was akin to being a Nazi. So my answer was predictable: "None of your business." The bigger of the two kids turned to his sidekick and said, "OK, let's pants him!" I had absolutely no idea why they wanted to take off my pants, but I didn't stop to think about it. I ran—the fastest I'd ever run in my life. And I was a very fast kid. They came after me. I tore around a corner, full speed, smack into the belly of a huge cop. Now back in those days, in New York City, the cops were all Irish and none was under six feet tall. There were no black, no Hispanic, and no women cops, and certainly no small ones. When I returned to the Big Apple in 1986 for the first time in thirty-eight years, one of the things that struck me as having changed was the size and the look of "Noo Yawk's foinest." Anyway, I slammed into this huge guy and he scooped me up with a hamlike fist and said, "OK, kid, whatsamatter?"

I was scared and crying, and I started screaming something about kids wanting to beat me up and take off my pants, and at that point the two bullies came running around the corner. Well when they saw him, they applied the brakes, but too late. The cop dropped me and in one smooth, uncannily swift motion grabbed them both by the collars, picked them right off the ground, shook them like a terrier shakes a rat, and roared, "You little bastards, you should be ashamed of yourselves! I'll talk to Father Clancy about you and see to it you get a proper licking!" Of course he knew all the Irish parishes in the district. Well, *they* began to bawl, and he just kept shaking them. Then he put them down with an audible thud and bellowed, "Out of my sight!" And they vanished. He then turned to me. "You too, kid, off you go. And don't ever let me catch you crying, shame on you." I'll never forget that guy. Every now and then I'd see him on the beat and he would just wink. I had no more trouble. And if I somewhat idealize the New York cops of my boyhood, I hope you won't hold it against me.

We didn't live long on Bleecker Street. When my father began making more money, we moved to East Forty-eighth Street between Second and Third, where we had a four-floor building to ourselves. It was a great place for a kid. Not that I remember much of it, except the kitchen on the ground floor where my mother gave me my first cooking lessons and where my father's Russian friends, people who, like himself, had been swept out of their country by the revolution, congregated to drink tea and talk politics. I spoke no Russian whatsoever, but every now and then they would lapse into French for my mother, and that's how I got the sense of their endless discussions. I do have one memory, although I would prefer to have forgotten it. Lining Third Avenue in the upper Forties were several antique shops. I used to love to look through the casements, coveting spyglasses, bronze writing sets, and the like. One day I spied a cavalry saber. My desire to have it was overpowering. I walked into the store and asked the man behind the counter how much he wanted for the saber. I couldn't have been more than ten, so he gave me a cold look and said "Five bucks." I could have killed for that saber, but instead of that I stole five dollars from my aunt's purse (she was living with us in those days) and then at dinner made up a cock-and-bull story about how I had found five dollars on the sidewalk and bought—guess what—an antique saber with it. I thought I had covered all the bases, but I hadn't counted on one thing: my aunt was anything but affluent. She was single and worked very hard for her money; she lived with us because she really could not afford an apartment. So she knew exactly how much money she had at any time in her purse. On the day I "found" five dollars in the street, her wallet was missing exactly five dollars. That's when I learned that crime doesn't pay. Like most people, I have learned most of my lessons the hard way. I will never forget the excruciating shame of being submitted to relentless questioning by my father and then having to go upstairs to my aunt's room and having to tell her that I had stolen the money from her purse. An integral part of that lesson was that moral punishment is far more painful than physical and leaves bigger scars.

In 1944, we moved into a beautiful duplex on East Tenth Street, between Fifth and University Place. It was and remains in my memory one of the most beautiful apartments I have ever seen. It belonged to a famous criminal lawyer, Arthur Garfield Hays, and had been designed by his wife, an extremely talented woman who was far ahead of her time in her interior decoration. When she died at a tragically young age, Mr. Hays could no longer bear living in this place, where everything reminded him of her. So he moved up to the fourth floor (he owned the entire building), we rented the duplex on floors two and three, and John Garfield, the actor, rented the ground floor.

Those years, 1941 through 1946, were a wonderful and positive time for me. I went to a truly fine school, City and Country, in those days an educational establishment for the children of wealthy—but progressive— parents. This was of course a private school; in fact, it was the second-oldest private school in America. In those days in New York City, most of the private schools were segregated. Yet we were taught early on that skin color made no difference. There were even a few colored kids (we didn't call them blacks then) in our school. That may not sound like much now, but it was then, believe me. Our teachers were wonderful. They not only liked children, they knew how to deal with them.

The director and founder of the school, Caroline Pratt, was an amazing woman.

I was a fighter. During my first two years at school—the grades were named according the age of the students, the Sevens, the Eights, and so on up to the last grade, the Thirteens—I fought all the time. I was big for my age, and so I beat up a lot of kids. What would have happened to me in most schools? I would have been disciplined in one way or another, they would have tried to break my spirit and, if that didn't work, they would have kicked me out of school. Not so Miss Pratt. At the end of my second year, she invited me into her office and talked to me. She told me that I was a fine boy but that I was too far ahead of my class. So she had decided I would skip a grade. Next year I would be with the Tens, she said. I implored her not to do this to me, I felt I was being cast out of my environment into a foreign and threatening world. Miss Pratt smiled, patted me on the head, and said, "Don't cry, Vlady, you'll be fine." So the next year I found myself in a class of kids who were from one to two years older than me and naturally bigger. That was Caroline Pratt's way of handling my aggressiveness. It was OK with her if I wanted to fight, but she didn't want to see me become a bully picking on kids who couldn't really fight back. As for my having academic problems, that was not even a consideration.

The way they taught at City and Country was not at all like the usual rote learning. As a matter of fact, it was like nothing I have ever encountered since. I don't remember reading a textbook in that school, and yet I came out of there with knowledge and especially an outlook that has permitted me to live in harmony with life, rather than in confrontation.

We had shops—for woodworking and pottery making—and our own baking and glazing oven. It was there that we got our aesthetic education without ever knowing we were being taught. We had our own printing presses—that was in the Elevens. One was manual, the other electric. We learned to set type, took exams, and became either apprentices or masters. We printed much of what the school needed in the way of invitations, flyers, etc. And it was in the Elevens that we learned about Gutenberg and his invention, about Europe during the High Renaissance. As a result, Gutenberg and his printing press was not just dusty, musty history to us, it was now and today, because we worked those presses, competed for the right to run them, to become master printers. Studying the Middle Ages in the Tens, we were taught how to write on parchment, we learned about vellum, we were taught how to mix and use colors as the monks did. Each of us chose a graduating student of the Thirteens and worked on his or her diploma, illuminating the capital letters with gold and carmine. As we did, we were no longer Vlady and Pete and Eve sitting in a classroom in New York City, we were monks in our cells somewhere in medieval England or France, monastery bells tolling faintly in the distance, as we worked on what generations would look upon with awe.

Our school involved us in all sorts of different activities. The Eights ran the school post office, selling stamps, envelopes, and paper to all the other kids. It was a concrete way of learning arithmetic and services simultaneously. The Nines ran the school shop, where you could buy anything from pencils, writing pads, and erasers to brushes and watercolor paints. The students bought the supplies wholesale, kept the books, learned about such things as fractions, percentages, being in the black and in the red. It was a pretty incredible place, but the most amazing part of it, its very heart as far as I am concerned, was the library and the librarian. I've forgotten her name, but I remember her face as if I'd last seen her yesterday instead of more than forty years ago. Whenever you had a spare moment, you went to the library—a large room with three walls lined with bookshelves, floor to ceiling. The fourth wall was lined with high windows that flooded the room with light. We were never told that we couldn't read a certain book because we were too small for it. But we would be guided, I would even say enticed, into reading the books we really needed. The librarian would walk up to you as you stood studying the bindings on one of the shelves, and leaning down, she would whisper conspiratorially into your ear, "There is a book I think you should look at before anyone else gets it. Interested?" Hell, yes! Of course I'm interested! And so it was that we spent hours reclining in the white, blue-cushioned wicker armchairs that lined the room, totally immersed in our "secret" finds, surfacing only to look around and gloat at being the sole keepers of these treasures. Literature led us into new and wonderful worlds. I have walked hand in hand with Winnie-the-Pooh, with Robin Hood and all of his merry men (especially Little John), with King Arthur and his knights of the Round Table, especially Lancelot and Gawain, I have fought the wars of the Red and the White Roses, battled for Maid Marian and shot both Guy of Gisborne and the Sheriff of Nottingham through the heart with my bow and arrow; I have sailed to Treasure Island with Jim Hawkins and the shrill cry of Long John Silver's parrot—"Pieces of eight! Pieces of eight!"—still rings in my ears; I have been with Tom and Huck and Jim on the Mississippi, fallen in love with Ozma, Princess of Emerald City, swayed to the Song of Hiawatha; I have fought shoulder to shoulder with D'Artagnan, Athos, Porthos, and Aramis (in that order, please); I have stood up to Wolf Larsen; I have wept over the fate of every animal ever written about by Ernest Thompson Seton; I have swung from the vines and branches of Mowgli's jungle, hugged Bagheera's velvet fur, and together with Rikki-Tikki-Tavi have felt my eyes grow red and my legs stiffen as I waited for the vile Nag and Nagina. Boy, I have lived—and that's only a small part of it. Yes, that library and the school that made it possible were pretty incredible places. And behind it all was the real care, the real love that the teachers had for the children. It was something I realized only much later, because as a child, I took it for granted. Still, I did remember my one year in French school in 1940, where I'd had teachers appointed by the Germans. Pupils were seated in class according to their academic performance. In the first row on your right, desk number one, sat your top pupil. Desk number two, the second best. So the kid sitting in the end of the fourth row was the worst student in the class. We kept moving up and down, back and forth, depending on our performance. It meant competition and envy cultivated in six-year-olds. The teacher had a long wooden rod with a ball on its tip, and when any of us misbehaved, he'd whack that child on the head. It was physically painful and morally degrading. That was the German method of instruction. Or the French method with a German slant.

When I finished City and Country, at age twelve, I went to Stuyvesant High School. It was and still is considered one of the top academic schools in New York City. At that time, you had to take competitive entrance exams to be admitted. Still, they had forty students to a class and most teachers, as I recall, didn't give a tinker's damn about any of us as individuals. The teacher taught and gave tests. If you did well, you did well; if you didn't, you didn't; if you failed enough tests, you were expelled. They couldn't have cared less. And that difference was very apparent to a child who had gone to City and Country.

Throughout those years, I knew very well that I was not an American. I don't know why I knew it, but I may have sensed it from my father. He didn't *like* America, although he did very well there, working for a subdivision of MGM called Loew's International. In 1946–47 he was making $25,000 a year, the equivalent of a quarter of a million today. As I said, we had a beautiful house. I was a snot-nosed kid with my own playroom, bedroom, and bathroom. So the fact that my father didn't like America didn't stem from career or money problems. I think it was because he was very European; he found Americans superficial and boorish. Many Europeans continue to hold that view.

So I knew I wasn't American. But I also knew I wasn't Russian. How could I be Russian if I didn't speak a word of that language? I knew what I was: French. My mother was French, I was born in Paris, and that was it. This view dovetailed very neatly with French law adopted after the Napoleonic wars decimated France's male population: any male child born in France of a French mother is automatically considered to be French and cannot change his citizenship without the specific permission of the government. As far as France is concerned, I am French and, what's more, a draft dodger who should have fought in Algiers. The French have a legal case against me whenever I go to France. I've been there several times, and they continue to show leniency. Vive la France!

But despite knowing that I was French, and despite my father's feelings, I loved America. I loved New York City and still do. I loved the streets, the smells, I loved the bustle. It was, and in a basic sense remains, my town. I didn't know that I loved it then, because children hardly ever think about such things. But that is where I felt at home.

Like any American kid, then or now, I loved baseball. My first memory of the number-one American pastime is of two baseballs my mother was given at the 1937 All-Star Game, one signed by the American League stars, the other by all the National League players, names like Hubbell, Gehrig, DiMaggio. Today those balls would sell for a small fortune.

We played ball at City and Country. Softball, but ball. The father of one of my classmates, a Wall Street broker, was a friend of the man who owned the New York Yankees. So his son, Bobby, knew everything about the Yankees, had met the players, had even been in their dugout at Yankee Stadium. My God, he had even shaken hands with Phil Rizzuto! Bobby invented, or at least greatly refined, a game called dice baseball. Every throw of the dice, every combination meant a play of some sort—a hit, a strike, a ball, an error, and so on. We all had notebooks with all the teams, and we played constantly, meticulously comparing notes on batting averages, RBIs, ERAs. The great things about this game were that you could play it alone and you made up your own teams. One of mine had the Three Musketeers in the outfield (minus D'Artagnan—the flashiest shortstop ever to ignite a triple play), Hiawatha at first, Mowgli at second, Sir Lancelot at third, with Huck Finn pitching and Tom Sawyer catching. My star relief pitcher was Jim—I desegregated my league long before the Dodgers brought in Jackie Robinson. This team was called the Story Greats. I had a bunch of other teams, but the only one that ever managed to beat the Greats was the Mighty Mythies, which boasted the likes of Hercules, Paul Bunyan, and Saint George—but let me not bore you with the details. Partly because of Bobby, I became an avid Yankee fan. But mostly it was because of Joe DiMaggio, whom I met once in my father's office and once at Yankee Stadium after a game.

It's hard to appreciate today what the Yankee Clipper was to baseball in the late thirties and through the forties. As far as I'm concerned, there simply are no ballplayers of that caliber around today. He was, literally, a walking, talking, living legend. You had other great ballplayers then too, like Ted Williams and Stan "the Man" Musial. But DiMage was special. He may not have been as great a hitter as Williams, his arm may not have been as good as Musial's, he may not have had the power of King Kong

Keller, but for the real aficionados of baseball, he was better than all of them combined. He was Mr. Baseball, my idol. There was dignity, poise, and respect, the magic that made him what he was.

Every Saturday and Sunday we used to go to Van Cortlandt Heights and play baseball with the guys. I was a fair fielder and a good hitter. Naturally, I played center field. Had it not been for Joe, I would have been a Brooklyn Dodger fan. The Yankees were, after all, the rich team, they were lily-white. I had real problems with that. And when the Dodgers fielded Jackie Robinson, the first black man to play in the majors, it almost made me switch my allegiance. But I couldn't. Because of Joe DiMaggio.

Even after leaving America, I continued to follow baseball. And when the Dodgers left Brooklyn, something really happened to the game—it lost the only team that stood for the little guy, for the underdog, the team that, by winning the World Series, loudly and clearly said Blaaaah! to the jet set, to the fat cats, to Mr. and Mrs. Rich Bitch. Sure the team and its players were someone's personal toy to play with or sell as his whim might be, and in that respect the Dodgers were no different from any other team then or today, for that matter. And yet there was *something*—some kind of populist magic about them that made them special, just as special as their fans, the Flatbush Faithful. And when the team moved to L.A., the mystique vanished, evaporated under the hot rays of the southern California sun, creating a new suntanned team with new suntanned fans. A good team, perhaps, at times even a great team, but a team that would never produce the likes of Duke Snider, Carl Furillo, Ed Stanky, or Pee Wee Reese, that would never have a fan who could raise his voice above the megadecibel level at Ebbets Field and instruct his pitcher to "stick da ball in da bum's ear!", "da bum" being none other than my idol, the Yankee Clipper. Gone is that team and gone are its wild and wonderful followers.

Today I still follow baseball, reading about it in the *International Herald Tribune.* I watch it avidly on television when I am in the States, and I also get it on cassette. But it has become a different game. They now having batting caps and fielding caps, batting gloves, for God's sake, they play on something called Astroturf, and only a few ballparks as far as I know, grow regular, normal grass—something now considered a bit of an anomaly.

Modern NBA teams could run circles around the best they could have fielded back in the forties. Ditto for football. But baseball? I think it used to be a game that demanded greater skill and better athletes than it does today. Take someone like Ty Cobb. Playing with the kind of super equipment and on the table-flat and flawless fields of today, Cobb would have broken the game wide open. Today, mediocre players bat .300 because the ball is livelier, the bats are better. Someone like Cobb or Ted Williams (whose yearly batting averages were sometimes over .400!), why they would probably hit closer to .500 nowadays. I am selecting incredible superstars, you say, and that's not fair? Fine, then how about my American League All-Star team, circa 1941: Siebert—1B (batting .334), Doerr—2B (.282), Travis—SS (.359), Tabor—3B (.279), Heath—RF (.340), Di-Maggio—CF (.357), Williams—LF (.406), Dickey—C (.284), Feller—P. Where's the All-Star team that could beat mine? Give me a break! I don't give a damn what anybody says: despite all the hype today, despite the outrageous salaries, the game has deteriorated.

Growing up in New York was like growing up anywhere else—a wonderful, exciting process of discovering the world around you and inside yourself. I first fell in love in New York. I was twelve or thirteen, and she was at least thirty-five. She was Irish, and I've always had this thing about the Irish, don't ask me why. She had the most incredible head of copper-red hair, the bluest sapphire eyes I have ever seen, and this impish, Irish smile. As far as I was concerned, she was by far the most beautiful and desirable woman on earth, with the exception of Linda Darnell, who occupied my erotic dreams like Joe Louis occupied the heavyweight box-ing title—knocking all competition out of the ring for years and years. But those were secret dreams. In real life, I was hopelessly in love with Mary, who had the intelligence and compassion not to make fun of me. She was happily married, but she would take me out to the movies or to a restau-rant, have me over for cocktails, treat me like an adult. I couldn't have been prouder or happier, except for that one time she took me to see *My Darling Clementine,* a new slam-bang Western starring Henry Fonda, Vic-tor Mature, and . . . Linda Darnell. Talk about conflict of loyalties. But with that one exception, that first love was a wonderful experience, and to this day I remember Mary with great fondness, and with love.

I got my first job in New York, my paper route. It was my first taste of capitalist competition. I had to get up at five in the morning to deliver the papers. The man who owned a little store around the corner on University Place, Sam was his name, had hired me for the job. On the first morning he had me follow him around as he delivered the papers. On the second day, he followed me to see how well I had remembered the route. From day three I was on my own, expected to be at Sam's by six sharp, pick up the papers, and have them all delivered by seven. When I say Sam had hired me, that is really not true. He didn't pay me a cent. "Remember, Billy," he said, calling me by my much Americanized name based on the faulty logic that Vladimir = William = Bill, "Remember, Billy, I don't want you ringin' no doorbells or knockin' on no doors, see? But on holidays, that's different. On holidays, you ring that bell and kick that door until someone opens up. And then you put a nice smile on your face and say, 'Good morning, sir or ma'am, I wish you a fine holiday and here are your papers.' They'll tip you, and you get to keep that money, no matter how much you get. I don't even want to know, see?" I saw. And on my first Christmas delivery, I received over one hundred dollars in tips—big money in those days. I bought myself a British-made three-speed bike and a delivery basket. There I was, ready to deliver by bike, which sure beat the hell out of walking.

One morning I overslept. I came dashing into the store, but Sam was gone, delivering the papers. I waited for him, and when he came back, I said, "Sam, I'm sorry, something happened to my alarm clock." Remember, I was just a kid, ten years old. Sam just patted me on the back and said, "Hey, Billy, don't worry. No problem. But the next time you oversleep, just don't bother coming. There's another kid who really wants your job. He needs it real bad, see?" Again, I saw. Sam didn't bawl me out, never even raised his voice, didn't preach. But he taught me one of the most important lessons of my life: either you perform or you're dead. Sam liked me, I know that, and he was a nice man. But from that time on I knew that regardless of how much he liked me, next time around, that was it.

Learning that lesson was part of growing up, and so were my encounters with racism. One happened on Long Island. I knew two young men who ran a gas station near the house we rented in the summer in a town called Miller Place. They were brothers in their early twenties. I was in my early teens. I loved to hang out with them, shoot the breeze, have a Coke. One day a black man drove up. They filled his tank, washed his windows, and he drove off. And they started talking about these "niggers" who were getting too big for their britches and who they'd just as soon shoot if they ever got the chance. So I said, "Hey, come on, guys, you don't really mean that," and gave them this fiery speech about the Declaration of Independence, equality, Abe Lincoln, and all the rest. At the end of which I expected we'd all shake hands and they would kind of hang their heads and say something like, "Hey, Vlady, thanks for setting us straight." Instead they said, "Kid, you are a nigger-lover. Get the fuck out of here and don't let us catch you comin' close again if you don't want the shit kicked out of you." It was very traumatic. I liked those guys. We had been friends. And I suddenly discovered that something abstract, as abstract as skin color, could turn a couple of friendly human beings into the meanest kind of bastards. You see, I knew they weren't kidding. They would actually attack and beat up a kid of thirteen. I have never forgotten that.

The same sort of turnabout I experienced happened to the Russians. It was unbelievable. During the war, there had been such an outpouring of friendship and warmth toward the Soviet Union. There was the Russian War Relief and the widespread admiration for the way the Soviet Union fought. All of that was very apparent. I was proud of being called Vladimir, clearly a Russian name. In fact, I so much wanted to be thought of as a Russian that I told lies. In the summer of 1942 or 1943, I was in summer camp in the Catskills, where we were visited by a delegation of Soviet women. All summer I had been telling the kids and the counselors that I was Russian and, of course, spoke Russian. Suddenly, here was this delegation, and I didn't speak a single word of Russian! I hid under my bunk but was found and literally dragged to be introduced to these Russian women, me, the pride and joy of Camp Hankus Pankus (God help me, that's what it was called), probably the only camp in the United States that could boast of having a Russian kid who could actually converse in that language with a bona fide group of Soviet Russians. Thanks to my dad and his Russian friends, I did know *da, nyet, spasibo, do svidanya,* and *pozhalusta.* How I managed the introduction with that kind of ammo, I'll never know. I suppose it was only because of the tact of those women. Later that day, we had a concert honoring the Soviet Union, and the kickoff piece was a Russian song called "Poliushko-pole," a song made famous by the Red Army Choir, a song I had listened to over and over again on my aunt's record player. Unfortunately, the only words I knew were the two that gave the song its name as well as its opening line. And who was the kid who did the solo? Right you are. You see, I never had any problems when we rehearsed, all I did was open with *"Poliushko-pole"* and then go into my own private Danny Kaye routine, making gibberish sound Russian and figuring nobody would know the difference. And right I was until those Russian women appeared on the scene. Well, what could I do? If Zeus had offered to destroy me with a bolt of lightning, I would have been delighted. But Zeus wanted to hear me perform. So he and everyone else got an earful of Pozner/Kaye, and I felt like falling into some small crack in the floor and disappearing forever. Those Soviet women bailed me out. They said I sung wonderfully, smiled, and patted me on the head. I write this and blush—forty-five years later.

The feeling toward the Soviets was very positive, warm. One of the Soviet marshals during the war was a man by the name of Timoshenko, and the joke going around was that the guy was not really Russian, he was Irish, and his real name was Tim O'Shenko. In those days, everyone knew it was the Russians who were in a life-and-death struggle with Hitler and that it was the Red Army and the Russian people who broke the Nazi beast's back. That was openly acknowledged in those days by people like Roosevelt, Churchill, and many more. Today, that has all conveniently been forgotten. It's not even in the textbooks. It's a distortion of history as crude as many for which the Soviets have rightly been condemned. As a result, many, if not most, Americans don't know who actually won the war against fascist Germany. In saying that, it is certainly not my intention to denigrate in any way the American wartime effort, of lend-lease, or anything else. But when it comes to what country actually bore the brunt of the Nazi onslaught and dealt the Nazi war machine the most devastating blow, there is no question about it. And in those days the American people *knew* that, they appreciated that, and it showed in their attitude toward the Soviet Union.

And yet, it took little more than one year to turn that spirit completely around. By 1947, I was getting beaten up at Stuyvesant High for being pro-Soviet. That's how quickly and how radically it changed. There was a deep, but dormant, anticommunism in people, dating from the late twenties or the thirties, and once aroused, it came roaring back. It was, in the main, irrational, based on the Red scares of earlier times. Today, when you talk about the Palmer Raids, 99 percent of Americans don't have the foggiest notion about what you mean. That reservoir of fear from the twenties and thirties had a great deal to do with how quickly and easily they turned the situation around, "they" being people who had a vested interest in fanning the embers of anticommunism, those who wanted to assume the imperial mantle of the British Empire, to justify the projection of U.S. economic and military power around the globe. And it worked beautifully. Stalin played right into their hands. Some of his actions—from his concealing the extent of Soviet wartime devastation to his crude and brutal repressions—made it oh so much easier to generate the image of the Red Menace.

Ironically, much of the international left-wing movement contributed to this. After the war, the moral authority of the Soviet Union in general and of Joseph Stalin in particular was extremely high. The Soviets had won the war against Hitler, and Stalin, it would seem, had almost single-handedly overcome stupendous odds and destroyed the mightiest war machine the world had ever known. The truth about his blunders that cost millions of Soviet lives, such as his refusal to acknowledge the information sent to him by both Soviet agents and people like Winston Churchill informing him of the exact date of Plan Barbarossa, his refusal to put the Red Army on the alert, was as yet unknown. As was the scope of the terrible crimes committed under his leadership in the Soviet Union between 1929 and 1938. True, much of this was anything but secret; however, to left-wingers who had had to stand up to years of Red-baiting, who had been persecuted, to them the Soviet victory over Hitler was akin to a personal vindication and triumph. It meant that they had been right to stand firm in their belief and turn a deaf ear to anything that might contradict it. One of these people, among so many others, was my father. But he was not a member of the Communist party. As for the western communist parties, U.S., French, Italian, British, or whatever, they just followed the Soviet line, no matter what Stalin said or did. This certainly reinforced the global-conspiracy image generated in the United States.

By 1947, the anti-Soviet atmosphere was such that I began to feel uncomfortable, and I started to want to leave America. It was not so emotionally troubling to me because I felt I was not an American. This, in a way, was brought into sharp focus by my friendship with a Soviet boy of my age, Yura, the son of a Soviet diplomat working at the United Nations. In those days, Soviet diplomats stationed in the United States were paid very low salaries. Consequently, they rented apartments in the less attractive neighborhoods of New York and led austere lives. My father made a special effort to befriend as many of these people as possible and invited them regularly over to our home on Tenth Street, a place that, even by New York standards, was considered posh. That was how I met Yura. To me he stood for all the wonderful things I knew about the Soviet Union, the things my father had told me. I was completely infatuated with him. Through Yura, I was able to visit the Soviet school, where I could compare the respect the Soviet kids showed for their teachers with the "up yours" attitude of my Stuyvesant classmates. As the U.S.-Soviet relationship rapidly deteriorated, gangs of local American kids began to assemble in front of the Soviet school waiting for the kids to come out so they could beat them up. On two or three such occasions, I found myself fighting on the Russian side, screaming every four-letter word I knew (a lot), seeing the expression of surprise in the eyes of the American kids ("What da fuck are you fighting on *their* side for?") change to one of disgust and hatred ("Fuckin' commie traitor"), this driving me crazy with a hatred of my own and alienating me even more. Yes, I was ready to leave America.

Life might have become even more difficult for me had we not left when we did, at the end of 1948. The worst was still to come for the United States. McCarthyism had not quite arrived, the House Un-American Activities Committee hearings were still something most Americans could not imagine. Of course, the FBI kept its watchful eye on us, and our phone was tapped. Nothing out of the ordinary, you understand.

My father was forced to leave his job. As he later told the story, his boss, who liked him very much and appreciated his expertise, informed him that he could no longer afford to employ a Soviet citizen. "Drop that Russian passport, apply for U.S. citizenship, and I'll double your salary. Otherwise, I can't keep you." My dad turned down $50,000 a year. He would have turned down $5 million. He didn't sell his principles—ever. For any amount of money. So he gave up his job.

We immediately moved into a much smaller and far less sumptuous apartment on West Twelfth Street, and I went to live with Maria Louisa Falcon, a Spanish woman who had fought in the civil war. She was a close friend of my parents, who asked her to take me in because the new apartment was too small for us since my brother Paul had been born in 1945. Living with Maria Louisa led to one of the more embarrassing incidents of my youth. In those days in the United States, there was no such thing as a porno industry. There were girlie magazines, and you could get dirty pictures if you knew where to look for them, but there was nothing remotely like what you have today on virtually any newsstand. I was going on fourteen and getting interested in sex. I began to buy a magazine, the name of which I long ago forgot, but I do remember it cost fifty cents a copy—a hell of a lot of money—and was filled with women in panties and bras, usually wearing silk stockings and pumps, always in the most suggestive poses. Of course, I hid these magazines from all eyes, reading them at night and stashing them under my bed. One day I came home from school to find a pile of my magazines stacked neatly on the shelf near my bed. Maria Louisa had done some housecleaning. I was mortified, so much so that I stopped buying the magazine.

We left the United States because we could no longer live there. My father had neither a job nor a future to look forward to; he was concerned about what would happen to his wife and children. And because of both his ideals and his illusions about the Soviet Union, that is where he wanted to go. Today, much is being said about the right of people to emigrate, to travel freely. It is a subject I have thought about many, many times. My own life has been dramatically influenced by the right to travel and the denial of that right, and it has certainly influenced my thinking. And my view is clear and unequivocal: the right to travel is a basic human right. Anyone who wishes to leave his or her country, be it for a while or for good, is born with the right to do so, regardless of the laws of the land. But personally, I have always felt that if you wish to leave your country, there is only one truly valid reason—the feeling that you simply cannot live there any longer. Either your life is in danger, the welfare of your children or your beloved is threatened, or life is so stifling that you cannot tolerate it. You don't leave because the grass over there is greener, or because there are more and better consumer goods, or because you want to make a million dollars. You go because you can't stand staying.

Clearly, a major factor in my family's decision was the shift in public attitudes in America, the beginning of the anti-Communist hysteria. I have asked myself many times what, in human terms, allowed that to happen. Certainly, the terrifying capacity to turn suddenly from warm, decent human beings into something quite different is not an exclusively American trait. Over time I came to realize that it is a basic human frailty, a weakness exploited for centuries by various power structures. Like racism and anti-Semitism, anticommunism is abstract, theoretical. Very often, the most vicious anti-Semites really have never met a Jew and haven't got the foggiest notion about Jewish culture, history, or religion. How many Americans have ever met—let alone know well—a single communist?

Creating the face of the enemy is an old, old, ugly game. The technique is to dehumanize that enemy so that ultimately he ceases to resemble a human being. Once that trick has been achieved, it is relatively easy to make people fear, hate, and kill. It is, of course, one of the ways soldiers are prepared for war. Historically, we have seen it happen in many countries.

What are the roots of prejudice? I don't think anyone has ever found the entire answer. Prejudice goes as far back in human history as we can see. According to psychologists, our individual characters are, in the main, formed by the time we are five. If we are taught by our parents and by our social environment that blacks, Catholics, and, say, bicycle riders are stupid, dirty, greedy, treacherous, and inferior, that is what we will accept and believe. If we suck that in with our mother's milk, it will contribute to shaping our psyche just as surely as the milk itself will contribute to the growth of our body. It will be a *belief:* "Bicycle riders are inferior." It's difficult to overcome that. I don't think a twenty-year-old can be indoctrinated deeply with that kind of concept. The adult will say: "Yes, some bicycle riders are inferior, others are not. But either way, it has nothing to do with their being bicycle riders." Deep-seated prejudice is a question of values instilled as one grows up. Prejudice has little, if anything, to do with logic and everything to do with ignorance.

As a former biology major, I understand that fear is a reflex, the age-old alarm bell of self-preservation. None but the psychologically abnormal are fearless. It is a basic, crucial biological reaction. But it is also something that can be exploited, manipulated. As it has been.

In the West, some have branded me a propagandist. This fear-laden label bears some examination. I am a Soviet citizen, and though critical of important elements of life in my country, I support socialism. That in itself does not pose much of a problem for those in America who have a vested interest in having Americans fear and abhor the Soviet Union. The problem with me arises because, in order to generate that fear and hatred, a one-dimensional, negative stereotype of Soviets was invented and propagated. We are cold, emotionless, brutal, cruel, untrustworthy, and so on. I don't fit that image. So some people go to the most extraordinary lengths to try to "unmask" me.

When I appear on American television or radio, some "expert" often comes on immediately afterwards to analyze me, to explain to that poor, gullible audience how well trained I am, what makes me effective, why I can't be trusted. They typically have a professorial look and say in sober tones that it is my knowledge of the language, mastery of psychology, intensive training, and gift for communication that make me so dangerous. The whole thing is quite amazing and reflects the insecurity of those who have bred the anti-Soviet stereotype. They are terribly afraid that, by seeing me as a normal, authentic, honest person, an honest *Soviet,* Americans will begin to question both the stereotype and, heaven forbid, even the policies that flow from it—anticommunism, massive military spending, the cold war itself.

The fact is, my popularity in the United States, my ability to reach Americans, came as a great surprise to me. After all, even though I did grow up in New York City, I left when I was fifteen and didn't return until thirty-eight years later. Yes, I speak the language fluently and have kept current on what has happened in the country of my youth. But why should that make me especially effective? I have given that question a great deal of thought, and the answer only came to me when I seriously began working on this book. What *really* make me effective, deep down inside, are my feelings about America. It is the fact that America is part of me, of who I am and what I believe.

Growing up in New York, I knew and loved Ebbets Field. But the home of the Brooklyn Dodgers stays in my mind not only because of baseball. I went there to hear President Roosevelt talk in 1944, during his last campaign. He had been attacked by the Republicans as an infirm old man no longer fit to run the country. So his response was to tour New York standing in an open car amid the thunderous applause and loud cheers of thousands of people who lined the streets and avenues. He stood bareheaded under the pelting rain. And at Ebbets Field, there he was, in his famous cape, the arc lights centered on him, accentuating the sheets of rain coming down. I don't remember what he said. But we cheered deliriously, and I felt a tremendous surge of pride in just being there, being part of it, and seeing him. And later, much later, I realized that he was and remains part of *my* America. By that I mean the America that means so much to me—Tom Paine and Thomas Jefferson and Abe Lincoln. And the great songs of America that celebrated John Henry, Joe Hill, Jesse James, Frankie and Johnnie, and hundreds of nameless others. And the people who sang them—Woody Guthrie, Leadbelly, Pete Seeger, Billy Holiday, Bessie Smith. And the Declaration of Independence and the Boston Tea Party, wellsprings of the great democratic tradition that was born in America and that has survived under the most adverse conditions. I say survived, not triumphed.

I didn't understand it then, but today I can say without doubt that FDR, though of course a patrician, was part of that democratic American heritage—the real America. I don't think it's something you can fully appreciate if you're not American, or if you haven't spent many years in America. If you aren't, or haven't, I don't think you will be as deeply affected by Paine's words: "These are the times that try men's souls." Either you are part of that and you get gooseflesh, or you are not. I am.

That day at Ebbets Field was the last time FDR spoke in public. I was very lucky to have been there. And for some reason I see Fala, his famous Scotch terrier, riding in the car beside him. But that may well be my imagination. FDR was immensely popular. He was truly loved by the nation, by those who one honestly may refer to as The People. The

Republicans, naturally, did their damnedest to discredit it. During the war, Roosevelt visited the troops in the Pacific, taking Fala with him. One day he sailed from an island and forgot his dog. Well, he had the captain or the admiral, or whomever, turn the ship around and sail back for Fala. The Republicans got wind of this and made a big stink about Roosevelt's spending the taxpayers' money to retrieve a dog. And I remember FDR addressing this issue on the radio and saying with the most wonderful disdain, "Not satisfied with vilifying and attacking me, my opponents now attack my little dog Fala." Needless to say, he was a great orator and knew exactly how to exploit those kind of things to the fullest advantage. I mean, to me, Fala was nearly as great as FDR himself.

But there is another America. Not long ago, I came across an example, ironically, a man who has the same name as I but spells it differently—Victor Posner. He is a very wealthy businessman. In 1984, *Fortune* magazine said he made more money than any other American. Recently, he was taken to court for tax evasion of roughly $1.3 million. He faced forty years in jail. But as things turned out, he will not spend a day there, let alone forty years. He'll just have to pay back taxes plus several million dollars to support a fund for the homeless. And he will have to work a certain number of hours once a week for charity.

If Victor Posner were not wealthy, if he were an ordinary American citizen, he would be in jail. But in America today, much more so than yesterday, some people are far more equal than others, and they hardly ever go to jail. There are special rules for such people. Everything the Declaration of Independence talks about applies to these people in spades. *Their* right to life, *their* right to liberty, *their* right to the pursuit of happiness is much more assured than that of Joe Six-pack—because *they* have the money.

When I say the Declaration of Independence is a truly great document, I mean it. And its greatness not only comes from what it says but from when it was said. It was written in the last quarter of the eighteenth century, a time when the world was ruled by kings, queens, czars, emperors, pashas, and shahs. And America declared that *all* men are created equal and have certain inalienable rights. The concept itself was mindboggling for its time. Beyond that, it was the foundation for an actual society, for a nation's law. Yet when you look at America today, I don't think you can honestly state that those great principles have been fully honored. The Declaration is still there, and most Americans maintain that all people are indeed born with those rights. But social, economic, and political reality make it impossible for all Americans to *enjoy* those rights with anything resembling equality. Depending on the kind of family you were born into and the status and money that your family has, it will be infinitely easier or incomparably more difficult for you to enjoy your inalienable rights. The American expression "to be born on the wrong side of the tracks" supports what I say. If you are born into a native American, a Mexican, Puerto Rican, or black family, with six kids, a junkie father, a prostitute mother, and drugs and crime all around—and that is the case for *millions* of American kids—your chances of breaking out of there and making a decent living are close to zero. To anyone who would dispute that claim, I ask this question: would you voluntarily have your child grow up in the ghetto? Of course not! And you wouldn't because you *know* that your child would not only suffer hardships, but would also be denied equal opportunity in education, in work, and in life. What does it mean when 15 percent of the population—30 million people—lives in poverty in America? Twenty percent of its children? Can that shocking reality be squared with the Declaration, with the claim of equal rights? It reflects an inescapable conclusion. In the most fundamental sense of the word, America is an unjust society. It has created unparalleled wealth, and yet it tolerates abject poverty and misery. We all know that the wealth of America, if distributed differently, would make it possible to provide a normal, human standard of living for every single American citizen. Everyone would have a decent home, no one would go hungry, all could enjoy a meaningful education and life.

There is a profound conflict of ethics and philosophy in all this. You cannot in good faith declare that all human beings are created equal and enjoy the same rights and then allow these injustices to happen. You cannot marry the two—the economics of survival of the fittest and the egalitarian, democratic philosophy of Thomas Jefferson. It is a conflict that cannot be resolved in a capitalist society.

Charity and soup kitchens aren't the answer. They not only don't solve the problem, they are degrading. I don't want to stand in a soup line. I want to enjoy the fruit of *my* labor. Yes, some people break through— the lucky and the exceptional. But the goal, the need, is for a society that works for the average, ordinary person. If one values the American tradition, its great human values, the situation is profoundly disturbing.

So is the reality of racial prejudice. My aunt lived and still lives in Alexandria, Virginia. I used to go down from New York to visit her. My mother would put me on the train to D.C., and from there I would take the bus to Alexandria. In the nation's capital, there was no segregation, but as soon as you crossed into Virginia, there it was. I must have been twelve years old or thereabouts when I decided to do something about it. The next time I went to visit my aunt, I got on the bus and took a seat in the back. That caused no problem until we crossed into Virginia. That was when all the blacks moved to the back of the bus and all the whites stayed up front. Actually, the way things worked was that the blacks sat in the back of the bus as soon as they got on, and the whites sat up front—why go to the trouble of changing seats only a few minutes after getting on? So I was the only white to sit in back from the beginning of the ride. Some people stared at me, but nobody said anything—until we crossed the Virginia state line. I stayed right where I was.

The bus driver got up, came over to where I was sitting, and looked me over. He was big and burly and spoke in a soft southern drawl. "Sonny," he said, "are ya'll lookin' for trouble? Well, you're gonna find it. You better move your ass outta there real fast. Hear, sonny?" And I felt in my bones that he was dead serious, that if I refused to move, I would get hurt. Interestingly, I could feel the same animosity from both whites and blacks. To the whites I was a smart-assed Yankee nigger-lover. To the blacks, I was a troublemaker who was making trouble for them.

I did this twice, and the second time I was thrown off the bus. I was really stupid. I wasn't doing any good, and I was jeopardizing my own safety.

I developed my horror of race prejudice because both my parents were color blind. At home, they discussed the race issue often and made it clear to me that it was a shameful, unacceptable thing, unworthy of a human being. They said, "That's what fascism and the Nazis were all about, except that for them it was the Jews."

The first black person I came to know well was our maid, Julia Collins. For me, Julia was boss. She called me Vladimary which, I suppose, made more sense to her than the strange-sounding Vladimir. She was about five feet, two inches tall and very fat, but she moved with incredible grace. She taught me how to dance, and I'll never forget the sensation of leading her through a fox-trot—she felt as light as a feather. As she worked, she hummed, sometimes breaking out into song. I could listen for hours—she had the most amazing voice.

I was nine when she first took me to Harlem. She lived on Lenox Avenue around 125th and had a huge family. They were great people—full of love, laughter, so warm and compassionate. I loved those people.

I could not for the life of me understand how some people could hate others or look down on them because of the color of their skin. One of my friends at school told me that "niggers stink," so the following day I came up to Julia, pressed my nose somewhere in the area of her generous bosom, and began to sniff. Julia immediately realized what this was all about. She threw back her head and let out a peal of laughter that made the windowpanes shake. And I burst out laughing too. Incidentally, she smelled great, kind of earthy and exciting.

It was Julia Collins who was the matchmaker in my love affair with American folk music. As I said, she would hum the blues when she cleaned the apartment. Sometimes she would break out into a spiritual. More often than not it would be "Sometimes I Feel Like a Motherless Child." I would pester her to sing another and then another song. One Sunday, with my parents' permission, she took me to church with her family in Harlem. Although I was baptized as a Catholic and had attended religious services before, I had never experienced anything like this. I had some trouble following the sermon, but the singing simply blew me away. I soared on the sheer poetry of it, the depth of feeling expressed had me laughing and crying. Here was joy and love, hope and sorrow of such intensity that I felt transported.

Soon, what I wanted most in the world was a record player, and my parents gave me one for Christmas. Automatic, RCA, ten-record—the big time. I began to collect albums. In those days, there was a market geared specifically to blacks. That's where I went. You couldn't find those records in white stores, but who wanted to listen to Bing Crosby and Frank Sinatra, let alone Perry Como? Not me. To this day I treasure my 78 rpm records of Billie Holiday, Art Tatum, Bessie Smith, to name just a few. Yes, I loved black music and still do and always will. But that was just my first gulp from that unbelievable fountain, the fountain that doesn't quench your thirst but whets it instead: American folk music.

Julia was the matchmaker. Pete Seeger finalized the marriage.

He taught music at City and Country School when nobody had heard of Pete Seeger, let alone the Weavers. The boom in American folk music was still to come, but thanks to Pete I discovered Woody Guthrie, Leadbelly, people who later became legends. All of this could not but be part of what shaped my view of and feelings about America, this incredible music, so living, breathing freedom, its human dimension. It reflected the American character as nothing else even came or comes close to doing. Through Pete I entered the world of white folk music, the ballads, the bluegrass, the cowboy songs, the ditties, the work songs, and they all blended with the chain-gang songs, the blues, the spirituals.

Back then, nobody but the real aficionados knew who Bessie Smith was. Ditto for Billie Holiday. Now, if you tell people about Billie, they'll tell you they saw Diana Ross play her in the movies. Well, better that than nothing, I suppose. But it isn't even remotely like the real thing. Ross is a product of the present. A fine singer, for sure. But no Billie Holiday.

In a certain sense, in respect to the voice of America as expressed through her songs, I have deeper roots, more American feelings, a more profound knowledge of America than most Americans. A lot of them don't really know where they come from. But that *is* where they come from—the Woody Guthrie tradition and his songs.

Woody was a uniquely American phenomenon. What he said and the way he said it epitomizes the American spirit.

"I hate a song that makes you think you're not any good. I hate a song that makes you think you're just born to lose, bound to lose, no good to nobody, no good for nothin' because you're either too old or too young or too fat or too thin or too ugly or too this or too that. Songs that run you down or songs that poke fun at you on account of your bad luck or your hard travelin'. I am out to fight those kinds of songs to my last breath of air and my last drop of blood. I am out to sing songs that'll prove to you that this is *your* world, and if it's hit you pretty hard and knocked you down for a dozen loops, no matter how hard it's run you down and rolled over you, no matter what color, what size you are, how you're built, I am out to sing the songs that'll make you take *pride* in yourself."

My America.

Pete Seeger and I remain close friends to this day. I remember the first time Pete came to Moscow to perform in 1961. One of his appearances was in Tchaikovsky Hall, one of the major concert halls in Moscow. Pete has a song about a logger, and to do it, he comes onstage with an ax and proceeds to chop a log in two while singing the song. Now this calls for a minimum of two things: knowing how to chop a log and having a log to chop. Tchaikovsky Hall has hosted the most famous musicians in the world and has had all kind of props on its stage . . . except a log. So Pete said, "Vlad, I need a log. The people at Goskoncert don't know what the hell I'm talking about and neither do the people at Tchaikovsky Hall." I said, "Pete, never fear. You need a log, you'll get a log."

So I went around Moscow looking for logs. Not too many lying around. But finally I found a very nice one, though it was rather big. I called my brother Paul, and together we carried it off to my home. Came the day of the concert, and the people of Moscow in the area of Gorky Street and Mayakovsky Square were treated to a rather strange sight: two guys dressed to kill walking along with a log on their shoulders, then trooping into Tchaikovsky Hall to set it on the stage. Nobody said a damn thing, but we sure got some strange looks!

Pete spent one night at our Moscow apartment with a bunch of my Soviet friends. All night long he sang. It was one of those incredible moments when the power of his music brought people together. It left an indelible impression on everyone. Today, nearly thirty years later, the memory is as fresh as if it all happened yesterday.

Pete has a nice voice (he calls it a split tenor), but it wouldn't bring any offers from La Scala. For folk music, the voice is really not what counts. Joan Baez, for example, has a truly remarkable voice—indeed, her voice is what made her famous. Yet, quite frankly, I doubt anyone will remember her fifty years from now. Pete Seeger is part of American history despite his split tenor, as are Woody, Leadbelly, Bob Dylan, and a couple of others whose voices sounded like sandpaper on glass.

What's the secret? In the case of Pete, I think the answer is that he is a uniquely beautiful person. And I'm not playing with words when I say that. He is a man of profound moral courage, unshakable integrity and honesty who has sung for everything but money. He has taken the American folk song to the American people. He's sung for the down and out, for the people on strike, he's sung for human causes, he's fought against the Vietnam War with his songs, his songs have been a power in fighting for a clean environment. Here is a man who organized people living on the Hudson River to work to build a sloop, the *Clearwater,* and sail up and down that river, stopping in towns and bringing out the people, regardless of politics, color, and creed, mobilizing them to clean up the Hudson and keep it clean. And, by God, it worked.

Pete uses the American folk song for what it is, communication of ideas, of feelings. Although he is a wonderful performer, he does far more than simply perform for his audience. He literally spreads the word. And that is what makes him what he is, a prophet in his own land. Never to be deterred by blacklisting or the McCarthys of this world. Yes, he was blacklisted, he was called to testify in front of the House Un-American Activities Committee, and he told them he would like to sing them some of his "subversive" songs. They didn't allow it. That was many years ago, but to this very day, Pete Seeger, a man any country should be proud to call its own, has not been invited to be on network television.

He is a freethinker in the American tradition. That, before all else, is what makes him great. He refuses to bend, and he never broke.

I have often asked myself why societies try to neutralize people like Pete. The conclusion I have arrived at is that every society or social system reacts to what it conceives of as a threat. It is totally indifferent to non-threatening activity. The stronger, the more sophisticated and sure of itself a society is, the less threatened it feels and, consequently, the less repressively it reacts.

You'll find that in the 1830s, people in the United States, were hung or tarred and feathered and ridden out of town on a rail for speaking favorably of the British. This was about seventy years after the War of Independence. But even so, Britain was still perceived as a threat, and pro-British feelings elicited violent reactions. Why so, in a land that had declared freedom of speech, of thought, as being the inalienable right of all people? Because the United States was still a relatively weak country, while the British were, by today's standards, the leading superpower. Britain presented a threat to the United States, at least in theory. Let's not forget that in 1812, the British had taken Washington and burned down the White House. The apprehension and the tension weren't totally baseless—hence, the reaction.

Today, if an American were to say, "Long live the Queen (or King)!" he would probably get a round of applause or be treated to a beer. Because today, the United Kingdom and the Royal Family pose no threat whatsoever to the United States. Now a superpower in its own right with two hundred years of experience behind it, the United States no longer reacts to such a "threat."

But what about communism? What about the Red Menace? Ah, that's a different affair. For that threat emanates from the Soviet Union, and the Soviet Union is a superpower. Yet the origin of the fear goes deeper. When the socialist revolution occurred in 1917, it set a very attractive example for a great many people all over the world, especially in Europe. In fact, there followed a powerful revolutionary movement in Europe, specifically in Hungary and Germany.

In the West, the wealthy saw socialism as a serious "disease," a mortal threat to their privileges and power and they were perfectly right. This period coincided with the new labor movement in the United States. In those years, the unions were still weak, the working man was still fighting for basic rights. People in America were working twelve and fourteen hours a day under the most terrible conditions, while over there, in Russia, the commies announced the world's shortest work day, eight hours, and shortest work week, four days of work and the fifth day off. Naturally this was attractive. Naturally the Morgans, the DuPonts, the Rockefellers, the so-called captains of industry saw this as a threat. How did the power structure react? It is history: they created the Red Scare.

Leaf through American publications of early 1918 and you will find a recurring cartoon theme: there stands a threatening figure, less man and more gorilla; it wears a bushy, bristling beard, a fur hat; it has a knife clenched between its teeth and holds a bomb with a smoking fuse in its right hand; with its left it lifts up the corner of the American flag it is preparing to crawl under. A band running across the fur cap proclaims BOLSHEVIK. There it is, the communist threat to America. The American people were having the fear of God put into them. The commies were going to share their wives, eat their children, plunder their homes.

Who owned the newspapers and magazines? The same people who still do, the wealthy. It should come as no surprise that their designated role—then and during the McCarthy years—was nothing short of vicious. Before the government could act, it needed the support of public opinion, and the media played a key role in whipping up the anti-Red sentiment and bringing it to boil. Once the kettle was boiling, the government started cooking.

The Palmer Raids, which I mentioned earlier, are just one example of that. They have been most conveniently forgotten in America. For instance, all the *Columbia-Viking Desk Encyclopedia*'s 1960 edition has to say on that subject is: "Palmer, A(lexander) Mitchell, 1872–1936, U.S. Attorney General (1919–21). Ardently prosecuted those suspected of disloyalty to U.S." Sure, and Vishinsky ardently prosecuted those suspected of disloyalty to the USSR. And the Holy Inquisition ardently prosecuted . . . For the record, the aim of the Palmer Raids was to wipe out the socialists, crush the working-class movement in America, and round up all the radicals and put them on a boat for Europe. But do this ardently, you understand.

Another symbol of those times was the execution of Sacco and Vanzetti. Today we know they were framed; the state of Massachusetts has acknowledged their innocence. These two Italian immigrants were used to show the "foreign," hence un-American, origins of socialism and were executed to "prove" to the public that the Reds were all murderers. Joe Hill was another victim, one whose case was sung and entered the annals of American folk music: "I dreamed I saw Joe Hill last night as live and you and me. I said, 'But Joe, you're ten years dead.' 'I never died,' said he, 'I never died,' said he." Joe Hill, originally Joseph Hillstrom of Sweden, was put in front of a firing squad for supposedly having killed a Salt Lake City grocer. In fact, he was what one would call a union activist.

There was a repetition of the Red Scare. I witnessed its beginnings in the late forties. As it matured and ripened, it brought such things as the blacklist, Joe McCarthy, and the intimidation of millions of Americans. The threat to those in power was revitalized in the immediate postwar world. The Soviet victory over Germany and the leading role that communists had played in the various underground European resistance movements led to a tremendous surge in the popularity and authority of the USSR and the communist parties, especially in France, Italy, and Greece. To make things even worse, the U.S. labor movement had budding socialist and communist elements. Clearly, what was needed was a deliberate, planned campaign to do what had been done after World War I—scare the hell out of the American people. And that is exactly what the McCarthy period was all about. According to the media of the time, the commies had infiltrated everywhere, there was a Red under every bed, even the U.S. government was being run by commies. Why, wasn't Eisenhower a card-carrying commie? Today we laugh at the idea, but instead of laughing, we should ask ourselves how could that happen and why did it happen? Also, why is it that to this day Americans react with fear to the word *communist?*

During the McCarthy period, it was no laughing matter. In that atmosphere, it is understandable why there was so little public outcry against the blacklist, against those who were jailed. True, no one was physically destroyed, although quite a few committed suicide. Most were destroyed morally and financially. Still, none of this remotely resembled the Stalin purges, either in substance or in style. However, this was taking place not in Soviet Russia of 1937, but in a society close to two hundred years old, a society whose security was, in reality, not threatened in the least. It was far and away the most powerful country on earth, economically and militarily; it stood head, shoulders, and belly button above all others. Americans had nothing to fear, and yet they reacted with paranoia.

When people ask me, "How do you know, how can you guarantee, that you won't have another Stalin?" I ask, in turn, "How do you know, how can you guarantee, there won't be another Joe McCarthy in America? Or even a fascist dictatorship?" How can any society *guarantee* something like that? It cannot. A Hitler can be elected to power democratically. It's already happened.

I bring these subjects up in the hope that people will look at them honestly. I hope that they will then agree that even in safe, strong social systems, there must exist allowable limits to the degree of dissent. Those limits evolve and, as society becomes more democratic and humane, they become less and less stringent. But people shouldn't pretend there are no limits.

Look at America. Yes, Americans enjoy a greater degree of freedom of speech than we Soviets do (that's the case today, but who knows about tomorrow?). But the greater one's access to the public at large, the greater the limitations. Network television in the United States will clearly not allow certain views to be expressed.

I had an interesting conversation about freedom of speech with a man who was then the president of one of the three networks. We argued back and forth for a while, and then I asked, "If I were your number one reporter and you sent me to the Soviet Union to prepare a series, and I came back, went on the air, and said, 'Ladies and gentlemen, I have discovered that we in the U.S. media have misled the American people, for socialism, as I have seen it function in Russia, leads to the creation of a society more just than our own.' How long would I still continue to work for you?"

He gave me an honest answer: "Not only would you lose your job with me, but no major television station in the country would want to touch you."

Simple as that.

On the other hand, the U.S. Communist party is allowed to publish its newspaper, the *People's Daily World.* With the kind of circulation it has, who cares? That's where the sophistication comes in, and it derives from the British tradition. They are the past masters of this art. Let the man get up on a soapbox in Hyde Park! Let him talk his heart out! Give him the satisfaction of knowing he said what he wanted to say! Allow him the luxury of coming home to his wife and boasting to her about how he told 'em all off! Let him do it . . . because he is not dangerous, not in the least. Now, if a movement begins, if he has a following, if it starts to grow, *then* comes the question of how to neutralize him. The more sophisticated a society is, the better it will handle something like that. If need be, however, society will kill. We've seen that happen. Of course, we are duly informed that these deaths relate to only one person, a madman at that.

What *really* happened to Martin Luther King? Does anyone honestly believe that a man by the name of James Earl Ray decided to shoot him?

Just like that? All on his own? I certainly don't. Martin Luther King had become a real force in America. There hadn't been anything like him since Abraham Lincoln (assassinated by one John Wilkes Booth, another "crazy" individual). He wasn't just consolidating the blacks, he was uniting the blacks and the whites, he was bringing together all the ethnic minorities of America. He was the first man in American history who was able to achieve that. His ideals, truly Christian ideals, led to social conclusions that threatened powerful interests relating to such different areas as the Vietnam War, military spending, vested interests, and the status quo.

There are always limits. The question is how sophisticated the system is in defining and enforcing them. Every system will protect itself. Never doubt that. The more insecure it is, the more violent will be its reaction—rather, its overreaction. The French Revolution of 1789 declared as its slogan Liberty, Equality, Fraternity—and proceeded to chop off many heads, including those belonging to the revolution's most ardent supporters. People were executed for protesting against senseless brutality, they were executed for expressing doubt. Today in France, people can and do say much harsher things without anyone really even taking notice.

The evolution of the limits of dissent has its own history in the Soviet Union, an issue I will deal with further on. At this point, I will only say that a new sense of awareness, a feeling of confidence and greater tolerance has begun to assert itself based on the realization that socialism, conceptually, is supposed to provide freedom of thought and speech and expression.

Nevertheless, limits certainly remain. In some ways, surprisingly, those limits are already broader than in the United States. The possibility of being publicly critical about one's own society and positive about others, for example, is more apparent in the Soviet media than in the American. But in most areas, our limits remain more strict. You will rarely find criticism of Gorbachev or of any member of the Politburo. If this were a consistent policy of neither praising nor criticizing ranking members of the party or the government, but criticizing or praising only *policies,* one might argue the merits of such an approach. But the fact is that there is a lot of praise for these people. Under glasnost and perestroika, we should be able to openly criticize the leader(s) of the country. The fact of the matter is, we do not. And the reason we do not has to do mainly with traditional fear of the consequences. In the past, such actions jeopardized your career, your freedom, even your life. Added to that is the tradition of respect, in a way analogous to the British attitude whereby one does not say nasty things about the queen. But that first reason—fear—is more important. Another taboo is Soviet foreign policy. Journalists, or more precisely editors, are reluctant to allow dissent in that area, as opposed to domestic affairs. Yet as I write this, I realize that between now and the time you, the reader, get to see it, things may have changed for the better.

And so the future. I doubt anyone here will ever have the legal right to advocate either the overthrow of the Soviet government or of the socialist system. In America, one has that right only if it does not pose "a clear and present danger"—whatever that means. Perhaps we too will adopt something similar. Perhaps we will take it even further. Who knows? It is hard to make predictions. Five years ago, I don't think many people would have predicted the changes happening right now in the Soviet Union. The ultimate limits of what can publicly be advocated depend on how *society* sees what is happening, whether or not society perceives these things as a threat. If it does, whether in the Soviet Union or the United States, that threat will be eliminated.

In both societies, we need to be honest in appraising the limits, not simply of expression, but of practicing human freedom in all areas of life. If we find that existing limits are not consistent with our ideals, we have the moral obligation to protest against them. In relation to socialism and the Soviet Union, that poses one set of issues. For America, the conflict is between her deep-rooted democratic tradition and an economic system that gives power and privileges to the few. Sooner or later, that basic conflict will have to be faced. Having lived in America, having grown up with its traditions and people, I believe that when those fundamental questions confront them, as they inevitably will, they will come down on the side of democracy.

2

⋖◆⋗

In Limbo

We sailed out of New York Harbor in December 1948, on the *Stephan Batory,* a Polish oceanliner of some thirty-four thousand tons. I remember looking down from the deck at the crowd that had come to see their friends and relatives off. Almost no one had come to say good-bye to us. In fact, the only person I recall was Uncle Beale, my aunt Jacqueline's husband. Everyone else, all our close friends, all those who had enjoyed our hospitality when my father had been making big money, all the people who came to our home to enjoy good wine and good company—none of them came to say farewell.

That last year had been hell. My father was out of work, and his prospects of getting a job were nil. A Soviet citizen with openly procommunist views, a man who carried his politics on his sleeve for all to see, my father quickly understood there was really no room for him in America. Most of all, he would have liked to return to the Soviet Union with his family. He had spoken about this to the Soviet consul general in New York on many occasions, but the man had put him off, giving evasive answers that drove my father crazy. Later, in Germany, this pattern was to repeat itself, only instead of the consul general it was the Soviet ambassador to the German Democratic Republic who kept putting my father off and incurring his wrath as a result. Today, I know that my father probably owed his life to these two men; that applies to my mother and myself as well. Had we arrived in the Soviet Union any earlier than we did, there is little doubt that we all would have wound up in one of the Gulag camps. My brother would have been put into one of those orphanages for the children of enemies of the people. Both the consul general in New York and the ambassador in Berlin knew this. Both couldn't risk telling my father (he would probably not have believed them anyway), so they did their utmost to stall him. I am eternally grateful to them and would like them to be known by name: Yakov Mironovich Lomakin and Gheorghi Maximilianovich Pushkin.

Out of work and unable to get permission to go to the Soviet Union, my father decided to return to France, a country he knew and loved. My mother wholeheartedly supported his decision. She didn't have to apply for a French visa, being a French citizen, as were my brother and myself— we were included on her passport. Not so my father. He had to apply. In 1948, the Communist party was extremely strong in France; in fact, there was a real threat of a leftist coalition coming to power. My father was a known quantity in France, certainly not a person the government particularly wanted to see again. Probably they would have denied his French visa anyway, but when he was denounced as a "dangerous communist" by one of his former colleagues, a man who envied him and hated him (the two usually go hand in hand), when this man sent the French government a letter warning it about my father, the decision was predictable. He was denied entrance to France.

It was then that my mother suffered her first nervous breakdown. Suddenly, in the street, she fainted, and from that day on for many, many years she was afraid of going out alone. I can only imagine what she went through, this woman who was so strong and so independent and yet had to ask her husband, her children, someone to accompany her every time she had to go out.

After the French visa was denied, we had one more choice: Mexico. That is where American leftists went to escape McCarthy and McCarthyite America, and my father had good contacts there. Then, like a bolt out of the blue, my father was offered a job by the Soviet government: to work as part of the Soviet Military Administration in Germany and rebuild the German film industry in that zone. Overjoyed, my father immediately accepted.

I have often wondered what would have happened to me if the French hadn't denied my father's visa application. Or if there had been no offer from the Soviets and we had gone to Mexico. Or if my father had decided to become a U.S. citizen. It's a little game I play with myself, a game that tickles my fancy, nothing more, for what happened happened and no one will ever know what might have been. But for some reason

I think of O. Henry's story "Roads of Destiny." If fate has it that you will be killed by the Marquis de Beaupertuys, then that will happen no matter what road you take.

Throughout that final year of 1948, we had had some new visitors and consequently lost most of our old ones. The new came from the FBI and asked the usual questions. I say "usual" instead of "stupid" because, contrary to folklore, they are not stupid—neither the questions nor the men who ask them. They have a logic of their own, one that may seem simplistic and obtuse, but do not underrate them. Like the Church, the police have been around for a long time and form one of civilization's most lasting institutions; they have accumulated great experience. Anyway, these regular visits, plus the fact that the FBI made calls on friends of ours and asked *them* questions about us, discouraged just about everyone from seeing us. Even the Windrows, people who had known us since the early thirties, even they vanished. The one person who refused to vanish was Uncle Beale.

I had really never liked him much. Whenever I visited my cousins in Alexandria, I tried to keep away from him. Even the way everybody called him by his last name, just Beale, kind of turned me off. He was a silent man, he rarely smiled, he wouldn't let me or my cousins touch the great electric train he had set up down in the basement. He was stern, strict, never showing any warmth. But when push came to shove, when all our liberal, leftist, progressive friends went running for cover, refused to be seen with my father or mother in public, asked us not to call them on the phone (ever!), this southerner, this man whose politics could only have been conservative, this American Mr. Straight who was so clean he squeaked (not to confuse with squealed) refused to be intimidated, refused to write off his wife's family just because the FBI didn't like them. No sir, he wasn't going to bow to any kind of pressure. And so he made a point of coming up from Alexandria, taking time off from his job with CBS in Washington, D.C., to come to New York City to see us off.

I never forgot that. And as the years passed and I saw people betray one another out of fear, the importance of what Beale had done gained stature, as did the feeling of guilt for not having loved him, not having known the real man behind the stern words, short temper, and cold demeanor. One of the greatest moments of fulfillment I ever experienced came forty years later, shortly after Beale had undergone cancer surgery and shortly before he passed away. I came to see him at the hospital, where I spent two hours with him and his family; then, when I said good-bye,

I hugged him and held him close. I *know* he understood what I was telling him.

But that was in 1988 and this was 1948, and I was leaning on the railing of the *Stephan Batory*'s main deck, looking down at the crowd and humming—I remember that to this day—"Mairzy doats an' goatzy doats an' little 'ams eadivey, a kid'll eadivey too, wouldn't you, yes, a kid'll eadivey too, wouldn't you?" Why that of all things? Why has that stayed with me all these long years? I have to believe it is because I was in a state of shock, even though I didn't know it and probably would have denied it. I have to think that deep down inside me, I knew my life was undergoing profound and dramatic change. I wanted to leave, that's true enough, but there must have been pain tugging in there somewhere, there must have been a sense of "good-bye America, hello what?" and the only way to keep an even keel was to sway to the asinine meaninglessness of "Mairzy Doats."

My memory of the voyage on the *Batory* is pretty much a blank. The ship docked in Southampton, Le Havre, Bremerhaven, and Copenhagen before reaching its final destination of Gdansk. The passengers reflected the hop-skip-and-jump nature of the voyage: Brits, French, Danes, but almost no Germans and only a few Poles (not counting the crew). The Danish women all struck me as being very pretty until I saw them smoking cigars, a sight that insulted my ideas of femininity. I have matured since then to the point where I can watch a woman light up a Montecristo without even batting an eye.

I had my first shave on the *Batory*. I figured that was the place to do it: my old friends wouldn't have to get used to my new face, and my future new friends would never have had seen the old one. I remember the pale and somewhat wide-eyed individual who looked back at me from the mirror after I finished shaving and had washed off the lather under my father's careful tutelage.

I remember Copenhagen as a toy city, warm and friendly, cobblestones and copper green with age, a bustling and yet peaceful city where we were allowed to spend a few hours roaming about. But my first real memory is of war, or rather the results of war. The skeleton buildings, the gaping empty windows, the heaps of rubble. These I first saw in Gdansk, then Gdynia, then Warsaw and Cracow. This was a truly different world. And I distinctly remember not liking it. It was grim, brutal, scary. And so I closed my eyes and my mind to it, knowing full well that I was just passing through. Why should I care? Still, a few things got caught in the web of my memory and have refused to be suppressed under the weight of time. The Bristol Hotel in Warsaw, the red rugs and cut glass that spoke of different, luxurious times. The food—good, yet unrefined and heavy. The prices—ten thousand zloty for a bowl of soup—and having my pockets crammed with money, all of which could buy very little. One of the waitresses in the Bristol restaurant—blond hair and eyebrows, piercing black eyes, red lips and, as they would say in New York, stacked—and my father catching my look, laughing and saying, "Polish beauties are very dangerous. Wait till you read Gogol's *Taras Bulba,* you'll see for yourself."

At that time I felt very close to my father in a way that had never been true before. A very stupid thing happened to me in Cracow, but it brought us even closer. I had always had an abhorrence of zoos and circuses. The sight of animals held in captivity or forced to do tricks literally made me sick (and still does).

One day in Cracow, we—my mother, father, a Polish friend, and I—went for a walk in the local park. The trees were bare and the temperature was below zero, but there was very little snow on the ground. As we walked along, I suddenly saw an antelope standing on what looked like a circle of faded grass surrounded by a rather wide strip of sidewalk. What a wonderful sight! An animal living unconfined amid human beings! Overjoyed, I ran toward it, onto that circular sidewalk and Crrrack! found myself up to my chin in freezing water. The "sidewalk" was really a moat that had frozen over, but the ice was still too thin to hold my weight. The antelope must have known, because it didn't budge, it just stared at me as I ran toward it.

My father pulled me out, soaking wet, teeth chattering. "Don't stand there," he said, "start running." And we ran. All the way back to the hotel, while my mother and our Polish friend flagged down a cab. We ran and ran, my father just behind me, speaking words of encouragement, keeping me going. We ran into the hotel, never stopping, up the stairs to our room, where my father had me undress and then proceeded to rub me down with vodka until my skin glowed. "You'll be fine," he said, "no cold can stand up to hot blood and strong vodka." And he was right. I didn't even have a touch of the sniffles. Together we licked that cold, and in a way it formed a bond between us.

Another memory of Poland was the Warsaw ghetto, or what was left of it. I won't even try to explain it. It's been done many times by people whose powers of description far exceed mine. I will only say that the desolation, the mounds of brick and rubble, the cold wind hissing over it all, the terrible sadness of it have never left me; the picture comes back, again and again, somehow reminding me of a Chagall painting and the plaintive sound of a lone violin holding a single note as the musician draws his bow back and forth across a string.

And a final memory. The apartment of a Polish filmmaker in Warsaw, where my mother and father had been invited for tea. I was sent off to play with the man's nine-year-old son. Among his meager toys, I found a tin cigarette box with several military medals, all Soviet. I realized that his father had fought in the Red Army against Hitler, which immediately made him a hero in my eyes. But why did he let his son play with something as sacred as these decorations? I asked my father, who really didn't know what to say. The boy's father smiled ironically and said something like, "Who gives a damn about such trinkets?" I was shocked and hurt, but at the same time his eyes, his voice told me much more than his words. I felt there was some kind of terrible pain there, and I resented knowing it, resented his making me aware of it. Looking back, I now understand that that was, perhaps, the first time in my life I experienced anger when encountering something that contradicted what I wanted to believe. In the future, it would happen again and again and again. I was to see it torture my father, and it would take me a good part of my life to deal with it. To say the least, it is a learning experience.

All told, we spent some two weeks in Poland. Then we left for Berlin. My very first impression, as our train pulled into the Ostbahnhof, was that of a vast number of military. They seemed to be everywhere—Soviet officers in long winter coats and fur hats, men with faces of granite who rarely smiled. When they did, they showed steel teeth, the likes of which I had never seen. I don't know what I expected, but whatever it was, it was different. And my very first thought, as I recall it, was "I don't want to be here." And for the entire four years we were to spend in Berlin, that desire to be somewhere else never left me. In fact, it grew. I say that today, as I look back upon the boy I was, and I realize that I kept this feeling locked away, refusing to acknowledge it. But deep down inside it gnawed away at me. Those four years were the most unhappy of my life.

I had grown up hating the Germans, nothing to boast about, to be sure, but a state of mind any child of my generation could not escape, especially if that child had experienced the German occupation of Paris and the intensity of the anti-Nazi feeling in wartime New York. But to make matters worse, because I did not speak a single word of Russian I was automatically a German to the Russians. The very thought of being considered German was unbearable. I could have killed for that—and once very nearly did.

It must have been in 1950. I was big for my age, especially compared with German boys who had undergone the privation of the war years. They were scrawny, small, undernourished, weak. One such German boy, Klaus, used to come around to our house to pick up his girlfriend, the daughter of our German cleaning woman, Frau Herta. One day I caught him admiring my boxing gloves, of which I had two pair. I asked him if he'd like to put them on. He did. Then I asked him if he'd like to spar. He would. So I took him out into the backyard. It all began innocently enough. I really had no intention, at least not consciously, of wanting to beat him to a pulp. But that is what I tried to do. I was at least a head taller than he, some twenty pounds heavier, and much stronger. In addition to that, I had done some boxing in a Catholic gym in the Village, while he had no boxing experience at all. I still don't remember how it actually happened—only the way we started horsing around with the gloves, then a total blank, and then my mother hanging onto my shoulders and screaming at me and Klaus' face, chalk white where it wasn't covered with blood. Had my mother not seen us from the kitchen window and come running out to stop me, I would have killed him. I really would have.

Klaus had nothing to do with it. I was hitting out murderously at my hatred of being in Germany, of not really knowing who I was: neither Russian, because the Russians would not accept me, nor German, because I could never accept them. I was striking out at my own unhappiness, at the circumstances that had so changed my life, at the feeling of utter helplessness of my condition. But I could never have explained it then.

Thus I found myself living in limbo, not with the Soviets, whom I loved in advance and desperately wanted to be loved by but who certainly didn't consider me as one of their own, nor with the Germans, whom I hated and whose acceptance, though in a way more forthcoming, I ferociously repulsed. I lived between the two. Perhaps that had something to do with my being outside and looking in, making mental notes, storing away information.

I found much to support my hatred of the Germans. The way they fawned, scraped, and bowed when addressed by Soviets and the insolent, insulting way any one of them treated a German of lower standing or rank. They way they were stingy, tightfisted, counting every pfennig, never treating one another to a drink, even expecting to be paid when one bummed a cigarette off another. The coarseness of the jokes, all about bowel movements and fat asses. The vulgarity of the voices, loud and aggressive. Their love of *Ordnung,* never mind what kind of order, order for who or what, but order as such, their respect for the notion of verboten. If it said Verboten on a door, you did not go in under any circumstances, and you did not walk on the grass if that was verboten, and most of all you did not question *why* it was verboten. The way the girls did little *Knicksen,* curtseys, when introduced and the boys bowed their heads and clicked their heels while I half expected them to snap their right arms up and yell out a "Heil Hitler!" I hated each and every one of them for making a point of saying that he had fought on the *western* front, and since only a select few ever admitted having fought on the eastern front, I was often tempted to ask who the hell the Red Army had beaten the shit out of at Stalingrad. But more than anything else, I hated them for not knowing. Concentration camps? A blank look. What concentration camps? Gas chambers? Ach, that's just a nasty story spread by those who want to vilify Germany. Ovens? Well, maybe, for baking bread. Which brings me to a wonderful story.

My father went to work for Sovexportfilm, an organization that was primarily designated to find foreign markets for Soviet movies and buy foreign films for distribution in the USSR. But in those postwar years in Germany, its main purpose was to help rebuild the local film industry. Of course, this was not just charity by any means. Film ranks second to none as shaper of outlooks, stereotypes, dos and don'ts, good and evil. No one has made that point better than Hollywood, which has not only created the image that people all over the world associate with America and Americans, but has indeed shaped most Americans' concept of who they are, what it is to look American and act American. I can think of no better example of that than Ronald Reagan. In short, film is a potent force that has been used for ideological purposes by every country that has a film industry. The Soviets were far from indifferent about what kind of movies they wanted the German film industry to produce and the German people to see. The problem was that the Germans were not going to the movie theaters. Not because going to a movie was *verboten,* but because the theaters were terribly cold: During the last year of the war, the heating systems had either broken down or been destroyed. My father was given the responsibility of doing something about that situation. He came up with a temporary solution of pure genius by getting the Soviet army command to lend all theaters as many blankets as they had seats. Potential moviegoers were offered a free blanket while they watched the flick. Free? Mein Gott, who could refuse that kind of offer? But the long-term solution called for installing new heating systems.

One day my father found himself in the old city of Weimar, the home of Goethe, among others. He sat in a rented office waiting for answers to the ad that had been published in the local paper. Sure enough, at eight-thirty on the morning after the ad appeared, two middle-aged Germans came knocking at his door. (They would probably have come at five, but the ad indicated that office hours started at eight-thirty. *Ordnung* is *Ordnung,* right?) They told my father that they the were exactly the people he was looking for: engineers who specialized in heating installations, descendants of a long line of civil engineers, highly respected by one and all. And to prove their impeccable credentials, they had brought along a few blueprints of some of the projects they had worked on in the past. Having said that, they spread one such blueprint on the table in front of my father. Now he knew next to nothing about heating installations. He had worked as a sound engineer for MGM, but that was many years ago and was far removed from this kind of engineering. However, as he looked at the drawing, he found himself wondering just what it depicted— because it certainly did not *seem* to be a heating installation. Consequently, he asked the two gentlemen to enlighten him. "Ach, Herr Pozner," one of them gushed, "this was really a very special project. It was commissioned by the very top people, the very top, you understand. We are very proud of it. We consider this to be our most outstanding achievement." Still, my father was not satisfied. He wanted to know exactly what this "outstanding achievement" actually was. To make a long story short, it was the blueprint for the crematory ovens of the Buchenwald concentration camp situated just outside Weimar.

When my father threw the two men out, threatening to have them put up against a wall and shot if he ever saw their faces again, they thought he had gone crazy. What was the matter with this uncivilized, insane Russian? After all, they had been commissioned to do a job, and they had delivered an outstanding piece of work. What more could anyone possibly ask? As for what might be the purpose of the machinery they had designed, that was neither their responsibility nor their concern. What *was* the matter with that Russian?

But as I was to discover, the ability to forget, to do one's job and ignore its consequences is not strictly a German attribute. This sort of self-serving justification applies to all of us who just do our jobs, just follow orders. We think that, by ignoring the consequences of our actions, the consequences will ignore us. They won't. They will return to haunt us and torture us as individuals and as nations—as has happened not only to the Germans.

And there were Germans who understood this.

Some I met when going to a special school that had been set up for the children of German political refugees who had escaped the Hitler regime and grown up in Moscow. These children had been tormented in Soviet schools during the war for being Fritzes and Krauts and fascists, so they hated their own Germanness. Now they had been brought back to the place their parents called home, taken back for good. Most of them cringed at the idea. Not only was Germany a foreign country to them, but German was a foreign language. They had been babies when their parents fled, and their natural language was Russian. The school was created to facilitate their transition back to German life. Many of the subjects were taught in German by Germans and followed the German school curriculum, but several subjects were taught in Russian by Soviet teachers. That was the school I went to, and it was there that I met the "other kind" of Germans. Those who had fought Hitler, those who had spent time in Hitler's concentration camps. These were the people who would soon become the leaders of the New Germany, the German Democratic Republic. Their children, my schoolmates, would graduate and be sent to the Soviet Union for their university degrees, all the while being groomed for future leadership—positions most of them actually never acquired because, ironically enough, they were looked upon as outsiders by the vast majority of "ordinary" Germans, those who had been born there, grew up there, gone to school and university there.

I can't say I disliked that school, but neither did I really feel comfortable there. It was a place I attended from nine to three, never spilling out into afternoons, as in New York, when we would hang out, go to a movie, pick fights in Washington Square, get together for a ball game on Sundays, visit one another's homes. There may have been a few occasions when I joined some of my classmates to go hiking or for a birthday party, but by and large we lived separate lives, they in their German environment, I with my parents. There was just one exception, a girl in my class named Dolores, in honor of Dolores Ibarruri, the famous La Pasionaria of the struggle against Franco. Her father, a Hungarian surgeon, had been killed in Spain during the civil war while serving the Loyalist Army. Her mother, one of the most strikingly beautiful, warm, intelligent, and kind women I have ever encountered, remarried in Germany. Her husband, Willi, was a German communist who had spent long years in concentration camps. Now he was a ranking law-and-order official. He went on to acquire top rank in East Germany's equivalent of the KGB. He was a man of principles and integrity, and when, several years later, I learned that he had committed suicide, I was shocked but not really surprised.

There is something truly amazing in the way a human being with a cause, with a belief, is capable of standing up to the most inhuman conditions, to physical and mental torture, to the carefully structured madness of a concentration camp, to fiendish devices aimed at breaking his or her spirit. But take away that cause, destroy that belief, and that very same human being almost invariably self-destructs. In some cases literally, as with Willi; in other cases through drink or violence or any of the other methods that all come down to the same thing: the destruction of the human in the being. That is perhaps what really makes us different from all other living creatures. We cannot live without a belief.

I attended that school for two years. As it gradually phased out classes in Russian, I left and began to go to evening school for Soviet officers and noncoms whose high-school educations had been interrupted by the war. If I was an outsider in the Russo-German school, I was even more so in this one. Virtually all of the students were in their mid- or late twenties, some even older, all fighting men who had gone through the hell of the war. But while they and I came from two different worlds, I found that I could relate to them in a way I never had with others. Perhaps it was the horror, the death and destruction they had gone through, perhaps it was also the pride of their achievement as soldiers, tempered by the wisdom of unparalleled suffering. Whatever the reasons, these men, though hard as nails and tough beyond belief, had a degree of compassion and gentleness the likes of which I have never witnessed since in any large group. What I say is a generality, yet it manifested itself in very concrete ways.

My Russian was poor. During a physics class, I was called upon by the teacher to describe the function of a solenoid, an electrical conductor that establishes a magnetic field once an electrtic current is sent through it. I mispronounced the word *solenoid* in Russian, and one of the officers started laughing at me. I could have died of shame. I stood there, red in the face, desperately wishing the ceiling would collapse and bury all of us. The classroom became deathly silent. One of the officers stood up and barked at me: "Get out and shut the door behind you." Looking neither right nor left, I walked out of the room, shut the door, and stood there, devastated. And then I heard the classroom erupt.

It must be said that Russian is a very rich language, but it excels and ranks second to none in its profanity. Its imagery is mind-boggling, it flies, nay, it soars into cosmic realms, its cadences are majestic, it is, when properly mastered, nothing short of an art form. I have been treated to some rather outstanding sermons and deliberations by past masters of this genre, but never before or since have I witnessed such unadulterated, pure, powerful Russian profanity.

As I stood behind that door, petrified by the sheer force of the oration, the officer who had made fun of me was informed about all his relatives, starting with his mother and including all of his ancestors; his intelligence was carefully analyzed, as was his standing as an officer; he was told what he might best do with the stars on his shoulder straps (as a captain he had eight—four on each strap) and where he should stick them. He was dissected internally and externally, his habits, facial expression, manner of walking and talking, and gestures were examined with great care and at length. This went on for about a quarter of an hour. Then a hush descended on the classroom, the door opened, and the officer who had ordered me out beckoned for me to come back in. The subject under discussion was standing in the middle of the room. His face was white and his hands shook. When he saw me come in, he walked toward me, stuck out his hand, and said in a hoarse voice, "Forgive me, please. I was wrong." And all the other men crowded around me, pumped my hand, slapped me on the back until the teacher, a woman in her early thirties, raised her head from the book she had been reading and said in a matter-of-fact voice, "Class is resumed."

That episode might strike some as being a strange example of sensitivity, but that is what it was. From that day on, the men made a point of treating me as an equal. This naturally had certain consequences, one of the most memorable being the first time I ever got drunk. It all began innocently enough when, one day, I bumped into a sergeant who attended the same evening classes as I. He asked me what I was doing and, upon hearing my answer—*"Nichevo,"* nothing much—said "Let's go toss a couple down." By that time I had had enough experience sitting at Russian tables to know that tossing a couple down was an understatement par excellence. I think it is fair to say that your average Russian can outdrink any other being, both terrestrial and extraterrestrial. But I was certainly

not going to show any sign of weakness. "Sure, let's," I answered noncha-
lantly. My new-found friend promptly led me to a soldier's canteen, sat
me down at one of the tables, and said he'd be back in a minute. And back
in a minute he was, carrying a tray with a bottle of vodka, two glasses (the
kind one usually drinks water from), and a plate with a stack of black bread
and two hard-boiled eggs. He put the tray down, opened the bottle,
emptied it into the glasses, filling them to the rim, clinked his glass against
mine, said "Here's to," exhaled loudly, and emptied his glass in three neat
gulps. He them dipped his egg into a dish of salt (there was one on each
table), shoved the whole egg into his mouth, bit off a piece of black bread,
and vigorously began to chew as I watched with fascination. "Come on,"
he said after swallowing. I don't know how I got that glass of vodka down,
but I recall having had no problem with the egg. I had once stuck five
plums into my mouth on a bet (nearly suffocating when I was unable to
either swallow or extract them), so one egg plus bread was easy enough.
"Good show!" said the sergeant. He slapped me on the back, took a look
at his watch, and said he had to go. So did I. I don't have any recollection
of getting home, so I must have been on automatic pilot. But I do remember spending the better part of the afternoon praying to the white goddess
and being miserably sick all night.

But I never held it against Sergeant Kovaliov. All he was trying to
do was to make me feel part of the team, and sharing a glass of vodka was
his way of telling me we were comrades.

But not all of my Soviet acquaintances were like Sergeant Kovaliov
or like the officers who took one of their own to task for laughing at my
poor Russian. Many kept their distance, clearly not wanting to seem
related to my family in any way, an attitude and a precaution I fully
understand and have understood ever since I came to learn of the dangers
associated then in the Soviet Union with having anything to do with
foreigners. Others were openly hostile. A few were friendly. And a very
small number went so far as to flaunt their friendship, hoisting it up as a
kind of challenging banner. But regardless of their attitude, they shared
one common trait I would have given anything not to see: they were
different. They were different from the Americans I knew; they were
different from the Russians I had known in America, the children of
Russian intellectuals who had fled the revolution between 1918 and 1922.
Most painfully of all, they were different from the way I had imagined they
would be. Most of them came from very humble origins, and this was
reflected in their manners, their way of speaking, their tastes. Most of them

had lived lives of such privation as was beyond my comprehension. For them, postwar Germany was a horn of plenty, a place of unbelievable material wealth. The vast majority of them had never enjoyed the luxury (and for them it was a luxury) of a private apartment, yet here the representatives of Sovexportfilm and their families occupied the entire floor of several two-story stucco buildings. To me, Berlin seemed desolate. Nothing caught my eye in the stores, the food was coarse, and the choice limited. To them, every day was like Christmas. I have often wondered what Russian people thought when they discovered that even after suffering defeat, the Germans lived better than they did *before* the war? It must have been a shock.

It must also have made some of them start thinking. Forty years later, when I was working on a documentary film based on the personal reminiscences of Valentin Berezhkov, a man who was Molotov's and then Stalin's personal interpreter from 1940 to 1944, Berezhkov answered the question I had asked myself so many years ago. "One of the reasons why Stalin resumed his policy of internal terror after the war had a lot to do with the millions of Soviet soldiers who had seen other countries with their own eyes—Austria, Norway, Hungary, Czechoslovakia, Germany. In a way, it was like what happened as a result of the Napoleonic wars. The Russian army, led by young and brilliant officers, defeated Napoleon and wound up in Paris, and even though France had changed since 1789, the spirit of the revolution was still very much present. It affected these young men, and they were the ones who led the Decembrist uprising of 1825 that nearly toppled Czar Nicholas I. Think now of the Soviet fighting men. Prior to the war, they had lived in a society where all initiative was fraught with danger, where the bureaucracy ruled supreme, where every step, every decision had to be verified and approved of by someone higher up, whose decision in turn had to be approved by someone above him, and so on. Then came the war. It liberated the people, strangely enough. It called for on-the-spot decisions, for creative thought, for independent ideas. Time was always a vital factor, a truth realized very quickly. And so the soldiers, the noncoms, the junior and senior officers were allowed to make their own decisions. They suddenly began to act like free men, and they found an enormous source of pride in this. Once bowed, head drawn into shoulders, flinching at every order, they stood tall, head thrown back. *They* were the ones who won the war.

"Stalin must have foreseen the danger they posed to his absolute rule.

"But in addition to that, we actually believed the propaganda we were subjected to, we were sure our standard of living was the best in the world, that, yes, in capitalist countries the "money-bags" wallowed in wealth but the working people lived lives of abject poverty and desperation. We believed that, never questioned it. Now imagine us discovering that, after seven years of war, after savage bombing and artillery shelling, after fighting on two fronts and going down in unconditional surrender, the average German still had whole hams and sausages hanging in his cellar, had heating and electricity, had hot water and even a telephone, had, in fact, far more than even those considered well off in the Soviet Union before the beginning of the war, let alone after it. People had to ask themselves, how come?

"Stalin must have understood where such questions could lead. And the only way to thwart the danger, as he saw it, was to break that new spirit, beat back the questions, create an atmosphere of xenophobia. And that is precisely what he did."

I agree with Berezhkov's analysis.

But in Berlin at the end of the forties and beginning of the fifties, no such thoughts crossed my mind. What's more, had anyone suggested such an idea, I would have hotly debated it. Because I was, as the French say, more Catholic than the pope. I think I had no alternative, this was my lifeboat, the safety belt that allowed me to stay afloat in the turbulent waters I had been thrown into by circumstance. The discrepancy between what I had expected and what I found gave me two choices: to admit there *was* a discrepancy, that I had been wrong in believing certain things, to accept that and go from there; or to close my mind and ignore the obvious. I chose to do the latter because the former was far too painful for a teenager in the process of adapting to a new life. Without any attempt to justify myself, I must point out (as I may have earlier and will do further on) that my decision not to see was made by virtually everyone who supported and sympathized with the socialist experiment going on in the Soviet Union, mature men and women well anchored in their lives and societies but who could not stand up to the pressure of acknowledging any shortcomings or criticism of the Soviet Union. These people had a siege mentality; it took enormous courage and integrity to be pro-Soviet in the West in the pre- and postwar years. The only way to deal with the anti-Soviet barrage was to close ranks and not yield. To give an inch was interpreted as a sure sign of unconditional surrender, a strange logic to be sure, but a logic nonetheless, one confirmed time and time again when western communists not only turned against the Soviet Union upon learning of Stalin's crimes, but left the party and became actively anticommunist.

My world was black and white (or should I say, red and white). It was a world of right and wrong, good and bad, friend and foe. No in-betweens, no shadings. I wholeheartedly embraced "clear," "axiomatic" truths. I put those words in quotation marks because, in reality, those truths were simplistic rather than axiomatic, superficial rather than clear. I loved to bolster my arguments with such slogans as "Enough for all, excess for none" (Robespierre), "He who is not with us is against us" (Mayakovsky), "If the enemy does not surrender, he is exterminated" (Gorky). I was, in the final analysis, an extremist, and as such I had what all extremists have—tunnel vision. Extremists are usually motivated by ideals, often of the noblest kind, in the name of which they commit the most atrocious crimes without batting an eye. When I use the word *ideal,* I am not automatically indicating something *good* (another word that often demands qualification); rather, I am speaking of the goal a given individual sets for himself and sees as the sense of his life.

Whether extremism is good or bad is really not for me to say. Even if I did have the authority to pass such a judgment, what difference would it make? Extremism is a state of mind almost everyone goes through at a certain age. Some outgrow it, others do not, but it will always be around— as long as we humans remain in existence. What's more, certain things cannot be accomplished without an extremist outlook. Revolution, for one. Or anything that demands singleness of purpose and the consequences be damned. The minute you begin to look at all the shadings, the ifs and the buts and the maybes, you may as well forget about immediate results. In that sense, extremism has its qualities. Then again, one might say that it has terrible drawbacks and is even self-defeating. Whether he acknowledges it or not, the extremist is an escapist, and what he attempts to escape is complexity. The extremist always goes for the easy solution. Thus, for example, the easy solution to the most abhorrent of all crimes, murder, is the death penalty. This is still accepted by the majority of people, as, I suspect, any referendum conducted anywhere in the world would show. Yet the history of human civilization demonstrates conclusively that capital punishment has not solved the problem. It could even be argued that it has, in certain cases, exacerbated it.

Aleko, the central figure of Pushkin's poem "The Gypsies," kills Zemphyra, the woman he loves, when she bestows her favours on another man. In a normal society, Aleko would be hanged, gassed, shot, in short, executed for his crime. The gypsies ostracize him. For them, he no longer exists. They shun him, shrink away from him, for by killing he has cast away his humanity. If society as a whole reacted similarly, the only life the Alekos of our world would ever take would be their own. But to react that way presupposes a willingness to think in terms of a complexity that most of us do not accept. We give certain people the authority to pass a law, others the authority to interpret it, and yet others the authority to put it into practice. We give Authority the authority to kill, thereby telling Aleko he may kill one of us, but we will kill him in return. The extremist solution. Instead of solving anything, it furnishes the illusion of having hit upon the perfect answer. In that sense, it is a kind of mental fix. With some, it becomes an addiction.

Berlin in the late forties and early fifties was certainly a haven for the extremist mind, for it reflected the contrasts, the extremes, the opposing views that had made it what it was: a city divided into East and West not just geographically, but ideologically and economically. The Berlin Wall had yet to appear. This structure should be allowed to stand for eternity as a three-dimensional illustration of the stupidity and inhumanity of the cold-war mentality. (In its own way, the Berlin Wall is no less a monument than the Great Wall of China, which, ironically, is simply celebrated today as a great engineering and construction achievement, although it too had the purpose of containment.) But at this time, the Berlin blockade was on, and U.S. transport planes roared low over the city every three minutes, bringing in the goods that would transform West Berlin into a glittering showcase built specifically to prove the superiority of western democracy over communist totalitarianism, to rivet the attention of East Berliners, and to tempt as many as possible to defect. It was not a struggle of equals. The Soviet Union had never had much of a consumer industry to begin with, and what it had built by 1941 had been destroyed during the war. The country saw one-third of its national wealth turned to ashes, found 25 million of its people forced to live in dugouts and tents because seventeen hundred cities and towns and forty thousand villages has been razed to the ground. Meanwhile, the United States had profited immensely from the war. Its losses in human terms were, by conservative estimates, forty times lower than those of the Soviet Union. Its continental territory remained unscathed. For the first time in the twentieth century, the United States enjoyed full employment; in fact, a case could be made that the war solved the problems of the Great Depression in a more basic and final way than any of the New Deal policies implemented by FDR.

America came out of the war richer than when she entered it, and she had been consumer oriented long before that. The United States could and did pour goods aplenty into West Berlin, stimulating local finance and industry. The Soviet Union could do nothing of the sort. It was no contest. West Berlin and, through it, the Federal Republic of Germany thus became seductive and tantalizing. The flow of people from East to West grew from a trickle to a torrent. This posed serious economic and manpower problems for the German Democratic Republic; the erection of the Berlin Wall was the solution. It was, in my opinion, a quick fix. It solved the problem of economic drain, but it created a far greater and much more difficult problem, both in terms of how it affected Germans on the inside of that wall and the kind of ammunition it provided for anticommunist ideologues all over the world. Extremism at its worst.

Living in Berlin, I found myself forced to take sides as never before. To be sure, I had taken sides in America, but that was different. It was more like taking sides in a classroom—you might have a fight, but you were still a member of that class, of that school, part of something bigger that all the differing parties belonged to. Now I belonged to something else. The GIs standing guard at Checkpoint Charlie seemed menacing to me. They were *the other side,* whatever that meant, and were, therefore, to be feared. I remember taking the S-Bahn and being jolted to my feet by the realization that I had gotten on the wrong train and was inside West Berlin. I got off at the first stop and began to walk back toward the Soviet sector. Suddenly I saw two policemen coming in my direction. My heart began to thud, and I felt my armpits go sweaty. I was wearing a Red Army cap with a star, and I was certain the *polizei* would arrest me as soon as they saw it. They passed by without a glance, and I made it back to "my" sector with no further adventures. What was I afraid of? I still don't really know. But I tend to think that I had subconsciously kept pushing myself to be part of this new "other side," the one that really didn't seem to be so keen on having me but which I had vowed to become part of. While pushing myself in that direction, I must also have been alienating myself from what I had once been. My newfound fear of Americans, my anti-American outlook, were, I think, the result of my locking out anything that might even appear to challenge my resolve to become someone else.

In addition to all this internal turmoil, all this ripping and tearing, I was moving from boyhood through adolescence. I was going on fifteen when we came to Berlin and was pushing nineteen when we left. Those are difficult years even in the best situations. Those are the years of the most severe strain on child-parent relations, the most demanding of parental love, understanding, and tact. My mother passed that test with flying colors. My father flunked.

When I was just a little boy, then a teenager, and even as a young man, my dad would tell me stories about growing up in St. Petersburg. His grandmothers always stood out in his memory. Grandmother Perl, on his mother's side, was born on the fortress-island of Kronshtadt, strategically situated in the Gulf of Finland to protect St. Petersburg from any enemy on the sea. To any Russian, the name Kronshtadt is synonymous with adventure, courage, independent spirit, the romantic hell-or-high-water attitude that was and remains the trademark of the Baltic Fleet. Grandmother Perl, as my father described her, had all of that—a daring charm, a romantic beauty, a taste for enterprise. In a paternalistic society, she danced circles around all the men, never fighting them with their own weapons, but cajoling them, making them laugh at their own pomposity, getting things her way so deftly and with such a light touch that it all happened before they realized it. Whenever she walked into a room, it seemed to light up, and wherever she was, there was joy and laughter and love. All the children adored her, my father included. And they all obeyed her, even though she never raised her voice, never scolded them, let alone inflicted any punishment.

Grandmother Pozner was a different story. Tall, large-boned, with powerful muscular arms and huge hands, her iron-gray hair tightly drawn back and knotted into a bun on the back of her head, she was Grandmother Perl's antithesis. Where the latter flirted outrageously and wasn't opposed to daringly low-cut necklines or showing a bit of calf, the former never wore anything but the most severe black dresses, floor length, long sleeves tightly buttoned at the wrists, high collars decorated with a bit of white lace. The only time she was out of uniform was in the morning when she would inspect how well her seven children had washed. Every morning she would line them up and, standing in her underwear, oversee their morning toilet. This included a careful scrutiny of first their nails and then, most painfully, their ears, which she would grasp with her enormous hands and turn nearly inside out to ascertain that there was not the smallest speck of dirt. When her children grew up, she turned her attention to their children, thus contributing to my father's personal experience.

One of the stories he told was about the time he asked for a second helping of dessert before being offered one. This happened at lunch. He was marched into the kitchen by Grandmother Pozner and given a huge bowl of the dessert and told he would not be allowed out until he had eaten the entire dish, which had been prepared for a family of ten or twelve. My father tried his best, failed miserably, and ended up weeping into the dessert he had loved but hated from that day on. He was thus taught "good manners": do not ask for a second serving until it is offered.

Another story concerns some dish—I don't remember exactly what it was, perhaps fish—that my father didn't particularly like. When he made this known (again, this occurred at lunch), he was told to leave the table. He got the same plate of cold fish for dinner, while everyone else enjoyed a new meal. When he refused to eat his fish, he was told to leave the table. When he sat down to breakfast the next morning, he was offered that same piece of fish. He was hungry, upset, miserable, and only nine or ten years old. He broke down and cried, and then his grandmother told him what the lesson was: if someone has been kind enough to prepare food for you, the least you can do is eat it.

I remember loving these stories, laughing, imagining this horrid old lady twisting my dad's ears, forcing him to wash in cold water to make him strong, sending waves of fear before her as she moved through her home. Both the dessert and the fish stories struck me as being examples of pedagogical wisdom. I suppose they were in a way. But more than that, they exemplified the authoritarian attitude of the parent toward the child, an attitude based on the unconditional acceptance of certain "truths"— that adults are always right, always know more, are more intelligent than children, and are, therefore, to be respected and obeyed. What that view fails to recognize is that obedience is predicated on fear rather than on respect. If you don't do what I tell you, I'll punish you. That has nothing to do with being more knowledgeable or more intelligent, it has to do with being physically stronger. The real message is: you will do as I say, or take the consequences, and there is nothing you can do about it. Fear takes the place of respect, and fear is *always* resented by those who experience it. Might that not be one of the reasons we so mistreat the aged in our societies? Are we perhaps not getting back at them for the way they mistreated us when we were little?

High in the mountain villages of Svanetia, in the Caucasus, young men dismount from their horses twenty paces away from any old person and walk their mounts past him or her. That is obeisance, as opposed to obedience, a sign of deep respect for age in a society where children are respected as human beings from the day of their birth, where experience is valued more than any gift other than the gift of discovery. The youngest and the oldest epitomize the two, and everyone else basks in the glory of this harmony.

Grandmother Perl was probably Svan-ish in her relationship with children. She never had to force them to do anything; in fact, they would do whatever she asked, overjoyed at the opportunity to demonstrate their love. Grandmother Pozner brought her children up to fear authority. They passed that on to their children, and my father tried to pass it on to me.

I'll never know why the Pozner strain was stronger in him than the Perl. But I do know that, deep inside, he must have resented having been reduced to tears over that bowl of dessert, forced to eat that fish, because to be forced in such a way is degrading. That resentment translated itself into his trying to do the same to me. He couldn't do it to his father, but he had to exorcise it. If I had accepted that, or at least not opposed it openly, not rebelled, we would have had a different relationship. Had I spent more of my formative years in his company, especially those first five years of my life, there is reason to believe that is exactly what would have happened. I would have accepted his authority because I would have grown up with it. But that was not the case.

My first recollection of conflict with him is a carbon copy of his own experience. I must have been six, and my father had just come home from the war. We were having dinner, and my mother had made cold leek salad. I had never tried that delicacy before and, after one look, decided I didn't like it, which I announced for all who might be interested to hear. My father looked at me silently for a moment and then asked in a low voice, "What did you say?" The tone of his voice, almost a purr, set off my internal alarm. Nevertheless, I repeated that I didn't want any leek salad. His eyes narrowed to slits, and his voice dropped almost to a whisper. "No one asked you what you like or dislike. Eat it." Again, I refused. I will not bore you with the gory details. I ended up swallowing the leek salad, then vomiting and crying simultaneously. As I write this now, nearly half a century later, I still don't know whether I have forgiven him. I think I have, but the anger is still there—not for having had to bow to force, but for my still being ashamed of him for what he had done to me.

Many years later, when I had a child of my own, I made a horrible discovery: the disease had been passed on to me. As a baby, my daughter was one of those who never seem to be hungry. Feeding her was pure torture. Like a chipmunk, she would tuck a spoonful or forkful of food behind her cheek and hold it there for what seemed like an eternity. One day, when she must have been five, and I had spent the better part of two hours trying to get her to eat, I lost control. I jumped up, dragged her from the table to the bathroom, and slapped her across the face. She didn't let out a sound. She just looked up at me with her huge dark eyes, and a trickle of blood began to run from her nose. I never again forced her to do anything, but to this day every time I see that scene, I squirm. I want to beg her forgiveness, and I despise myself.

I don't think my father ever experienced any such guilt.

One day in Berlin, when I was seventeen, what had to happen happened. I had gone for a walk with my brother Paul, eleven years my junior, promising to be home by six. Along the way, I met some friends who invited me to join them for a beer. As a result, I started back for home at least two hours late. It was a thirty-minute walk, and we were about halfway home when a car passed us and then came to a screeching stop. My father jumped out and came running toward us. His face was white with anger. "Where the hell have you been?" he shouted, "Your mother is sick with worry! Not about you, you idiot, about your brother!" If he had not added that last insult, I would probably have said I was sorry. But I just shrugged. Infuriated by that gesture of disrespect and indifference, my father hit me. It wasn't a strong blow, and I certainly don't remember feeling any pain. But it broke what by now had become the very thin wall that dammed my pent-up resentment. In a flash, I grabbed my father by the shoulders, shook him violently, and hurled him from me, sending him reeling and stumbling backwards and crashing into the car. We stood there panting, facing each other like two fighters, each waiting for the other to make his move. Then my father got a grip on himself. "Get into the car," he said to my brother, who stood there, petrified. Then he turned to me and said, shortly, "I'll take care of you later."

The way he took care of me was to ignore me. For several weeks he did not speak to me. Then, very gradually, things got back to a kind of normalcy. He never mentioned the incident again, but from that day on something came between us. It wasn't the only thing, or the one that was to divide us most deeply, but it never completely disappeared, not even when we finally sorted out our differences and buried the hatchet only a few years before his death.

In Russian fairy tales, Ivan the Fool, a homely, hapless fellow, is forced by the cruel Czar to jump into a cauldron of boiling water and then, if he is still alive, into a cauldron of freezing water. Ivan does it and emerges transformed into a handsome prince who marries the czar's daughter and lives happily ever after. In a sense, Berlin was my cauldrons of boiling and ice-cold water. That is not to say I emerged transformed into something better than I was. But I was transformed, and the process was just as painful. It included the loss of a way of life, the loss of a bond with my father, the loss of my own identity. But Berlin played a crucial role, preparing me for things to come. I am not sure I could have dealt with Moscow without those four years in Berlin, without that intermediary point where the rules of the game were completely different from the ones I had played by in the past but were not quite the same as those I would play by in the future. Berlin tempered me for things to come, it taught me lessons—not through the didactic dos and don'ts of the classroom, but through daily experiences and encounters.

Such as the time Gherman, a young KGB operative who had befriended me, sat in his Spartan living quarters cleaning his gun and caught me staring at the weapon with admiration and envy. "You dumb son of a bitch," he said. "Thank God you have no gun and pray to him that you'll never have one or be forced to do the job I do." That was not the first time I had heard negative comments about the KGB, but coming from someone inside the organization, it not only startled me, it forced me to challenge some of the assumptions I had never before doubted.

Such as the time I complained to the daughter of the Soviet high commissioner about how desperately I wanted to go to the Soviet Union, and she said, "You should write to Comrade Stalin." "But does he read English?" I asked, and she just stared at me, stunned by such sacrilegious doubt, then gave a short laugh and said, "Yes, you really are a foreigner, aren't you? Of *course* Comrade Stalin knows English. How could he have conversed with Churchill and Roosevelt if he didn't? Comrade Stalin knows *everything.*" I recall thinking that nobody knows *everything,* that it is impossible. But I also distinctly remember a voice inside me telling me to shut up, not to express any doubts whatsoever about Stalin. Mind you, I had no knowledge of any danger, I was just as crazy about Stalin as she was. My incredulity at anyone's knowing everything came from my western education. So why didn't I respond? Only because of the other education I had been getting, whose subtle message (and, yes, it was subtle) was: keep your mouth shut if you don't want problems.

And I did learn another lesson in evening school, although it certainly was not part of the curriculum. It had to do with the course on Soviet literature, where particular emphasis was put on Maxim Gorky's novel *Mother,* Vladimir Mayakovsky's poem "Vladimir Ilyich Lenin," and Alexander Fadeyev's novel *The Young Guard.* The choice of literary works was in itself instructive, for it was based on ideological considerations. In the first two cases, while the writers were outstanding, the selected works were far from their most significant literary achievements. In the last, the writer was, at best, second rate. But that is not my point. Upon completing the reading and discussion of each writer, we were supposed to write a composition on the subject. The theme of the composition was always strictly formulated: "Gorky as the founder of Socialist Realism," "Lenin as portrayed by Vladimir Mayakovsky in his poem 'Vladimir Ilyich Lenin.' " What you were expected to do was to put into writing whatever the textbook and the teacher had told you, walk the mental straight and narrow, never digressing, never introducing any of your own ideas.

As I said, this was a new ball game. It readied me for the hardball that was still to come.

3

⊰⬥⊱

Father of the People

I have known joy in my life, but on few occasions have I experienced such a feeling of pure exhilaration as the day we boarded the train from Berlin to Moscow. The nightmare was over. Now it was time for the dream. The aching, the yearning, the pent-up frustration of being neither here, nor there, the waiting, the praying—now it was all over. Finally, I was going home. To be sure, a home whose threshold I had never crossed, much less lived in, but a home I had built in my mind's eye, the most desirable home in the world.

I don't remember what the scenery looked like as our train steamed through East Germany and Poland, stopping briefly in Warsaw and then moving on. I probably never looked out of the window. I didn't care. As far as I was concerned, it didn't matter if I never saw those countries again. In fact, I vowed never to set foot in them and, as fate has had it, I never have, except for a week in 1969, when I traveled to Dresden and Berlin when I was urgently summoned by my mother. She and my father had been vacationing there when he had a near-fatal heart attack, and I went there to help my mother bring my dad home. That trip stands out in my mind not only because of its reason—my father's desperate situation—and not only because it was my first trip abroad since arriving in the Soviet Union sixteen years earlier. I remember it most of all because it nearly did not happen.

Until very recently, the Soviet population was, and to a certain extent still is, divided into two categories—*viyezdnye* and *ne viyezdnye,* that is to say, those who have been cleared to travel abroad and those who haven't.

This division into the equivalent of first- and second-class citizens is a subject of special and personal interest to me, an issue calling for discussion in a future chapter. But suffice it to say that at this point I knew I was second class, that in some KGB cubbyhole my file was marked with whatever they marked in the files of subversives or suspicious individuals. Yet when I received a telegram signed by the chief doctor of the Dresden hospital informing me that my father had suffered a near-fatal heart attack and that the sooner I came the better, I could not believe anyone would have the stupidity, let alone the lack of compassion, to refuse me. I still had a lot to learn about stupidity and lack of compassion. It took less than a day to have my request refused. I recall being in a state of blind shock and blind hatred, both stemming from a feeling of complete helplessness, of complete dependency on people and organizations I could neither see nor speak to but who pulled the strings and decided my fate. They would decide whether or not I could see my father for what might well be the last time. They would look at my record, at the different reports written about me by the finks and stoolies who were commonly referred to as rappers—people who rapped on whichever of their friends, family, colleagues, and acquaintances the KGB asked them about—and decide whether I was too much of a security risk, not loyal enough, too independent to be allowed to travel to the German Democratic Republic to see my ailing father. How can I describe my fury and feeling of futility?

The Russians say, "If something is not allowed but you want it bad enough, you can get it," roughly the equivalent of the English "Where there's a will, there's a way." My father had left me the phone number of a ranking KGB officer I was to call only *in extremis,* one Victor Alexandrovich (probably just one of his many aliases). The call got results, although it did take nearly a week before I received my passport and was able to board the Moscow-Berlin express.

However, that is a different story pertaining to a different time. At the time I was speaking of earlier, we were going in the opposite direction, leaving both Germany and Poland behind. Leaving them behind, as I said, with no regrets.

When the train crossed the Polish-Soviet frontier and pulled into the Brest station, we all had tears in our eyes. Being on Soviet soil left me weak but left no visual imprint on my mind. Had I been asked to describe what the Brest station looked like, I would have found it difficult to do two days after passing through it, let alone today. (Small wonder that when I passed through Brest sixteen years later on my way to Berlin and Dresden, I recognized nothing.)

The trip from there to Moscow was uneventful. I spent most of the time in a compartment of our sleeper car playing dominoes with a young Soviet woman. She worked for Intourist as a guide and had accompanied a group of foreigners as far as the frontier. She struck me as pretty and intelligent. She was also quite a domino player, ultimately defeating me forty-seven games to forty-six. Naturally, during the long hours while we played and drank strong, black tea in glasses placed in metal holders, we did a lot of talking. As we talked, I realized I was telling far more about my life than she was about hers. However, she did give me her address in Moscow with the promise that when we met there, she would tell me more about herself. I was very naive. One of the first things I did in Moscow was to go looking for the young lady. Imagine my chagrin upon discovering no such address existed! Oh yes, the street did, but it was a short one, and the house number she had given me was far too high. There was no such house. Domino Lady, if you are reading these lines today, know that I remember you and bear you no rancor. I soon came to learn that working for Intourist in those days, having any contacts with foreigners, as your job demanded, automatically meant having regular, if not permanent, contacts with the KGB. I soon came to understand that any unsanctioned contacts with a foreigner could be used against a person, could, in fact, pose a mortal threat. I soon fully understood why you gave me a false address, and to this day I wonder at your courage when you allowed me to spend so many hours in your compartment playing dominoes, because you had to know that the chances of your being watched and reported on (by any of the Soviet passengers, by the steward, or by a host of others) were far higher than of remaining unobserved. The false address at first puzzled me, but I soon got over that.

Getting over some other things turned out to be much harder. When we were living in postwar New York, my father made a point of cultivating Soviets working for the United Nations. They often visited our home on East Tenth Street, a home that even by American standards was luxurious. To my father's Soviet friends, it must have been positively dazzling. They came to enjoy company they would not otherwise have met, to enjoy drink and food they could not afford. Of course, they reported to their superiors—that was a must then and remained one for many years—but diplomatic personnel all over the world, Americans included, report to security officers about their contacts. It is really nothing to get upset about. It goes with the turf.

As I said, these people visited our home regularly, and we became friends with several families. For me, they were special precisely because they were Soviets. I yearned to see them in Moscow—and now, finally, that was going to happen! I played out my fantasy in my mind. Would I just look up one of them, ring their doorbell, and stand there smiling when they opened the door and stared at me unbelievingly? Or would I call them on the phone and pretend I was someone else, a friend of Vladimir Pozner's who was calling at his request to find out how they were? I played this little game over and over again, anticipating the thrill of the real thing. On our second day in Moscow, I decided to call the Borisovs, one of the two families we had become friendliest with in New York. I have never forgotten that conversation:

"Hello? How are you?"

"Who is speaking?"

"Three guesses.

Impatiently. "Who is speaking?"

"Me. Vova" (I used the diminutive for Vladimir that I was always called by at home).

"What Vova?"

"Vova Pozner."

It was the moment I had been waiting for. The response had to be a combination of surprise and delight. I'm sure I had a blissful smile on my face. Most people at one time or another have experienced biting into something they fully expected to be sweet, only to be shocked by the sour taste that floods their mouth. That's the only comparison I have for what followed. There was a long pause.

"Oh. I see. You are in Moscow?"

"Yes! Yes! When can I see you?"

Another long pause.

"We're very busy right now. Why don't you call up in a week or so? And give my regards to your parents. Good-bye."

The phone clicked off and I stood there, stunned, listening to the dial tone buzzing into my ear. Slowly I put down the receiver and looked at my father.

"So?" he asked.

"They are busy," I answered. "They said to call back in a week."

A few days later, over dinner, my father said, "Don't bother calling the Borisovs."

"But why?" I asked.

"Just don't," my father said shortly, and I suddenly understood why they did not want to see us. They were afraid.

My first impressions of Moscow are a jumble of things, each one clear but unrelated to the next. Stereotypically, what stands out most is Russian winter. The snow squeaking and crunching at every step. The snowflakes swirling down, the light of street lamps sifting through them. The trolley buses, the insides of their windows sheathed with ice, a perfect place for graffiti that would disappear with the thaw of spring. That memory brings back another: my mother sitting in a trolley next to a window and putting to practice her recently acquired knowledge of the Cyrillic alphabet. "Ha," she says, deciphering the first letter of the inscription scraped on the frosted coating, then "Ou," then "Ee kratkoye," the last letter, and loudly and triumphantly "Huy"—the word itself. Her achievement is greeted with a few snickers and suppressed laughs. There should have been loud applause, for she had just mastered one of the most commonly used and popular words in the Russian language: *Prick.*

The cold that froze your nostrils together if you breathed too deeply and wreathed your face in steam when you spoke. And, most amazingly, people eating popsicles in the streets. When Churchill saw Muscovites consuming ice cream in the dead of winter, he supposedly remarked, "Now I understand why the Russians are invincible." Whether he said those words or not, I do not know, but I did eat ice cream in the streets of Moscow when it was twenty-five degrees below zero, Centigrade, and I came down with a major case of quinsy.

Moscow, unlike Berlin, was a living, bustling city. There seemed to be people everywhere, shoving, pushing, always in a hurry, somehow reminding me a little of New York. On one of our first days there, I found myself in Gastronom (Food store) Number One, more commonly referred to as Yeliseyevsky, the name of its prerevolutionary owner. It blew me away with its barrels of black, pressed, and red caviar; its array of smoked sturgeon, beluga, and lox; its heady aroma of freshly ground coffee and mounds of apples, oranges, and pears; its rows of salamis, sausages, hams, pâtés; all of this set in an unbelievable turn-of-the-century interior, all of this offered at incredibly low prices: ninety roubles for a kilo of the best caviar, eighty kopecks for a can of Chatka king crab. Moscow was stocked, Moscow ate its fill, and it would be nearly three years before I realized what an exception this was to the rule. In the summer of 1955, I traveled with a group of fellow students to the Altai region of the country. In the city of Barnaul, I saw people standing in bread lines at five in the morning, people who probably lived their entire lives without ever seeing, let alone tasting, smoked sturgeon.

But all of that was later.

We moved into the Metropol Hotel, a splendid monument to nineteenth-century Russian architecture situated in the very center of the city. My parents' room looked out on the Bolshoi Theater and the Maly Theater, on the House of Trade Unions (formerly the Aristocratic Club), on Revolution and Sverdlov squares and then, further down, the building of the Council of Ministers, designed by Le Corbusier, the National Hotel, the Moscow Hotel, the History Museum, the Lenin Museum, and, behind it, the domes and spires of the Kremlin. My room offered a view of the interior yard. We spent about a year living in the Metropol. We had no apartment in Moscow, no relatives who could take us in. Nor did we have any real sense of the housing crisis until we visited a family my parents had become friends with while in Germany. I still remember my discomfort at seeing how they lived. It was in a one-story, barrack-like wooden building, a long corridor running from front to back, doors facing each other the length of the corridor. The Gridnevs, a family of four, shared two rooms, one of which had a sink with running water and served as a combination bedroom/washing place. There was just one communal toilet, situated at the end of the corridor, and one kitchen, a huge room with at least twenty gas ranges, one for each of the families who shared the premises. Mind you, this was not by any means the worst of situations, four people to two rooms. Eight, ten, and even more living in one room was no rarity as I was to discover. As for private apartments, in those days less than 10 percent of the capital's population enjoyed that luxury.

Such hardships, such lack of the most elementary necessities of life, are beyond the comprehension of most Americans. Living in Harlem in the late forties and early fifties was definitely more comfortable than the way most Muscovites lived when we arrived in the Soviet capital. But what would have totally confounded Americans was how happy these Muscovites seemed, how little they complained, how ready they were to accept their privation. There were, I think, two reasons for that. One was the war. After what the country had gone through, people did not have to be told they would have to pull in a couple of hitches on their belts. Nor did the government need to invent any excuses for the hardships of the nation. The war was to blame. That explanation for all kinds of shortages and problems was used for years, even decades, and for a long time, most people accepted it without any argument. They started to question it only much later, when they began to realize that it had become nothing more than a justification for bureaucratic indifference, economic stagnation, unwillingness to admit serious deformation of the political system. The second reason had to do with the commonly shared belief that tomorrow would be better than today, a belief based on past experience. Regardless of the famine of the postcollectivization years, regardless of the Stalinist terror of the thirties and late forties, the vast majority of Soviets saw their standard of living improve over the years; they had experienced the thrill of fulfilling and surpassing the goals of the first five-year plans, of transforming their land from a backward country to a superpower. Their view of the future was optimistic, even though it did mean going through more than a few lean years.

In a strange way, this brings to mind a comparison with the Reagan years in America. One of the results of Reaganomics was not only that the poor got poorer but that their number increased to over thirty million. A large number, to be sure, but a minority of the population; the majority enjoyed a boost in living standards. The prevailing view in America, one very much supported by the government, has been and is that the poor are poor because they want to be poor. It's their own fault or choice, which is basically the same thing. In the Soviet Union, millions suffered from the repressions, but they too were a minority. The majority sincerely believed that it was their own fault because they were enemies of the people, a point most forcefully, not to say ferociously, brought home by the government.

Amid the hardship and poverty of life in the Soviet Union in the early fifties, the Metropol Hotel stood out like a glittering jewel. The tinkling fountain and delicious food in its huge glass-domed restaurant, the plush, soft carpets, the burnished bronze fixtures, the crystal chandeliers—this was a different world accessible to a select few, to Soviet dignitaries in town for special occasions and to foreigners, only a small number of whom were tourists. Most of the others were accredited journalists and diplomats whose countries had yet to acquire or build embassies and apartments. If you did not live in the Metropol, you needed a visitor's pass signed by the senior administrator to get in, and to get the pass, you had to state your business and present your passport. This screening kept everyone out except the most foolhardy and those whose visits had been sanctioned. In addition to the senior administrator in the lobby, every floor had its own administrator whose desk faced the elevator and the stairway. There was no way you could pass without being asked what room you were going to and who was expecting you. That kind of blanket security, so typical of the Stalin era, disappeared in later years, only to reappear not long ago after a major fire in the Rossiya Hotel. Today one needs a pass to get into any hotel, and the floor administrators are once again strategically situated opposite elevators. Supposedly this measure pursues the noble aim of protecting hotel clients from undesired intruders, but I sometimes wonder, considering the ubiquitous prostitutes and underworld characters that have become a hallmark of Moscow's better hotels.

As the first days of our life in Moscow stretched into weeks, I realized that my father was not working. At first I had paid no attention, being too caught up in the enthralling novelty of Moscow. But my father, who had always been out of the house by eight-thirty in the morning and rarely returned before eight in the evening, was now spending much of his time in his hotel room, something so unusual that I could not fail, finally, to notice it and wonder what the reason was. He had been employed by Sovexportfilm in Berlin. Why wasn't he working for the same organization in Moscow? When I asked my father, he said they were overstaffed. He applied for a job at Mosfilm, the country's largest and most important studio, then at Gorky Film Studio. Both turned him down.

One day he told us he was going to Minsk, the capital of Byelorussia, to look for something there. The idea of moving to Minsk made me sick to my stomach, and I was overjoyed when he returned with no offer, although I did my best to conceal my feelings. He was then advised to go to Tbilisi, capital of the Georgian Republic. He came back empty-handed. I couldn't make heads or tails of what was going on.

Vladimir A. Pozner was a very well known and respected name in the film industry in both North America and Western Europe. He was considered one of the most expert and brilliant professionals in the area of distribution and production. Yet for some reason his talents were not needed in the USSR. During the years in Berlin, he, like all Soviet citizens, had been paid part of his salary in the local currency, while a large percentage was accumulating in a rouble account in Moscow. When we arrived, he had something like eighty thousand roubles waiting for him, a tidy sum in those days. But two rooms in the Metropol and eating in restaurants, coupled with no regular income, bit deeply into his savings. With no job and money running out, things began to look desperate. They were far more desperate than we imagined.

This period of our lives coincided with one of the most vile and notorious manifestations of Stalinism, the so-called Doctors' Plot. A group of leading Soviet physicians were accused of being spies, agents of enemy powers responsible for the death of statesmen, artists, and writers, including Maxim Gorky, whom they allegedly poisoned in 1936. For years, these "murderers in white robes," as they were immediately christened by the media, these traitors, these hired killers of imperialism, these Judases who had sold their Motherland for thirty pieces of silver, had clandestinely and systematically taken the lives of their country's finest. But now, thanks to the vigilance of Lydia Timashuk, an ordinary general practitioner, they had been unmasked, apprehended, taken into custody and had confessed to their heinous crimes. Timashuk became a celebrity overnight, children wrote poems in her honor, journalists spewed out endless copy extolling her virtues. She was awarded the highest of all honors: the Order of Lenin.

Reading the names of the killer-doctors, I recall being struck by the fact that they were almost all Jewish, something that made me uneasy. However, I was aware of the predominance of Jews in the medical profession in the western world and tried, though not very successfully, to allay my apprehensions with that thought. Somehow the idea of a group of doctors hatching such a diabolical plot, masquerading as physicians while actually serving as undercover hit men for some unnamed foreign organization, struck me as being rather incredible. But while I had my doubts, I never came close to divining what the Doctors' Plot was really about. It was the first act in a drama conceived by an evil genius, a drama the final act of which was to have been the deportation of all Jews far beyond the Ural Mountains, a final act that, in a certain way, was comparable to Hitler's final solution—but with a difference. Hitler actually did hate the Jews, believing they were evil. His crime, horrendous as it was, was that of a man possessed by hatred and prejudice. To be sure, it was executed in cold blood with Teutonic exactitude, but it was based on irrational hatred. Not so for Stalin. We have no reason to accuse him of harboring a particular abhorrence for any ethnic or religious group. The Georgians suffered as much as, if not more than, any national group in the Soviet Union, and Stalin was a Georgian. He was preoccupied with one thing only—power. And if one person or ten million had to be sacrificed for that cause, so be it. What Stalin saw as a threat to his power may well have been based on a paranoic premise, but from that point on, every step was meticulously planned with cold logic. It would take a far more profound person than myself to read Stalin's convoluted mind, but it seems to me that, unlike other absolute dictators, he employed fear not for the purpose of subjugating people to his will (something he succeeded at brilliantly, since the people loved and venerated him), but to keep the nation in a permanent state of what might be called beleaguered awareness. There was the enemy from without, always planning to destroy the first socialist state, and the enemy from within, scheming the downfall of the workers' and peasants' paradise. The Trotskyites, the rightist deviationists, the enemies of the people, the kulaks, the cosmopolitans, the Zionists—they all served the same purpose. As long as the nation felt threatened, slipping and sliding across the wet, treacherous deck of history-in-the-making, people would have no time to think and, most importantly, to question. And as long as they did not question, Stalin's supreme power remained assured. Other ethnic minorities had been sacrificed before, the Chechens and the Ingush, the Kabardins and the Balkars, the Kurds and the Crimean Tartars. Now it was the Jews' turn.

My father's Jewish origins, his "foreign" past, his French wife, each was reason enough to pack him and his family off to some Siberian gulag. The combination made it a certainty. Conditions being what they were, there is nothing surprising in his not having been able to land a job. In fact, what is surprising is that the noose tightened so slowly. Had Stalin not died on March 5, 1953, just two months and a few days after our arrival, I feel certain we would have suffered the same fate as millions of Soviet citizens before us.

I will never forget the day of Stalin's death. We were still living in the Metropol when the news was announced on the radio. It must have been between five and six in the morning when the phone rang, waking me from a fitful sleep. Ever since the first announcement of Stalin's illness had been made three days before, I had asked the maid on our floor to call me if anything important was broadcast. I jumped out of bed and grabbed the receiver. "It's all over, Stalin is dead." I hardly recognized the voice of my favorite maid, Polina, muffled by tears. I put down the phone and hurriedly began to dress. I distinctly remember wondering why I wasn't crying, too. The thought made me uncomfortable, as though something were wrong with me. I left my room and went down the hall to wake my parents, passing Polina along the way as she sat weeping at her station in front of the elevator. The early hour notwithstanding, I was far from the only one up. People scurried hither and yon, most of them foreign journalists and diplomats. I remember the *New York Times* bureau chief, Harrison Salisbury, charging down the hall, his bristling red whiskers and ferocious expression reminding me of a fox closing in on its prey.

My parents didn't have much to say. We spent most of the morning sitting silently, each wrapped in our own thoughts. Not having been brought up in the Soviet Union, I had not been subjected to the pervasive indoctrination my peers had received. Much as I emotionally desired to merge completely with this new society, there was something inside me that rebelled at the adoration and adulation I encountered whenever Stalin's name came up. I certainly believed Stalin was a great man, someone I admired profoundly, a man who had, I thought, almost single-handedly defeated Hitler. I yearned to march across Red Square on May Day and see him and his comrades, all comprising the leadership of the country, standing on the upper level of the Lenin Mausoleum, waving to the crowd. But Father of the People? Of all the people? The infallible judge of all things, from linguistics and cybernetics to genetics and the most complex questions of nationality? My brain refused to accept such notions. Much in the same way, I could not feel love for Stalin, and while I grieved at his death, I did not, unlike most Soviets, experience a sense of personal loss. This discrepancy between what I was and what I wanted to be was a source of acute discomfort and I attempted to hide it not only from all others, but from myself as well.

Stalin lay in state for three days in the Hall of Columns of the House of Trade Unions, and for three days, round the clock, an endless procession of Muscovites passed by his bier. I was one of them, and it must have been my guardian angel that introduced me to a Stalin Prize laureate living in the Metropol who, thanks to his medal, managed to get the both of us onto the head of the line. If I had attempted to get in on my own, I would perhaps have been killed in the process.

No one knows the exact number, but at least three million people converged on the House of Trade Unions. They came from all parts of Moscow, rivulets of humanity merging into streams, flowing into turbulent rivers that all funneled into a narrow torrent. These bodies of humanity, like bodies of water, had their banks. Some were natural, such as the buildings lining the streets. Others were artificial—hundreds upon hundreds of army trucks parked bumper to bumper, blocking all entrances to side streets and yards that might serve as shortcuts to that final stretch down Pushkin Street leading into the House of Trade Unions. The vast crowds surged along, and as they moved, people were crushed to death by the sheer weight of this multiheaded and multilegged monster. Some died gasping their last breath, rib cages cracking, plastered against building walls and cast-iron fences. Others, shoved into the sharp contours of the army trucks, snapped in two like matchsticks. Others slipped on the ice—the winter of 1952–53 had been exceptionally cold, and though it was March, the streets of Moscow were still covered with ice and snow—

and were trampled to death. This nightmare acquired apocalyptic proportions around Trubnaya Square. The boulevard leading to it from Stretenka Street dipped steeply, and as the multitudes advanced, people lost their footing and fell—first one, then another, then several, all going down with muffled cries. As the bodies piled up, more people tripped on them and fell. The crowd panicked and surged forward, literally lifting the mounted police, horses and all, into the air and then trampling them, too. The plunging terrified horses, the cursing police swinging their clubs in a last desperate effort to stave off the inevitable, the black masses of people swirling and eddying along, engulfing everything in their path like some terrifying maelstrom—who could have imagined a more fitting final rite for the monster who even in death took so many with him?

Inside the House of Trade Unions, everything seemed to be draped in black. Perhaps my memory plays tricks on me, but I think there were armed military guards standing at attention, as well as officials, who saw to it that the crowd kept moving. No one was allowed to stand still and look around for more than a couple of seconds.

Stalin's coffin stood slightly propped up so that people could get a better view of the body. As I looked up at it, I was suddenly mesmerized and horrified by how big Stalin's nostrils were. They looked liked caverns: deep and black, yawning open to engulf the individual who might be foolhardy enough to venture too close. But while these thoughts were passing through my mind, I was jolted by another one: you were supposed to be awestruck, profoundly shaken by this experience, by seeing the great Stalin lying there in state, surrounded by a sea of flowers. Yet there I was, staring at the man's *nostrils,* for God's sake! What was I, some kind of pervert? It was very strange, because in fact I was grief-stricken. But within that feeling, something very important was missing.

Soon after Stalin's death, my father got a job at Mosfilm Studio—not much of a job, to be sure, for he was put on the payroll as a simple engineer, a station far below his standing in the profession and a situation he must have found painful. Still, it was better than nothing. Meanwhile, I diligently prepared for the entrance exams to Moscow University's Department of Biology, a choice I had made based on my interest in Pavlovian theory and conditioned reflexes. I realized my great disadvantage compared to all the other applicants, for whom the Russian language was their mother tongue and who had had ten years of good Soviet schooling. Knowing that my chances were slim, I worked like someone possessed. As a result, the events between March, when Stalin died, and

August, the time of the exams, did not really register in my mind, with one exception: the arrest of Lavrenty Beria. I remember it clearly because of the tanks on Gorky Street, Moscow's main avenue. I had no idea why they were there, but since it was neither early November nor late April, when the final rehearsals for the November 7 and May Day military parades take place, I had to wonder what those vehicles were doing there. I saw the tanks one evening. The next morning they were gone, and the news of Beria's arrest and trial was announced. I really did not understand the importance of the arrest, and the scope of Beria's criminal activities was described only several years later. I have no intention of dwelling on them in any detail now, since they have been well documented. Anyone with a particular interest in that subject should have no problem finding reading material. But I cannot refrain from making a few *nota benes*. One of the crimes the head of the KGB (from the day of its foundation in 1918, that organization went under different names—Cheka, GPU, NKVD, MGB and, finally, KGB. From here on, I'll use only the latter for simplicity's sake) was accused of and sentenced to death for was spying. The absurdity of the charge is obvious, as is the significance of the anti-Beria group's finding it necessary to use it. In 1953, three years before Khrushchev's famous de-Stalinization speech to the Twentieth Party Congress, Beria could not be accused of being what he really was: a mass murderer. Beria was also a sadist who enjoyed torturing his victims personally. According to one story, a Georgian composer (Beria, like Stalin, was Georgian) whose eyes had been put out because Beria did not want to be recognized by him, was brought before this monster for interrogation. No sooner did Beria ask the first question than the man said, "Ah, Lavrenty, it is you." "How did you recognize me?" Beria asked. "You have destroyed my sight but not my hearing. I am a composer and I have perfect pitch." In a fury, Beria called for a hammer and nails and personally drove the nails into his victim's ears. Beria was also a pervert who had squads of operatives cruising the streets of Moscow in search of attractive women. They were picked up and taken to his mansion on Kachalov Street where they were forced to have sex with him. As a memento of each encounter, he kept their bras, a vast collection of which was found in his personal safe after his arrest. It boggles the mind to think that this man was only an inch away from inheriting Stalin's throne. The tanks in the streets bore testimony to his power: they were brought in to thwart any attempt Beria might have made to strike with the military units that were then (and still remain) under the command of the KGB.

In the first six months I lived in the Soviet Union, I had witnessed the death of two men whose power had been as absolute as that of any potentate in history. Stalinism, though, did not die with Stalin and Beria. A vast, complex, and interrelated structure of institutions and attitudes had been created. That structure so skillfully exploited human weakness, human frailty, that it has survived and evolved for three and a half decades. When you cut through all the rhetoric, it is that living legacy of Stalinism that forms the opposition to perestroika today. The struggle for renewal is really a struggle against Stalinism.

My first brush with Stalinism came soon enough.

As I said, I had decided to become a biologist. Throughout the winter, spring, and most of the summer, I prepared for the competitive entrance exams everyone had to take, except those who were graduated from high school with a gold or a silver medal (the equivalent of graduating with straight A's or just one B in America). There were five exams one had to take to be enrolled in the Department of Biology, and since the top grade was a score of five, the ideal was to amass twenty-five points. The minimum score necessary for enrollment depended on the number of applicants—the more there were, the higher that score had to be. That year it was extremely high—twenty-four, meaning you had to get four perfect marks and one four. Assessing my chances, I felt I could get that score. In one subject, Russian composition, the best I could hope for was a four. But in the others—physics, chemistry, foreign language, and Russian/Soviet literature—I believed I could score all fives.

The first exam was physics, and I managed only a four. I was very depressed, feeling certain I had been knocked out of the running. Nevertheless, I decided to stick it out, and, miracle of miracles, I somehow got fives in all the other subjects, including Russian composition. I had received the needed twenty-four points! I was deliriously happy and immensely proud.

The day the admittance lists were posted, I raced to the biology building, tremendously excited. A crowd of would-be students stood in front of the huge bulletin board scanning the column of names on the white foolscap tacked up for all to see. I pushed forward, heart racing, mouth dry, palms wet, anticipating the surge of joy I would experience when I saw my name on that list.

It wasn't there.

"Don't jump to conclusions," I said to myself, "they may have misplaced your name, don't look only at the P's, start from the beginning." I did.

My name was not there.

I found myself staring into space, eyes unfocused, the letters on the lists blurring. I closed my eyes, rubbed them, and looked again.

There was no Pozner on that list.

I must have looked like an automaton as I turned away and moved toward the auditorium where the members of the exam committee were handing out admission papers to those who had been admitted and answering the questions of those who hadn't. I approached one of them—I don't remember whether it was a man or a woman—and said, "My name is Pozner—"

"Yes?"

"Well, I received twenty-four points, but my name is not on the list."

"You're not the only one, you know. A lot of people scored twenty-five. I'm sorry, but there is only room for so many. Try again next year."

Next year? I couldn't believe my ears.

"But I was told I would be accepted if I got twenty-four! Something is wrong!"

"Too many people apply, that's what is wrong. Now, if you'll excuse me, I'm very busy."

I turned and walked away, my head spinning. All that work, all for nothing. As I reached the door, I heard someone call, "Vladimir." I looked back and saw a woman—about forty-five, gray-blue eyes, light brown hair, a nice face but nothing special, yet a face I would never forget. "Follow me," she said, motioning with her head, and led me out of the auditorium, through the entrance hall, and out into the street, past the groups of buzzing teenagers. We walked about halfway down the block, she in front, me about three paces behind her. She stopped, turned to me, and, looking me straight in the eye, said, "I must tell you something. Your performance warrants that you be accepted. Twenty-four points was, in fact, more than enough. But your biography—the fact that you came from abroad, that your father was the son of an émigré, and that your name is Pozner, a Jewish name—is the reason you were not accepted. I am telling you this confidentially. Do something if you can. But if anyone ever comes to me about this, I'll deny every word I said. Good luck." And with that she turned on her heels and walked back toward the biology building.

I stood there paralyzed. It wasn't that I had never encountered prejudice and discrimination, both of which were and remain part of growing up in New York. But prejudice, I had been taught, was a product of capitalism! And here I was in the Soviet Union, the land of socialism!

What's more (a saving thought?), I had never thought of myself as being Jewish! How could this possibly be happening to me?

By the time I got back to the Metropol, I had reached the boiling point. As luck would have it, my father was waiting for me.

"Where have you brought me?" I erupted. "What kind of a country is this?" And I proceeded to tell my story. My father had two levels of anger. The first, when he would raise his voice, impressed only those who didn't know him well; the second, when his voice would drop to a whisper, his face would go white, and his eyes would narrow to slits, would alert anyone in their right mind to take pains to be very, very careful. When I finished my story, the look on his face scared me. "Remember what I am telling you," he said. "They will admit you, even if it's the last thing they do in their lives." With that, he stalked out of the room, slamming the door behind him.

Later I learned that he went straight to the building of the Central Committee of the Communist party and demanded an appointment. He had no connections there. In fact, he was not (never had been, never would be) a member of the Party. But such considerations never stopped him. He would bang on anyone's door—or table, for that matter—if he felt so inclined.

And so I waited for a decision. August merged into September. One day I received a conscription notice ordering me to report to the local Soviet army recruiting office for military service. Once I got there, I was told to report to Major Rys'. With a name like that (in Russian the word *rys* means "lynx"), I should have been forewarned. When I entered his office, the major got up from behind his desk, stretched out his paw, and said, "Welcome, Vladimir Vladimirovich." For the benefit of non-Russian readers, it must be said that the use of the patronymic—a Russian's middle name, derived from the name of his or her father—is a very subtle thing. It is, first and foremost, a form of politeness, a way to address older or senior people or someone you are not on intimate terms with. But it can also be used alone, without the first name, on a man-to-man or woman-to-woman basis, as a sign of close friendship between adults. Thus, if the major and I had been approximately the same age and good friends, he could have called me simply Vladimirovich. But addressing me by my name *and* patronymic when I was at least fifteen years his junior was totally out of the ordinary. I was immediately on my guard. And, as I soon found out, for good reason.

"Sit down, sit down," said the major. "Smoke?"

I declined.

"Good for you," said the major, lighting up, "It's a disgusting habit." He blew some smoke and then said, "We've looked into your file and we like what we see. Since you're being called up for military service, we want to offer you something special. How would you like to go to intelligence school?"

So that was what the Vladimir Vladimirovich bit was all about! I was surprised, amused, and angry, all at the same time.

"You know, Comrade Major," I said, "this is very interesting. They won't accept me at Moscow University for my being suspect, but the army wants me to become an intelligence officer?"

The Lynx smiled. "We are a different organization."

I thanked him for the offer and the trust it reflected. I told him I was very honored, but no, I couldn't accept.

The Lynx raised his eyebrows. "Are you not a patriot of your homeland?"

"Sure I'm a patriot. But why can't a patriot be a biologist instead of an intelligence officer? I'm just not cut out for that kind of work."

The Lynx gave me a long, hard look. "Go out into the corridor and think about it. We don't make these offers to everybody."

I left his office and sat down on one of the chairs lining the long hall. About five minutes later, a young lady in civilian dress walked up to me and said curtly, "The commanding officer will see you now."

The head of the recruiting office was a colonel—a huge man with a distinctly leonine mane of gray hair. The conversation was brief, not as congenial as it had been with the Lynx. He asked some questions, which I answered as I had earlier. Once again I told him that I refused to go into intelligence. He sent me back to the Lynx. This time the claws were distinctly out.

"So you refuse, do you? Well, let me tell you something. You had a choice, but you lacked the intelligence to make it. So you are going to learn the hard way. You are going to serve not in the infantry or the artillery, where it's three years, but in the navy. Five years. Now what do you say?"

I was quaking inside, but if there was one thing I had learned in New York, it was that you never allowed fear to show. So, cocky as hell, I said, "The law's the law. But I think you're wasting your time. I expect I'll be accepted by Moscow University before you draft me."

As luck would have it, I was. Thanks to my father's refusal to give up, my case was reviewed by someone at the Central Committee who decided in my favor. I don't think it bothered anyone at the Department of Biology—after all, they had only been covering their asses. Someone else had made the decision, so it was no longer their responsibility. If I turned out to be OK, so much the better. If not—well, they hadn't wanted to take me in the first place. All the bases were covered.

That was my first brush with the army. The second occurred a little more than one year later, when I was expelled for flunking two out of the three winter-session exams.

I had finished my freshman year well enough, but when the time for summer vacation came, I had nowhere to go. We were new to things Soviet and had no idea what one did during holidays, how one applied for reservations at a resort or whether it was possible to rent a place in the country. These were things we would learn soon enough, but then, during that second summer in Moscow, we were still testing the waters. My parents had made some friends, and one of them suggested I go spend August in Leningrad with the sister-in-law of one of my mother's colleagues at work (she had gotten a job as a news reader for Radio Moscow's French-language service). Having nothing better to do, I agreed. The overnight ride to Leningrad was uneventful, there was nothing that even remotely gave me reason to believe that I was on my way to one of the great adventures of my life.

The train pulled into Leningrad's Moscow Station at precisely 8:25 in the morning, and a glorious morning it was, the kind Leningrad does not offer often: the sky and the sun looking freshly washed, the purest blue and the most shining gold, the air rushing into your lungs and ballooning you off your feet. As I stood there, somehow feeling like a tree in spring, I heard a voice call, "Volodya?" The voice, somehow too deep and throaty, spun me around, and I found myself staring at a face that left me tongue-tied. I can visualize it now: slate-gray eyes (set much too far apart), high cheekbones (too pronounced), a pug nose (too small), a full mouth (too full, too big, the upper lip just one sweeping arch with no V in the middle), and a chin (somewhat too heavy), the head crowned with auburn hair (too curly) and perched on a neck Modigliani would have sold his soul for. I could describe the body in minute detail, for I came to know it well, but I will leave it all to the reader's imagination. This was the sister-in-law of my mother's colleague. She was thirty-four, married to a naval officer, and was, as I soon discovered, in the process of being divorced. Depending on how you looked at it, I had arrived at the best or the worst time.

That month in Leningrad was one of the happiest in my life. Zhenya, that was her name, was far more than my cicerone. She did not simply show me around Leningrad, she taught me Leningrad, opening my eyes and heart to its unique beauty, its magical proportions and symmetry. As we walked the streets of the Venice of the North, she took me back in time. I saw Peter the Great stalking like a crane across the flat marshlands, staring moodily toward the Gulf of Finland, putting his will of steel to the test as he built his city, St. Petersburg, pushing himself beyond human endurance and showing pity for no one, built it where no city should be built, setting it on the bones of countless nameless Russian peasants who died of disease, hunger, and heartbreak, cursing the day they had been born. I saw the Peter and Paul Fortress go up, its spire challenging the leaden skies. I saw the mansions line the Neva River, and I saw the river shrugging its defiance, swelling, rising up to flood, drowning the man-made attempt to steer it between granite banks. I saw Alexander Pushkin, that pure genius of poetry, unmatched as Shakespeare, I saw him moving like quicksilver, small, graceful, his features bearing testimony to his Moorish ancestor, Pushkin, that most un-Russian of all Russian poets in his lust for life, in his delight in simply being, in the lightness of his touch, in the easy compatibility of the sensual and the spiritual in his verse, simple and transparent as a raindrop, complex and opaque as infinity; Pushkin, that most Russian of all Russian poets in his wisdom, in his understanding of, and compassion for, the human condition.

I saw Gogol furtively walking down Nevsky Prospekt, cloak pulled tight around him, foxlike face peering back over his right shoulder at some future denizen of his stories. I heard Paul I gasping out his life under the pillows the murderers pressed to his face while his son, Alexander, waited for the news that would make him czar. I smelled the acrid odor of gunpowder on Senate Square as the artillery of Nicholas I dispersed the Decembrist uprising, ending a chapter that hardly began and that could have led Russia to democracy and opening one of the longest and darkest chapters of Russia's dark history.

All this and more I saw, heard, smelled, felt, and all the while I was looking into those slate-gray eyes and listening to that voice, too husky, too low, and altogether too overpowering.

Have I made it clear that I was in love?

We returned to Moscow together, she to live with her sister and brother-in-law, me to join my parents in the two-room apartment we had received and to begin my second year at Moscow University. But rumors about us had arrived earlier, and the reception we got was hardly cordial.

Zhenya was crucified by her relatives for seducing an innocent boy. The innocent boy was told by his father that either he would stop seeing this harlot or he would be kicked out. The upshot was predictable: Zhenya rented a room in a communal Moscow apartment and I moved in with her. Needless to say, I had no time or desire to study. I attended classes only in body. I lived for the moment when I came back to that tiny little room, transformed into a fairyland by the presence of this woman. Nothing else mattered, nothing else existed.

Then came the time for winter exams, and I flunked the first two. I was promptly expelled. I told Zhenya nothing. I knew she would find out, but I could not bring myself to admit that I had failed her. One evening I came back to our room carrying a cardboard box of our favorite pastries. I opened the door, came in, and stopped short, as if I had come up against a wall. Zhenya was sitting on the couch, looking at me with an expression of utter contempt. "So you are a liar," she said in that throaty voice that drove me crazy. "You are a coward—what's more, a stupid coward because you think your exams are so important that you have to lie about them. I despise you. Get out. I never want to see you again."

I said nothing. I could not have spoken to save my life. I turned, walked out, and shut the door behind me.

As I look back, I think she had decided to end our relationship well before the occasion presented itself. She had decided there was no future to it and that was that.

Ten years later, during the intermission of a ballet, the name of which escapes me, I saw Zhenya again. It was in the Kremlin Palace of Congresses, on the second floor, and she was standing some thirty yards from me. She was nearsighted and refused to wear glasses, so she probably didn't see me, for which I was thankful. My knees began to tremble, my heart began to pound wildly, and for a minute I thought I would faint. Time stopped. Then she turned away and disappeared in the crowd.

Another ten years elapsed before I saw her again. I was taking the up escalator in the metro, looking at the people gliding downward, without actually registering anything, when suddenly a face jumped out at me: Zhenya. She must have been fifty-five, but I saw the same face that had mesmerized me twenty years earlier. She was staring off into space, immersed in her own thoughts, and did not see me. That was fifteen years ago, as of this writing. I have never seen her since. Probably I never will. Nor will I ever forget her.

All this explains my second encounter with the Soviet army.

No sooner had I been expelled than I received a summons to the local recruiting office. When I arrived, the place was packed with young men of my age, most of whom had failed the competitive entrance exams to this or that institution of higher education. Some, like myself, had flunked out. Among the latter was my buddy from the Department of Biology, whom I will refer to as Kolia—he has become a television personality in this country and would probably prefer to remain anonymous.

We were all herded into a large room and ordered to strip for a medical examination. Now I had never before undressed in public, even in the presence of men, so it should not be difficult to imagine my mortification at having to stand naked in front of women. Yet that was the case, since all the doctors who were seated at the tables lining the walls and all the paramedics were women. Each of us moved from doctor to doctor— neuropathologist, surgeon, dentist, ophthalmologist, and so on. I was prodded, punched, pinched, every nook and cranny of my body was looked into and commented upon, I was questioned, spun around, appraised, and categorized (very much like the All-American kid from New York City in Arlo Guthrie's "Alice's Restaurant" who was injected, inspected, detected, infected, neglected, and selected). Had it not been for Kolia's indomitable sense of humor, I don't know how I would have gotten through it all. Finally we approached the last table, where the doctor, a woman in her late twenties, sat studying a list of names. Without even looking up at Kolia she said, "Spread your legs and lean forward." He did. "Put your hands on your buttocks," she said, getting up and positioning herself behind him, "and pull them apart." Kolia complied. She leaned forward and looked into his anal aperture. "Do you smoke?" she queried. "Yup," said Kolia. "Do you drink?" Kolia look back at her with a lascivious grin. "Why? Do you see a cork?"

Once that ordeal was over, each of us was marched separately into an even larger room, where a group of military officers was seated on a dais behind a long table. We were made to stand at attention while our physiques were discussed—much in the way one might discuss the merits of a racehorse or a thoroughbred bull. When my turn came, the officers went into a huddle. Then the senior officer told me I would be inducted into the navy. By that time, I knew my father had talked the dean of the Biology Department into taking me back for one term on a provisional basis. If I did well during the spring exams, I would be fully reinstated; if not, I was out for good. Overcoming my feelings of helplessness and shame, I said, "Don't count on getting me. My case has been reconsidered. I'll be going back to university." This caused a bit of discussion behind the table. It seemed that once the navy was promised a recruit, it demanded prompt delivery and made a great big stink if anything got fouled up. Nobody gave a hoot in hell about me, but nobody wanted to incur the navy's wrath. Finally, they decided to assign me to the infantry, because if things didn't work out, that branch of the armed forces really wouldn't care about getting one person less.

That was my second and last contact with the army, my first and only experience of what serving might actually be like, how from the outset things were geared toward breaking your spirit, making you despise yourself, suppressing the individual in the individual. I have always hated regimentation, and I always will. If I had ever entertained the slightest romantic idea about the military, that one day in the recruitment center not only cured me, but made me immune to the appeal of the military for the rest of my life.

Strangely enough, recollections of my student years seem shaped by events, conversations, and people far removed from my principal activity, studies. Perhaps that is because I soon discovered that biology was really not my thing. I must have made this discovery by the end of my freshman year, but I hid it deep down inside me. I did not want to know about it, especially considering how it would disappoint my parents. Out of those five long years at Moscow University, only two study-related events stand out. One was the winter-session exams of 1955–56, which I passed with straight fives, thereby proving to my parents, to my fellow students, to my professors, and, most importantly, to myself that if I put my mind to it, I could be a brilliant student. *Vanitas vanitatum.* The second is filed away in the up-yours section of my memory and has to do with a running feud I had with a teacher of Marxism, a certain Ootyonkov, who embodied the most typical negative traits of those in his profession: obtuseness, dogmatism, agressive ignorance, and a pettiness of mind matched only by a fear, bordering on horror, of independent thought. Perhaps that statement calls for clarification.

There are three subjects, and only three, that are mandatory for *all* Soviet university students, regardless of what they major in: Marxism, economics, and philosophy. The first is really a euphemism for history of the Party; the second consists of the economics of capitalism (based on Marx) and the economics of socialism (until recently based on black magic, voodoo, and other similar exact sciences); and the third introduces students to dialectical and historical materialism. Whether knowledge of these subjects is of vital importance for a future astrophysicist or aviation engineer is, shall we say, debatable. What is not debatable, or at least not during my student years, is the content of the subjects themselves: it was set in stone, indisputable by virtue of having supposedly been formulated by Marx, Engels, Lenin, and Stalin. These were subjects to learn, not to probe, and as such they attracted a certain kind of teacher. While there was some room for discussion in the philosophy course, which at least touched on the ancient Greeks and the great German thinkers of the nineteenth century, among others, and while the economics course inevitably led to an examination of real life, however perfunctory, the history of the Party was a catechism. To question any part of it was heresy, to disagree was a mortal sin. Not surprisingly, many of those who taught this subject had to be of the Ootyonkov ilk, true believers in the most fundamentalist sense. Not surprisingly, they were the faculty least respected and most despised by the student body. And none, as far as I know, were less respected and more despised than Ootyonkov. One of my favorite Russian jokes tells the story of a woman who can no longer stand her husband's stupidity. "If there was a world schmuck championship," she said to her spouse, "you would come in second." "Why second?" he asked. "Because you are such a schmuck you could not be first." That story was about Ootyonkov. I couldn't stand the man, and I didn't even try to conceal my feelings during seminars. Things got to the point where students came to these seminars to hear our exchanges. Came the day when the subject of discussion was the Communist party's agrarian policy. This was at the height of the Khrushchev period, marked in agriculture by his pet project: corn. He had visited the Garst farm in Iowa and had been deeply impressed by this wonderful plant that could feed both humans and animals. He returned to the Soviet Union dead set on making corn the number-one priority. Actually, it was not a bad idea, were it not for the bureaucratic psychology that is always predicated on the principle of pleasing the boss. Because of the Stalinist legacy, this assumed epic proportions in the Soviet Union. When Khrushchev called for growing corn, the suggestion was interpreted by Party bureaucrats all over the country as an order. All other produce was virtually forgotten, all state and collective farms were told to plant corn, regardless of whether the climate and the soil were suitable. The results of this policy need no description on my part. Suffice it to say that after Khrushchev was forced out of office, corn stopped being planted almost completely, a backlash that was and still is as detrimental to Soviet agriculture as the event that provoked it.

The subject of discussion in class that day was, as you must have guessed, corn. Ootyonkov proceeded to go into a litany. But the more he spoke, the clearer it became how little he knew about it. I must have had a sarcastic smile on my face, for suddenly Ootyonkov interrupted his oration and turned on me. "I take it Comrade Pozner, as usual, does not agree? Could it possibly be that he knows something about corn that we need to be enlightened on?" I just kept on smiling. "Come, come, do not allow this welcome, but unexpected, bout of modesty keep you from sharing your wisdom with us." Ootyonkov was clearly having one of his better days. I became very serious and said, "Well, I was just wondering whether you, Comrade Ootyonkov, had ever seen a corn tree?" Ootyonkov looked around at the class, which had become deathly quiet, then back at me. He proceeded to crash triumphantly into my elementary trap. "I am not a city slicker like some in this room. Yes, I have seen a corn tree." At which statement pandemonium broke loose. When the laughter finally subsided, Ootyonkov gave me a look so charged with hatred that I felt the hair on my neck prickle. "The time of reckoning will come, Comrade Pozner," he said softly. "The time of reckoning will come."

And so it did in the form of the spring exam session, which included the history of the Party. I had prepared well, diligently reading not just the required texts but extracurricular material as well. I don't know what seventh sense prompted me. After all, I knew Ootyonkov would flunk me even if I knew the textbook by heart, as well as all the Marxist classics and pseudoclassics in the bargain.

Came the day of reckoning, an unusually cold day for May, so cold, in fact, that Ootyonkov sat at the examiner's table in his coat. The tactics and strategy for oral exams have a history as old as exams themselves. Should you go first, thereby impressing the examiner with your confidence? Or should you go last, when he will be too tired to ply you with questions? Perhaps you should bide your time and wait for the first bunch to come out so as to get a feel for the examiner's mood but not wait too long? Should you answer in a loud, no-nonsense voice, or should you speak in a this-is-between-you-and-me tone as if sharing something of particular importance? These are just some of the stratagems that are the subject of endless and heated student debates. But they did not concern me on that day. They were irrelevent. I just wanted to get this over with as quickly as possible. When Ootyonkov opened the door and told the first five students to come in, I was among them. Thirty-five oblong rectangles (we called them tickets), each bearing two questions, lay face down on the examination table. Each of us approached the table and picked up one ticket, read out its number, and then sat down to prepare for about twenty minutes. When I picked up mine, Ootyonkov gave me a venomous look and said, "I can't bear to hear what you have to tell me." I was fourth in line, so that meant I had much more than twenty minutes to think about the questions, which was usually a good position. But I knew it meant nothing in my case, so I hardly gave any thought to the matter at hand. Twenty minutes ticked by, and Ootyonkov called on the first in line, a straight five student who always went first, to begin. I sat there doing nothing. The student was about two-thirds of the way into his answer when suddenly in walked a man in a dazzling blue suit. Immediately, Ootyonkov jumped to his feet and said, "Comrades, this is Professor Raiskii who heads our department of Marxism-Leninism." Raiskii nodded, gave us all a warm smile, and said, "I will be helping Comrade Ootyonkov with exams today. If any of you are ready to answer, I am at your service." I was on my feet almost before he had finished his sentence: "I am!" Raiskii sat down at a table in a corner of the auditorium and motioned me over. I had broken one of the unwritten rules of conduct by jumping the exam order, but not one of the students ahead of me showed the slightest sign of displeasure. They knew what was happening. I don't remember what my questions were, but I distinctly recall being brilliant, so much so that when I finished, Raiskii said, "It's really a pity you chose to major in biology, you have a gift for Marxism." Exulting inside, I put on my most modest face and shrugged, as if to say, "You are so right, but what can one do? The die is cast." Raiskii took my exam form and opposite the name of the subject, Marxism, wrote "Excellent" and then inscribed a large five. "Thank you," he said. "Now have Comrade Ootyonkov sign that." How can I describe my feelings as I walked up to where my would-be executioner was seated and put the form down in front of him? All I could think of were the words uttered by Beetles in Kipling's wonderful novel *Stalky and Co.:* "Je vais gloater. Je vais gloater tout le blessed afternoon. Jamais j'ai gloaté comme je gloaterai au jourd'hui."

Oh did I gloat! And when Ootyonkov refused to sign the form, something that made Raiskii raise his eyebrows (of course Raiskii signed it), I no longer gloated, for I was in paradise. Just for the record, in English the Russian word *rai* means "paradise," and the name Raiskii can be translated as "Paradisiacal."

Another memory relates less to studies than to a student activity, that of the so-called *agitbrigades.* While the concept of agitation has always seemed pernicious to most Americans (even though Tom Paine, Thomas Jefferson, and Abraham Lincoln rank among the greatest and most effective agitators in history), this has not been the case in the Soviet Union, where agitation has been, and is, seen for what it is: an attempt to win people over to a certain attitude or viewpoint by actively addressing them on the issue. Agitation, like so many other things, is neither good nor bad; it all depends to what use it is put. The creation of an army of Party agitators in the Soviet Union, of people who mainly parroted the party line without any attempt (or ability—probably one of the reasons they were selected for the activity) to question, analyze, or engage in a serious exchange with their public, has, to be sure, tarnished the figure of the agitator but not the concept of agitation. Similarly, public relations is accepted in the United States as a legitimate and, in fact, extremely useful activity, but the con artist is looked upon with contempt.

During three of my five student years (minus the first, when I was just learning the ropes, and my last, when I was too involved in writing my graduation thesis to do anything else), I was a member of an *agitbrigade,* a group of about fifteen Biology Department students who toured the country during their vacations, offering audiences a mixture of songs, dances, skits, recitations of satirical verses written on the spot by our "poets" as a comment about local practices, and so on. My first major involvement with such a brigade was in the summer of 1956, when we traveled beyond the Urals to the Altai region, where we toured a series of agricultural and industrial sites. What sticks out in my mind is the beauty of the roaring Katun' River, a white-waterer's dream if there ever was one, and the ugliness of the two largest cities, Biysk and Barnaul. The latter will remain embedded in my memory forever thanks to an experience I would rather forget. It was in Barnaul that I got drunk on *chernogolovka,* literally "little black head," the local vodka thus named because its corked top was sealed with black wax. For the edification of non-Russian vodka drinkers, including those who, may the good Lord have mercy on their misled souls, sip, dilute, and put ice into their drink, it must be stated unequivocally that vodka should be consumed in one gulp, chilled to the point when the liquid almost becomes syrupy, and followed by food. Drinking vodka as you would a gin and tonic or any other aperitif is to ask for trouble. And a final piece of advice: sipping vodka is far more lethal than drinking the same amount in one gulp. For the adventuresome, the doubting Thomases, and those with suicidal tendencies, I recommend the following experiment: try drinking one hundred *thimblefuls* of vodka.

Only please don't forget to have an ambulance handy. Also, don't say I didn't warn you. By comparison, drinking the equivalent of one hundred thimblefuls poured into one glass is no big deal.

What I have related are really ABCs, the most basic of basics. The connoisseur will tell you that the best-tasting vodkas are made of wheat and have been purified to the point that they actually have no taste at all. The fewer filters a vodka has been put through, the worse its taste and the more lethal its kick. And of all the vodkas ever produced and foisted on the public, "little black head" was the least filtered, if it was filtered at all. What's more, in Barnaul in 1956, there were virtually no refrigerators, which meant downing that vodka at room temperature, which boosted its awful taste to stunning proportions and turned what might be called a deadly potion into one capable of creating raving homicidal maniacs.

Anyway, that is the drink I consumed on our first evening in Barnaul. The consequences were nothing less than shattering. Feeling ill, I staggered out of the house where our group had been put up. Under the star-studded summer Siberian sky, I searched desperately for the outhouse. Even though Barnaul was one of the largest cities in that entire region, plumbing was a luxury then available to the select few. After negotiating the terrain, which, for some uncanny reason, seemed to lurch this way and that under my feet, I finally stumbled up against the object of my quest.

Were I Homer, I would at this jucture launch into an epic description of The Outhouse in the Soviet Union. Not because I have any particular, let alone perverse, interest in the disposal of human waste, or because of any belief on my part that the study of this subject might lead to profound and enlightening philosophical conclusions. I would do it out of a sense of compassion for my fellow humans. As I would warn them not to undertake an expedition to the North Pole or the Sahara Desert without certain precautions, so would I advise them of the dangers and rigorous demands posed by The Outhouse. I would strongly recommend such equipment as a gas mask, rubber boots, an alpenstock, and a wet suit. I would also underline the importance of psychological preparedness to see shit. Not just here and there, you understand, not even everywhere, but all over, including places you would not dream of in your wildest fantasies. Had I, I repeat, the epic genius of Homer, or at least the ingenuity of Gargantua, who, at the tender age of five, amazed his father by relating to him a series of in-depth experimental studies that led the boy to the discovery of the most soothing and voluptuous torchecul, or ass wiper (a tender, young, and well-feathered bird that worked wonders, provided one clamped its head between one's knees, lest its beak inflict unpleasant sensations), I would attempt this literary feat. Being, however, neither a Homer nor a Rabelais, I will limit myself to this: The Outhouse in my country blows you away.

I hope you now have a general picture of what I stumbled up against in that Barnaul backyard. I then stumbled into it, slipped, and fell. What more can I say? The torture chambers of Torquemada pale in comparison.

But of all the memories of my student years at Moscow University, the one that stands out is the day in 1956 when we were assembled in one of the largest auditoriums and read Khrushchev's famous secret speech to the Twentieth Party Congress. Its revelations about Stalin and his reign of terror were not a total surprise to me because of my friends, the Gordons.

A year earlier, my parents had returned to Germany, where my father had, once again, been offered a job by Sovexportfilm. Quite frankly, I was happy to see them go. My relations with my father had become quite strained; what's more, I was twenty-one and chafing at the bit, and I looked forward to living in our two-room apartment without my parents and my ten-year-old brother. However, that was not to be. Shortly before his departure, my father informed me that an old friend of his, Iosif Gordon, and his wife, Nina, would be moving in. There was nothing I could do about it, but I immediately developed a wholesome dislike for the Gordons. Had I been given a choice, I would have refused to live with Iosif and Nina—and would thereby have almost certainly deprived myself of a relationship that ultimately changed my life.

Iosif was two or three years older than my father. He, too, had been born in St. Petersburg; he had emigrated to Paris in 1925 for health reasons (he had the beginnings of tuberculosis, the curing of which called for the kind of nutrition and climate that could not be found in Leningrad, as the city had been renamed in 1924). Once in Paris, Iosif found work at Paramount as a cutter, and it was through the film business that he met my father. Iosif, like many other Russian émigrés, had strong pro-Soviet sentiments and was, in fact, a Soviet citizen. In 1936, he returned to Moscow, where he began to work for Mosfilm Studios. It was then that he met Nina. It was love at first sight, not an uncommon event, but it was also, for both of them, love forever, the one and only love, a far rarer matter. Within one year, Iosif was arrested, accused of being a British spy (!), put on trial, and sentenced to ten years in a labor camp. Ultimately, he spent seventeen years in prison camp and in Siberian exile before being rehabilitated and returning to Moscow in 1954.

When Iosif and Nina first met, she was working for one of the Soviet Union's most famous journalists, Mikhail Koltsov, who headed the Zhurgaz conglomerate of newspapers and magazines; it was through him that Nina met the entire Soviet literary elite of that time, such people as Yuri Olesha, Ilya Ilf and Yevgeny Petrov, Osip Mandelstam, and many more whose names have since become legendary. When Koltsov returned from fighting on the Loyalist side in Spain against Franco in 1939, he was soon arrested and sent off to some camp or prison where he probably was killed—the actual circumstances of his death remain unclear. Many, if not the majority of those who fought in Spain, suffered Koltsov's fate, for reasons that also have not been clearly established. Was Stalin simply fearful of those who had enjoyed such a deep gulp of democracy while defending the Spanish Republic against fascism? Or did he have a secret motive in Spain that differed radically from the official Soviet position, a secret motive that might have been uncovered by such men as Koltsov? The questions are all there, and they beg an answer.

By the time Koltsov disappeared into the gulag system, a majority of the literary figures Nina had befriended had already gone that way. All around her people disappeared overnight, yet she was not touched. Perhaps that was because she soon moved to Siberia to be closer to Iosif. She spent many, many years living in Krasnoyarsk, in de facto voluntary exile. Probably that is why she was never arrested. Out of sight, out of mind. When the Gordons finally returned to Moscow in 1954, Nina went to work for Konstantin Simonov, another famous Soviet literary figure. He had been named Kirill, not Konstantin, by his mother, but because of a speech impediment, he could not pronounce either the letter *r* or *l*, causing his name to come out "Kiwiw." He changed it later to Konstantin. I would not bring this up if it were not for a strange thought. Besides being a writer, Simonov was a prominent and influential public figure, a man of principles and courage, yet a man who, to use test-pilot lingo, never really pushed the envelope. He espoused many a good cause but never engaged himself beyond the point of his own security. The courage he demonstrated was never really of the sort that could be dangerous or threatening to him—as his career demonstrates. When the situation would become sticky, as indeed it did, he would back off and thereby join, perhaps without even planning to, the very forces he had been opposing. In a way, it might be said that his character was flawed—as was his speech. However, it must also be said that he did everything in his power to help Nina and her husband, and she always was, and still remains, fiercely loyal to him (Simonov died in 1979).

I'll never forget the day I first met Iosif. He was of medium height and thin to the point of being scrawny. His hands were large, sensitive, and of a reddish color, the result of frostbite. He was bald except for a fringe of gray hair that had once been red—as his eyebrows betrayed. But these were all details I noticed later. I was riveted by his eyes—enormous, of the purest blue, and totally penetrating. Eyes you could not look into and lie. Eyes that made you squirm at even a dishonest thought, let alone action. The eyes of your own conscience, full of kindness and compassion, encouraging you to be everything you could be. Eyes that appealed to your integrity, eyes that made you stand tall and take pride in being a human being, eyes that made you cringe inside when you failed to measure up to their standards.

Iosif and Nina lived with me for three unforgettable years. Their relationship, the way they interacted with the world around them, their delicacy and tactfulness, and their moral standards affected me profoundly. Iosif became a second father to me, a person I could and did bare my soul to, knowing he would never betray my confidence, a person who would never hurt me but would always be honest, a person whose feelings of love and sense of responsibility I could rely on without any qualification, a man who had gone through hell's crucible and emerged as pure gold.

Iosif died in 1968 of a heart attack, his second, died at least ten years before his time, ten years lopped off his life by Stalin's concentration camps. That was over twenty years ago, but the empty space in my heart that he once filled has never stopped aching. I still look into his eyes for guidance.

On that first day of our acquaintance, Iosif gravely looked at me and asked, "May I call you Ghenrikh?" (the Russian for Henry). Seeing my surprise, he explained, "I once came across a French Russian-language textbook that featured the following dialogue in Russian: 'How are you?' 'Thank you, Ghenrikh, I am in good health.' Ever since, I have dreamed of meeting someone by the name of Ghenrikh who would ask me how I am. However, fate has not seen fit to steer any such person my way, and now I no longer wish to leave it to chance. I am asking you to be Ghenrikh." I remember the feeling of warmth that literally flooded me as I stuck out my hand and said, "How are you?" Iosif shook it firmly and, with an impish twinkle in his eye, solemnly answered, "Thank you, Ghenrikh, I am in good health."

Over the next three years, I met many of Iosif and Nina's friends, most of whom had gone through the gulag and Siberian exile. Evening upon evening I would sit there listening to them tell the countless stories of their experiences while they sipped Iosif's famous tea. He called it b-slash-b, a weak translation of which into English would be "no-shit tea." It was strong, fragrant, and altogether wonderful, brewed as only he could brew it, one teaspoon of tea leaves per person plus one for the pot. I recall once asking Iosif to tell me his secret recipe. He gave me a long look and said, "Once upon a time, there lived an old Jew who was famous far beyond the confines of his *shtetl* for the tea he brewed. People came from far and wide, including gentiles, to drink his tea and learn his secret. Some begged, others offered large sums of money, but to no avail. Finally came the day when the old man lay on his deathbed. The entire community gathered around him, and the rabbi told him that to leave this world without sharing his secret would be an unpardonable sin. The old man looked around the room at all the people who had gathered and made a sign that they come closer. They came up to his very bedside, straining to hear his words, for he spoke in a barely audible whisper. 'Listen, for now I will tell you my secret,' the old man said, 'Jews, do not scrimp on your tea.' "

The world Iosif, Nina, and their friends reminisced about was one of horror and inhumanity, yet the stories they told were full of humor, profoundly human, a testimonial to the all-important truth that the spirit is indomitable. These are stories I cannot repeat, simply because I have the wrong voice. I can, at best, approximate the tune, the inflections, but my song would be false, the tone fuzzy. I was an outsider looking in, listening to these men and women describe a system designed to snuff out that sacred spark with which we all are born. Instead of dying, it became a burning flame.

A paradoxical thought: those who went through the camps and survived came out better human beings than those who were spared that calvary. Stronger, more compassionate, wiser, kinder, less cynical. Is there a moral to this? I don't know, but as I reflect on it, two people come to mind. One is Kyrill Henkin, a man my mother met in the French Section of Radio Moscow. His mother, Yelizaveta Nelidova, came from Russian nobility and as a young woman had been part of Czarina Alexandra's retinue. After the revolution, she emigrated to Paris, where she met a young and very talented Russian Jewish actor, Victor Henkin, whom she married, much to the horror of the highly anti-Semitic White Russian community. Their son, Kyrill, was born in Paris, given the best education money could buy, and brought up with a very pro-Soviet outlook. He fought on the Loyalist side in Spain and returned disillusioned with what he saw as the betrayal of democracy by the "free world." In 1939 or 1940, the entire family returned to the Soviet Union. Unlike most people with similar pasts, people "corrupted by bourgeois ideology," neither Kyrill nor his parents were persecuted. His father became a well-known actor who died young, but of natural causes; his mother passed away when she was over eighty; and Kyrill had a comfortable life, at least by Soviet standards. He adapted to the circumstances, compromised, and taught French (which he spoke brilliantly) at the Military Institute of Foreign Languages, one of the prime training centers for military espionage. Later, working at Radio Moscow, he translated texts he found stupid and offensive and read them over the air. He had a keen mind, the most biting and ironic sense of humor, and a tongue like a rapier. With the hint of a sneer on his lips, he relished taking the entire Soviet establishment to task—the bumbling bureaucrats, the party hacks, and especially the mind-numbing stupidity of the very propaganda he participated in dissipating.

I think Kyrill considered his life to have been a failure, or perhaps, more correctly, that somehow life had failed him, had not provided him with the successes, the recognition he believed he was worthy of. In a certain sense he was right, for he was endowed with an exceptional intelligence, a flair for literature, and a rare gift for languages; had he lived in a different time or place, there is reason to believe his talents would have been appreciated to a much greater degree. But Kyrill lacked the courage to admit that, while life may not have treated him fairly, it did not necessarily follow that life was, in general, not fair. In a way, he reminded me of those men I have met who have never loved or been loved, or, as the case may be, whose love was betrayed; not being able to endure the thought of others being happy, they retreat into a psychological fortress of protection, every turret of which flies a banner proclaiming Love Does Not Exist. As a result, their mentality toward the other sex is that of a fighter pilot: the more kills, the better, for every score proves their point. Ironically, the deeper they sink into their self-created quagmire, the slimmer the chances of their ever loving.

Kyrill seemed to take a masochistic delight in wallowing in the filth he so despised, in diving to the bottom and coming up holding something particularly despicable for all to see, the living proof of one of his favorite adages: "All is shit, except urine."

Once, when I had decided that I could no longer live in the Soviet Union, that I wanted to go home to New York City, I asked Kyrill what to do. I told him what my father had said—that he would sooner see me put behind bars than allowed to leave the country—and that I was desperate. Kyrill responded with the wry smile I have never seen anyone else come close to mastering (the corners of his mouth actually turned down when he did this), a smile that said, "You see? I told you so." He then advised me to attempt to escape across the Soviet-Norwegian border. He was not joking. He told me that the Kola Peninsula, where the Soviet Union bordered both Finland and Norway, was the ideal place for escaping, for it was less tightly guarded than other areas. Let us note that Kyrill wanted out as much as I did (he emigrated from the Soviet Union in the late seventies and, after failing to find meaningful occupation in either France or the United States, wound up in Munich working for Radio Liberty, indulging in the same kind of propaganda exercise he so despised when working for Radio Moscow), but he never attempted to follow his own advice. He knew it was far too dangerous. Had I been foolhardy enough to try it, I would have either been shot or apprehended. And Kyrill, hearing of the sad news, would have smiled his famous I-told-you-so smile. All is shit, except urine.

Compared with what life had done to Iosif, Kyrill was born not with one but with three silver spoons in his mouth. Iosif was twenty-nine when he returned to the Soviet Union, he was thirty when he was arrested and sent off to forced labor, and he was forty-seven when he came back. Those seventeen years robbed him of a career, of fatherhood, of a family, of a home. Life had treated him with the most atrocious injustice. Yet he was not bitter. Nor was he cynical. It would have been so natural, and so easy, for him to play to my disappointment with what I found in the Soviet Union, to my desire to leave, to destroy whatever ideals I still had. He did the opposite. He taught me—not just through words, but by his example—the true meaning of what it is to care, to believe in something, to be committed, to realize that there are things much more important than your personal interests. "Ghenrikh," he once said, "you can flunk any test, except one, the mirror test. Every morning when you shave, you look at yourself in the mirror. God forbid that you should ever want to spit at your own face." I think of those words every morning. And if I can still look myself in the eye without feeling sick to my stomach, it's thanks to Iosif, a man who never betrayed himself and therefore did not betray others, a man who did not bend and refused to break.

Iosif guided and prepared me for many things. Khrushchev's de-Stalinization speech was one of them. The uprising in Hungary, the student protests against Soviet intervention, and the following government crackdown on the students was another. Coming to grips with Stalinism and its consequences was an extremely complex process consisting not only of major events, such as the ones I have mentioned, but also of almost accidental, inconsequential incidents.

In the summer of 1956, our Biology Department brigade went to Siberia. Our goal was to reach the city of Irkutsk, near Lake Baikal, and then hike to one of the country's major construction sites, the Bratsk hydropower station, some four hundred and fifty kilometers away. We slogged through the taiga—the endless, almost impenetrable pine forest of Siberia. It was tough going. During the day, we were attacked by clouds of gnats and the biggest and most vicious horseflies on earth. We had to wear horsehair masks, gloves, and thick padded jackets to keep from being eaten alive. As if this were not enough, we carried backpacks that weighed, on the average, thirty-five pounds. Under the hot summer Siberian sun, we sweated profusely, which drove the flies and gnats into a feeding frenzy. When night finally came, we would sleep under nets to ward off the mosquitoes. The Siberian brand is big as a bumblebee, sucks blood like Dracula, flies in military formations, and attacks like a kamikaze.

Once, after a long day's hike, we arrived in a lumber camp where we were due to give a concert that evening. More than anything else, I wanted to rest up, so I went to one of the tents. I recall lying down on one of the bunks and seeing a man sitting across from me and thinking, "He sure doesn't look like a lumberjack." He was perhaps ten years older than I, wore a thin mustache and a small, pointed beard, and had a sensitive, chiseled face. I was on the point of dozing off when he asked me something about where we were from. When I told him we were a concert brigade, he asked me what I did. I tried to make my answers as brief as possible because, more than anything else, I was dying to go to sleep. But when he heard I sang French and American songs, he asked me if I spoke English. I just nodded, hoping that would be the last question. At which point he said in perfect American English, "Wheredja pick it up?" I nearly fell out of my bunk. Then he told me his story.

His parents were from Russia, his father having been a Cossack who fought in Kolchak's army against the Reds during the civil war. Along with many others, he retreated into China, where he met and married a Russian woman. He worked for an American company there, and that was where my new lumberjack friend was born. As a boy, he had attended an American school in China, finished high school, and was then sent to continue his studies in New York. He then returned to China and enlisted in the Nationalist Chinese army to fight the Japanese. After 1945, he fought in the Kuomintang against Mao, winding up as a POW in Shanghai in 1949. Discovering that he was a Russian, the Chinese authorities handed him over to the Soviets. He was immediately arrested and sent to Moscow and the infamous Lubyanka Prison. In short order he was accused and convicted of being an American spy. He was sentenced to twenty-five years in a labor camp. This was in 1950 or 1951. When Stalin died, he was rehabilitated, a free man with a clean bill of health. A man who was trilingual, speaking Chinese, English, and Russian. Working as a lumberjack.

After I heard his story, I said, "What the hell are you doing here? You speak the three most important languages in the world. Get your ass to Moscow! You've got things to do." I gave him my address and phone number and we parted friends. And I never heard from him again. Lumberjack-linguist, what happened? Why did you disappear? Wheredja . . . wheredja . . . ?

By 1957, I had begun asking myself some not-so-trivial questions. Did I really want to become a biologist? Was the Soviet Union really such a great place? Did I really plan on living here all of my life? Different questions, but all with the same answer, which sounded like no. Then, that summer, came the World Youth Festival, and I spent two weeks living with the American delegation. It was a strange group, a hodgepodge of card-carrying communists, radicals, liberals, freebooters, FBI informants—you name it. There were endless debates about such profound and relevant issues as to whether this actually was a United States delegation or a delegation of Americans, whether or not they would carry the American flag in the opening parade and ceremonies. But despite the craziness, I felt totally at home with these people, as well I might. The festival, combined with all that I had experienced since leaving the United States, forced me to confront myself in the most agonizing way. I had been in the Soviet Union for less than five years—long enough to understand how different its reality was from what I had been taught to expect, but not long enough to become deeply attached to the country. I hadn't lived there very long, wasn't part of the culture, and had only recently mastered the language. It was a foreign country. In addition, I had had certain personal experiences, some of which I have related, others that have yet to be told, that forced me to begin to see the United States in a different light. Not that my political views changed. Not that I accepted anticommunism or the racism or the injustices that I had seen in American society. But that country, as I discovered, was the one I was tied to emotionally. That was where I had grown up. It was home.

What does the sound of bat meeting ball mean to most people in the world? Zero. Nothing. A sound, period. What does it mean to an American? A whole world. You see the field, you smell the leather glove, you hear the roar of the crowd, you see the outfielder fading back as that white sphere arches into the blue sky. It is a world that lives inside you invisible to others, a world brought to life, conjured up by that magic Crrrack!, the sweet, clean sound of wood on horsehide.

Or you take a gulp of Coke and suddenly you're back in Washington Square playing stickball with the guys.

That's what homesickness is really all about. No matter what the politics, there's a place you call home. That's where you come from.

In that summer of 1957, at age twenty-three, I said to myself, "Shit, I've had it. I gotta go back." I had no illusions about what would happen. I was politically committed, pro-Soviet, procommunist, I knew things would be tough for me, I knew all about Joe McCarthy, I knew that emotionally, financially, politically I was in for one hell of a trial. But that wasn't the point. I was going home. I had no intention of making a big deal about this, I could only guess how painful my decision would be to my parents, but I felt I had no choice. The Russians say, "Man supposes, God disposes." I am not religious, but I do believe in fate—which, in my case, intervened right after the festival by introducing me to the girl who would become my first wife. Had I not met her, what would have happened? Would I have heeded Kyrill's advice and tried to cross the border illegally? Who knows. What's more, it's of no importance at all. What is important is that, after having decided to marry, I had to ask myself: would I try to make this person I loved tear up her roots, leave everything she loved behind, go through the same agony of adaptation as I had? Or would I try to stick it out? I opted for the latter, and, as a result, my encounters with Stalin's legacy continued.

In 1963, when I was working for *Soviet Life* magazine, I returned to Irkutsk and Lake Baikal. This time, though, I was a journalist from Moscow, status that gave me, among other things, a car and a driver. More than a quarter of a century later, that driver remains etched in my mind. He was about five-seven or five-eight, whether you measured him from head to toe, shoulder to shoulder, or spine to belly button. He made a brick shit house look fragile. His head was large and bald, and when he smiled, about once every seven hours on the average, he showed big, square, yellowish horse teeth. A jagged white scar, much like a bolt of lightning on his swarthy skin, streaked down from behind his right ear to the corner of his mouth. I don't know how much he weighed, but every time he sat down behind the wheel, the Volga sedan would list badly to the left. He had small, light-blue eyes, almost the color of Lake Baikal ice in winter when the sun hits a flat plane and a hint of the water underneath comes flickering through. And he made a clam seem gregarious. When you're in the back country, driving for hours on barren roads with never a house or a human in sight, you want to strike up a conversation. Trying to talk to him was hopeless. The best I got was a grunt or a humorless grin.

Late one night, after I had finished collecting data from people living near and on the shores of Lake Baikal, we drove back to Irkutsk. There was a bright moon out, and I started to drop off. Suddenly the driver began to talk. At first I thought I was dreaming. Even now, as I look back, the story has a dreamlike character, bathed as it was in the silvery light of that shining moon hanging over the inky-black silhouettes of the Siberian cedars.

He was born, he said, in a little village nearby. He was a boy in the early thirties when forced collectivization came to Siberia and people were arrested by the hundreds. Kulaks they were called, he said, but in reality they were farmers who had started out the same as everyone else after the revolution and the civil war, when the land was evenly and fairly distributed according to the number of people in a family. They had started out even but had worked their butts off and, as a result, prospered. The lazy, the good-for-nothings envied them and so, when their chance came, reported them to the authorities as being exploiters of the people, or kulaks. They were arrested, shot, their property was divvied up, becoming kolkhoz—collective farm—property. Thus the best farmers were destroyed and the goldbrickers took over. In the late thirties, as a teenager, he witnessed the mass arrests and then saw them repeated about a decade later. "Believe it or not," he told me, "there was a quota to fulfill, a plan. We had been told there were enemies of the people everywhere, right?

The trials of the thirties had proven that, hadn't they? So those whoresons came up with a great idea: whoever arrests more "enemies" is the greatest patriot. The bastards competed with each other to see who could arrest more, and the winners were praised and received a bonus for their patriotic activities. They didn't care who they arrested, all they thought about were numbers. They took fifty percent of all of those living in my village, fifty fucking percent!"

We drove on in silence for a few minutes, the driver staring straight ahead, unblinking. "I knew I had to get out of there," he said, "and I needed a job that would give me protection. And the job I got was as a truck driver in the gulag. I drove trucks from camp to camp, transporting all kinds of things, as well as people. That was in 1949. Then came 1953, when Stalin died. A few months later, I was ordered to drive a truckload of zeks [camp slang meaning an incarcerated person, an inmate] to another camp. We always drove our live cargo at night. So we headed off. There were guards, all armed with Kalashnikovs, one up front with me, and two more in the back of the van with the zeks. It was a night like this one. The steppe was as flat as a plate and the moon was full and shining. At one point, a guard began to bang on the partition that separated us from the back of the van. It was a signal to stop and let the zeks take a leak. I stopped the truck and we all got out. The zeks weren't shackled—where the fuck could they escape to? And suddenly, as if for the first time, I actually saw these poor bastards. In the light of the moon they looked like ghosts. They were pale, gaunt, so underfed they reminded me of scarecrows floating over the snow. They were, I realized, just like the people from my village, they had never done anything wrong, they were just a number, a statistic that some son of a bitch dreamed up to please Stalin, may his soul fry in hell. And in that moment I knew I couldn't do this any more. I jumped back into the truck, leaned out and yelled at the guards and the prisoners, 'Get the fuck out of here, you fucking bastards!' And I drove off. I just left them standing there in the snow.

"Well, I figured it was all over for me—I would be arrested and stood up against a wall. But I didn't care. I drove to Irkutsk, left the truck on the outskirts of the city, and walked to where my sister lived. I got there at the crack of dawn. I knocked on her door, and she opened it, and the first thing she said was, 'Have you heard the news? Beria has been arrested!' Yeah, I guess I was born lucky. If Beria hadn't been taken then, I wouldn't be around to tell you my story," he concluded with a mirthless laugh.

*   *   *

How can an American understand the phenomenon of Stalinism, a tyrannical political system *supported by the majority?* For someone living today, there simply is no analogous experience. But for those who lived in the United States before 1861, a parallel might be drawn. Here was a society born on the principle that all men are created equal, but yet it accepted slavery. How did people rationalize that? How did they see themselves, their parents, how did they—farmers, preachers, professionals, politicians, all decent people and responsible citizens—find it possible to support simultaneously liberty, independence, and slavery? It is a stunning experience to read how the Bible, the Constitution, and even the Declaration of Independence were quoted again and again and again to defend slavery. How many people were publicly vilified, run out of town, lynched, murdered because they took a stand against slavery or, much later, fought for equal rights for the blacks? To pass after-the-fact moral judgment is not the point, nor is it enough. We need to look deeply into the human character, the human experience, and the ethics of our economic and political systems to find real answers.

That seems especially hard for Americans. They are a change-oriented people in a society that stresses the here and now. This has its benefits and shortcomings, one of the latter being a short historical memory and the reduced understanding that results from a loss of historical perspective. Many Americans are probably mystified at the importance attached here to the Soviet rehabilitation of Nikolai Bukharin some fifty years after his trial and execution by Stalin as a "spy and wrecker." So what they think? But to Soviets, the connection between past and present is very evident.

To make an analogy in American terms, let us imagine that John Fitzgerald Kennedy was the victim of a conspiracy. Let's imagine that Lee Harvey Oswald was gunned down by a man sent to do that job, by a man whose death in prison was no accident, that a score of other witnesses to all of this died accidentally in the following years. Let's imagine that JFK was the victim of a plot hatched by people in the military, in the industrial sector, in the world of organized crime, and even in the government. If this were the case, and if that truth were made public today, some twenty-five years after the assassination, I think it would have a profound impact on the American psyche—much deeper than, say, the trauma of the Vietnam War or the shame of Watergate. It would mean having to come to terms with something very frightening, for it would mean having to acknowledge the existence of an all-powerful oligarchy that will not tolerate a president who goes too far. In short, it would mean that "government of, by, and for the people," a concept central to Americans' faith in their system, is a hoax. I posit this scenario as a way of trying to communicate the magnitude of Bukharin's rehabilitation.

One has to understand that Stalin became to the Soviet people what Lenin had been—the founding father of their new society, the flame of their revolution. Mind you, this was not some remote figure, such as George Washington, who had lived two centuries earlier. Lenin was a contemporary, he had been seen and heard by many who could tell that story, who lived in the twenties and thirties. Even today, there are still people around who saw Lenin. It would be like meeting someone in America who can say, "When I saw George Washington . . ." But this is even more true of Stalin, a man who lived much longer than Lenin and who left his mark on virtually every aspect of life in this country, shaping not just institutions, but individuals as well, so powerfully that we continue to feel it today.

It is one thing to state that Stalin is responsible for having masterminded the persecution of millions of innocent people: painful as this may be, this fact was admitted more than thirty years ago. But it is an entirely different thing to say that Stalin set out to destroy the party leadership, that he planned the murder of Lenin's closest associates, that he was obsessed with only one thing, power, and that in acquiring it, he lured the overwhelming majority of Soviets into supporting a system that was inhuman, corrupt, and vile—all the while fooling them into believing that they were suffering, struggling, sacrificing to make the dreams of the revolution come true. It is, I repeat, a completely different thing to sweat and strain for your leader, only to be told that he misled you, that your life had been wasted, that had it not been for him and what he did, your country would be a very different and much better place than it is today.

So rehabilitating Bukharin and all the others, stating officially that they were not guilty of any crime, that they were the victims of total fabrication, is more than simply that. It is the ultimate, final, irrefutable condemnation of Stalin and Stalinism. If, prior to this, some people could argue, "Yes, but look at the opposition he faced. Those people were really against socialism, they were plotting, for him it was do or die," now that discussion is over. The rehabilitation is important if one simply believes in justice. But it is far more important if it finally enables people to grasp that what Stalin did could have destroyed—or, indeed, may have destroyed—the chances that socialism would ever be possible in this country. I am not sure that was Stalin's intention; probably it wasn't. But that's irrelevant. He destroyed the farmer, exterminated the intellectuals, transformed the Party from a revolutionary power into a ponderous bureaucratic superconservative machine. It is my opinion that the major problems the Soviet Union faces today—and they are major—have nothing to do with socialism and have everything to do with Stalinism.

Was Stalin an evil genius? Such as, say, Hitler? Not really. Hitler lasted for twelve years, from 1933 to 1945. His impact on the world was terrible but not of long duration. It didn't really affect the psyche of the German people in a lasting way. Hitler openly advocated vicious, lethal racial supremacy, he made his intentions clear early on, and, despicable as those intentions were, the majority of the German people supported them. Hitler did not pretend to be what he was not. He told the Germans they were Aryans, the master race, that together with them he would build the Third Reich, which would last one thousand years. He told them that the Jews were the cause of all evil and should be destroyed. And the majority of the German people bought that view. They were not being sold a bill of goods. The product was certainly evil, but it wasn't packaged to look different. What you saw is what you got. Not so in the case of Stalin.

He donned Lenin's mantle and sold the Soviet nation (as well as many people around the world) on the idea that he was carrying the torch. In fact, he sold the nation out.

There is a scene in Mikhail Romm's brilliant documentary film, *Ordinary Fascism,* that shows Hitler standing on an outdoor podium, about six feet above street level. Throngs of cheering people are passing by, their hands stretched up toward their führer. Every now and then, Hitler bends down and lowers his hand. This leads to great excitement as the people, almost like trained seals jumping for fish, leap up and try to touch it. Playfully, Hitler pulls back or moves his hand around, forcing the jumpers to miss. He laughs and they chortle back. What a marvelous, truly Aryan pastime!

Stalin would never be so frivolous. He would appear atop the Lenin Mausoleum with other members of the Leninist Guard, often standing modestly in the second row. Then he would step forward and wave, while the crowd in Red Square would roar. Stalin always appeared retiring, modest, he never wore medals except for one gold star, the Hero of the Soviet Union, on his tunic. That was all. He rarely spoke in public, and when he did, the speeches were short, to the point, the delivery dignified, free of any theatricality.

Yes, Stalin did transform the Soviet Union into an industrial power.

Yes, he did ultimately lead it to victory over fascist Germany. Yes, he did alter the face of a once-backward country. And each of these things was accomplished at a horrendous price of millions of human lives and even more millions of warped souls. The millions who sacrificed, whose heroic labor made it all possible, personified everything they achieved in one man, Stalin. In doing so, they committed a fatal mistake. The human act of blind faith, whether in a god or a man, is both noble and tragic. Tragic, because it demands the sacrifice of the very essence of our intellect—the ability to question.

But the bottom line? Was this man an evil genius? Yes. In a unique way, he may have been the greatest criminal in history. But if this is true, as not only I believe, why, more than thirty-five years after Stalin's death, after the countless disclosures of his crimes, are there still more than a few people in the Soviet Union who proudly call themselves Stalinists? While not pretending to have all the answers to that question, I would like to share a few thoughts.

One has to do with national pride. Stalin was certainly a figure who commanded respect, both at home and abroad. He was always number one, overshadowing all others, including FDR and Churchill. Love him or hate him, you could not deny his stature. This could not be said of those who followed. Khrushchev was a country bumpkin compared to Stalin, a man who shot his mouth off, who promised his compatriots they would be living in a truly communist society by 1980, who predicted that the Soviet Union would catch up with and then overtake the United States in a matter of years, who banged his shoe on the UN rostrum and became the laughingstock of the world. Brezhnev was even worse. Here was a state leader who had a yen for flashy sports cars and medals. He astounded and insulted the nation by having himself decorated *four times* Hero of the Soviet Union (one more than the wartime hero Marshal Georgi Zhukov, winner of the battles of Moscow, Stalingrad, and Berlin). Brezhnev's public appearances, especially in his last years, when he had trouble walking without support and when his speech impediment was so great that he mispronounced virtually every word he spoke, made people cringe with shame. Neither Nikitka, as the people condescendingly referred to Khrushchev, nor Sissimasissi (a rather vulgar reference to the way Brezhnev mispronounced the Russian word for systematically) commanded respect. Stalin did.

Another answer has to do with the loss of ideals. In the "good old days," as some still refer to those times, Stalin set the example his bureaucracy, and the entire country, followed willy-nilly. If Stalin lived a Spartan life, or at least made people believe he did, so did everyone else. If Stalin worked fourteen or sixteen hours a day, it meant that the entire country did the same. There was no being late for work—in fact, during the war years, people were shot for that crime. There was no shirking responsibility or goldbricking. Things worked—or else. But when Stalin left, so did the will of iron that held the country together. His successors were of another ilk. Their main concern was to grab as big a piece of the pie as possible. All they cared about was number one. At that point, the entire system that Stalin had created and that had run on the fuel of his terror began to function purely for the satisfaction of those who controlled it. Grab, grab, grab.

This climaxed under Brezhnev, a period that saw the almost total corruption of Soviet society. Payola became the name of the game, graft was everywhere, organized crime, supposedly impossible without private ownership, flourished, spreading its tentacles from the cotton farmer in Uzbekistan to the Kremlin. The contradiction between the slogans about a just society and its reality were an insult to people's intelligence. One of my favorite jokes was born at this time. It tells the story of a man who applies to see the eye-ear doctor. The clinic nurse tells him there is no such thing. It's either the ophthalmologist or the otologist, she says. But the man keeps insisting, so the nurse finally asks, "Look, there is no such doctor, but if there were one, why would you want to see him?" "Because," says the man, "I keep hearing one thing and seeing something very different." When this applies to society, it destroys ideals as nothing else.

I have always held that the more one is idealistic, the more a society is idealistic, the greater the danger of chaos when those ideals are perceived as being false or having been betrayed. The higher you fly, the harder you fall. In a capitalist society, greed is, de facto, sanctioned, at times even praised (though the word for it is enterprise). So having it operate isn't so corrosive to public morality. But discovering greed as the raison d'être of a body that preaches selflessness and modesty can be devastating. This was the case in the Soviet Union.

No doubt, life under Brezhnev was far less oppressive than under Stalin. There is no comparison. Yes, there were dissidents. Some were tried and incarcerated, others were shut away in mental wards. But in Stalin's days, there were no dissidents—they were shot *before* they ever came close to dissenting. Stalin's repressions were replaced by corruption, by a view that said forget about the country, forget about the goals, screw all the talk about the noble this and the noble that, grab whatever you can while the grabbing is good. That is why, at least in part, the system began to go to pieces and went to pieces everywhere. In Stalin's times, society had been held together by a two-part glue. One part was terror, the other was ideals. When both went, things fell apart. That falling apart has been so painful and so frightening to some that they think back with nostalgia about the good old days (the main reason, I believe, for Andropov's great popularity during his short tenure as general secretary, when he had posses checking peoples' documents in broad daylight in stores, movie theaters, and public bath houses to see whether they were taking time off from their jobs).

And a final point.

As I write these words, the Soviet Union is in a time of turmoil. Changes are happening daily, sometimes even hourly. There are no unambiguous answers, much less simple ones. Stalin spelled, among other things, stability. Everything was black and white: friend and foe, good and bad, hot and cold, no in-betweens, no curving or wiggly lines. Those who are not with us are against us. Things may have been hard, but at least they were clear. All the answers you might ever need were in *Pravda,* in the infallible writings of the Father of the People. Not a few people today in my country feel insecure, cannot adapt to, nor deal with, the constant change, the fluidity, the lack of ready answers, the need to think for one's self. As the Christians of old would ward off evil with a sign of the cross and whisper "God is with us," my countrymen close their eyes to reality and repeat "Stalin is with us."

And they are not completely wrong.

4

◄◆►

A Coach to England

My love of literature has two sources. One is my mother, who started reading to me when I was three or four (the story of Ferdinand the Bull is the first one I remember). The other is the librarian at City and Country School in New York, whom I mentioned earlier. But with the exception of A. A. Milne's *When We Were Very Young* and *Now We Are Six* and the *Rhymes of Mother Goose,* I developed no interest in poetry until the age of seventeen or eighteen, when I began to study the Soviet school curriculum. That was how I made the acquaintance of the great Russian poets— Pushkin and Lermontov, Tyutchev and Nekrasov, Baratynsky and Fet, to name a few. I was lucky to have started so late, when I was old enough to begin to appreciate and understand what these men wrote about, as opposed to the students who "go through them" at the ages of fourteen or sixteen. Also, I read on my own, unconstrained by the didactic and politicized approach to teaching literature that was then, and still remains, one of the less-attractive features of the Soviet school system. I was not instructed to interpret Pushkin's *Bronze Horseman* this way or that, I was not told to read Fet with the understanding of his having been a cruel master to his serfs. I simply read their magnificent verse and reveled in it. This discovery of Russian poetry whetted my taste for more and so prepared me for a meeting with English poetry, which influenced my life in a very profound, though not obvious, way. One rarely remembers the exact chain of events that led from A to Z, but in this case, I remember perfectly. Though I was very much a Hemingway fan, especially of his short stories, I had never read *For Whom the Bell Tolls* (which, by the way, was not translated into Russian and published in the Soviet Union for many years because of Hem's not overly enthusiastic description of the communists' role in Spain during the civil war). I had been too young to read it in the United States, I had had no opportunity to read it in Germany, so when I found an English-language copy in Moscow, soon after our arrival, I jumped on it like a famished wolf. I turned the first page and saw this quote from John Donne: "No man is an *Iland*, intire of it selfe; every man is a peece of the *Continent*, a part of the *maine*; if a *Clod* bee washed away by the *Sea, Europe* is the lesse, as well as if a *Promontorie* were, as well as if a *Mannor* of thy *friends* or of *thine owne* were; any mans *death* diminishes me, because I am involved in *Mankinde;* And therefore never send to know for whom the *bell* tolls; It tolls for *thee.*" The words blew me away. They were *my* words, they were *my* thoughts, they said everything I wanted to say, but oh, how much better!

I read the novel and loved it (still do), but all the while I kept asking myself, who is John Donne? Now it just so happened that I had bought Hemingway's book in a second-hand bookstore on Kachalov Street, almost exactly opposite the Moscow Conservatory. It was a unique place, a treasure house of beautiful foreign editions, some very old, most of which had probably been confiscated from the libraries of arrested intellectuals, while others had been brought in by old ladies of the ancien régime who had somehow survived the upheavals of the revolution and the terror of the Stalin years, old ladies who had been born with French nannies and British masters to teach them languages, old ladies who still dressed in the sadly tarnished finery of their past, who wore little lace frills around their throats and wrists, little hats and veils in the summer, old ladies who twittered like birds in a cage, little, frail old ladies who never had enough to eat, who lived on a pittance and gradually sold everything they still had from "those times," including their beautiful books. You could buy them cheap, for very few people had any interest in them. I recall picking up the complete works of William Shakespeare in one leather-bound volume for eighty roubles—the equivalent of about ten dollars today. It was also there that I bought an 1837 edition of the works of Byron, with the most amazing engravings, for fifty roubles.

The store was run by two ladies, one who stood at the counter on the first floor, the other who worked on the second floor, pricing the books people brought in for sale. I rarely had anything to do with her, but the first-floor lady was special. She looked like a gypsy witch from some Bohemian fairy tale. Her black hair, streaked with gray, was always pulled tightly back and tied in a bun, which gave a clear view of her rather large ears, from which always hung the biggest pair of earrings I have ever seen. Her eyes were black, elongated, and somehow sculpted by the thin, arching eyebrows that spread nonstop, much like a child draws a sea gull, almost from temple to temple. Her nose was large and hooked, but finely shaped, while her mouth was small, the lips thin. She spoke French, and when she overheard me speaking French to my mother the first time we visited the store, I immediately became her favorite customer. In those days, all modern foreign books, especially thrillers and detective novels, were hard to get. After all, they were shoddy examples of bourgeois decadence, certainly unworthy of the attention of a builder of socialism. While such books were not officially banned, neither were they allowed— it was a gray area. They could not be sold openly, but when trusted clients brought in a pocket-book copy of Agatha Christie or Erle Stanley Gardner, the second-floor lady would accept it and pass it down to the first-floor lady, where the book was sold from under the counter to some other trusted client for a standard price of fifty roubles—the same as I paid for *The Complete Works of Lord Byron*.

"Voulez-vous quelque chose d'intéressant?" she would say to me in a low, conspiratorial voice. She would bend down, her enormous earrings swinging, and emerge from behind the counter with what she thought was a book-lover's find. "Regardez," she would say, shielding the book from whomever else might be in the store, "regardez," she would say, clearly meaning "for your eyes only," and she would flash Mickey Spillane's latest.

It was in that store that I bought Hemingway's novel. And it was there, after having read the book, that I looked for, and found, the writings of John Donne.

How can I describe being hypnotized, getting gooseflesh as I read

> *Goe, and catche a falling starre,*
> *Get with child a mandrake roote,*
> *Tell me, where all past years are,*
> *Or who cleft the Divels foot,*
> *Teach me to heare Mermaides singing,*
> *Or to keep off envies stinging,*
>   *And finde*
>   *What winde*
> *Serves to advance an honest minde.*

Or this:

> *Busie old foole, unruly Sunne,*
> *Why dost thou thus,*
> *Through windowes, and through curtaines call on us?*
> *Must to thy motions lovers seasons run?*

Read that, savor it, roll it around with your tongue: "Must to thy motions lovers seasons run?." Great God, what is that divine gift that enables a man to put such mundane words together and produce the inimitable?

Donne led me to Shakespeare, to Chaucer, to Ben Jonson, to Blake, Bunyan, Browning, to Hood, Moore, to Keats, Byron, and Shelley, Yeats, to Emily Dickinson, to Dylan Thomas. And so it came that by the time I realized I was not, nor would I ever be, a biologist at heart, I was spending more and more time translating English poetry, mainly Elizabethan, into Russian. During my last two years at Moscow University, I worked on my graduation thesis—"On the Evolution of the Respiratory Center in Fish." I spent long hours implanting electrodes into a specific area of the brains of carp and then watching and recording the electric signals that flashed on the screen of the oscillograph in front of me while simultaneously trying to find the Russian equivalent for "Blasted with sighs, and surrounded with teares, / Hither I come to seeke the spring, / And at mine eyes, and at mine eares, / Receive such balmes, as else cure everything."

During those two years, I became a very popular person in the student dorms. I don't know how many carp I disposed of before being able to come to a scientifically grounded conclusion concerning their respiratory center, but I do know that many of the Biology Department students who lived in the dorms counted on me to provide them with a steady supply of fresh, tasty fish.

I was awarded top marks for my thesis and received an offer to go on to graduate studies. Much to my parents' disappointment, I declined. According to the law of the land, every institution of higher learning must offer its graduates a job; on the other hand, every graduate student must repay the country for five years of free university education by working no less than three years in his or her area of training. The law, however, is one thing—reality is another. Very often, the institution will offer something it really cannot guarantee, while the graduate will accept it, knowing he has no intention of taking that job. That way the law is formally respected and personal interests are satisfied. When I turned down the graduate-studies offer, I was officially given the option of a job at the Institute of Scientific and Technical Information. I signed a paper accepting the offer only when I was informed (unofficially, of course), that the institute actually had no openings, for I did not have the slightest interest in making a living by translating foreign scientific papers on biology into Russian, which is what the job entailed. I went through the motions, received a written refusal from the institute, and that made me free—as well as one of the very few unemployed people in the Soviet Union.

I began working as a freelance translator of medical and biological texts from Russian into English—not that I did this with any feeling of satisfaction, but at least it paid much better than English to Russian and I had to make a living. After all, I was a married man and a father. While still in my last year at Moscow University, I had married Valentina Chemberdji, a senior of the Philology department, and two years later our daughter Kathrin was born. Like the overwhelming majority of young married couples, my wife and I did not have a home of our own. Our only choice was whose parents to live with, hers or mine? The awful housing shortage (it has not changed thirty years later) is one of the prime causes for the high divorce rate in this country. It certainly contributed to our divorce in 1968. But that was ten years later and certainly not something either of us thought about when I moved into the apartment that belonged to my wife's mother, a well-known pianist and composer, Zara Levina.

The only way I can describe my mother-in-law is as a force of nature, an Antaeus who took her strength from the earth, a person whose daily life was ruled by what her body told her to do. She ate when she was hungry, slept when she was tired, never giving a damn about generally accepted rules of behavior. I don't think she ever brushed her teeth, and I know she never washed her hair, but her teeth were strong and white and without a cavity until the day she died, well into her seventies, and her hair was thick and gleaming—it had that wind-blown look long before blow dryers made it fashionable. She was supple as an acrobat although by no means slender (she could not have cared less about diets with all their dos and don'ts), and she moved as naturally as an animal. When she tripped or slipped on something, as all people do now and then, she never hurt herself, for she fell like a bag of bones, utterly relaxed, the way stuntmen are taught to fall. She was in a way the epitome of the absent-minded professor. She could, for instance, stick her glasses in the fridge instead of the butter and then spend the better part of the day looking for them high and low and muttering about the vile people who have nothing better to do than to hide her glasses. One evening, when the phone rang while she was eating a sandwich, she grabbed the receiver, put the sandwich against her ear, and spoke into the earpiece. She could be delightfully amusing and totally unbearable. She was suspicious, tempestuous, egocentric, dictatorial, unpredictable, unfair; she was also kind, broad-minded, generous, loyal—in short, she was a true cocktail. But above all else, she was talented. And it was she who, reading some of my translations, took it upon herself to get in touch with Samuel Marshak, one of the Soviet Union's foremost literary figures, famed for his children's prose and poetry but especially renowned for his translations of Robert Burns into Russian.

One can argue about how faithful Marshak's translations of Burns are to the original. But what is undeniable, is that thanks to those translations, Burns became a Russian poet, or rather a part of Russian culture. Marshak was also famous for having translated Shakespeare's sonnets and the verses of Keats, Shelley, Blake, Kipling, and many others. Marshak was a national icon, so you can imagine my excitement when I received a call from his housekeeper who told me that Samuel Yakovlevich would be pleased to see me on such and such a day and time, if I could make it. If I could make it? Hell and high water could not have stopped me.

Marshak lived on Chkalov Street almost exactly opposite Kursk Station. I was ushered into his apartment by Rosalia Ivanovna, the woman who had called on his behalf. She was a German from Riga, well into her seventies, who spoke in a high, creaky voice and who seemed permanently displeased with everything, but most of all with Marshak. Their's was a love-hate relationship that had nothing to do with any sort of man-woman situation. She had worked for him for decades, going through thick and thin, seeing his wife pass away, his beloved younger son Yasha die of tuberculosis at the age of twenty. She knew him inside out and felt it was her duty to guide him along the right path. I think he was deeply attached to her, yet at the same time resented her nagging. Both of them had short tempers, and so I was often to witness bouts of name calling, where Rosalia would be hopelessly outclassed and outmatched. She knew this and so doggedly, or should I say Teutonically, stuck to her one invective, "old fool." She would call him that again and again in her creaky, shrill voice, while he would counter with such flights of fancy as "Madame Jump-Jump," "Hitler in a skirt," and "Shakespeare's unwritten tragedy."

All this, however, came later. On that first day, I recall being stunned by Marshak's library. Shelves of books lined the walls. They were everywhere, they dominated the space. Then Marshak came out of his study to greet me. He was past seventy and very small, not more than five-five. Once he had been portly, but now he was thin, almost frail. On this small body sat a leonine head. Small gray-green eyes bored into me from behind thick glasses. Later, I discovered that those eyes could be cunning, or full of laughter, or blazing with anger. When he was angry, his nostrils would begin to flare and he would snort and puff like a dragon. He had unusually large, wrinkled ears, like an elephant's. I imagined them as being warm and soft. Many is the time I fought the desire to reach out and touch them. His face was deeply lined with age—and, yes, he did somehow remind me of an elephant. It was a wise, nice face.

Marshak told me that he had read my translations and felt I was not without talent. I had, however, a lot to learn, he continued, and if I were willing to work as his literary secretary (the position turned out to be that of a glorified pen pusher, answering letters he got from abroad), he would teach me the tricks of the trade and help me publish. I was delighted and accepted immediately. For the next two and a half years, I worked for him.

Those were my graduate studies in the most privileged school one could imagine. For starters, I was in constant contact with a cultural dinosaur, a member of a dying species. This was a man whose childhood and adolescence were rooted in prerevolutionary Russia, who, as a boy, had been introduced to Leo Tolstoy, who had later studied in London and returned to mingle with the greats of Russian literature. He had lived through the revolution of 1917, witnessing the upheavals in the artistic and literary world that brought to the fore an incredible array of writers, playwrights, theater and film directors, painters, and architects. The first two and a half decades of Russia's twentieth century make one think of a magnificent carnival where the heavens explode with dazzling fireworks. Each spark is a name any country would be proud to call its own. Akhmatova, Blok, Tsvetayeva, Yesenin, Mayakovksy, Soutine, Chagall, Kandinsky, Petrov-Vodkin, Filonov, Serebriakova, Lisitsky, Tatlin, Eisenstein, Vertov, Tairov, Meyerhold, Vakhtangov, Stanislavsky—the list goes on and on of the Russians who stunned the world with their innovative genius. Who knows what forces come into play to produce such explosions of creativity? Why did this occur in Elizabethan England? Why the Renaissance in Italy? The unbelievable flowering of ancient Greece? Of Roman art and letters? Of France's golden age? We don't know and, I hope, never will, but what a thrill and what a blessing to be there when it happened! Marshak had been there.

He had also witnessed the gradual destruction of this edifice during the Stalin era, the decapitation of the country's intellectual/artistic community. He had seen it all, and he knew so, so much.

In reality, Marshak was a tragic figure, a lonely man who came from a different time and who could not but have been sickened by what he saw. He overcame this loneliness by constantly being surrounded by people—editors, would-be poets, budding translators, reporters. On the one hand, he never ceased complaining about being hounded by people who didn't care about his health and had no respect for his old age; on the other, he made sure that the steady stream of visitors and phone calls never stopped. He would become extremely agitated and concerned when the flow would, for whatever reason, ebb.

Marshak loved to talk, and I listened for hours on end. Thanks to him, I went through an entire new course in Russian literature and Russian history. I began rereading the writers I had perused in preparation for my Soviet high-school exams. Now I read with a completely different approach, rediscovering Pushkin, Gogol, Tolstoy, Dostoevsky. No less importantly, I encountered scores of writers of whom I had never heard before, writers who were taboo, whose names had been deleted from the textbooks, whose works had been taken off the library shelves. As far as Soviet society was concerned, those writers never existed. Some were outstanding, such as Bulgakov, Platonov, Babel, and Zoshchenko, while others were less good but still important in helping me develop an understanding of what had occurred in Russia at the beginning of the twentieth century, develop some sense of the currents and undercurrents that eventually led to the downfall of the Romanov dynasty. Almost none of these books were available in stores or libraries, but they were in Marshak's library.

In addition to being what he was—a fine writer and an outstanding translator—Marshak was also a cultural magnet who pulled as-yet-unknown talents into his orbit: Young Yevtushenko, Voznesensky, Akhmadulina, to name just a few. He was a close friend of Alexander Tvardovsky, the great poet and legendary editor of *Novy Mir* magazine who published Solzhenitsyn's *One Day in the Life of Ivan Denisovich.*

Tvardovsky's fame rested on his wartime poem, "Vasily Tyorkin."

Tyorkin was the quintessential Soviet GI of World War II, the guy who takes beating after beating but always comes out on top, who goes through the hell of war and comes out human. The poem had such an impact that Vasily Tyorkin gradually assumed legendary proportions akin to Paul Bunyan or Pecos Bill.

But very few people knew that Tvardovsky had been discovered by Marshak back in the thirties. A country boy from the Smolensk area, Alexander Tvardovsky came walking into Moscow in birch-bark shoes (*lapty,* they are called in Russian), carrying some food wrapped in his mother's shawl—or so the legend goes. He came because he thought he could write poetry as well as anyone else around, and he came to Marshak, whose name he had known from his childhood. As Marshak told me, he nearly fell off his chair when he began to read "the bumpkin's scribbling." It was, he said, the most wonderful poetry he had read in years—and that was saying something.

Tvardovsky's poetry has the simplicity of true genius. As I write those words, I realize all too well that I should, but cannot, illustrate them: Tvardovsky has yet to be translated into English in a way that would do him justice (the same applies without exception to all other Russian poets). And yet, when I make this point about the simplicity of genius, I feel it must be expressed in concrete form. These lines from Byron's "Don Juan" should serve my purpose:

> *I had my doubts, perhaps I have them still,*
> *   But what I say is neither here nor there:*
> *I knew his father well, and have some skill*
> *   In character—but it would not be fair*
> *From sire to son to augur good or ill:*
> *   He and his wife were an ill-sorted pair—*
> *But scandal's my aversion—I protest*
> *Against all evil speaking, even in jest.*

Try expressing those thoughts as eloquently, as elegantly, and as simply. Actually, don't—unless you are a genius. And please keep in mind that even though you are reading just one stanza of a poem written in the first quarter of the nineteenth century, the language, which has generally changed enormously over the past 175 years, is as fresh as a mountain brook. That is the way Pushkin wrote (incidentally, he freely admitted that his masterpiece, *Eugene Onegin,* was influenced by Byron's *Don Juan*). And that is the way Tvardovsky wrote. Snobs tend to look down their noses at such simplicity. They think it is too easy to understand, it is not elitist enough, you don't need a university degree to enjoy it. As far as I am concerned, that view is laughable. The greatest art is as simple as Mount Everest. It is as simple as the sun, the moon, and planet earth. It is that simple and that complex. Therein lies its beauty, its power, and its immortality.

When Tvardovsky would drop in on Marshak, which was often, I was allowed to sit quietly in a corner of the study and listen to them talk. Like many people, Tvardovsky had venerated Stalin. Like not so many people, Tvardovsky confronted himself on that issue. The result was a jewel of a poem, "Za Dalyu—Dal'." The title, like any poetic phrase, is extremely difficult to render in a foreign language. The word *Dal'* means "the distant" or "the far-off," so a literal translation would be something like "Beyond the Distance." You will simply have to trust me when I say how little this reflects the Russian original. The first time Tvardovsky ever read that poem to anyone was at Marshak's, and I was privileged to be there. And that is just one example of the way I was treated to a unique opportunity to experience literature in the most direct way, to listen to the Soviet literary giants of those times express their views.

I was also allowed to sit in on what I called Marshak's laboratory and watch him work on translations. I watched him edit, re-edit and re-re-edit. We all know that writing is a difficult trade, but you have to experience it—or at least watch someone else suffer—before you can even begin to grasp what that really means. I saw this man sit for hours on end at his desk, wracking his brains, driving himself to a state of utter exhaustion as he searched for the one right word that eluded him. Mind you, Marshak's reputation was carved in stone. He no longer had to worry about anything, he had made his mark. But he kept pushing himself to the limits of his powers. That was in itself an education about what it is to be an artist. The man who said it best of all was William Faulkner.

> By artist I mean of course everyone who has tried to create something which was not here before him, with no other tools and material than the uncommerciable ones of the human spirit; who has tried to carve, no matter how crudely, on the wall of final oblivion, in the tongue of the human spirit, "Kilroy was here."
>
> That is primarily, and I think in its essence, all that we ever

tried to do. And I believe we will all agree that we failed. That what we made never quite matched and never will match the shape, the dream of perfection which we inherited and which drove us and will continue to drive us, even after each failure, until anguish frees us and the hand falls still at last.

Marshak knew this anguish. It took him twenty years to translate Shakespeare's sonnets, yet when that volume came out and was greeted with universal praise and awards, I know he was not satisfied with it. He was tortured by the thought of not having achieved perfection.

As I said, he was a lonely man whose younger son had died of tuberculosis during the war. His relationship with his older son was not the best. His wife was dead. The woman he loved, and had loved most of his life, was married. When I appeared on the scene, she had just been diagnosed as having cancer. Not surprisingly, he latched on to me as a second son.

He always treated me as an equal, addressing me by my name and patronymic, Vladimir Vladimirovich, never using the thou form—something that would have underlined his superiority, for there was no way I could have answered in kind.

He smoked heavily, at least two or three packs a day, even though he had weak lungs. He often came down with pneumonia, and the minute he began running a temperature he would become delirious. He always demanded that I be by his bedside when he was ill. Once, after a bout of fever, he came to and, looking at me, weakly said, "Vladimir Vladimirovich, let us go to England." "By all means, Samuel Yakovlevich," I answered, thinking he was still delirious. "When we get to England, we shall buy a coach and horses," he continued gravely. I nodded. "And you," he went on, "will sit up front as the coachman and attract all the beautiful young ladies." "Very well, Samuel Yakovlevich," I answered. "But," he said, his eyes twinkling mischievously, "I will sit inside the coach, because you don't know what to do with beautiful ladies!"

Typical Marshak.

I worked hard on my translations and gave them to him for critiquing. One day, after examining several of my latest efforts, he said, "These are worthy of publication. I can make a few phone calls, if you wish." But being the proud young man I was, I thanked him but said no thank you. "All I ever wanted to hear," I said, "was your judgment. I will get these published on my own."

Now in addition to being proud, I was a sly son of a bitch. I retyped the four translated poems he had selected (two by Donne and two by Blake), but I also typed out four of Marshak's published translations. That made eight. I took them and presented myself to the head of the poetry department of *Novy Mir* magazine. I was a nobody, someone who had walked in out of nowhere and was asking to have his translations printed in the most prestigious literary magazine in the country. The department head, a lady who, as fate would have it, was married to a second-rate Soviet poet, looked at me, as the Russian expression goes, like a soldier at a louse, and said, "We're not really interested." But I pressed a little, suggesting that perhaps she might just take a look at them. She shrugged and told me to leave the translations and come back in a week. Which I did. She informed me that she had looked the material over and had found it very pedestrian, of no interest whatsoever.

"That's too bad," I said. "Maybe there are one or two of those eight translations that stood out a little?"

"No, none of it was interesting. These are rather poor translations, excuse me for being so brutal."

"Not at all," I answered. "On the contrary, I am truly grateful and thank you from the bottom of my heart."

She gave me a puzzled look. "I'm afraid I don't understand."

"Well, you see, these four are my translations, but the other four were done by Samuel Marshak. And if you were not able to tell the difference between the work of a great master and mine, that is a real compliment."

Need I describe the hysteria that followed? Need I make it clear that my translations were not published in *Novy Mir?* When I confessed my crime to Marshak, he was at first very angry and called me a hooligan, but he later burst out laughing. "I knew you had progressed and learned much from me," he said with a twinkle in his elephant eye, "but I never realized you were exactly as good as I am."

Translation is mechanical only when the subject is technical or scientific. In the case of literature, be it prose or poetry, you must realize that you are cocreating. Sometimes the task is formidable, virtually impossible. How can anyone translate "Tiger! Tiger! burning bright / In the forests of the night"? Look at that image. Close your eyes and see that Tiger! Tiger! burning bright—and you want to say to William Blake, "Hey, come on, Bill, give me a break! You don't know what the hell you are writing about because there *are* no tigers in Britain, OK? And tigers don't burn!" Only the trouble is, this particular tiger does. Thanks to the magic image created by Blake's language, you have no problem, your mind doesn't stumble on that burning tiger—on the contrary, it accepts it and applauds it. But how do you render that in another language? Never mind the rhyming, never mind the rhythm, just tell me how you translate "Tiger! Tiger! burning bright" without make a fool of yourself. There is really only one way, and that is to put the image through the prism of another language so that what comes out will look different but convey the same feeling. There is no other alternative.

It is a challenge. And if one loves language, the meaning of the challenge is to give people the chance to enjoy the flavor of a totally new dish. It is a wonderful and maddening occupation—literally. I know of one Soviet translator who became insane and had to be committed to a mental institution as a result of his trying to render Faulkner faithfully into Russian. But if the translation of prose presents a problem, poetry is the real crusher. To attempt to translate poetry is nothing less than an act of courage and of love. Edward FitzGerald, the man who enriched English literature with Omar Khayyám's *Rubáiyát,* has a statue erected in his honor in London. Quite fittingly, too, for his work was an act of literary heroism.

My exposure to the literary world subtly intensified my interest in the world around me. The flowering of Soviet society at this time was like a renaissance. It had all begun in 1956 with the Twentieth Party Congress and Khrushchev's de-Stalinization speech and had led to a creative explosion in the arts, which, though nothing like the period of the early twentieth century, brought to the fore a new generation of writers, poets, painters, film and theater directors, and composers. It was, to say the least, a heady time, a time of exuberance and hope. It was also, however, a contradictory time. I remember Marshak fuming with outrage at the persecution of the then-unknown poet Joseph Brodsky (later a Nobel Prize laureate). I remember his refusal to agree with the charges that Brodsky, who was not a member of the Union of Writers and could not therefore qualify as a professional writer, was a parasite because he did not have a job. As a matter of fact, Brodsky earned a living by translating poetry, but the authorities refused to admit that was a job. They were out to get Brodsky because of what he wrote; since that was the case, no logical defense, no arguments were taken into consideration. Ultimately, the Soviet Union lost Brodsky, just as it lost a host of other brilliant artists and scientists who could no longer bear the stifling political climate.

On the one hand, this was the period of the so-called Thaw marked by Dudintsev's novel *Not by Bread Alone,* Solzhenitsyn's *One Day in the Life,* Tvardovsky's poetry, the *Novy Mir* magazine under his editorship, the Taganka Theater with Yuri Lubimov, and, of course, Ilya Ehrenburg's *The Thaw,* which gave the period its name. On the other hand, you had, almost simultaneously, the bloodbath in Hungary, the crackdown on Moscow University students, the first dissident trial of Siniavsky and Daniel. Despite the contradictory nature of the times, there was genuine excitement in the air, a feeling of great expectations. It was, except for the most recent period, the only time I ever saw spontaneous demonstrations in support of anything. According to what I had been told, such outpourings of mass support had been typical before Stalin's death; the annual May 1 and November 7 parades across Red Square had been spontaneous affairs involving hundreds of thousands of people who wanted to see The Great Stalin. I believe that. But after Stalin's death, the parades became a formality—and I say this as someone with firsthand knowledge.

I participated in those parades twice, once as a student and once, much later, when I was working for Radio Moscow. In both cases, I was selected to be the right-flank man, the person who is closest to the mausoleum, the one who marches eyes front while the entire row marches eyes right, depending on the right-flank man to keep them in a straight line. It is a place of honor. It also entails a certain amount of briefing. Thus, when I marched for what I think will be the last time, I was asked to attend a party committee meeting with all the other right-flankers. We were each given a slogan to shout out, this to be followed by the entire contingent from Gosteleradio roaring "Hooray!" The slogans were the usual kind that insult the intelligence of any normal person. I was supposed to yell something like "Long Live Our Beloved Soviet Women!" I refused. After much bickering, the local party official backed off, figuring nobody would be able to hear a thing anyway, which was absolutely true. We were also given artificial flowers to wave but told to wave them carefully or else they would fall apart. Why might that happen? Because they were not held together by a solid piece of wire, as had been the case in the past, because some functionary had decided that the wire could be used as a dangerous weapon. Against whom? That became clear to me during the parade. The closer we got to Red Square, the more plainclothesmen lined the sidewalks. In Red Square, there seemed to be as many of them as there were demonstrators. They stood in lines, forming corridors through which we marched; they watched us like hawks, making sure no one stopped, no one did anything out of the ordinary. As a result, they were the most formalized and least spontaneous public demonstrations I have ever seen.

But during the Thaw, things were different. In 1957, Sputnik went up; four years later, Gagarin became the first man in space. People in Moscow went wild. They came out of their homes, their offices, their places of study, they came out singing, dancing, ten abreast, arm in arm, cheering, hugging whomever happened to be there. This was joy expressed in the most spontaneous and natural way. The same thing happened in 1965, with the twentieth anniversary of victory over fascism in World War II. It was, believe it or not, the first genuine celebration of that victory since the famous parade of 1945. For reasons I still do not fully understand, Stalin had not seen fit to celebrate Victory Day annually in any major way. So this was really the first time in twenty years that people could come out and express themselves, and it was the most amazing spectacle. The men and women standing in the little square in front of the Bolshoi Theater holding signs with the names of the military units they had served in, or pictures of their buddies lost in action; the tragic hope in their eyes that now, suddenly, out of the blue, these people would appear and heal the aching wounds of the past. It was one of the most moving spectacles I have ever seen. It told me more about the Soviets' attitude toward war and peace than any speech can ever hope to convey.

I repeat, those were contradictory times, and they could not have found a better person to embody them than Nikita Sergeyevich Khrushchev. One the one hand, he had genuinely democratic, or should I say populist, impulses; he had principles, he displayed both those principles and real courage when he went against the Politburo's decision and delivered his de-Stalinization speech. On the other hand, he was a product of the system, not just a bystander, but an active participant, someone who had the blood of many innocent people on his hands; to expect him to break with Stalinism would be the same as expecting a lizard to part with its tail. Even when that happens, the tail grows back.

Although Khrushchev was cunning and nobody's fool, he was (as were almost all party leaders until Gorbachev) poorly educated and unsophisticated. He also lost his temper easily, especially if he thought someone was trying to make him look like a fool. He was easy to read and, for those who had the opportunity, easy to mislead. A classic example is his notorious visit to the Manezh, the former royal stables situated opposite the original Moscow University building. The stables had been transformed into one of Moscow's largest and most prestigious exhibition halls. In this particular case, the exhibit included many paintings and pieces of abstract and nonobjective art. Khrushchev had been primed for this by the entrenched leaders of the Union of Artists, all true followers of the Socialist Realism School, who saw their positions being threatened by a new generation of revolutionary painters and sculptors. As soon as Khrushchev saw the abstract works, he hit the ceiling. He was truly outraged, and the focus of his anger became the only man who actually had the courage to scream right back at him: Ernst Neizvestny. Ernst was a war veteran, a man who had been twice written off as killed in action, a man who was not afraid of the devil himself. Khrushchev screamed and Neizvestny shouted right back. Many years later, when he was no longer in power, Khrushchev acknowledged that he had been wrong, and, as the ultimate expression of his repentance, he asked that Neizvestny design his gravestone—which the sculptor did. Visit Novodevichy Monastery cemetery and you will see Khrushchev's tomb: a piece of marble, half white and half black, and, in a niche, Khrushchev's head sculpted in a golden metal, realistic in every detail—to the point when the realism becomes its own joke.

Khrushchev was a peasant, a man of the most simple upbringing. He had worked the land, he had worked in a coal mine, he was, as the song goes, a man of muscle and blood whose entire life had been a fight for survival that left no time for anything else. Take that kind of person, lead him into an art gallery, show him a canvas on the wall—a white square with a black dot in the center—and tell him that painting is titled *Horse Eating Hay.* This man has lived with horses on the farm, he has carried bales of hay on his back, he has seen horses and people starve because there was no hay to be had. He knows all about life and nothing about art. If he turns around and says, "You are a bunch of charlatans trying to make a fool out of me. Well, it won't work," if he says that and then proceeds to explode, you should not be surprised. He is being honest—as was Khrushchev, except that he was manipulated by people who were counting on him to do just that and who capitalized on it.

Their plan worked perfectly. When Khrushchev called all the nonrepresentational art trash, an insult to the people, they got what they wanted. Immediately, the Ministry of Culture, the diverse unions of artists, composers, writers, etc., cracked down on a whole generation of the most talented people around. Their works were no longer exhibited, performed, published. They found themselves isolated, pariahs. Not surprisingly, when emigration became possible, they were among the first out the door.

If Khrushchev was a reflection of those times, so were the people he appointed to office, such as the Minister of Culture, Yekaterina Alexeyevna Furtseva. She was a plain worker, someone who, I believe, had started out as a weaver in a mill. Today, many look back on her with sympathy. But I tend to think that's really a comment on the kind of people who replaced her and who were even worse. She certainly was not suited to head the Soviet Union's cultural development. It may well have been during her tenure that the famous anecdote was born about a reception during which Czechoslovakia's secretary of the navy is introduced to the head of a visiting Soviet delegation. "Excuse me," says the Soviet dignitary, "but how can you have a secretary of the navy when Czechoslovakia is landlocked?" "But," replies the Czech host, "the Soviet Union has a minister of culture, doesn't it?"

After the revolution of November 7, 1917, the first Soviet government adopted a policy of encouraging access to all art forms by the broadest possible spectrum of the population. This decision represented a radical and enlightened departure from both the czarist and the bourgeois tradition of viewing the fine arts as the province of the intellectual and wealthy elite (a mentality still pervasive in the West).

The man charged with implementing that policy, Anatoli Lunacharsky, was, however else one might view him, an exceptionally erudite and cultured person. By and large, he played an important role in supporting the experimental character of Russian and Soviet postrevolutionary art and literature. However, as Stalin's hold on power became stronger and stronger, as the artistic avant-garde either emigrated or was suppressed, Soviet cultural policy assumed a different function and demanded a different leadership. This led to the appearance of ministers of culture who were cultureless, who spoke Russian as illiterates, who had read two books in their lives (one being Stalin's "short history" of the Party), maximum three; they became the laughingstock of the Soviet Union's artistic world, but the laughter was akin to Gogol's famous "laughter through tears," for the artists were controlled by these administrators.

Furtseva was probably one of the less offensive ones, not a bad person at heart. But that was about it. She actually believed the day would come when amateur art would replace professional, a point she made time and time again until Boris Livanov, one of the Soviet Union's most famous actors, publicly asked her, "Tell me, if you had to have an abortion, would you go to an amateur or a professional gynecologist?" This, of course, led to a scandal because, in addition to being insulted in public, Furtseva was extremely prudish—as many so-called simple people are. But simple people do not usually make the decisions that affect a country's culture, while Minister of Culture Furtseva did. One example concerns a British movie, *That Sporting Life,* shown at the Moscow Film Festival in 1961. In one scene, Albert Finney's girl tells him she is pregnant. "How do you know?" he asks, and she says, "I've missed my monthlies." The simultaneous interpreter repeated that line, and Madame Furtseva, who was present, had a fit. To her way of seeing things, to mention anything as private as monthlies in public was pornography! And this was a typical response of someone raised in a peasant culture. One simply does not talk about such things in public.

That type of bigotry is typical also of Pamyat, an organization that pretends to base its views on the old Russian spiritual ideals. Chauvinistic and pathologically anti-Semitic, Pamyat loves to play the purity card and castigate television for showing any uncovered part of the female or male body. It has attacked movies for having nudity and sexual scenes, it describes beauty contests as obnoxious (something I agree with but for completely different reasons). In short, Pamyat is the kind of organization the Ayatollah Khomeini would have blessed. But sarcasm aside, Pamyat has an audience—as did the Ayatollah.

Furtseva was no more fit to head our cultural affairs than I am fit to be the minister of naval construction. Sure, I like boats, but that's about as far as it goes.

One of the starkest examples of the contradictory nature of the Khrushchev period was the Boris Pasternak case—his expulsion from the Union of Writers for having allowed his novel, *Doctor Zhivago,* to be published abroad. For the record, the novel was slated for serial publication in *Novy Mir,* but Konstantin Simonov, who was then the editor, had asked Pasternak to make some changes. Because of this and certain other issues, publication was delayed. Meanwhile, a manuscript of the novel had been acquired by Feltrinelli Publishers in Italy, who had agreed to bring the book out immediately after its appearance in the Soviet Union. But when the date of the Russian publication was moved back, Feltrinelli went ahead and published, and all hell broke loose. Of course, the fact that the West heralded the novel as some kind of anti-Soviet manifesto certainly did not make matters easier, but I have no doubt that Khrushchev's violent reaction and the resulting vicious anti-Pasternak campaign in the Soviet press were the result of the same kind of intrigues as those that triggered Khrushchev's fury at the Manezh exhibit of 1961. Besides being detrimental to Soviet art and literature, the Pasternak case was exploited to the hilt by western propaganda. It was an ace in the game of cold-war politics at a time when the anti-Soviet establishment was looking for strong cards.

In a way it reminds me of a story I first read in *Time* magazine and later in one of the major Soviet national dailies about the history of the first dissident trial of Siniavsky and Daniel. It concerns a conversation the poet Yevgeny Yevtushenko had with Robert Kennedy during a reception in New York. At one point, Kennedy led Yevtushenko to a bathroom, where he turned on the shower to neutralize any bugging devices. Then, through an interpreter he had taken along, Kennedy shocked the poet with the following revelation. The trial of Siniavsky and Daniel, he said, was the result of a deal made between the CIA and the KGB. For several years, U.S. magazines had been publishing stories by a certain Abraham Terts, a dissident Soviet writer. This was clearly a pen name. The KGB had not been able to discover the real man behind the alias. The CIA had let them know that it was Siniavsky. There was a method to this madness. At the time, the anti-Soviet hysteria of the McCarthy period was a thing of the past. Americans were becoming fed up with cold-war saber rattling; they were also becoming more and more concerned by the growing U.S. involvement in Vietnam. In search of something that could radically turn that tide, the CIA had hit upon a truly diabolical plan: induce the Soviets to start a McCarthy-like witch-hunt of their own and use that to outrage the American people. Cold-blooded beyond words, the scheme worked like a charm. *Time* was skeptical of Yevtushenko's claim, so before printing the story, they looked up Kennedy's interpreter. He confirmed every word.

In a way, the Pasternak affair has the same smell.

Most of the people I knew in Moscow were horrified by what was done to the author of *Doctor Zhivago*. Pasternak, as I said, was expelled from the Union of Writers, to the everlasting shame of that organization. It is a black page in its history that the union will never wipe clean. This man was a poet of genius, one who stands with the greatest in Russian letters. That is not saying a little, for Russian poetry, in my opinion, has no equal (with the possible exception of its English counterpart). For the Union of Writers to expel Pasternak was, in a sense, ridiculous. In a way it was like a flea "casting off" the dog it had been sitting on. For Pasternak's stature was far greater than that of the Union.

Many writers spoke up in Pasternak's defense, though at their own risk. One of them was Ilya Ehrenburg, a contradictory figure, to be sure, but someone who, in the last years of his life, tried to make up for his apologetic Stalinist past. Ehrenburg was highly erudite and had a mind and a tongue like a razor. He was a formidable debater, and I had the opportunity to witness his talents during a discussion at Moscow's Library of Foreign Literature, where he took on a then-prominent Soviet art critic on the subject of French Impressionist painting. In those days, the only accepted art was Socialist Realism (a term that has been discarded with much of the other mumbo jumbo of the Stalin era), something none of the Impressionists qualified for. While Soviet museums, especially the Hermitage in Leningrad and Moscow's Museum of Pictorial Arts, had fantastic collections of these painters, they were kept in storage (that, too, is a thing of the past, and now we can feast our eyes on masterpieces acquired by such patrons of the arts as Savva Morozov and other prerevolutionary Russian capitalists). Ehrenburg, who had lived for many years in France, was a true connoisseur, a man who had known Modigliani, Braque, Chagall, Léger, had been a close friend of Picasso's. In short, he was someone who appreciated painting, in particular the Impressionists, and knew the subject inside out. The debate was a debacle. Ehrenburg wiped up the floor with his opponent, while I, along with most of the audience, applauded wildly. I remember the laughter when the proponent of Socialist Realism, as a kind of last resort, challenged Ehrenburg to prove that Degas was a better painter than Reshetnikov. Ehrenburg gave him a look of contempt and said: "Allow me to quote Chekhov who said, 'You cannot prove that Pushkin is better than Zlatovratsky.' " Which is like saying that you cannot prove that Shakespeare was a better writer than Tom Clancy.

The Library of Foreign Literature was an oasis in an environment otherwise barren of foreign literature. Besides books, it offered foreign-language tapes of songs and poetry readings, as well as monthly lectures on the latest English, French, and German books, delivered in those languages. The lecturers were either literary critics or professors of literature. But in those days (the end of the fifties and beginning of the sixties), they didn't have anyone to speak on American authors. Thanks to an American friend of the family, I had been presented with a three-year gift subscription to the Book of the Month Club. Always an avid reader, I was thus able to keep up with the American literary scene. Interestingly enough, I received everything I ordered except on two occasions, when the parcels were confiscated. One was a deluxe edition of the Bible with illustrations by Rembrandt (it still hurts to know that someone else probably has it); the other was William Shirer's *The Rise and Fall of the Third*

Reich, a classic study of Hitler's ascent and downfall that has yet to be translated into Russian.

I decided to offer my services as a lecturer on modern American fiction and asked for an appointment with the library's director, a wonderful woman by the name of Margarita Rudomino. She received me warmly and immediately accepted my proposal. I thanked her and said there was a condition, namely that I did not want to be paid for my lectures. She looked at me with surprise and asked why. "Because," I said, "if I accept your money, that means I must abide by certain rules. If I don't, I'm my own boss and can say what I want." Talk about being immature! Had she been another person, she would have shown me out or laughed at me or both. She did neither. She nodded, smiled, and said, "It's a deal."

I began lecturing and became very popular almost overnight. In part, this popularity was because of my American English, something language students came to hear (to this day, all English-language students are taught British English, although most want to speak like Americans. What would Professor Higgins think?). Also, the things I said departed from tradition—I did not review books from a purely political or class point of view. Finally, I did not hesitate to bring to my audience's attention books that, while not anti-Soviet per se, were not available in libraries because of their subject matter. One that comes to mind was Leon Uris's *Exodus.* This could have gotten me into trouble; in fact, I was asked by one of the librarians not to discuss "subversive" literature—something I flatly refused not to do. I'm sure there would have been problems had it not been for Madame Rudomino's influence. She was a typical representative of Russia's prerevolutionary intelligentsia, one of those who had cast her lot with this new society, one of the very few who had not been swept up and destroyed in the purges, a woman of exceptional personal courage and integrity. Her outlook had nothing in common with that of the "cultural" functionaries.

Working for her was a pure delight. After a year of doing exactly what I wanted, she called me in and asked whether I would now allow her to pay me for my work. Feeling extremely stupid, I said yes. It certainly wasn't much (seven roubles per lecture, or twenty-eight roubles per month), but it was something.

The Library of Foreign Literature, like all other major libraries in the Soviet Union, had, in addition to public reading halls, a very special room called the *spetskhran,* the special depository. It was reserved for those who, because of their work, had access to books and periodicals that were not available to the public. A special organization, Glavlit (State Censorship), was authorized to determine which printed matter was too subversive for the ordinary Soviet citizen. This included all noncommunist western periodicals, all non-Soviet Russian-language publications, and a host of literary works. The fact that Uris's *Exodus* was banned should suffice to furnish a general idea of how broad that protective blanket was. I say was, because today those rules no longer exist. Glavlit is still with us, but its function is to keep military and economic secrets from appearing in the press. The *spetskhran* has been abolished.

Whether books are burned or banned or simply removed from the shelves of school libraries, as still happens in the United States and elsewhere, there is one common denominator for all of these actions, even if they differ in degree. That common element is intolerance of dissenting opinion, which, in turn, is based on fear that accepted views and traditions will be challenged. The less secure a society, the more violently this is manifested. Soviet history provides a case study. The Pasternak affair, Brodsky, and Solzhenitsyn are the most well-known and obvious examples. But there are scores of others: Bulgakov, Pilnyak, Zoshchenko, Akhmatova, Tsvetayeva, Platonov, Harms, Mandelstam. Any society that, for whatever reasons, fears independent thought is schizophrenic in its attitude toward the writer. On the one hand, it perceives the writer as a possible asset, someone who, through the power of the written word, can further the society's goals in a much more profound way than politicians or a controlled media. But by the same token, the writer can just as effectively undermine the establishment view and therefore is seen as a potential threat. That schizophrenia manifests itself, I believe, in all societies to a greater or lesser degree, depending on historical tradition.

For reasons that go far beyond the scope of this book, it could be said that Russian literature developed as part of the counterculture, a current of thought that clashed with the czarist establishment. The Russian writer of stature rarely, if ever, espoused the concept of art for art's sake. Rather, he saw his role as that of taking a stand on issues of social importance. Invariably, that led to retaliation.

The writer and publisher Nikolai Novikov was incarcerated in the dreaded Schlüsselburg fortress for five years on the orders of Catherine II. That was in the last quarter of the eighteenth century.

That same empress exiled Alexander Radishchev to Siberia for his classic attack on serfdom, *Journey from St. Petersburg to Moscow*. Written in

1790, the book was banned and appeared in print only in 1905. Threatened with new reprisals when he returned from exile, Radishchev committed suicide.

The poet Mikhail Lermontov was exiled to the Caucasus by Czar Nicholas I in 1837 for his poem "On a Poet's Death" (the subject being Pushkin's death in a duel). Lermontov himself was killed four years later in a duel.

Dostoevsky was condemned to death in 1849 for his political activities. The sentence was commuted to five years of hard labor and military conscription.

Count Leo Tolstoy was publicly excommunicated and anathematized by the Russian Orthodox Church.

Perhaps the most graphic example of the attitude and relationship being discussed is that of Russia's greatest literary genius, Alexander Pushkin. Not only were many of his poems banned, not only was he banished from the capital and sent into exile, but the czar himself became Pushkin's personal censor! Nicholas I personally read every line the poet submitted for publication, personally blotted out what he disliked. Without the czar's signature, Pushkin's work could not be printed. This unique situation speaks most clearly about the role of literature in prerevolutionary, czarist Russia as perceived by the Establishment and the writer. Sometime around the last quarter of the eighteenth century in Russia, a tradition was born and continued to develop that a writer either fought the system or served it. The revolution of 1917 did not change that tradition.

The writers and poets whose works were banned, who were forced to write, as the Russian expression goes, "for the drawer," who were drummed out of the literary ranks, who were purged were not the accidental victims of some bumbling censor. They were deliberately silenced by an establishment that regarded their voices as dangerous. This is not a purely Russian or Soviet phenomenon. Both Molière and Byron suffered from their kings' displeasure. In more recent times, "leftist" American writers were hauled before the House Un-American Activities Committee in a kind of modern auto-da-fé. Nevertheless, I know of no other country where the writer and the poet have, as a matter of principle, assumed the role and responsibility of the nation's conscience—a role and responsibility acknowledged by both the Establishment and the people, albeit with polar reactions.

During the Thaw of the late fifties and early sixties, such poets as Akhmadulina, Voznesensky, and Yevtushenko packed Moscow's fifteen-thousand-seat Winter Stadium. People came not simply to enjoy poetry, they came to listen to a passionate commentary on their times, on the human condition, something that addressed them directly and helped them understand what their lives were about. Make no mistake, these were not just poetry readings, artistic events tailored to suit the tastes of the select few. These were unique mass rallies, venues for expressing sentiments and thoughts that otherwise had no outlet.

Much in the same way, the balladeer, poet, and actor Vladimir Vysotsky carried that torch throughout the seventies. When I think of Vysotsky, I am reminded of Woody Guthrie, whose songs were all political and social statements. Not many people in America today remember that Woody wrote a regular column, "Woody Sez," for the *Daily Worker,* the U.S. Communist party's newspaper. Why? Because no other paper would run his stinging and articulate commentary on the injustices of American society. Guthrie has become an American legend, but his radical political aspect—which was central to who he was—has been glossed over and conveniently forgotten. We Soviets have often been criticized, and quite rightly so, for painting historical figures whatever color best suits our purpose. But the same has been done in the United States, admittedly more subtly—and Woody is just one of many examples. In any society, the establishment finds ways to silence or neutralize its critics, whether they are in the arts or in politics.

Vysotsky was a Russian Guthrie living and working in a society that allowed less freedom of expression. The ingredients of his early songs were vodka, gangs, prison, and labor-camp life, songs rife with underworld argot, songs that extolled the virtues of the outlaw—much like the ballad of Jesse James. Gradually, he evolved, turning to the theme of war and ultimately to his own philosophy of life.

This short, powerfully built man with a voice like a hoarse foghorn, this man who sang like John Henry drove steel, the chords of his bull neck standing out and straining like ropes in a storm, this man who had a broader appeal and larger audience in his country than either Elvis Presley or the Beatles in theirs saw only one album of his songs come out in the Soviet Union before his death. He was never allowed to perform on radio or television. Yet at the same time, every new song he wrote spread over the country like wildfire as people copied their friends' audio cassettes. His songs had a universal appeal and message. They were collected by Politburo members and coal miners.

They tell the story of Vysotsky's arriving in a town on the Volga

River with the Taganka Theater (he was its star actor) and walking down the main street to the deafening sounds of his own music blasted out by the tape recorders, put out on every windowsill of every floor of every house.

Like so many other Russian artists, Vysotsky drank; he probably used drugs. He burned the candle at both ends, driving himself like a man obsessed. When he died during the Moscow Olympic Games of 1980 in his forty-second year, the outpouring of grief was spontaneous, authentic, and universal—with the exception of the Establishment, which tried to ignore the whole affair. "The poet treads barefoot on razor blades," wrote Vysotsky, certainly alluding to himself. He spoke out with brutal honesty, the entire country hanging breathlessly on each of his poetic metaphors. He was caustic, humorous, tragic, lyrical, passionate, and, above all, he was supremely Russian.

One can hardly exaggerate the role literature has played, and continues to play, in the Soviet Union's history. It certainly was a prime factor, a catalyst, in the revolutionary movement. Of course, the artistic and intellectual community always plays a leading role in social ferment, is always at the forefront of major social upheavals and revolutions in particular, but this is especially true in Russia. Its intellectual community was extremely small but of the purest water. It was a flame of such heat that a profoundly backward, politically and economically underdeveloped nation caught fire and set out to create a society that had never before existed. The high concentration and low numbers of Russia's intelligentsia were both its power and its weakness. Like a ray of sun focused through a magnifying glass, this searing pinpoint of light could serve to ignite almost anything. But it could also easily be snuffed out. And that is what Stalin did.

Stalin, as always, knew exactly what he was doing and why. The intelligentsia is by definition the social group that questions, analyzes, doubts. It is the yeast in the social dough, the force that refuses to be contained by any lid. But it is also a divided force. Very rarely can it act in concert, assemble under one banner. And so its greatest asset—the willingness and ability to examine, assess, question—is also its greatest weakness. Stalin made that weakness his most powerful weapon, turning one group against the other, using one to destroy the other, until, finally, all the meaningful opposition had been wiped out. Then he set out to tear up whatever roots were left. It was intellectual genocide, no more, no less, a crime that has yet to be shown for what it really was.

Fifty years later, I question the extent to which we have a true intellectual community to provide moral leadership and integrity today. Have we had the time to develop a new intelligentsia? If not, then what are the implications for perestroika? Without the support of the people, no attempt at social renewal can hope to succeed—but is that support sufficient? If we agree that the revolution could not have succeeded without the intellectual leadership of the Bolshevik party, as I believe we do, then we must ask ourselves whether the same question does not apply to the success or failure of perestroika. Has the yeast come back into the social dough? The success of perestroika depends on a host of conditions, the most important being radical economic reform, profound political restructuring, and a solution to the nationalities issue. But in my opinion, all of these depend on the probing, skeptical, questioning role of the intellectual in general and the artist in particular. Without their participation, without their existence, we cannot hope to create a truly democratic, humanistic socialist society in the postindustrial age.

In 1988, I was invited to participate in a Ted Koppel special. In forty seconds, I was asked to explain why I do not support religion. Here is what I said (this is not a quote, but it's very close): "I do not support religion because it demands that we give up our most important human asset, the ability to question. It demands that we simply believe."

Isn't that true of any dictator, of any totalitarian society?

Insofar as social development is concerned, nothing is of greater importance than the human function of questioning. It is the prime expression of thought. Thought *means* to question. Whether you are looking for an answer, analyzing an event, thinking about a book you've read or a movie you've seen, examining your own relationship with your wife, your kids, the world around you, *you are questioning.* There simply is no greater, no more important function of our minds. Questioning led to the development of civilization. The greater the ability to ask the most penetrating questions, the greater the intellect, a point illustrated by people like Einstein, Darwin, Hegel, and Marx.

It all comes down to one simple word: *Why?* Banish it from the human vocabulary and you will have succeeded in changing the human animal into an animal. I am thankful that no one has succeeded—nor will they ever. But a nation can be decapitated effectively and for generations by the destruction of its intellectual elite. I agree with what Carlos Fuentes said to Bill Moyers: "In the name of certainty, the greatest crimes have been committed against humanity." Those who insisted they had all the answers to all the questions that might ever be asked, those who said they had a lock on the truth, they are the ones who committed the most atrocious crimes. Hitler, Mao, and Stalin are just twentieth-century examples. Go back in time, look at all the kings, the emperors, the religious fanatics, look at the Crusades, look at the millions of human lives, the tens of thousands of cities, the civilizations destroyed over the ages because some group or some person had ALL THE ANSWERS, or THE ANSWER. We must never accept anyone's word for anything—not if we hope to live happily ever after.

In that respect, Marxist theory must be scrutinized carefully, as must Lenin's ideas. The only constant thing, according to dialectics, is change. Nothing remains static for fear of dying. Dialectics, as a method of social analysis, demands constant questioning as the only possible means of evaluating complex and ever-changing relationships. As such, it is truly an intellectual doctrine and concept. Yet there is a profound contradiction between the openness and thought-provoking character of Marxist philosophy and its practical implementation. In virtually every case, this philosophy has led to the destruction of the intellectual community, the ending of all discussion, and the emergence of a so-called Marxist state that was in effect the antithesis of Marxist thought: the replacement of debate and questioning by one point of view.

This was true of the Soviet Union. It was true of China. It applies to virtually every country where a socialist revolution triumphed or where a socialist government was established by other means. From Cuba to the Democratic People's Republic of North Korea, from Romania to Vietnam, from Albania to Mongolia, the rule applies. True, all of these countries started out as underdeveloped, backward countries, including Russia. Contrary to what Marx predicted, we have not seen a socialist revolution in any of the industrially developed countries. Why not? And if there were to be such a revolution in such a country, would we see the same pattern emerge? Is this shutting down of intellectual freedom an intrinsic, inevitable feature of socialism?

When a new social order is struggling for its very existence, when it is under attack from without and within, as was the case with Soviet Russia between 1918 and 1921, the situation is the equivalent of war. This is not the best venue for democratic debate, to say the least. Had Soviet society evolved in a less hostile international environment that supported internal hostility on the part of those who had lost power, it may well have taken a dramatically different course. Then again, it may not have.

Once Marxism has become the state philosophy, does it retain its central and truly unique element of consistent questioning? That is not a moot issue, especially keeping in mind that, historically, institutions do not encourage probing thought and critical analysis.

We know that Lenin made debate central to his concept of the Party. We also know, however, that he limited debate through what he called "democratic centralism." Democratic in that open debate was essential for the production of new ideas. Centralized in that once a vote had been taken, the debate was over and all members of the Party, whether they agreed or not, were duty-bound to support the majority opinion and act accordingly.

I joined the Party in 1967, at the age of thirty-three, unlike most Soviets, who almost automatically went the entire route from member of the Pioneer Organization (from age nine to about thirteen), to member of the Young Communist League, or Komsomol (from fourteen to twenty-eight), to member of the Party. Naturally, I was never a Pioneer. I joined the Komsomol in the winter of 1954–55, during my second year as a biology student. Two things stand out about that experience. My candidacy was discussed at a general meeting of all second-year biology students, about three hundred people—that was standard procedure. Anyone had the right to ask me whatever they wanted and hear me talk before deciding whether to vote yea or nay. At one point, a girl stood up and asked me, "Tell us, did you fight against capitalism when you lived in the United States?" Caught totally unaware, I thought she was joking. However, no one laughed, so I asked her what she had in mind. "Were you in the underground movement against capitalist exploitation?" she asked. At that point, I began to realize that any explanation was hopeless. She had been brought up to believe certain things about the United States, and no matter what I said, it was not going to change her mind. So I simply said that I had not been the member of any clandestine resistance movement. "Comrades," she said, "my father is the Soviet ambassador to the People's Republic of China, he knows such things very well, and he told me never to trust people who were brought up in the West, such as Pozner."

I have never forgotten that moment, even though the overwhelming majority of the students voted for me.

The second item has to do with the Biology Department's Komsomol Committee, the ruling body, a kind of local mini-Politburo at the Komsomol departmental level. Its members have to endorse the decision of the general meeting. They ask you a few questions, some of which can be very unexpected, such as, "What did Marx say at Engels's funeral?" Most would-be Komsomolers break into a cold sweat because they cannot remember, or they stammer out some absurdity. Very few have the sang-froid to recall the simple fact that Marx died well *before* Engels and could, therefore, have said nothing at his funeral.

I was not asked anything so insidious. Had I recently read the papers? What international events of importance had occurred over the past week? Now it just so happened that during that week we had been in the process of moving into the new apartment my parents had finally been given. Because of that, I had had no time to read any newspapers whatsoever, a failure I candidly admitted. My statement produced shocked silence. Then one of the committee members cleared his throat and solemnly said, "We cannot endorse your application. A Komsomol belongs to the politically most active, most well-informed youth. We give you one week to catch up on your reading." With that I was dismissed. A few days later, I bumped into that same person. "What the hell is the matter with you?" he asked. "Couldn't you say you read the papers every day? Even if you didn't know much about current events, we would have let you off the hook. Who gives a shit about your moving and all that? Use your head!" Sure enough, a week later, after confirming that I had read the papers all week, I was accepted by the committee. The vote was unanimous. And I got my first inkling of what a formality being a Komsomol member really was—although I could hardly imagine what a laughing matter it would become.

Joining the Party was anything but a formality as far as I was concerned. On the one hand, there was so much about its leadership (this was in 1967—Khrushchev had been replaced by Brezhnev three years earlier) that I did not like, so much about Soviet society that I found oppressive and unacceptable. But, on the other hand, how was I to be an active participant, how, if at all, could I influence things without joining the Party? It was a maddening puzzle. My decision was made thanks to two people. One was Iosif Gordon, the other Nikolai Yakovlevich Tillib, a party member from way back who had served in the legendary Latvian Sharpshooters, a military formation created during World War I that played an active role in helping the Bolsheviks seize power, fought with consummate skill and total dedication in the civil war, and delegated its men to serve as Lenin's bodyguards. Tillib was anything but loquacious. "If you really want to improve things and improve the Party," he told me, "join it. But make sure you have the will not to sell out, because you will not find it easy."

He was right, I haven't found it easy—which really doesn't bother me at all. I didn't join in search of relaxation. But throughout all the years since 1967, I have been uncomfortable with that principle of democratic centralism and unable to solve the dilemma it poses.

If you are a member of a team, you can debate issues of tactics and strategy to your heart's content, but when the coach and the team have made a decision, you have to go out there and play according to the game plan, even if you disagree with it. Either that or you leave the team. But how can you honestly go out there and follow a game plan you profoundly disagree with? This is not simply a theoretical question. We have, after all, witnessed more than one occasion when the Party made a decision that turned out to be a disaster for the country—forced collectivization and going into Afghanistan are just two cases that come to mind. Of course, in both those cases, no debate was allowed even prior to their being decided. Dissenters were arrested, shot, and exiled to Siberia in the former case, locked up in insane asylums in the latter. Just for the record, let it also be noted that, until the most recent past, when the Party made a decision, society at large, its individual members, the mass media—they, too, stopped debating.

Marxism holds that a scientific method of analysis, if properly used, can elucidate the most vital political and social truths. The communist parties in countries belonging to the so-called socialist camp invariably have become the sole repository of these "truths." But the Party, like all institutions, has internal dynamics that have nothing to do with anything close to objective analysis. What's more, these dynamics have clearly discouraged the sort of questioning that is central to the Party's intended function.

One of the causes of the Party losing its questioning role, I would argue, was the shift from a *political* function—of trying to articulate the right political program and mobilizing public support for it—to one of *government/management.* Under Stalin, the Party began to manage everything from arts to zoology. This situation began to change only with the advent of perestroika, but change has been slow, for the party apparatus has absolutely no desire to part with its job as supreme commander in chief of everything. The party bureaucrat does not wish to part with the total control without responsibility that he so enjoys. And the so-called party worker is in a cold sweat—for good reason.

For decades, that party worker was a person who in his lifetime could aspire to occupy any post—minister of foreign affairs, chairman of the KGB, chairman of Soviet TV and radio, minister of culture, ambassador to any foreign country, whatever. The reason? Because a party worker is an expert in nothing, a specialist in nothing, except leadership, running whatever needs be run as the Party sees fit to run it. Hence the minister of cinematography whose knowledge of that art and industry has been limited to going to the movies. Yet until recently, this man made all the final decisions on everything pertaining to film. Decisions based on the infallible wisdom of the Party. But now, when we are finally returning to Lenin's view about what a political party is and should do, what can the party worker hope for?

If I were to lose my job, I can find another one because I have a profession. I am a professional journalist. Plus I am a linguist. If worse should come to worse, I will be able to make a living by working as a translator. But what happens to a party worker who loses his or her job, especially if he or she has been a party worker for years and years and has forgotten the professional training he or she once upon a time received? All they know how to do is manage—in a very strange way indeed. All they usually do is get in people's way. Take the local regional party chairman in a rural area who, until recently, actually told the farmers when and what to plant, when and what to harvest, and so on. This man doesn't care about rain, hail, or snow, that's not his department. Neither are such things as organic fertilizer versus chemicals. He just gives the orders.

The head of a collective farm does one of three things in response. The more courageous one tells the party functionary to go fuck himself— but that could spell prison or even death for the obstinate farm manager (in fact, before perestroika there were many such cases), because the party functionary cannot risk being proven wrong. It is better for the party worker to find a way to put that farmer behind bars than to let him go ahead with his own plan, turn out to be immensely successful, and thereby undermine the party worker's position. The less courageous farmer, but one who still cares, says "Yes, sir!" and snaps off a salute, then goes back to the farm and does what he thinks is right anyway. Finally, the farmer who has learned the hard way says fuck it and does what he's told. The result has been total chaos in agriculture. It is even surprising that it hasn't broken down completely, what with incompetent people telling farmers what to plant and when.

Similarly, party functionaries have told artists what to paint, writers what to write—with the same results as in agriculture.

All this is changing radically, but the concept of democratic central-ism is still very much part of the Party's rules and regulations; also, at least as of this writing, Article 6 of the Constitution of the USSR specifies the "leading role of the Party." If the right to question and to dissent is recognized as the primary vitamin necessary for a society's health, then both of those concepts must be reconsidered. But even that is not enough—as demonstrated by the situation in the United States where, as we know, there is no such thing as Article 6 of the Soviet Constitution or any concept of democratic centralism.

The overwhelming majority of Americans are convinced they enjoy the right to question. And they do . . . sort of. How many Americans would feel comfortable questioning the policies of their company? How many oil-company executives, for example, would feel at ease when questioning the oil industry's ecological policies (or the absence thereof)? How many executives of the National Rifle Association would have no fear of questioning the real aim of their organization (which is to make money, not to protect the constitutional right of American citizens to bear weapons)? American propaganda has been extremely successful and so-phisticated in leading Americans to *believe* rather than to *act.* One finds examples of this everywhere, including American chauvinism—not an aggressive or violent feature, simply the utter belief in being special, a chosen people. Look at the lyrics of such songs as "America the Beautiful," "God Bless America," and all the rest of them. The same attitude surfaces again and again. President Reagan was quite explicit about it when he spoke of America as the "city on the hill," set there, as it were, by God for all other people to look up to. In an ironic way, that line reminds me very much of what Stalin was able to convince the Soviet people of—that they lived in the best of all worlds. Most of them believed him. That same propaganda has been much more effective in America, where it has existed for a longer time and where the art of selling a product or an idea is far more of a science than it has ever been in the Soviet Union. Perhaps the real clincher is the argument I have heard from certain Americans who have proudly said, "I have the right *not* to work, I have the right to live in the street if I so wish!" These people were trying to prove the superiority of their system over mine. The fact that they didn't have the right to work or to a roof over their heads didn't even cross their minds. They did not question (although they are proud to tell you that they have the *right* to question) what they had been programmed to believe: that unem-ployment is the right not to work, and homelessness is the right to live in the street, and both of these are proof of American democracy.

In modern society, television and film have powerfully affected public perception of social reality. But in mid-nineteenth-century America, the relationship was reversed. Social reality had a tremendous influence on social commentary, especially literature. When American literature came into its own, it carried a very strong social and political message; it also demonstrated great social commitment. That applies to Mark Twain just as it does to Herman Melville. This was no escapist literature. Far from saying "pay no attention, look the other way, leave your troubles at the doorstep," this literature told you to get involved. The muckrakers were, let's not forget, an American literary phenomenon. They looked at American reality and showed it with a brutality, honesty, and pain that is hard to match. American literature gave the world some of the greatest writers of this century—Twain, Melville, Dreiser, Faulkner, Steinbeck, Hemingway, Thomas Wolfe. All wrote about the human condition. They were *involved,* they *questioned.* The same applies to America's greatest poets: Walt Whitman, Carl Sandburg, Robert Frost.

A frightening thought: most Americans have never read *any* of these authors. The men who have asked the biggest questions, who have been their nation's conscience, are unknown to the majority of their people. And please don't tell me about Americans reading more than ever before, because what they are reading has nothing to do with literature, no meaningful social function. The latest blockbuster novel is to literature what the Classic Comics is to Shakespeare.

The average Soviet knows more about American literature than the average American. Amazing but true. I remember Phil Donahue taping a show with a Soviet audience in 1987 and asking all of those who'd like to visit America to raise their hands—which everyone did. "Where would you like to go in America?" Phil asked, approaching one of the participants.

"New York."

"Fine," said Phil, moving to the next person. "And you?"

"Las Vegas!"

"Very good, and how about you?"

"Oxford, Mississippi."

"Very good," said Phil almost automatically as he turned to the next person. Then he caught himself, spun around, and asked: "Oxford, Mississippi? Why there of all places?"

"Because," came the answer, "that is where William Faulkner lived."

Phil's jaw dropped. "How many Americans would know that?" he subsequently remarked. Not many, to be sure. Probably even fewer than the number who have read Faulkner's major works. This is in contrast with polls demonstrating how well acquainted Soviets are with the major American classics, as well as with their contemporary authors.

Why are Americans so unfamiliar with their own great literature, which speaks so profoundly to the human condition? And why does America thrive on what can only be called trash literature? Part of the answer has to do with the changes in American society, a society that has become almost completely market oriented, where everything, including literature, is a commodity.

The pattern is similar in American film where, with some notable exceptions, the recipe has been Hi-Tech, Hi-Sex, and Hi-Vi (for violence). Compare movies of the seventies and eighties with those of the thirties and forties and you cannot help but be amazed at today's obvious backing away from social issues. Then the subjects were politics, democracy, the plight of the little guy—at least up to a point, because, let's not forget, that was when Hollywood became known as the Dream Factory. But if that is what it was then, what is it now? It is, as it always has been, a reflection of America's social pulse, social conscience, a pulse that today beats evenly and strongly, as should the pulse of a health-conscious society that has stopped smoking and is jogging, running, pumping iron, aerobicing itself to the limit so that when its members are old they will die looking young, a conscience that basks in the certainty of America's being special. The pulse likes its beat, and the conscience feels comfortable; the first does not really want to start beating faster, let alone miss a beat, while the second prefers not to be bothered.

Why this change in American film and literature? As is always the case, there is no all-encompassing answer, but part of it has to do with politics and goes back to the origins of the cold war. Who was blacklisted when Hollywood was attacked by McCarthy and the other superpatriots in the late forties and early fifties? Certainly not those who made escapist movies, not the makers of B-movies, not those who wrote, directed, or produced the rootin', tootin', shootin', flag-salutin' nonentities starring John Wayne. No, the ones that were hung up and put out to dry in America's greatest political witch-hunt were those writers, directors, and producers who did have a social conscience, who did care about the human condition, who cared enough to put their money and talent and time and energy into bringing that concern to the American people. And for that, they got shafted. The studio heads got the message, which was, basically, stick with apolitical entertainment, but if you want to be political, be anticommunist. Television was just starting out, and it, too, took the cue.

A new ethic has emerged in literature, film, and television in America, an ethic that somehow frowns upon delivering a message, on being committed. It's great to be an entertainer, because that designation is both positive (who doesn't like to be given a good time?) and value free. If you are an entertainer, it doesn't matter that you are participating in something that is, by any human standard, amoral or immoral, that's not your responsibility. The fact that entertainment without social commitment is a value-laden position, a revealing statement in itself, seems to escape many people. It is the mirror image of the objective-journalism syndrome I will discuss in the next chapter. People convince themselves and others that they are neutral, and, what's more, that neutrality represents the highest level of professionalism and art. The socially committed actor, producer, or director is now somehow suspect, somehow not a true artist! Who hasn't heard the criticism that so-and-so is "too political," or that so-and-so's politics get in the way of his or her art? But have you ever heard anyone criticized for being too committed to entertainment?

The New Deal concept of social commitment is gone, stored away in the attic of the All-American house along with a great many other things that were once as integral a part of the American image as Reaganomics became. For instance, labor unions.

In their heyday in the thirties and forties, unions were a major social force. And now? Less than one in five working people is a member of a union (this is more than in Taiwan, Turkey, South Korea, Greece, and even France, but a lot less than it used to be). And the unions themselves? In the beginning, they were committed to social justice, to fair distribution of wealth. But after the war and with the onset of the cold war, the socialists and the communists, the people who played a key role in organizing and building the unions, were kicked out. And union leadership cut a deal with business: give us bigger paychecks and we won't rock the boat. That worked as long as the economic pie got bigger, but it cut the heart out of the union movement. Instead of being united by social ideals *and* the fight to improve working conditions, it became "What's in it for me?" The public sensed the shift, and support for the unions waned. Then, when the pie stopped growing in the seventies, and management moved shrewdly, in different ways, to weaken the unions, to bleed off their membership, and to blame them for inflation, the unions had no way to fight back. They had sold out.

What has that got to do with art and literature and with questioning, you ask? A whole lot.

Lack of political commitment, absence of questioning, whether in the labor movement or in art, contains an implicit assumption: that the society in which one lives has no serious social problems demanding public attention and focused action. Things are hunky-dory, we have arrived. There is no need for art that probes and questions the human condition, stimulates people's thinking on fundamental moral questions.

In Brezhnev's Soviet Union, we had an analogous situation. Though serious, deeply probing work was written, it simply was not produced in any form (except the samizdat, "underground," press). For us there were no basic problems to be explored. Only for us? Our theater, poetry, prose, film, television suffered terribly—as did our minds. Only ours?

Art and life are one. Art reflects, embodies, and, at its best, predicts the human experience. It is part and parcel of the human condition. If one goes back to the most ancient times, art has always been a comment—an intensely powerful comment—on human existence. This includes escapist art, the desire not to comment, or the fear to comment, both reflections of the human condition. Banal, value-free, apolitical art—whether in the Soviet Union or the United States—reflects a society wearing blinders, a society hiding from the truth.

5

⊶◇⊷

Of Pine Trees and Telegraph Poles

I never had any intention of becoming a journalist. By 1961, at the age of twenty-seven, when most people have already achieved at least some degree of success in their careers, the only thing I knew for sure was that I did *not* want to do biology or translations. But what did I want to do? One of my favorite literary characters, Tigger, of A. A. Milne's *The House at Pooh Corner*, thought Tiggers liked everything. He was much dismayed when he discovered they decidedly did not like honey, acorns, or thistles. It was by a stroke of luck that Tigger stumbled across what Tiggers really like: extract of malt. I stumbled onto journalism the same way.

One day I received a call from a friend. Would I like to try out for a job with Novosty Press Agency, he asked? Novosty had just been created as a public, nongovernmental entity in place of Sovinformbureau. It would be geared to foreign consumption, so they were looking for people with a knowledge of foreign languages. You have nothing to lose, my friend said, go for an interview. I went, and that decided my professional fate.

It would be uplifting and noble to say that my reason for applying for a job with Novosty was the result of soul-searching, of an attempt to find myself. It wasn't. Some subconscious process may have been at work, but I have no memory of it. What I do remember is that Marshak, while a marvelously interesting human being, was also stingy in the extreme. After two years of work, he was paying me seventy roubles a month, a salary that would have barely sufficed for a young man fresh out of college. But, as I have already noted, I was married and I was a father and there was simply no way I could support my family on seventy roubles a month. So, as did a great many other people in the Soviet Union, I indulged in moonlighting. I translated scientific papers into English, a job that paid as much as I hated it—which means, a lot. I went to the Novosty interview hoping I would get a good offer. That was my main incentive. Imagine my delight and astonishment when I was proposed the princely sum of one hundred and ninety roubles a month and the position of senior editor! I owe my breaking into journalism to the man who was then vice-chairman of the board of Novosty, who soon after that became the vice-chairman of Gosteleradio, the USSR State Committee for Television and Radio, and who, at a later date, played an active role in nearly drumming me out of the journalistic ranks. His name is Enver Mamedov, and I will relate that story in its proper place.

Because of my fluency in English, I was assigned to work for *Soviet Life* magazine, which was born as part of the first postwar cultural agreement between the Soviet Union and the United States. Published only in English and only for an American audience, it is the counterpart of *Amerika* magazine, which appears only in Russian for Soviet readers. Both are well-designed, slick publications whose aim is to present its society in a favorable light. There are two ways to achieve this: one is to doctor the facts to make negative aspects of society look much less negative than they really are; the second is to ignore those negative aspects and to focus only, or mainly, on the positive. In both cases, truth is not the objective. During their thirty-plus years of publication, both magazines have, by and large, adopted the latter course.

However, these were things I would start thinking about and ultimately confront at a later date. At first, I found journalistic work to be exciting and immensely satisfying. I had been debating political and social issues since childhood, and they were a central part of my being. Now I could share my views about what I felt to be important with thousands of people. True, they were all Americans, but that fit perfectly into my scheme. While working for the Library of Foreign Literature, I had been able to give Soviets a better understanding of America, a feeling for a country they knew very little about; in the future, I would continue to do this, lecturing on American literature, on jazz, on African American folk music. Working for *Soviet Life* gave me the opportunity to make this a two-way street.

Working for *Soviet Life* also meant writing about the Soviet Union, which in turn meant doing research for articles and traveling around the country. I had traveled before, as a student, but this was different. For the first time since my arrival eight years earlier, I was exposed to the immensity and the diversity of a country of which I had only a fragmentary experience. I had come to Moscow with an abstract, idealized view of Soviet socialism. My first experiences of Stalinism, as well as my university years, had required a painful personal and political reassessment. My work with Marshak had exposed me to the richness and humanity of Russian literature and poetry, to the unique features of Russian and Soviet literary tradition. But I still lacked a real sense of this country's stunning complexity—geographic, ethnic, and cultural.

In the Soviet Union, as in the United States, the position of journalist opens many doors, although perhaps for different reasons. In the United States, the press has enormous power. It can make you or break you. Hence, the journalist is either feared ("better talk to the SOB or he'll *really* make trouble for us") or sought after. Until the spring of 1985, a journalist in the Soviet Union could make trouble for no one unless he was assigned by the powers that be to do either a serious piece of investigative journalism or a hatchet job on someone; both were relatively rare, especially the former. Most of the time, reporters were sent out to do positive stories, pieces showing how good things were, what a wonderful society we were all living in. Obviously, everybody wanted to figure in that type of reporting. That is not to deny the existence of some bona fide investigative journalism, but it was usually limited to exposing local wrongdoings invariably defined as "exceptions to the rule." With the inception of glasnost in 1985, that situation underwent a radical change.

There is, in my opinion, at least as much if not more real investigative journalism being done in the Soviet Union today than in any other country, West or East. As a result, society has become divided in its attitude toward the press. The majority of the people see the journalist as some kind of hero, at times even as a Don Quixotesque figure, more often as a Bayard, *le chevalier sans peur et sans reproche,* while the minority perceives them as a threat. It would be an oversimplification to say that that very vocal minority consists only of party bureaucrats, for it includes a broad spectrum—writers, veterans of World War II and Afghanistan, members of Russian chauvinistic organizations such as Pamyat and other superpatriotic groups. Neither should one forget that the new role being played by the media is the result of the revolutionary reforms initiated by the Party. Nevertheless, of all the untouchables in the past, the least touchable, the most protected from any sort of criticism, was the Party and its apparatus, people whose conduct was based on the knowledge of their impunity. They praised glasnost with the absolute certainty that it did not apply to their activities. They were outraged when things turned out differently.

The battle between the media and the bureaucracy surfaced for all to see during the Nineteenth Party Conference of 1988, when every speaker who attacked the media was greeted by thunderous applause; the same is true of the first Congress of People's Deputies (June 1989), where the conservative minority of the country was able to win a majority of the seats thanks to an electoral process tilted in their favor—something the press has been quick to bring to the nation's attention. But back when I broke into journalism, in 1961, the media would have looked the other way.

I think Khrushchev's de-Stalinization and liberalization efforts reached their zenith at that time. There was a tremendous feeling of enthusiasm, which was justified by what the people saw. The standard of living was improving by leaps and bounds, labor productivity spiraled—so much so that, what with western economies looking stagnant, Khrushchev predicted that the Soviet Union would soon catch up with and then overtake the United States in per capita income, quality of life, and economic production. This outlook seemed to find confirmation in the mind-boggling achievements of Soviet science and technology: the TU-104 became the world's first passenger jet; in 1957, Sputnik proclaimed Soviet preeminence in space; and in 1961, Yuri Gagarin, the first human being to go into space, dazzled the world with his boyish smile, the perfect PR symbol of the New Post-Stalin Soviet Man. There was magic in the air, perhaps akin to the magic of the Kennedy days in America, an uplifting optimism, even a certainty, that things were going to be absolutely wonderful.

Traveling across the country, I was struck again and again by the upbeat atmosphere I encountered. When you asked people about how things would be done, about the problems, they would laugh. The response was the equivalent of the American "a piece of cake." This was genuine euphoria on a national scale. Having experienced those times, one cannot but be struck by the contrast posed by today's perestroika. The scope and depth of perestroika's reforms cannot even be compared to those, not any more than revolution can be compared with reform. Their potential for fundamental, far-reaching change affecting the life of every single citizen in the most positive way is immeasurably greater today. Yet the public reaction is much more divided and skeptical than at the height of the Khrushchev reforms. Why?

Part of the answer has to do with the passage of some thirty years.

Then, the nation had its hopes raised, only to see the country slide into stagnation and moral putrefaction. The nation was, to put it bluntly, jilted. The profound skepticism existing today is a conditioned reflex that, like all reflexes, is an adaptation to a new condition. Either you adapt or you suffer. It is, thus, a kind of psychological lifesaver, and most people are loath to let go of it. But there is another factor. In the words of Politburo member Alexander Yakovlev, perestroika represents "a breakthrough into the unknown," a multiplicity of changes so basic that "we must change our way of thinking" about ourselves, our social structure, about the world around us. Can anything be more challenging? Or frightening? Tens of millions of Soviet citizens complain (with good reason) about shortages, shoddy consumer goods, poor housing. "Fix the system!" they clamor. But when told that confronting the problems will involve *them,* that *they* will have to change the way they live and work, even the way they think, that *they* will have to assume greater personal responsibility, many back off. In a sense, this is true of people in general, but it has a special meaning in the Soviet Union, a country that comes from a absolutist, czarist tradition compounded by its own totalitarian Stalinist legacy. Until recently, complaining about life was fine precisely because you couldn't do anything about it. You had no power, you could justly claim it was all "their" fault. Also, it was "their" business to change things for the better. But when Gorbachev made it clear that perestroika couldn't work without the personal participation of the individual citizens and called for change in attitudes, that represented a upsetting departure from all past experiences, including those of the late fifties and early sixties.

The thing that struck me most in my first journalistic travels was the discovery of a country I did not know, a patchwork quilt of wildly diverse peoples and cultures. Of course I was fully aware that the Soviet Union is a multinational land, but the knowledge was theoretical. I was not prepared for the differences I encountered. To begin with, the people did not look alike, even those who lived in the same geographical area. A Georgian resembles a Basque or the typical Frenchman from Gascony much more than he does an Armenian, who, in turn, reminds one more of a Greek than of an Azerbaijani, whose features are distinctly Iranian. Yet all three are neighbors and occupy a mountainous area between the Black and Caspian seas. The same may be said of the Estonians, Latvians, and Lithuanians, although they all are Baltic people. In Soviet Central Asia, Uzbeks, Tajiks, Turkmen, and Kirghiz look the same only to those who believe that all people whose skins are not white are identical. Ka-zakhs, Buriats, Yakuts—a bewildering kaleidoscope of ever-changing faces. But the facial features are only the first difference that jumps out at you. What about the languages, as different as English and Vietnamese? What about the alphabets—Latin, Cyrillic, Georgian, Armenian? And all of these reflect different histories, cultures, and traditions, which are much less obvious to the eye but far more important to understand.

It was during these initial encounters that I fully came to appreciate the wisdom of the Russian adage "We all look at the world from our own belfry." We automatically, subconsciously interpret everything from our own frame of reference; whatever we see must fit into the Procrustean bed of our experience, and if we must stretch it or lop it off to make it fit, so be it. Thus, instead of interpreting we misinterpret; thus, we create our own prejudiced view of another people, race, and nation.

I remember being hosted by a group of Georgians in their capital city of Tbilisi. The food was delicious (one of the best cuisines in the world, as far as I am concerned), the wine was wonderful, the toasts were endless and flowery—and almost all to my health. People whom I had never met before got up and said the most incredible things about me. They praised my honesty, my courage, my kindness; they saluted my many talents, my wisdom. I remember thinking to myself "Georgians must be terribly devious people. They met me fifteen minutes ago, yet they speak as if we were old friends. This is all show, they are trying to buy me—for whatever reason." As the eulogy continued, I got more and more upset. Something must have shown, because when the womenfolk came in to clear the table (another shocker for me: in the Caucasian and central Asian republics, women, as a rule, still do not sit down at the same table with men—and never mind about socialism, equal rights, and all that), one of my new acquaintances, a local journalist named Vakho, took me aside and asked me what was wrong. I shrugged and said nothing. But he would not be put off. "I can see you are not comfortable. Tell me why." So I told him. "How can all those people honestly say such wonderful things about me without even knowing me? They can't possibly be sincere, so I can't trust them, and that's an unpleasant sensation."

Vakho looked at me the way an old man might look at a child, a look full of compassion at the knowledge of the pain and travail awaiting this little human being. Then he said in a gentle voice, "Volodya, everything you heard at the table today was as sincere as anything you have ever heard or will hear." "But what if I am a despicable son of a bitch?" I exploded. "How do they know who I am?"

Again Vakho smiled that smile of an ancient, long-suffering poeple. "If you are everything they say, then that is fine. If you do not quite satisfy all of those virtues, that gives you something to work for. And, finally, if you are a despicable son of a bitch, it's been a long time since you have heard anything halfway nice said to you. Hearing people speak that way about you may make you want to live up to those things and change your ways. Kindness does more to make the world a better place than does brutality."

I had felt slightly uneasy at nailing Vakho with my statement about the Georgians. Now I felt profoundly ashamed of myself and stupid. I had been right on target in my judgment as it applied to the cultures I had experienced, and I had applied that frame of reference to a culture I knew nothing about. The conclusions I had drawn—negative conclusions about the national character of an entire people—were the product of my ignorance. As is all prejudice.

Once, late at night, I found myself high in the mountains of Armenia, not far from Lake Sevan, a breathtakingly beautiful body of water of volcanic origins threatened by the construction of a tunnel. All day I had gathered data for the story I was preparing to write on that subject. It had been a long day, hot as an oven, and the minute I got back into the car taking me to Yerevan, I conked out. When I opened my eyes, I looked out of the window and saw the sky—a black velvet blanket studded with the largest and brightest stars I had ever seen. They seemed so close, it was as if I could stretch my hand out and touch them. Then I suddenly saw the moon—a half crescent *lying on its side!* As a teenager reading *The Thousand and One Nights,* I had seen illustrations of the moon floating like a canoe over mosques and minarets. I took that to be a flight of imagination, quite fitting for the tales of Scheherazade and just as faithful to reality—after all, I *knew* the moon never looked like that. Yet there it was, right out of the *Arabian Nights',* hanging over my head, a sobering comment on my limited knowledge. But I had more to learn that night.

As we were driving through a village, my driver applied the brakes and stopped in front of a house perched on a mountain slope. When I asked him why we had stopped, he told me he had friends here, that he was hungry, and that they would be happy to feed us. There wasn't a light to be seen anywhere; clearly, everyone was in bed and sound asleep. I knew how I would react to being hauled out of bed at some ungodly hour to feed anyone, let alone a stranger. But I knew better than to argue. My driver got out, walked up the narrow path leading to the door, and knocked. A light went on, the door opened a crack, and I heard fragments of a whispered conversation. They could have cursed, for all I knew, because they were speaking Armenian and I wouldn't have understood a word. The driver returned, lit a cigarette, and said, "They were expecting us a little earlier." "Tell me another one," I thought to myself. We waited there in total silence, not even a dog barking in the distance. Then all the lights in the house went on, the door opened wide, and a man's voice called out in Russian, "Come in!"

The house was small, not more than four rooms, sparsely furnished, the floors and walls made of wooden planks. In a way, it made me think of a Depression-hit Oklahoma farmhouse of the thirties—not that I had ever been in one, but I had seen pictures of them and read Woody Guthrie's *Bound for Glory.* But this was not the Dust Bowl, and these were not Okies. When I entered, the first thing I saw was a table, set for at least eight, loaded with food. The master of the house welcomed me and asked to be excused for a few minutes. As I soon discovered, he went out to slaughter a lamb and prepare shashlik for the guests he had been "expecting." As we waited, I looked around the room. In the far corner, on a bed, there lay a woman so old that she could not be called that. She was ancient. She stared back at me, unblinkingly, with huge dark eyes of infinite sadness, eyes that had witnessed the glorious times of Armenia's flowering and the centuries of its suffering, its heroic struggles against wave after wave of would-be conquerors—the invincible Roman legions, the archers and horsemen of Parthia, the tyrants of Byzantium, the relentless Tartar war machine, the steel regiments of Tamerlane, the curved scimitar of the Ottoman Empire—all of this she had witnessed. She had walked the endless sands of history, her eyes bespoke the wisdom of the ages, and as I stared into them, I felt small and naked. I turned away and found myself looking at seven figures standing shoulder to shoulder, seven boys all dressed in identical suits and what must have been their Sunday best, the shortest on the far left, the tallest on the far right, but even he was short. I would have said he was eleven at the most, except that he had the face of an adult and so simultaneously looked both much younger and much older than his actual sixteen years. But what paralyzed me was their eyes, seven pairs of eyes all exactly like the old woman's. There was something profoundly disturbing about being watched by children who seemed to have been born older than I would one day die. I came to realize then and there that my culture, my civilization were nothing to these people who had survived as a nation, preserved their language, their culture, their land, who were the direct descendents of generations that had lived before

Rome was born, before ancient Greece put its magic spell on us, at the same time as the pharaohs of ancient Egypt.

When we sat down to eat, the only other female in the room—the children's mother—did not join us. The old woman continued to lie silently in bed, never looking away, while the mother of the family sat next to her and watched us eat. This angered and upset me, a fact I shared with my driver a couple of hours later, after we had bade them all farewell—the old grandmother, who slightly inclined her head in reply, the mother, who smiled but did not step forward, all seven boys who, strictly in age order, eldest first, solemnly shook my hand, and the father, who gave me a bear hug. "Why the devil wasn't that poor woman allowed to sit at the table with us? This is supposed to be the last quarter of the twentieth century in a modern country, damn it!" The driver shook his head. "You don't understand," he said. "What's more, you are blind. Didn't you see how every time our host got up to toast us, he looked over at the two women for permission? Don't you understand that his wife allowed him to slaughter that lamb? That he had to have them say yes before he let us in? You make such a big thing about having women sit at the same table with you, but you treat them like inferiors. My people obey women because they are life itself."

Once again, blinded by the conceit of my culture and tradition, I had judged another by my standards. I had concluded that these people treated women as second-class citizens. I still think I was right, at least in part, but so were they in looking down on my way—the western, "civilized" way—of putting a premium on appearances. I was taught a lesson in humility: before making a judgment, be sure you know what you are talking about.

Today, the nationalities issue is one of perestroika's major challenges. If no solution is found to the strife and centrifugal forces at work, perestroika will fail as surely as if radical economic reforms do not serve to liquidate our tremendous deficit, convert the rouble to a hard currency, feed the nation, and provide it with a choice of quality consumer goods. There are many reasons for what some consider to be a totally unexpected eruption of nationalism, and one of them, in my opinion, has to do with the lack of understanding of other cultures Moscow has demonstrated for decades. While complaints on the part of ethnic minorities concerning Russification are not without justification, I do not believe that this has been a deliberate, long-term plan; rather, it is the result of a conceited majority's disregard for, and unwillingness to understand, other cultures.

Both the Soviet Union and the United States are multi-ethnic societies, an important similarity. But the difference is, perhaps, even more important. All the different nationalities and ethnic groups that live in America *came from somewhere else* (with the exception of the native American), but the vast majority of those living in the Soviet Union (with the exception of a small number of Germans, Greeks, Koreans, Bulgarians, and a smattering of others) *are indigenous.* It is one thing to deal with racial, religious, and cultural prejudices in a country of newcomers, people who have torn up their roots and turned a new page, but quite a different matter to deal with these issues among people who have lived side by side for centuries, fought with one another, people whose cultural stereotypes are set in the cement of history. But even with that advantage, plus over two hundred years to realize it, has the oldest existing democracy on the face of the earth solved the problem and created a family-nation?

That is what the so-called melting pot was supposed to be about: the immigrant came to the United States, was thrown bodily into the melting pot, and came out . . . American. That cozy bit of mythology became one of the tenets of the American way of life. It was put to bed for good by the civil-rights struggles of the sixties and replaced by the salad theory: the American nation isn't a homogeneous entity of the *Homo americanus* species, it's a fruit salad, a cocktail, a wonderful mix of ingredients, each one complementing the other. It is an attractive picture—much more so than the reality it supposedly portrays. In the fall of 1987 in Seattle, KING-5 TV helped me produce a series of five one-hour shows. The series, "Meeting With America," featured five different audiences, each one discussing a specific issue—the American family, the American woman, American attitudes toward the USSR, the American school system, and ethnic minorities in America. The audience for the last was a mix of native Americans, African Americans, Hispanics, Chicanos, and Americans of Asian origin. They were all patriots, they all, without exception, loved their country and made that clear. And they all agreed, to differing degrees, that they were not choice morsels in the American salad, that, because of the color of their skin, where they came from, and how well or poorly they spoke English, they were, in many ways, second-class citizens. On the average, they had fewer educational and job opportunities, lower incomes, lived in less attractive neighborhoods, and were more likely to be harassed by the police and less likely to get a fair trial than "white" people. This is not to deny progress. But it has been terribly slow, and even if there is light at the end of that particular tunnel, it seems awfully far away. With all the talk about liberty and equality for all, none of the so-called democracies have even come close to solving minority problems.

The Soviet Union has had about seventy years to deal with the nationalities problem—roughly one-third as much time as the United States. But the roots go back to Russia's early history.

As the grand dukes of Muscovy gradually subjugated the other principalities of Russia, as Moscow took the lead in throwing off the Tartar yoke, the Russian state was born. It came together under its first czar, Ivan IV (the Terrible) in the mid-sixteenth century and began to grow, incorporating other nations into what became the Russian Empire. Typically, the Russian Empire competed with others, spreading its influence and presence in virtually all directions. Smaller nations faced with the unhappy choice of being engulfed by larger ones often turned to Russia for what they hoped would be a better deal. Georgia and Armenia, for example, as Christian countries, felt far less threatened by Russia than by the Ottoman Empire. Christian Orthodox Ukraine saw her independence threatened by the Muslim Crimean Tartars to her south and, more immediately, by Catholic Poland to her west. The decision to join Russia in 1648 was, first and foremost, an act of self-preservation. But such choice between the lesser of two evils was not always the case. As Russia became a major military power under Peter the Great, it expanded south and north as well as west, engulfing ethnic groups that had never wanted to be under the Russian two-headed eagle. That process continued throughout the eighteenth and much of the nineteenth centuries.

Like all empires, Russia exploited her subject nations both politically and spiritually. While the local nobility was allowed to exercise power, real authority was concentrated in the hands of the Russian viceroy. Also, since Russian Orthodoxy was the official state religion, one had to be a member of that church to qualify as Russian. The consequences of being a non-Russian were officially sanctioned discrimination in education, in holding office, in job opportunities, and so on. The dominant view was succinctly formulated by professor N. M. Korshunov in 1910: "Regardless of the scope of any subservient area's autonomy, the legislative power of the Russian monarch is superior to that autonomy, and that is what guarantees the sufficient predominance of Russian interests over any and all local, particular aspirations."

This view eventually led to a situation where the ethnic minorities of the Russian Empire, especially those living east of the Urals, in the far north, and in central Asia, found their cultures, their sense of national identity (no matter how limited) and their way of life being destroyed. In many of these areas, the local language wasn't taught, books or newspapers weren't published in anything but Russian. In what is today Soviet Central Asia, illiteracy was close to total; the small ethnic minorities of Siberia and the far north had no alphabet and were on the verge of extinction. While the czarist policy of anti-Semitism is well known and has been publicized for reasons having little to do with genuine sympathy for the Jews of Russia (more on this later), the plight of all the other ethnic minorities in this "dungeon of nations," as Lenin called prerevolutionary Russia, was never an issue of international concern.

As I traveled on assignments around the Soviet Union, I witnessed the remarkable achievements of what has been, and continues to be, referred to as Leninist nationalities policy. Nonexistent alphabets had been invented, languages had been restored, the republics were represented in the country's supreme legislative body; elementary and secondary education was offered in the local languages, as were newspapers, magazines, books, radio and television programs; film studios produced movies directed by local directors based on scenarios written by local writers, featuring local actors. Local theaters staged the works of local playwrights. And literacy throughout the Soviet Union was officially one hundred percent. But if all this was the entire truth, then the speeches about a "Union of equal, independent sister republics" should have sounded right. Somehow, they didn't. Because there was an additional dimension to what I have just described, and it took a while before I realized what it was.

Yes, tremendous changes had occurred, affecting once extremely retarded nationalities politically, economically, socially, and culturally, but Russian control remained as omnipotent as during the czars' times.

Officially, power was exercised by local government. In fact, it was concentrated in the Party. In Russia proper, the top party authorities were Russian, which was logical. In the fourteen other republics, the first secretary of the local Central Committee was always of the local nationality; however, the number-two man, the so-called secretary for ideology, was invariably a Russian—and that person was the real authority. This was a far more sophisticated and less brutal way of establishing Moscow's rule than having a viceroy, but it was no less, if not more, effective.

I also noticed something else: the Soviet army troops quartered in the national republics were not of the local nationality. Uzbeks did not serve in Uzbekistan. Georgians did not serve in Georgia. Byelorussians did not serve in Byelorussia. The concept behind this was simple enough: should it ever become necessary to use military force against the local population, it would be far more difficult and even dangerous to order Latvian soldiers, for example, to shoot at Latvians, than to have that job done by people of a different nationality, foreign to the culture, with no knowledge of the local language or of local problems.

It would be a mistake to interpret all this as a continuation of czarist policy that gave no consideration whatsoever to the plight of the ethnic minorities and made no effort to improve their lot. When the Bolsheviks came to power, they adopted what might well be considered the world's first affirmative-action program. Formulated by Lenin and basically adhered to by Stalin, it was based on the concept that the Russians had been the oppressor nation and were duty-bound to make certain sacrifices because of that. Per capita government allocations for the other republics were higher over the years than for the Russian Federation. More effort was put into developing and preserving the national cultures and arts than into those of Russia proper (in more recent times, Russian dissatisfaction with this has led to the rise of nationalism and extreme chauvinism, as reflected in the activities and slogans of Pamyat).

This approach was as different from czarist policy as day is from night. But one aspect was preserved: control. Perhaps preserved is not the right word; reinstated would be more appropriate. It was only after Lenin's death and Stalin's consolidation of power that elements of the prerevolutionary past began to creep back into society. Films appeared extolling the virtues of such czars as Ivan the Terrible and Peter the Great, of czarist generals and admirals—Suvorov and Ushakov, Kutuzov and Nakhimov. Traditional military ranks and awards were restored: the ribbon of the czarist St. George Cross became that of the Soviet Order of Glory; the gold-colored shoulder straps of czarist officers, once despised by the Red Army, were brought back in; even the uniforms were similar. I remember my father's shocked reaction of disgust when he saw his first Soviet general. "That is a czarist uniform!" he exclaimed. "What the hell is going on?" Even the colors were the same: light blue for the czar's infamous Third Department (the secret police) and the same for the KGB. This reinstatement was accompanied by a gradual resurrection of Russian nationalism.

Lenin's concept of a federation of equals living together of their own free will never got off the ground. In reality, Stalin's theory of autonomization triumphed. He had proposed a Soviet Union in which autonomous national entities would all be incorporated in the Russian Federation, a view Lenin called unacceptable. Stalin backed off and bided his time. With Lenin too ill and too isolated to interfere, Stalin managed to push his plan through, with one tactical change: the autonomous entities were called constituent republics. In reality, this was simply a cover, a glorified title whose only function was to make the local people feel good. In a very personal way, it reminds me of my years with Marshak, when he referred to me as his literary secretary. In fact, I was his pen pusher, someone hired to prepare drafts of answers to the letters he received from abroad and from readers in the Soviet Union. I have to admit that I too felt good when I was presented to others as Marshak's literary secretary because it made them think I was more important than I really was. But by the end of my two-and-a-half-year stint, the discrepancy between what my title inferred and my real station in life began to irk me far more than if I had from the outset been called simply a secretary. Much in the same way, the nationalities, once proud of being called sister republics and equals among equals have become profoundly dissatisfied with being referred to as what they are not (independent) and with being denied what they demand to be (equal partners).

These are the less obvious factors that have contributed over the years to the exacerbation of the nationalities problem in the Soviet Union. The more obvious ones include such Stalinist measures as the recarving of national territories and the forceful removal of whole nations from their hereditary homes.

When parts of Tadzhikistan, in particular the areas including the ancient cities of Samarkand and Bukhara, were "incorporated" into Uzbekistan, and when parts of Armenia, including Nakhichevan, Nagorny, and Karabakh, were "presented" to Azerbaijan, seeds of national strife and discord were planted. The seeds would flourish in this fertile soil, producing poisoned fruit, which would be eaten and would lead to hatred, to bloodshed; it didn't induce minorities to act together against the oppressor, but to play into the oppressor's hand by fighting one another.

When entire peoples—the Crimean Tartars, the Volga Germans, the Kalmuks, the Chechens, the Ingush, the Kurds, to name just some—were accused of having collaborated with the Nazis, stuffed into cattle cars like pickles in a barrel, and carted off to Siberia or Kazakhstan, another smoking fuse of national dissent was lit.

Today we are witnessing the explosions in the riots and tragedies of Sumgait and Nagorno-Karabakh, of Alma-Ata and Tbilisi, of Fergana and Kokand, of Novy Uzen.

But besides the deliberately planted seeds of discord, I also encountered prejudice bred by erroneous economic policies. This was especially apparent during the nearly eighteen long years of Brezhnev's rule, when extensive economic development was practiced as the prime means to combat stagnation. Of course, it did the reverse, but it also led to an increase in national tensions in two profoundly different regions of the Soviet Union: the Baltic Republics and Soviet Central Asia.

Central Planning officials regarded the Baltic Republics, which were more advanced than most other areas of the Soviet Union, as the perfect place to develop new industries. These, in turn, called for a work force none of the Baltic Republics could provide. The ensuing influx of Russians and other non-Baltic people soon reached threateningly high levels: they composed slightly over one-fifth of the population of Lithuania, some two-fifths of that of Estonia, and nearly half of Latvia. These newcomers worsened what was already a bad housing shortage, an insufficient number of day-care centers, and the like. Local people who had had to wait for years for a new apartment saw themselves pushed even further back by these intruders. To make things even worse, the intruders as a rule made no effort to learn the local language.

I remember a discussion I had in Tallinn, the capital of Estonia, with a local woman who told me about the case of a young married couple who had taken their six-year-old boy to the local children's hospital only to discover that the doctor could not speak and did not understand Estonian. "This was a very fine doctor," she said, "but that he did not speak Estonian, just as some of the clerks in the stores or in the ticket agencies, is something we cannot accept. Not any more than a Russian would accept the existence of a doctor in Moscow who did not speak Russian." She was absolutely right. Without saying the words, she was politely commenting on Great Russian nationalism, something Lenin called "the worst of them all."

I encountered it myself, I think it was in Riga, capital of Latvia, when I met a Russian who had been living there for twenty-five years but who still could not speak a word of Latvian. "But how is that possible, how can you communicate?" I asked. "Let 'em speak Russian," was his reply.

The Russians are not to be blamed for being in that part of the Soviet Union—after all, they cannot be held responsible for the bureaucratic decision to develop industries in an area that did not have the work force to run them. But it decidedly is their fault that most have made no effort to adapt to the local culture, to learn the language, that they have behaved like colonists.

Some might argue that that word is too strong. Perhaps it is, economically speaking. But the policies and economic decisions of the past bespeak the mentality of a colonist. And that mentality, I believe, has served as the prime detonator for the nationalist explosions in all three Baltic Republics.

The colonist mentality is even more apparent in Soviet Central Asia—Uzbekistan, Turkmenia, Tadzhikistan, and Kirghizia. Economic outlooks based on everything but local interests have transformed these republics into an overwhelmingly cotton-growing area. His Majesty Cotton rules supreme here. Tremendously labor intensive, cotton harvesting has been the work of women and children, the latter being exempted from school from September through December. Cotton has served to create one of the most powerful criminal organizations in the world, one that has permeated both government and party structures, one that has siphoned enormous wealth into the pockets of underworld kingpins and ranking officials. Cotton has also bled the people dry. Purchased by the government dirt cheap, cotton has brought no revenue to the people, but it has spread over three million hectares of land that could grow fruit, vegetables, and grain. It has locked out any major industries and, as a result, it has brought about the factual unemployment of roughly five million adults. This is the way a metropolis treats its colony, and such treatment invariably leads to unrest.

Over the years of its existence, Soviet society saw these issues appear and grow but refused to acknowledge their existence. This desire to ignore the problem took on Swiftian proportions during the Brezhnev era, as the following quote from one of his major speeches should make clear.

> The whole world is aware of the results of the Leninist nationalities policy. All nations and peoples of the Soviet Union have emerged on the road of prosperity and have achieved major successes in the development of industries, agriculture, science and culture . . . The unity of the multi-national Soviet people is as solid as a diamond. And, as a diamond sparkles with all the colors of its many facets, so does the unity of our people sparkle with the many nations it consists of, each of which lives a rich, fully equal, free and happy life.

Five years later, in connection with the fiftieth anniversary of the Union of Soviet Socialist Republics (December 1972), Leonid Brezhnev announced the birth of a new historical entity: the Soviet people. Instead of facing the problem, instead of diagnosing the illness, acknowledging its existence, and taking measures to cure it, it was drowned in bombast, in slogans about "the eternal friendship and brotherhood of the Soviet people." Centuries-old, rooted deeply in the hearts and psyches of millions, exacerbated by Stalin's deliberate divide-and-rule tactics and by the mindless economic policies of the Brezhnev period, nationalistic attitudes were internalized. They festered. When glasnost took the lid off, they poured out with a special fury and violence.

I gradually took all these things in, for I was no stranger to ethnic and racial prejudice. I knew the signs—as anyone who has lived in America does. And came the day when I had to ask myself a key question: is this an empire? Because if it is, then it must fall, as have all previous empires.

If by empire one means a political unit comprising a number of territories or nations, ruled by a single central authority, then the answer would seem unequivocally to be yes. Yet that single central rule has always been challenged, has never been able to fully establish itself because of the officially declared federal status of the Soviet Union. To be sure, that status has never been completely established. It has been infringed upon, bastardized, but the ideological need to stress its character along with concrete policies has served, as I see it, to make the Soviet Union neither a true empire nor a true federation. No true empire has ever put so much effort into the education of its minorities, no true empire has gone so far as to spend more per capita on them than on the majority nation. But neither has any true federation attempted to impose such centralized power on its supposedly equal members. The two tendencies—central rule and federal independence—have been in constant conflict, and the fate of the union depends on which of the two carries the day. Should the former win out, the union will cease to exist; should the latter triumph, we may witness the first true union of equals, the first true federation of what are, indeed, historically different countries.

I did not have to start traveling around the country as a journalist to discover anti-Semitism. I had had my first taste of it in the Soviet Union early on, when Moscow University refused to admit me. But there is another story I must tell, for it gives this volatile issue a different and fuller dimension.

During my freshman year at Moscow University, I spent most of my time in the old Biology Department building in the center of town, on Herzen Street. However, as biologists, we also attended lectures and took laboratory courses in chemistry. These were conducted in one of the new university buildings on Lenin Hills. Usually they ended around six or seven in the evening, by which time darkness had fallen on winter Moscow. It was on one such evening that three of us emerged from the chemistry building and walked to the bus stop: myself, Semyon, and Vera. Semyon was the son of a prominent Jewish economist, a very bright young man, but one whom Nature had not endowed with a powerful or attractive physique. As is often the case with such people, he always gravitated toward bigger men, like myself, and went after the most attractive girls, such as Vera. As we stood near the bus stop, talking, a young man walked up, a geology student, as testified to by his black uniform (in those days, certain professions offered uniforms to their future graduates). He had been drinking and he was looking for trouble. He ogled Vera and proposed she drop those "two dopes" and go with him. Vera turned away, but Semyon said, "Watch your mouth." That was exactly what the future geologist had been hoping for. "What if I don't, Jew-boy, what are you going to do about it, kike-face?" he said with contempt.

Now I knew there were only two answers to that. One was to run for cover, the other was to attack. Without waiting for Semyon to respond, I attacked. I put everything I had into that punch, knowing that if you are going to hit someone, you may as well hit him as hard as you can. It was a perfect uppercut, right on the button, and the geologist went down like a felled tree. Expecting him to get up, I moved in to put him away for good. But he just lay there on the sidewalk near the bus stop.

In Moscow, as all over the world, the police are never anywhere in sight when you need them most. It's when you don't want them that they appear. A patrol car drove up out of the blue, two militiamen jumped out, and five minutes later, after a useless attempt to explain things, I found myself in the backseat of the squad car headed for the local precinct.

When we arrived, I was led into an interrogation room and questioned by a uniformed officer and a plainclothesman. They took down my statement, read it back to me, and had me sign it. Then they walked out, telling me to wait.

I was, need I say, scared. This was my first brush with the forces of law and order in the Soviet Union. I had been very nervous, and as a result, my accent had become more apparent than usual. I had made some mistakes when speaking, and the two men had looked at me suspiciously (this was in the winter of 1954—Stalin was gone, but Khrushchev had not yet arrived). I didn't know what would happen. Would I be whisked off to some Siberian salt mine, as my friends John Sandusky and Harry McCormack had predicted on the day I said good-bye to them at Stuyvesant High?

The door opened and the uniformed officer asked me to come out with him. We walked down the hall and stopped in front of a door covered with what looked to me like phony black leather. "In you go," the officer said, opening the door. Giving me a slight push, he closed the door behind me. I found myself staring at a man seated behind a desk. A portrait of Dzerzhinsky, the founder of the Cheka, hung on the wall behind him. The room was dark, just a bright pool of light covering the desk, thrown by the swivel lamp clamped to the desktop. The man, also in uniform, was reading my statement. He put it down, gave me a quizzical look, and barked, "Pozner?"

I nodded.

"Tell me what happened."

I thought it was strange he should ask me to do that after having read my verbatim statement, but this was not the place or the time to argue. When I finished, he nodded.

"Do you know what happened to the guy you hit?"

I said I didn't know and didn't care. He stared at me for a minute and then said softly, "You should. Because you broke his jaw. He is in the hospital. You can get five years of jail for uncalled-for violence."

I didn't know what to say, but I began to feel sick to my stomach.

"How come you talk like a foreigner?" he asked.

I explained.

"Pozner," he said, "I want you to understand something. You are in the Soviet Union, not in America. In this country, you don't go around beating up people, socking them in the jaw—unless you want to go to jail. In this country, there is a law against race slur. The next time you hear anyone call your friend a kike, report him, take him to court. But don't start throwing punches. You understand?"

I nodded.

"Good, Pozner." He took my written statement and carefully tore it into two, then four, then eight rectangles. He then put them in a huge ashtray and set them on fire. "Go home now," he said, "and forget you've ever been here." He looked me straight in the eye and with just a hint of a smile at the corners of his lips said softly, "The guy you stood up for, he didn't come down to the precinct with you, did he?" I shook my head. "Well," he said, with that same hint of a smile dancing around the corners of his mouth and in his dark eyes, "that poor bastard with the broken jaw was right. Your pal really is a lousy kike. Now go home."

I turned and walked out of his office, head swirling, trying to figure out what this had really been about. For some reason, I turned to look back at the door—and saw, immediately to the left, a sign on the wall that said:

CHIEF OF PRECINCT
LT. COLONEL A. B. KOGAN

The man who had saved my ass was the first and last Jewish police officer I ever met.

For many years, I told this story as an anecdote, stressing Lieutenant Colonel Kogan's punch line and playing down my own jaw-breaking punch. I wanted people to see this as modesty on my part. But in reality it was false modesty, for I portrayed myself as a truly noble human being who came to the rescue, fists swinging, of a victim of prejudice, something that had absolutely nothing to do with me. Not only was the modesty false, but so was the premise. The question I had to ask myself, had to face sooner or later, was this: was I defending Semyon, or was I reacting to the word *kike* because it applied to me as well? It took me a long time before I could honestly answer that question. Because to answer it, I had to answer another question: am I a Jew?

The following exchange between Phil Donahue and myself, when I was the guest of his show in the fall of 1986, speaks volumes concerning how ill-prepared I have been to deal with that issue.

DONAHUE: You are a Jew.

POZNER: That's what you say. What is a Jew? Just determine . . . define it for me.

DONAHUE: Were you bar mitzvahed?

POZNER: Never!

DONAHUE: You say that with some enthusiasm.

POZNER: No! Look, I was born to a Catholic mother and a Russian father. When I say Russian, his father in prerevolutionary Russia became a Russian Orthodox, although he was Jewish, he became a Russian Orthodox because in czarist Russia you couldn't go to a university if you were not a Russian Orthodox, a Jew could not go to a university. So his . . . my grandfather, as it were, became a Russian Orthodox because that would make him Russian, 'cause that was a state religion. So I'm born to a Russian father and a French Catholic mother. How does that make me Jewish?

DONAHUE: Well, so . . . So it's important to you that you . . . that the record be straight on this matter?

POZNER: I don't care what I am, that's not important to me, but I wish someone would define, does it mean being religious, basically, or is it the blood that runs in your veins, or what is it? Because I'm not religious. So therefore . . .

DONAHUE: Well, you know the reason for the inquiry.

POZNER: Oh sure, I know what I've been called.

DONAHUE: Well, now let me . . . What *have* you been called?

POZNER: A little Jew.

DONAHUE: A little Jew?

POZNER: A little, betraying . . .

DONAHUE: A traitorous Jew is . . .

POZNER: A little, betraying Jew is what . . . I think that was it.

DONAHUE: And you reject, and you object to that because? . . . Because what? You're not Jewish?

POZNER: I laugh at it. I laugh at it. And I find it strange that a U.S. official can use that type of language publicly.

Believe me, I was not laughing. I was hot and flustered, not the Mr. Smooth-'n'-Cool of "Nightline" fame. I clearly had a problem, an identity crisis of sorts.

Ever since I can remember, I always got the impression that my father repudiated his Jewishness. I don't know why that was, but I can guess. I think his attitude had to do with two very Russian conditions. One was that the Jewish intelligentsia in Russia made a deliberate attempt to become assimilated. In that desire, it shared what was considered to be the progressive view as expressed, for instance, by Lenin in the following passage from his article "The Situation of the Bund in the Party":

> The Jewish question stands precisely thus: assimilation or isola-
> tion? And the idea of a Jewish "nation" is clearly reactionary

in character not only on the part of its consistent supporters (the Zionists), but also on the part of those who attempt to combine it with the ideas of social-democracy (the Bundists). The idea of Jewish nationality is counter to the interests of the Jewish proletariat, for directly or indirectly it gives birth to a mood hostile to assimilation, to a "ghetto" outlook.

As far as the intellectual community was concerned, Jews really had one of two choices: either stay within the Pale (that is to say, within a certain geographic area where Jews were forced to live under czarist law), remain foreign entities, lead separate lives, and remain isolated from the mainstream of Russian existence, or join that mainstream, become active contributors. This meant giving up Judaism, often it meant converting to Russian Orthodoxy. It also involved a spiritual breaking with the *shtetl* Jew, the man with the black hat, the long black coat, the black beard, and the dangling earlocks. I could be wrong, but I think the majority of those who opted for assimilation despised their past, their heritage—at least subconsciously. I think they threw themselves into Russian life with an energy and a passion generated by their desire to leave the degrading climate of the Pale behind, forget it, exorcise it from their memories. It is no accident that the percentage of Jews in the Bolshevik party, in the leadership of the first Soviet government, in the top echelons of the Cheka, the "Revolution's sword," was extremely high.

These people refused to speak Yiddish, they brought their children up on the treasures of Russian culture and deliberately ignored their Jewish legacy. In a way, they shared the view, although they never would admit it, that there *was* something shameful about being Jewish. Not that any of them condoned anti-Semitism. But they condemned it the same way a Wasp might condemn antiblack prejudice: as a phenomenon that does not directly involve them.

I picked these insights up over a period of years as I watched my father's reaction of denial and disdain whenever he suspected that someone considered him to be a Jew. And part of that rubbed off on me. I knew his parents were both Jewish, but for some reason I doggedly repeated my father's story about his father having come from converts to Orthodoxy, while his mother was of Russian stock. It took me a while to accept the fact that my last name—Pozner (also Posner or Posener)—comes from Poznań, a Polish city that was a center of Jewish culture as early as the fourteenth century.

I grew up regarding myself as French, my mother's nationality. But when those two Catholic toughs tried to pants me in the Village back in 1942, I did not say no when they asked if I was Jewish. Nor did I argue when the lady from the exam board at Moscow University told me in private that I had been denied entry because of my Jewish last name. Yet I never felt Jewish. I never had any interest in the language, in the culture. I never felt a surge of pride (as did many non-Israeli Jews) at the military prowess demonstrated by Moshe Dayan. If anything contributed to a feeling of Jewishness on my part, it was anti-Semitism.

In Yevtushenko's poem "Babi Yar," there is a line in which the poet says he will consider himself to be Jewish until the last anti-Semite has disappeared. It's a good line, a typically Yevtushenkoesque piece of rhetoric. It is easy for someone to say who knows he is not, and is not considered to be, Jewish. It's the white guy defending the black guy all over again. But there is much to say for the view that anti-Semitism consolidates the very object of its prejudice.

With the exception of when I was turned down by Moscow University, I have never felt I was the victim of anti-Semitism. But I have no intention of generalizing my personal experience and stating that anti-Jewish prejudice is rare in the Soviet Union. Supposedly—and this is something I have been told over and over again by Jewish people—visible anti-Semitism had become virtually nonexistent by the thirties. That would seem to be corroborated by Stalin's answer to the Jewish Telegraph Agency in 1931:

> National and race chauvinism is a vestige of misanthropic mores peculiar to the period of cannibalism. Anti-Semitism, as an extreme form of race chauvinism, is the most dangerous vestige of cannibalism.
>
> Anti-Semitism is profitable to the exploiters as a lightning rod which helps the capitalists escape the working people's wrath . . .
>
> In the USSR anti-Semitism is strictly prosecuted by the law as being profoundly hostile to the Soviet system. Soviet law punishes active anti-Semites by the death sentence.

I have never heard of a single person being put behind bars, let alone sentenced to death, in the Soviet Union for anti-Semitism. And if that most ancient of all existing prejudices was no longer manifest in the USSR by the thirties, which I find hard to believe, it had certainly not disappeared from the national psyche. Otherwise, how can one explain the undeniable fact that Hitler's propaganda found a receptive audience and a positive response on occupied Soviet soil? This is certainly not to say it was a universal response, or even a majority response. There is solid evidence to the contrary. But the number of Soviet citizens who turned Jews in to the Nazi oppressors, who collaborated with the Germans in the slaughter of hundreds of thousands of Soviet Jews, testifies to the sad truth that, at best, anti-Semitism had been dormant and that even propaganda from a cruel and relentless foe was enough to reawaken it.

In postwar times, the angry fires of anti-Semitism were deliberately fed by Stalin's campaign against cosmopolitans and, in particular, by the notorious Doctors' Plot, the prelude to the planned mass deportation of Jews to Siberia of which I spoke earlier.

Although the post-Stalin period was, generally speaking, far less oppressive, the situation for Jews did not improve. In fact, a case could be made for its having worsened. Between 1953 and 1972, anti-Semitism remained at a relatively low level. One rarely heard stories of anyone's being discriminated against for being Jewish—even though it was common knowledge that in some prestigious institutions of higher learning (such as Moscow's Institute of International Affairs) and certain government offices (the Foreign Ministry, for example) Jews were not welcome. But with President Nixon's summit meeting with Brezhnev in Moscow in the spring of 1972 and the signing of a series of agreements, one of which specified the rights of Soviet Jews to emigrate to Israel, the situation took a turn for the worse—something most people in the West still find inexplicable. To understand it, one must see emigration as the majority of Soviets have perceived it for more than seventy years.

Prior to the revolution, most of the emigration out of the Russian Empire was Jewish—Jews fleeing the pogroms of the 1890s and early nineteen-hundreds. Most Russians felt that it was good riddance to bad rubbish. Came the revolution and the first major exodus from Russia. The majority of those who departed did so for *political* reasons. It was not just to better their condition, as was the case for Italians, Germans, Irish, and other people who left their homelands in search of a better life. In the case of postrevolutionary Russia, the emigrant was, as a rule, either someone who had actually fought the Bolsheviks and the Red Army or someone who had banked on the Bolsheviks losing. These were people who did not agree with, did not accept, the new system. Not surprisingly, they were called traitors by those who remained. Thus the first link between emigrant and traitor was forged in the national mind.

The second wave of emigration coincided with the end of World War II. As the German troops retreated under the Red Army's onslaught, many people fled with them: collaborationists who knew all too well what would happen if they were apprehended; people whose relatives had been suppressed during the purges of the late thirties and who wished to escape before the same fate befell them; opponents of the Soviet system who, for whatever reasons, had not been able to get out in the early twenties and who then saw the door slam shut. Considering the nature of this second wave, it could not but reinforce the concept of emigrant as traitor.

The third wave of emigration came as the result of détente, the cooling of cold-war tensions that was met with mass approval. Even so, any individual who would have emigrated, taking advantage of the improvement in U.S.-Soviet relations and the ensuing agreements, would have been branded a traitor by his former countrymen. But emigration policies were based on the concept of homeland. Thus ethnic minorities whose forebears had originally immigrated to Russia or the Soviet Union were allowed to return to their ancestral homelands. This included the Spanish, Greek, Bulgarian, German, and other minorities who had never had much of a presence in this country, who generally kept an extremely low profile. An exception to that rule was the Armenians. Because of the genocide perpetrated by Turkey in 1915–1916, millions of Armenians had fled abroad. As a result of the Armenian diaspora, a kind of second homeland open to all Armenians had been created. But just as there had never been a Spanish question or a German question in Russia, neither had there existed an Armenian question. Finally, and most importantly in this case, there were the Jews. They were the focal figure in this third wave of emigration, both in numbers and in their visibility. As they began to depart, a new equation took hold: emigrant=traitor=Jew.

The reaction to Jewish emigration was extremely emotional. It focused all the anti-Semitic prejudices and created a hostile atmosphere that convinced many Soviet Jews to emigrate who had never entertained the thought of leaving the country and finalized the decision of those who had been undecided. But as the flow of Jewish emigration increased in the early and mid-seventies, the hostile atmosphere translated into concrete expression. Universities closed their doors to Jewish applicants, regardless of their qualifications. Job opportunities became more and more limited. Anti-Semites who had previously refrained from openly practicing their prejudice now had a field day.

I witnessed this at my place of work, Gosteleradio (the USSR State Committee for Television and Radio), where the chairman of the board instructed the personnel department not to hire Jews. When the Gosteleradio Symphony Orchestra came up for review—like most symphony orchestras around the world, it had a disproportionately high number of Jewish musicians—the chairman personally crossed out the names of virtually all the Jews. Others, working in the many departments of television and radio, found themselves under pressure to leave.

When I write "I witnessed," I am not being precise. The head of personnel (whom I knew) never told me in as many words about having been instructed not to hire Jews. Nor did I see the chairman crossing out names. But this was information that became known, not just rumors. Those of us who heard about it did not doubt its truth. But we did not verify it. Why? I can only speak for myself, but had I been provided with factual, visible evidence, I would have had to react.

When Rostropovich was a student at Moscow's Conservatory of Music in the late 1940s and his professor Dmitry Shostakovich was fired for being a "formalist," the young man protested by leaving the Conservatory. When the Russian Academy refused to accept the writer Gorky as a member, Chekhov and Tolstoy resigned.

When one sees people being victimized, one is duty-bound to react. The only real excuse for not reacting is lack of evidence. That, I think, is why most of us prefer not to know anything that could force us into a dangerous (or shameful) situation.

I was no exception.

A push-pull mechanism was established: the increase in Jewish emigration led to greater anti-Jewish feelings and actions, which in turn stimulated emigration. This was, of course, compounded by the political situation, as the United States used the Jewish emigration issue for its own political purposes.

Perhaps this is the time to state unequivocally that the official United States position concerning Jewish emigration from the Soviet Union had little, if anything, to do with concern for human rights, passionate statements to the contrary notwithstanding. When in the late seventies the gates of emigration from the Soviet Union began to close, it affected not only the Jews, but the Germans, the Greeks, and others as well. Had the

United States really cared about the plight of those whose rights to travel had been abrogated, it would have protested no less vehemently about those other ethnic minorities. Or, for that matter, about the Russians and all the others who have never qualified for emigration because they didn't have roots elsewhere, a diaspora, or a newly founded homeland. The American Jewish community never lifted a finger or its voice in support of any group except Soviet Jewry. The American press never brought anything but that subject to the attention of its readers. The American government never made a case for any other nationality or religious community. The U.S. Congress passed the Jackson-Vanick Act only with the understanding that a refusenik was a Soviet Jew who had been refused the right to emigrate.

I remember being invited to meet with a group of extremely influential Jewish leaders from the United States who had come to the Soviet Union to speak to government and party officials. The thrust of their message was that if the Soviet Union did not change its Jewish emigration policy, they would see to it that the Soviet government would regret the consequences. When I expressed my feeling that such pressure could only worsen the situation, that no country would stand for any kind of blackmail, that, personally, I was appalled by their lack of compassion for non-Jewish Soviets whose chances to emigrate were nil, I was made to understand they did not give a tinker's damn about them.

Perhaps this is also the time to point out that the change in Soviet emigration policy, a major change that now makes it possible for *any* Soviet to leave*—and return, a no less important human right—is the result of perestroika, "new thinking," of initiatives born *inside* the country. External pressure has been a secondary factor, if even that, something those who pat themselves on the back for having "forced the Russkies to say uncle" should never forget.

The opening up of emigration in the Soviet Union has served to take the edge off the refusenik issue and its Jewish connotation. But discrimination at the university and job level still exists, while the emergence of openly and violently anti-Semitic associations, such as Pamyat, has injected an element that did not exist before: the threat of physical danger.

In the mid-seventies, the following anecdote supplied the rationale

---

*Except those whose work involves national security and who have been forewarned as to how this will affect their right to travel.

for Jewish emigration. A well-known Soviet Jewish scientist applied for emigration papers. Because of his international stature, he was invited by the local party authority to talk things over. "Are you dissatisfied with your job?" he was asked. "Not at all," he replied. "Then, maybe, you need a larger apartment?" "No, I am quite satisfied with my dwelling." "Could it be that your children have had problems finding a job?" Again, the professor answered in the negative. His son was doing graduate studies and his daughter was a successful concert pianist. "So what do you want, you lousy kike?" came the answer.

Basically, the anecdote still stands. As long as it reflects the situation in this country, Jewish emigration will continue.

With the exception of groups such as Pamyat, which have their U.S. counterparts in the Klan, the Nazi party of America, and several others, anti-Semitism has never been overt in the Soviet Union, nor has there ever been a stated anti-Semitic government policy. However, anti-Zionist campaigns have served as a cover for that purpose. The following definition of Zionism, culled from the *Soviet Ecyclopaedic Dictionary* (1980), speaks for itself:

> ZIONISM (from name of Mt. Zion in Jerusalem), a reactionary chauvinistic ideology and policy of the Jewish bourgeoisie. Appeared at the end of the 19th century. Formulated the slogan calling for the creation in Palestine of a Jewish state and the migration of all Jews. Zionism's characteristic features: bellicose chauvinism, racism, anti-communism, anti-Sovietism. The supreme Zionist body is the World Zionist Organization, founded in 1897. The ruling bodies of Zionism are situated in Israel, where Z. is the state doctrine, as well as in the USA.

I must acknowledge being no supporter of Zionism, or of any doctrine that demands of its followers that they live in a certain geographical area and supports the concept of a chosen people. I tend to agree with what Albert Einstein wrote in his essay "Our Debt to Zionism" (1938): "To be a Jew, after all, means first of all, to acknowledge and follow in practice those fundamentals in humaneness laid down in the Bible—fundamentals without which no sound and happy community of men can exist . . . Judaism owes a great debt of gratitude to Zionism. The Zionist movement has revived among Jews the sense of community." But, he goes on, in discussing the issue of partition of Palestine, "Just one more personal word on the question of partition. I should much rather see reasonable agreement with the Arabs on the basis of living together in peace than the creation of a Jewish state. Apart from practical consideration, my awareness of the essential nature of Judaism resists the idea of a Jewish state with borders, an army, and a measure of temporal power no matter how modest. I am afraid of the inner damage Judaism will sustain— especially from the development of a narrow nationalism within our own ranks, against which we have already had to fight strongly, even without a Jewish state."

As I grappled with my personal identity crisis, I was outspoken in my condemnation of anti-Semitism—and I paid a price for it. In the winter of 1968, I was invited to dinner by the then counselor for cultural affairs of the West German embassy in Moscow. Up until the most recent past, contact with foreigners was allowed only to a select group—people who had been cleared for that purpose by the KGB, people whose jobs necessitated such contacts, and dissidents. My work for *Soviet Life* and *Sputnik* magazines put me in the second category, so that invitation was nothing out of the ordinary. But the dinner itself most definitely was. There were only five couples present, including my wife and myself. The others were our host and the counselors of the Finnish, Indian, and Japanese embassies and their wives. We were the only Soviets, which should have set my internal alarm ringing. That four counselors should want to spend an evening with me, a person of no official standing or influence, should have really triggered all my early warning systems. Nothing of the sort occurred. On the contrary, I basked in the glory of my falsely assumed importance. Throughout the entire dinner, I pontificated on different aspects of life in the Soviet Union, including the issue of anti-Semitism. I still do not know why I was chosen as the guest of honor for that dinner. Perhaps it had something to do with my reputation for speaking my mind (shooting off my mouth?), perhaps with the lack of contacts with Soviets that embassy people experienced. As the Russian saying goes, in a fishless situation even a crayfish will pass for a fish. Diplomatic personnel always fish for information; in the absence of the real thing, I would do. But whatever the reasons for that invitation, a few days later my father called and asked me to come over immediately. The sense of urgency in his voice was clear.

When I arrived, I discovered he had company in the person of one Victor Alexandrovich—the same man who later made it possible for me to go join my parents in Dresden when my father had a heart attack. I never knew him by anything but that name and patronymic, although several years later I learned what I had always suspected: that both were aliases. Victor Alexandrovich was a ranking KGB officer, probably a lieutenant general, with whom my father had a relationship I never asked about. I tend to think the KGB took an interest in my father because of his background and knowledge of the West, an interest that flattered his ego.

On that particular afternoon, my father told me that Victor Alexandrovich had something important to discuss with me privately. "Let's go have lunch," he ordered (in my experience with him, which was limited to fewer than ten encounters, I never heard him use any other tone). We left the house and got into a waiting car, which took us to the Prague Restaurant on Arbat Square. There we went to a small private dining room. The table was set for two, an indication that things had been ordered in advance. We sat down. "Here," he said, taking several sheets of paper, folded in four, out of his coat pocket, "read this." What I proceeded to read was a handwritten report describing the entire evening at the West German counselor's house, describing everything I had said, exact to the last word. Speechless, I looked at Victor Alexandrovich. He gave me a mirthless smile. "When you figure out how this was done," he said, "I will believe you are intelligent. But what this says is that you are a fool. It says that you preen your feathers in public, you undress like a whore in front of anyone who will pay enough attention to watch. You think they were impressed with your liberal outlook? Why, they despised you, they laughed at you, they couldn't believe how stupidly full of yourself you are. This report could mean the end of your career, you could go to jail for this. I intercepted it and persuaded my superiors to take no action. I did it for your father, not for you, I did it because your father is a man of integrity, a man who had the courage and the principles to return to his native land so as to contribute to our cause. You I don't care about. But I care about your parents, I know they could not live if anything happened to you. Thank them for still being a free man, for not being kicked out of the Party, for not losing your job and worse. Now eat and think of what you are. And remember, your 'friends' wanted your head for this, now they won't get it. But they will make you pay."

I was devastated. The revelation that one of those four diplomats worked for the KGB left me cold. But I despised myself for the fear that paralyzed me and, even more, because I realized he was right. Yes, I was a pompous fool, yes, I did take myself far too seriously, yes, that whole evening had been an ego trip for me. Had I taken a public stand on anti-Semitism, had I protested to Soviet officialdom, had I addressed myself to my own people—that would have been an act of courage. Considering the times, the risks would have been enormous, the price high. But that was a risk and a price worthy of respect. But deep down inside, I was afraid to take that risk or pay that price. My taking the issue to a foreign audience was a way to prove to myself that I was not afraid. In fact, it proved the opposite. And, as Victor Alexandrovich had said, it also proved my stupidity, for the people I addressed could not have cared less. They used me—with my full compliance.

A word about my "friends."

One evening, in 1956, when I was living with Iosif and Nina Gordon, I received a phone call from a man who said he had just arrived from Berlin and had brought me a letter and a parcel from my father. Could I come by and pick up the stuff at five on the following day? The Ural Hotel, which no longer exists, was situated in Stoleshnikov Street in the center of downtown Moscow. Even by the low standards of those days, it was a second-rate facility, its usual clients being provincial employees sent to Moscow by their local bosses with instructions to wangle some minor concession from the all-powerful ministries under whose rule their particular plant or enterprise struggled. The elite corps selected for foreign service was a cut higher than these poor devils and would hardly be found in a place like the Ural Hotel. But these were thoughts I had later.

After climbing two flights of stairs (there was no elevator) and walking down what seemed like endless winding corridors, I found the room I was looking for and knocked. "Come in," called a voice. I opened the door and stepped inside, where two men were sitting at a table. One walked toward me, shook my hand, then dropped it and locked the door behind me. The second man stood up as I approached, whipped a red leather ID wallet out of his breast pocket, stuck it in my face, and said, "KGB. Sit down."

What followed had a nightmarish quality. On the one hand, it was like a B-movie about the KGB. On the other hand, it could not be happening precisely because I knew that B-movies were never true to life. On the third hand (which is impossible, but not for a nightmare), this was for real.

For four hours they questioned me about my life. Every time I forgot or omitted a detail, they supplied it. They knew more about me than I did. It gradually dawned upon me that I had been watched since the first day we arrived, that people I had become friends with had reported everything I had ever said, everything I had done, including very private and personal affairs. They knew all about Zhenya.

The man who had locked the door played the good cop. He was short and stocky, with light brown wavy hair and a perfectly nondescript face. His smile was quick and furtive, as were his movements; he seemed to be ducking something all the time. His voice was soft, conciliatory. The only hard thing about him was his handshake—like a vise.

His colleague was the bad cop. Tall, thin, and balding, with coal-black eyes and a hard, unsmiling mouth, he sat coiled in an armchair, somehow reminding me of a cobra about to strike.

Together they played me like a piano. Whenever I began to show any sign of anger or irritation, Nikolai Antonovich, the good cop, would duck in with something soothing. As soon as I got back onto an even keel, the bad cop (I don't remember his name) would spit out something that knocked me back off balance.

When all the details of my life had been held up, examined, and hung out to dry, the bad cop uncoiled, stood up, and solemnly said, "We are asking you to cooperate with the Committee for State Security. Do you agree?" I asked what that entailed. He gave me a withering look. "It means many things you have yet to learn—when we see fit. But at this point it means giving us information on the foreigners you frequent in Moscow and on your fellow students."

I remember not having been able to believe my ears. I was being asked to be a fink, a stoolie. Did they really expect me to agree? I tried to contain my fury and said, "As far as my fellow students are concerned, or any Soviet citizens, for that matter, the answer is no. And that's final. And I promise that, should I ever encounter a foreigner who strikes me as being suspicious, I will let you know. But I refuse to report on any of my foreign friends."

"Don't play games with us," hissed the Cobra. "You'll regret it."

"He's not playing games," interceded Nikolai Antonovich, "he's an honest young man who is a little confused. He should be given time to think things over."

The other man nodded. "Just remember, you will share this meeting with no one. Also remember that divulging state secrets is an act of treason."

As was always the case when boxed into a corner, I became cocky. "What happens if I do tell someone? My father, for instance. Will you shoot me?"

The bad cop sneered. "Worse," he said shortly. He unlocked the door and motioned for me to get out.

I never saw him again. But for several years after that, I would get a call every now and then from Nikolai Antonovich. We would meet in an apartment on Pushkin Street in a building opposite the attorney general's office. There he would ask me about people I had met. Invariably, I would give them the highest recommendations. After one such discussion, a few days before my birthday, Nikolai Antonovich presented me with Kafka's novel *Metamorphosis,* which had just been published and was impossible to get in Moscow. It still stands in my library, and every time I see it, I think of the irony of a KGB officer giving me a book written by a man who described as no one else the horror of the ulti-mate state machine of repression. Was Nikolai Antonovich trying to tell me something?

In 1963 or 1964, he called me for what turned out to be our last meeting. This time he was not alone. There was another man, a person he clearly deferred to. The conversation, throughout which Nikolai An-tonovich never said a word, was short and to the point.

"Vladimir Vladimirovich, would you consider taking a vacation abroad? For instance, to an international resort like Varna in Bulgaria. You would go under a different name with a Swiss passport. Of course we will provide you with the necessary training. What do you say?"

For an instant, I wasn't sure I had understood him correctly, but almost simultaneously I knew that I had. They were recruiting me, and the enormity of what they were asking me to do led me to lose my cool for the first time ever when dealing with those people.

I could hear my heart thudding in my ears as I said, "Are you serious? Look, you know who I am, where I come from. I have friends all over the world, I have relatives abroad, I don't know how many foreigners I've met in the past few years, and I don't think my face is easily forgotten. You say Varna is an international resort. What if some-one recognizes me? What if someone comes up and says, 'Hi, Vladimir, what are you doing here?' Am I supposed to say, 'My name is William Tell?' Either you are trying to set me up, or you are a bunch of god-damn fools. I am sick and tired of this. Isn't it time you recognized I've never cooperated with you? Enough is enough. Let's forget about each other. I've had it."

I'll always remember the look he gave me (Nikolai Antonovich had been studying his shoes. He never raised his eyes, not even when I got up to leave). "Yes, Pozner," he said, "enough is enough. But we will not forget about you. Now go."

Those were my "friends." I'm sure they were put through the wringer by their superiors for having lost me. And I know they could not forgive me. I'm sure they did a nice standard piece of character assassination on me, that my file was stashed away in some cubbyhole reserved for disloyal individuals. I have no doubts they were responsible for my not having been allowed to travel until 1977. Even then, it took the personal intercession of the chairman of Gosteleradio, a member of the Central Committee of the Communist party, to unlock that door.

In a strange way, the discussion concerning my attempts to come to terms with my being, or not being, Jewish led me into the story of my dealings with the KGB. Therefore, I take this opportunity to conclude both issues.

Just as all Arabs are not Egyptians, or Algerians, or Syrians, neither are all Jews Israelis. To be Jewish, as I see it, is the same thing as being French, or Russian, or Norwegian, a matter of what is unscientifically referred to as "blood." Yes, I am partly Jewish. And French. And German. And probably a great many other things, as are most people. As differing from citizenship, it is something neither to take pride in nor be ashamed of. But far more importantly, one is what one feels. Most people have no trouble determining that. My case is more complicated. As far as I know, I have neither Russian nor American blood. Yet I feel Russian (up to a point) and I feel American (but not completely) more than any other nationality. I feel French—sometimes. But I have never felt Jewish (I do not speak Yiddish or Hebrew, have had no contact with Jewish culture, and am not a religious person) except when I have encountered anti-Semitism.

The CIA and the KGB are governments within governments. They are dangerous because of the vast power they have been allowed to assume. The KGB has perpetrated crimes against the Soviet people. The CIA is guilty of crimes against other people—such as the Chileans, to name just one example. Let us not, however, place the blame at the wrong door. Neither the KGB nor the CIA "just grew" like Topsy. They were created by the Soviet and the U.S. governments, initially created for one purpose, later used for a variety of purposes. The two governments invested these creations with the power and the authority that has made them almost unaccountable for their actions. The governments are to blame. The KGB and the CIA are not jinnis, they can be forced back into the bottle—and they well should be. Both have been the tail that wags the dog—but only because the dog wanted to be wagged. The change in the Soviet outlook today is evident: the KGB has come under the control of the new Congress of People's Deputies, it has been attacked and vehemently criticized in public by elected officials in session, on television, and in the press. In short, these organizations have been, are, and will be the creations of their governments—neither more, nor less.

I broke into journalism at the height of de-Stalinization, during the Thaw. The area was new to me, a kind of terra incognita for me to conquer. I had, until then, not given much thought to what the function of journalism was, to the relationship between freedom of the press and responsibility to the reader. I was naive enough to believe that a journalist could write anything and have it printed, provided he had integrity and honesty. I embarked on my journalistic career with gusto, focusing on subjects that, by their very nature, protected me from facing any of the "to be or not to be" questions of journalism. As I noted earlier, *Soviet Life* was created to present Americans with a positive image of the Soviet Union, a view I supported. Americans never encountered any scarcity of negative coverage of the USSR. What they lacked was balanced coverage. As I saw it, *Soviet Life* was a drop of positive information in a negative sea, which, in the general context of what Americans got, made it a legitimate publication.

With that attitude, I didn't encounter any obstacles in writing what I desired and having it printed—not, that is, until 1964, when I went to Lake Baikal in Siberia to do a story on the world's largest body of fresh water and the people who lived around it. I had been there eight years earlier as a student, and I was shocked by the changes. Baikal was in trouble, threatened by the construction of a mammoth celluloid factory. Supposedly it had all the necessary purification installations, but a closer look showed this was nothing but a smoke screen. In reality, the plant was designed to suck up Baikal's uniquely pure water and spit back poison. The story I wrote focused on the conflict between state planning interests, which allegedly coincided with those of the people, and reality. It was, as I look back on it a quarter of a century later, one of the best stories I ever wrote. I was proud of it and said so when I handed it to the editor. A few days later, I was summoned to the office of the executive secretary of Novosty. If I had to describe him in one word, that word would be *fat*. That would include not only his short body but also his face, his lips, his nose, and somehow even his eyes—two small oily black pools surrounded by layers of lard. But inside it all lurked an astonishingly keen and sophisticated mind, a rollicking sense of humor, and compassion for people like me who had so much to learn and who would be battered and bruised in the process.

"Volodya," he said, after having greeted me and waved me into an armchair, "Volodya, I want to congratulate you." I glowed. "You have written a whale of a story," he continued, "but I want you to read it carefully, always keeping in mind who your readers are. They are Americans, right?" I nodded. "Now what do Americans know about our country? Zero." He drew a great big circle with both hands. "If you had written this for a Soviet audience, it would be a different matter. They know about central planning. But Americans? To them it's Greek. What I want you to do is go over what you've written, read it as though you were an American who picked up *Soviet Life* at a newsstand. When you do that, I'm sure you will cut whatever your reader would find confusing. But, please, do not make a telegraph pole out of your pine tree." "I'm sorry," I said, "but I don't understand." "There are editors," he said, beaming at me, "who are afraid of their own shadow. Instead of using their pencil like a scalpel, they use it like a buzz saw. They lop off anything that sticks out; they want uniformity above all. They take a pine tree of a story and they cut off all the branches with their needles and cones. They turn it into a telegraph pole—smooth, no individuality. Don't do that. I'll tell you what, let me show you what I mean. Leave your story with me, I'll work on it."

Two days later, I found the story on my desk with a note that said, "A fine piece of work. I shake your hand."

I must admit, he did a wonderful job. He had used his pencil like a scalpel. At first glance, very little seemed to have been cut away. Everything was there—except the conflict. The story had no balls.

I immediately recognized it for what it was—a snow job. But my reaction was tempered by a combination of vanity and accumulated knowledge. This was my first major piece for *Soviet Life,* and I couldn't wait to see it printed. Everything in it, I said to myself, is true—it's not all the truth, but then what is? I knew certain areas were taboo insofar as voicing a dissenting opinion was concerned, including foreign policy, government policy decisions, any member of the leadership (until that person had fallen into disgrace). This was nothing I had been told. No one was ever handed a list of instructions, these were things one learned, codes of behavior, unwritten rules. The rationale was simple enough. Had the

West not declared war on us? A cold war where victory and defeat depended on who would succeed best in the struggle for human minds? Were we journalists not referred to as "soldiers of the ideological front"? Privately we might agree that all was not well, that there was room for improvement, but could a soldier locked in battle with an implacable foe permit himself to complain publicly about his commanding officers? Of course not! True patriots would close ranks and stand as one until the battle was won. To do otherwise was to play into the enemy's hands (have not American conservatives expressed the same view vis-à-vis public criticism of the same things in the United States?).

Finally, there was another dimension to this argument: the issue of self-preservation. The Stalin era, with its ruthless suppression of any criticism except that sanctioned by Stalin himself, was far from forgotten. The first dissident trials gave a clear signal as to what to expect for anything that might be qualified as anti-Soviet propaganda. Fear lurked in the corners of people's minds—and I was no exception.

Like everyone else, I found myself between a rock and a hard place. I knew I would despise myself for compromising on my principles—whether the compromise be on the left or on the right. I had to create an ecological niche of my own, develop a modus vivendi that would allow me to retain my honesty without giving up my freedom. Gradually, this led me to a tactic that was formulated a few years later by the old Bolshevik Nikolai Tillib when I asked his advice about joining the Party. "Most of what you encounter today has nothing to do with Lenin's ideas, with what the revolution was meant to be. Some things will make you sick to your stomach. But you will have to suffer in silence. You will have to walk the razor's edge, never letting them know what you really think. If you really believe Socialism has the potential to provide a better life for people, you will prevail. If not, you will either sell out or go over to the other side."

I made a promise to myself that I would not lie. I would not disinform. I would not sing hosannas to the Party or to its general secretary. I would select the kind of material that served to destroy prejudice and the false stereotypes Americans had about the Soviet Union. And, whenever the opportunity presented itself, I would do the same for Soviets and their distorted views of America.

I made that promise in all honesty, but I cannot honestly say I kept it. It was not that I deliberately misinformed my audience. Rather, I censored my statements, I deleted passages that could be threatening to me, I rarely spoke my mind fully. More than once I questioned what was really influencing my decisions—fear for myself and my family's well-being, the desire not to furnish the "enemy" with ammunition, a false sense of patriotism, or a real lack of courage? Probably, a bit of each.

Those were lonely and trying times, made even more bleak by upheavals in my private life and the breakup of my first marriage.

I had met Valentina in the summer of 1957, hard on the heels of the World Youth Festival, when I had spent two weeks living with the U.S. delegation. Those two weeks had solidified my decision to return to America, not an easy decision to make, considering that it meant leaving my parents, yet it gave me a sense of relief once I had reached it. I had a month of summer vacation left after the festival but nowhere to go. So when the parents of a university friend proposed that I move into their dacha for the month of August (they were spending that month in the Crimea), I jumped at the offer.

A dacha (pronounced DA-tcha) has been presented by the American media as a kind country manor accessible only to the Soviet elite, a status symbol. In reality, a dacha can be anything from a mansion to one room in a village cabin without running water, gas, or heating. The place I was offered was an attic in Nikolina Gora, a settlement twenty-five miles from Moscow where the artistic and scientific elite own beautiful country homes. Most of the dachas there were built before, or immediately after, the war. Since then, prices have skyrocketed and only the superwealthy can afford even a small home there. Having a dacha in Nikolina Gora is like owning property in Southhampton. It is a statement about your station in life. Those who cannot afford to buy a place but aspire to breathe the same air as the celebrities are ready to rent a room, porch, and kitchen at outrageous prices from local residents, who move into crude abodes for the summer season and try to cram as many Muscovites into their regular homes as possible.

The place I was offered was an attic—just a room and a bed, not a facility I would have considered paying for, but this was a gift horse. It was there that I met Valentina.

She was twenty-one, a brilliant senior in Moscow University's Department of Classical Languages. We hit it off immediately, finding we had similar tastes and much to talk about. We spent day after day together playing tennis, rowing up and down the Moskva River, taking long walks through the woods and fields. In September, we returned to Moscow for our fifth and last year of university studies. We continued to see each other every day. We were married in March 1958. We were divorced ten years later. The reasons? I could probably tick off a whole list. Each would make sense. I refrain from doing that for one reason only: sense has nothing to do with why people get married and even less with why they separate. As Tolstoy put it, "All happy families resemble one another; every unhappy family is unhappy in its own fashion."

More than twenty years later, I remember to the last detail our final evening together. We had been invited to a private showing of Stanley Kramer's *Ship of Fools*. We returned home and, as was the family ritual, sat down in the kitchen for a cup of tea. We shared our impressions of the movie, which I still consider to be one of the best I have ever seen (Kramer, in my opinion, is one of Hollywood's most socially committed and, because of that, least appreciated directors). At one point, I said, "You know, the real message in *Ship of Fools* is that we all lie. Not only to each other, which is bad enough, but to ourselves. We think we can fool life by refusing to admit the truth. Ultimately, that destroys us." Valentina looked deeply into my eyes. "Yes," she said, "you are absolutely right." And I suddenly realized that her response to my general observation was concrete and final and related to the two of us.

I remember my feeling of despair, of my world falling apart. The pain was terrible; life didn't seem worth living anymore. Had I been capable of analyzing my reaction, I would have understood what I came to recognize much later: what hurt most of all was that this was happening to *me*. It was a blow to my ego, to my certainty that, while such things happened to other people, I was immune because I was somehow special.

Don't most of us feel that way about ourselves deep down in our hearts? Haven't we all reacted with outrage and pain when life has proven us to be wrong? Have we not employed our energy and intelligence to lay the blame for what befalls us at any doorstep but our own? But, by the same token, are we not prone to ascribe all of our successes to our special personalities? Humility is not a quality we are born with. We are poor students of that science; rarely does even an entire lifetime suffice to fully master it. The one exception I have ever encountered is Mother Teresa.

Marrying Valentina meant giving up returning to America, and no matter how sound my reasoning may have been, it could not make the homesickness go away. The only compensation I found was in palling around with as many Americans as possible—and in those days, the opportunities were few and far between. Thus I found myself drawn to the American correspondents based in Moscow, people I could legitimately meet with because of my work. They were, in many ways, strange relationships. Since their contacts with Soviets were limited (with the exception of the dissident and, later, refusenik community), they could not be choosy. I wasn't much of a catch, but I was better than nothing. At the same time, they knew by experience that any establishment figure, no matter how minor, would not frequent foreigners unless he was authorized to do so. And the only authority in that respect was the KGB. Understandably, they were wary of me. Had I had the intelligence to realize this, I probably would have stopped seeing most of them without regrets and certainly would never have shared with any of them my inner turmoil. I was a fool and have no one to blame but myself. Many years later, when Nick Daniloff was interviewed by CBS's "West 57th Street" for a piece about me, he commented that I used to visit him and would "cry in my beer"—a remark that is par for the course for Mr. Daniloff, but one I fully deserved.

My American "colleagues" pumped me for everything I was worth (not much, in those days), and I, in my vanity, was more than willing to satisfy their curiosity. That the situation got me into trouble is not surprising; what is surprising is how long it took.

One day in June of 1963, I got a phone call from the Moscow ABC bureau chief Sam Jaffe, one of the American correspondents with whom I had developed what I believed to be a friendly relationship. "Vlad," he said, "there are rumors all over the place about a Soviet woman going into space. Do you know anything about it?" I had heard the rumors but naturally had no access to concrete information, especially considering the cloak of secrecy in which the Soviet space program was shrouded in those times. "Hell, Sam," I said, "my guess is as good as yours. For all I know, she could fly next Thursday." I had said exactly what I meant, namely, that I had no idea whatsoever when the event would take place—it could be any day of any forthcoming week. But Jaffe read a special meaning into my words, understanding them to be a hint. Why he came to that conclusions, I will never know. Had I been privy to secret information, I would never have divulged it. I have difficulty believing that Jaffe could have thought otherwise.

Time and time again, reality puts the most fertile imagination to shame. On the Thursday of that week, Valentina Tereshkova blasted off from the Baikonur launching pad to become the first woman cosmonaut— and ABC News predicted the event hours before it happened. On the following day, I was summoned to the office of one of Novosty's deputy chairmen, where I was questioned for over an hour by several other gentlemen whom I had never seen before and never saw again. Where had

I gotten my information? they wanted to know. I repeated, word for word, my conversation with Jaffe. "Why did you say Thursday?" one of them asked sternly. I shrugged. "I could have said Tuesday or Sunday, I just said what first came to mind. You know I had no information!"

Of course they knew. But they also knew that one of my colleagues at Novosty, a man I often had coffee with in the snack bar, had been assigned to cover the event. He did have access to the information I had hit upon by accident. They were making sure it was just that—a coincidence, not a leak. When I finally convinced them, I said, "I'm sorry this ever happened. But tell me, how did you know I was the person who gave Jaffe his lead? Is his phone tapped?" It was such a naive question. They all stared at me, then one of them said, "Why bother to tap phones when some people blab? When ABC News refused to run his story without his furnishing his source, he named you."

I was flabbergasted. Revealing sources was supposedly one of the things no journalist ever did. I had to think they were out to poison my relationship with Sam. I called him immediately. "Sam," I asked, "why did you give my name as your source for the Tereshkova story?" His answer was a gem: "Why, Vlad, I wanted you to share the credit."

I was far less shocked and upset a few years later, when rumors began to circulate about Jaffe's having had affiliations with the CIA. I do not know whether the matter was ever resolved, but that is really irrelevant, at least in my opinion. By then I was older and wiser. I knew that there were journalists who did "extracurricular" work. Learning about life was not an easy process, or a painless one, for that matter, but it definitely helped. As they say in Russia, "One person who's had his knocks is worth two who haven't."

My contact with American journalists was a learning process in more ways than one. I had the opportunity to observe the way they worked, how they put bits and pieces of information together, searched out, even in the adverse circumstances of those times, people and events to finally come up with the story they were after. I marveled at how good they were, how professional. But the more I learned, the more I found myself in fundamental disagreement with them on the most basic issue of so-called objective journalism.

At first glance, it appears unfair on my part to criticize someone for simply wanting to report the facts. But the realities of journalism don't involve just facts, for if they did, computers would replace journalists. Journalism always involves *choices*—choices among subjects, treatment, words. As a result, the claim of objective reporting functions simply to camouflage what is in fact a value-laden activity. It is not only the readers who are misled by the claim. The journalists too can be blinded by their own cover.

A telling illustration of this phenomenon can be seen in nearly the entire postwar period of American reporting on the Soviet Union. Polls have consistently confirmed what was obvious: Americans have rather negative views of their Soviet counterparts. Soviets are believed to be less happy, less family oriented, less patriotic, less satisfied with their work, less prone to enjoying a good laugh. Not because they were born that way, but because of the system they live in. I am reminded of a television talk show I participated in in New York City with a woman who had recently returned from Moscow. "The people in your city don't smile. I sensed how oppressed they were. I had the most terrible experience in my hotel one day. When I said hello to a Russian woman in the elevator, she just stared at me like she was afraid to answer." "Ma'am," I answered, "I invite you to join me when this show is over and go down into the streets of this great city. Let's count how many people we see walking around with big smiles on their faces." The audience broke out into laughter and applause—they immediately got my point. If Soviets don't smile in Moscow, that's because they are oppressed. But if they don't smile in New York, that's because . . . ? "As for the lady in the elevator," I pursued, "in most countries, mine included, one does not say hello to strangers. To do so is interpreted as either your being not quite normal or trying to make a pick up. Take your choice." Again I got a round of applause.

Americans were not born with such perceptions. They were taught them by objective reporting.

Ironically enough, American journalists acknowledge the depth of the misconceptions their fellow countrymen have about the Soviet Union but refuse to acknowledge the connection between their own work (the cause) and the distorted perceptions (the result). David Shipler, former *New York Times* bureau chief in Moscow, related in an article how he toured U.S. college campuses in the mid-eighties and was astounded and troubled by the false, negative Soviet stereotypes he encountered. It didn't seem to occur to him that his own writing had contributed to the problem!

In all of my conversations with Moscow-based U.S. correspondents, I have never heard any of them say, "I don't like this country and I'm going to make sure my readers feel the same way." I am sure many did not like the Soviet Union (sometimes for good reason). But I am willing to wager that few, if any, ever admitted to themselves, let alone to anyone else, that they were slanting their work to reflect their bias. Most, I think, actually believed their own I-simply-report-the-facts line—even while they selected only facts that fit their views.

Of course, sometimes they were not above doing a little deliberate distortion.

I recall an article on the subject of inflation in the Soviet Union written for *U.S. News and World Report.* The topic was inspired by the high rate of inflation in the United States (this kind of thinking has been typical for both U.S. and Soviet media and is based on the view that if we show that they have the same problem as we do, somehow that makes ours less of a problem). In this particular case, the story featured a price index for a number of goods and services pertaining to two different years—I don't remember which two periods were compared (which is irrelevant anyway), but let's say it was 1978 and 1980. All prices were given in U.S. dollars and cents. Thus, the metro fare for 1978 was indicated as five cents. For 1980 it was six cents—an increase of twenty percent. That same increase, or even more, was apparent for all the other items as well—a loaf of bread, a pound of butter, a car, and so on. At face value, inflation in the Soviet Union was a walloping 10 percent annually. What the reader didn't realize was that Soviet citizens didn't pay for goods or services in dollars and cents; that they paid in roubles and kopecks; that in *Soviet currency,* metro fare, the price of a pound of butter, of meat, etc., was exactly the same in 1980 as in 1978. What had changed was *the official exchange rate of the dollar vis à vis the rouble.* The dollar had gone down. Hence it was worth less in 1980, in Soviet currency, than in 1978. Objective reporting.

For decades, Americans didn't get any positive stories from their reporters in the Soviet Union. I have met only one U.S. correspondent, whose name I will omit (I don't reveal my sources), who had the honesty to admit, albeit in a very private conversation, "Sure, I know there are positive things to write about. But I know what the editor wants. Look, we are judged by how often we get on television or on page one. And we know what it takes to make that happen. The dissident story, the refusenik story, alcoholism, drugs, corruption. We get good vibes or bad vibes, and we act accordingly. And so do you."

He was absolutely on target. But I must say that I have met only one Soviet reporter who, after filing story after story about the downside of life in the United States—unemployment, the homeless, crime, police violence, poverty, discrimination, drug abuse—claimed with a straight face that he was "simply reporting the facts." All the other colleagues with whom I ever discussed this at least had the courage to say they were doing what was expected of them.

That is what Americans scornfully call toeing the party line. But, one might ask, have they not been guilty of the same crime? Would it be an exaggeration to propose that the American media have, by and large, toed the government line in foreign policy, especially in relation to "communist" countries? (I put that word in quotes because it is a staggering misnomer, seeing as there is not a single communist country in the world—a subject I will return to.) The classic case is China.

For nearly a quarter of a century, Red China was portrayed by the U.S. media as the land of the crazies, the human ant people, a nation bent on domination of all Asia. That image was a mirror reflection of U.S. foreign policy, which refused to recognize the government of Mao Zedong and prevented its entry into the United Nations. To Secretary of State Dean Rusk, the underlying goal of American intervention in Vietnam was to prevent Chinese expansion.

Then Richard Nixon and Henry Kissinger decided to capitalize on the Sino-Soviet rift in hopes of using China as a strategic card in the U.S.-Soviet power game. Nixon went to China, met with Mao and Zhou, slugged down a couple on the Great Wall, said nice things about the Chinese people and Chinese culture. Virtually overnight, the American people began receiving a very different picture of China. So different, in fact, that one might have thought it pertained to a different country. The Chinese were courteous, industrious, family oriented, modest to the point of being shy. They had the most wonderful and ancient cultural tradition, as demonstrated by such sophisticated games as mah-jongg. They were wizards at ping-pong. And, ladies and gentlemen of the jury, they *loved* giant pandas (when was the last time you heard that Russians loved *any* animal?). In less than a year, American public opinion turned completely around. Everyone loved the so-recently hated and feared Chinese.

It took the June 1989 massacre in Beijing before the U.S. media finally grappled with the issue of human rights in China. But what was the situation like in the seventeen long years between 1972 and that event? Were there no limitations on dissent? Weren't dissidents incarcerated, physically exterminated? Were there no political prisoners in China? Of course there were, far more than in the Soviet Union. But one would have a real problem coming to that conclusion on the basis of what the U.S.

media had to say. Again, the media followed the government lead—which is a more acceptable way of saying they toed the party line.

This is not to say that we have done a better job. On the contrary, the Soviet media has followed the government lead even more closely. Even in these times of glasnost and perestroika, the breaks with that dispiriting tradition have been few and slow to come. In the past three years, they have been most apparent in the opening up of the media (both print and electronic) to uncensored statements by western spokesmen. Such officials as the commander-in-chief of NATO, West Germany's minister of defense, the U.S. secretary of state, the speaker of the House, the chairman of the Joint Chiefs of Staff, leading columnists, Congresspeople, and the likes have been given space in Soviet newspapers and magazines and time on Soviet television. Often this has been accompanied by a catch of sorts in the form of a follow-up commentary or editorial furnishing the Soviet view (much as the way my appearances and those of other Soviets are usually rebutted in the United States).

Beyond giving uncensored exposure to the western point of view (a major breakthrough for the Soviet media), things have gradually moved to the point when Soviet foreign policy, through virtually all our history an anointed sacred cow, is gradually becoming an acceptable subject for public debate. Afghanistan and the deployment of the SS-20 missile, Czechoslovakia in '68 and Hungary in '56—these are some of the major areas of foreign policy that have been discussed, pro and con, in the Soviet media. But one is quick to note that these are all, so to speak, in the past tense. They cannot be attributed to the present leadership.

There are, in my opinion, two major obstacles to achieving the same level of dialogue, openness, and difference of opinion on foreign-policy issues as we now have regarding domestic policy.

The first has to do with the unwritten rule that has always forbidden explicit criticism of the top leadership. If erroneous domestic-policy decisions could belatedly be blamed on this or that ministry or minister, foreign policy was always the prerogative of the inner sanctum, the Politburo, the general secretary—who, like Ceasar's wife, was beyond suspicion. Even though editors and journalists have been briefed by top party and government officials and called upon to speak their minds, they have been reluctant to do so. I was present at one such briefing during which we journalists were repeatedly reminded that we were not government officials or spokesmen. "Tell us what you think about all issues, including those of foreign policy," we were told. As we were leaving the premises after the briefing, I overheard the following exchange between an *Izvestia* columnist and his editor: "I'll give you a story tomorrow," said the columnist, "that will knock you out of your socks." "Go right ahead," countered the editor, "I won't print it." The editor was a wise old fox. He knew the ropes, he remembered what had happened to the gullible in the past. The future? Let someone else take the risk.

The second obstacle is what I call the boomerang effect. For years and years, anything and everything published in the press or stated on television pertaining to Soviet foreign policy was official. While this was never openly admitted by the Soviet government, neither was it ever denied. Whenever a foreign country encountered anything it considered particularly revolting or distasteful in the Soviet media (which was often enough), it interpreted it as being the official view and lodged a protest with the Soviet government. After all, was not the Soviet press government controlled? This view gradually became "standard knowledge." It applied not only to the media but to all Soviets—whatever they said was official policy (the one exception being dissidents). I recall being invited to address the American Enterprise Institute (one of the most conservative U.S. think tanks) in 1986 and creating a mild furor when I criticized Soviet emigration policy and the jamming of foreign shortwave radio broadcasts. My audience could simply not believe that I was expressing a personal opinion. Soviets, by definition, could not do that. So for those gentlemen I was very much like the giraffe whose existence the New Hampshire farmer refused to accept. When the farmer was taken to a zoo and shown a live specimen, he took a long look and said with finality, "There ain't no sich animal!"

Today, the Soviet media is a very different animal indeed. What appears in the press or on television may at times be government inspired (as in all countries, the United States included) but, by and large, it is no longer the official view. However, that rapid and radical change has not been matched by a similar change in the mindsets of foreign governments—West and East. When I produced a highly critical television documentary on the inside story of the Soviet-German relationship in 1939–1940, the German Democratic Republic lodged a protest with the Soviet ambassador in Berlin. That was a typical reaction. And because of such reactions, the Soviet Ministry of Foreign Affairs, while encouraging journalists to speak their minds, has actually been reluctant to have them do so, fearing that this might lead to complications with our allies. The most recent example that comes to mind is Soviet coverage of the student uprising in Beijing. In that coverage, Soviet television has been, at best, noncommittal. The Soviet TV correspondent in the Chinese capital repeated the government statement that "not a single person was killed in Tiananmen Square."

In short, we once convinced the world that Soviet journalists who wrote on affairs of international policy were nothing more than mouthpieces. We convinced everyone so well that now, when things have changed, we have become our own victims—the boomerang effect. Foreign governments either do not believe those changes to be true or choose not to believe them when that suits their purpose.

There is, I must add, yet another obstacle along the way to what, for lack of a better word, I would call decent coverage of foreign policy. The obstacle is shared by both Soviet and American journalists and by journalists in general. It has to do with journalists suffering from the same personal sense of nationalism and national competition as do their governments and other members of their societies. The power of those sentiments must not be underestimated. In almost any country, people are far more tolerant of internal criticism than of dissent over foreign policy. To criticize one's country in relation to another, to go so far as to admit that, on a given issue, another country is right and yours is wrong, smacks to many of disloyalty. The American phrase "Our disagreements end at the water's edge" illustrates my point just as well as the Russian "Why strip in the cold?"

Taking their cue from their respective governments, the mass media in the U.S. and the Soviet Union stood for decades in confrontation. Now, with the change in governmental relations, we begin to see a change in media treatment of the other side. To me, one of the most important questions is whether the media will demonstrate the motivation, the resolve, the kind of new thinking that goes far beyond the "you pat my back, I'll pat yours" attitude and bespeaks a real sense of responsibility. Bespeaks the understanding that we are not "just" Soviets or "just" Americans, but that, as journalists, we are citizens of the world who can and do, whether we admit it or not, influence and shape public opinion. Will the media and journalists rise to the challenge and break out of their narrow national egoism?

For that to happen, some sacred cows will have to be put out to pasture, one being the concept of value-free reporting. Naturally, I accept the premise that we journalists have the obligation to communicate facts and opinions that contradict our personal beliefs and values. We are duty-bound to be impartial and report the picture we see, not the one we would like to see. But I do not and cannot accept the premise that we must be neutral. More precisely, that we must pretend to be neutral, for in reality we always are partial, we always have sympathies and antipathies, and ninety-nine times out of a hundred, the reader/listener/viewer knows whose side we are on.

Besides, doesn't the journalist have the moral obligation to society to communicate his or her point of view—or absence of any, for that matter? The journalist who pretends to be neutral reminds me of the young man who was sunbathing in the nude on a riverbank. Looking about, he suddenly saw a very attractive young lady approaching. Not having the time to put on his pants, he looked desperately around and saw an old rusty pot lying nearby. He grabbed it by the handle and covered his private parts with it. The young lady was now quite near. She walked up to the young man, smiled, and said, "I bet I know what you are thinking." "W-what?" stammered the young man. "You think that pot has a bottom." Our "concealed" bias sticks out in the same way.

The obligation to report the facts honestly and express views openly poses some serious questions for all journalists, but for none are they more serious than for a Soviet journalist who happens to be a member of the Communist party. As a party member, I accept Lenin's view that after an issue has been democratically debated within the Party and a decision reached, party members have the duty to work in good faith to carry it out. But as a professional journalist, I also feel that I, and I alone, must make the final decision about my approach to a story. My personal morality must be the ultimate arbiter. The potential for conflict in these two views is clear—but when I was starting out in journalism, it wasn't apparent to me. Then, when the problem established a presence I couldn't ignore, I relegated it to the back of my mind, I tried not to think about it. I pretended it did not exist and thus lied to myself (*Ship of Fools* all over again). The pine tree to telegraph pole story is just one example of how I sidestepped the issue early on.

When the limits imposed by *Soviet Life* began to get to me, fate threw me a lifesaver in the form of *Sputnik,* a monthly digest of the Soviet press for international distribution, a kind of Red *Reader's Digest* (as differing from the red, white and blue original).

Sputnik was born in 1967, but it was conceived several years earlier during a period when Khrushchev was gone but the Thaw was still there. Very few people realized they were basking in an autumn sun that would soon sink under the horizon to be replaced by a long chill. Launched by

Novosty Press, this magazine immediately caught people's eyes. It was the first digest in Soviet history. It took the best the Soviet press had to offer, cut away the fat, wrung out the water, and presented a highly readable cross section of articles on a vast array of topics. Printed in Finland, it seduced readers with its bright colors, fancy artwork, and sophisticated layout. In a matter of two years, *Sputnik* became the first-ever Soviet publication to actually sell in the West. Rights for its publication and circulation were bought by publishers in Great Britain, West Germany, France, and Spain. Japan was next in line. By the end of 1969, *Sputnik* was actually selling over one million copies abroad!

Its popularity soared in the socialist countries of Eastern Europe as well, where it sold at newsstands in the Russian-language edition and was gobbled up faster than you could say *da*. Or *nyet*, for that matter. In Moscow, black-market copies of *Sputnik* sold for as much as five roubles each; Central Committee officials and lesser bureaucrats demanded, asked, and pleaded for their monthly copies.

Novosty's chairman, Boris Burkov, saw *Sputnik* as his claim to fame—provided that he could get it distributed in the Soviet Union. There he had a real problem. Novosty's publications, much like those of the U.S. Information Agency in America, could not as a rule appear on the Soviet market. Besides, the vast majority of magazine editors were dead set against *Sputnik*'s being allowed to appear because, as they correctly feared, it would capture the market. There was no way Soviet weeklies or monthlies could compete with *Sputnik*—first, because it looked so much better, second, because it actually was so much better. But there was another, much more dramatic reason.

Traditionally, the media had always been controlled by the Propaganda Department of the Central Committee. Khrushchev changed that—in part. Propaganda for internal consumption was separated from propaganda for external consumption. The latter became the responsibility of the new Department of International Information. The creation of this new entity, charged with the same functions (supervising propaganda) as its far more traditional and more powerful counterpart, could not but lead to a life-and-death battle between the two. Looking back from today's vantage point, one realizes that the outcome of that struggle was predetermined. With the Soviet Union's high priest of ideology on its side in the person of Mikhail Suslov, a man who came to personify the Brezhnev years even more than Brezhnev, the Propaganda Department could not lose.

Burkov was a wily man. He had been in the intrigue business for years; he was also a bit of a gambler. One of his initial strategies was to have the sons and daughters of top Soviet leadership working for Novosty. There was a period when one of Khrushchev's daughters and Brezhnev's daughter were working for Novosty at the same time! Carefully playing his cards, Burkov used those whom he privately called "my zoo" to get to their fathers—in particular, to Brezhnev. Soon all of Moscow was talking about Burkov's regularly having tea with Leonid Ilyich. And that, I think, is when Burkov lost control, when he figured he was home free. From that point on, instead of going through the proper channels, he would apply directly to Brezhnev for whatever he wanted. He made a point of rubbing the Propaganda Department's nose in the dirt—and they did not forgive him. They bided their time, waiting for the opportunity to present itself. And it did—in the most unpredictable manner.

The layout for *Sputnik* was always done in Moscow. Since this was a commercial publication for western consumption, it allowed ads, and a certain number of pages were left open for that purpose. The only limits, insisted upon by the Soviet side, was that ads could not be anti-Soviet or pornographic. Lenin's one-hundredth anniversary was marked in 1970 and, not surprisingly, it was the *Sputnik* cover story for the April issue (Lenin was born on April 22). The West German art director changed the layout slightly to fit in an extra ad that was to occupy the page opposite the one that opened the Lenin story. The ad showed a young man standing nude behind a fence, one of the bars of which had conveniently slipped to a forty-five-degree angle, thus hiding the gentleman's private parts. It was a deodorant ad. The German editor saw nothing wrong with it. He couldn't possibly have guessed how the Propaganda Department would use it.

The anti-*Sputnik* campaign that was launched concentrated on just one point: ideology and money do not mix. Ideology is pure, money is crass. Any attempt to sell ideology must invariably lead to a compromise on principles. Now that truth had been demonstrated once again. To put Lenin, the leader of the world proletariat, to put this unique human being opposite a pornographic piece of capitalist advertising—was that not the most damning testimony, did that not unequivocally show to what level of decadence *Sputnik* had sunk? A special meeting of the Moscow City Party Organization was called. Its participants outdid each other in branding *Sputnik* everything from a "bourgeois rag" to an "ideological two-faced Janus." Naturally, everyone took pot shots at the magazine's editor, but what most people did not realize was that he and the management of

Sputnik were small fry. The real game plan was to bring down Burkov. And it worked.

Burkov was dismissed, and the organization he had founded and headed for just under ten years, an organization that even by western standards, had been vibrant and efficient, soon became a swamp of stagnation. Chairman after chairman followed Burkov. Most were completely indifferent to Novosty's fate; all they cared about was not rocking the boat. In more recent times, some have attempted to revive the organization. But it will take much more than mouth-to-mouth resuscitation to breathe real life into what was transformed into a zombie.

Naturally, *Sputnik* suffered too. The editor was drummed out of journalism. Several people were fired. All contracts with western publishers were canceled. Sales plummeted. Soon the magazine found itself back at square one—having its entire Russian, English, French, German, and Spanish circulation printed in Finland and footing the bill for that, as well. Novosty also had no choice but to be *Sputnik*'s distributor, a function it never performed well at all. Thus *Sputnik* too became a kind of zombie. It continued to appear, but in reality it was dead.

I left the magazine in February 1970, just two months before the deodorant ad appeared in the West German edition. Again, my guardian angel saved me. There is not the slightest doubt that I would have been drawn and quartered in public as the living proof of western infiltration, the seditious element that had led to *Sputnik*'s downfall.

However, it wasn't intuition, not some inner voice that prompted me to hand in my resignation. There were three reasons. The first related to my wanting to do more writing and to be responsible only for myself. Managing editor was an exciting job, and it certainly taught me all there was to learn about putting a publication together, but it left no time for writing. The second reason was the gradual strangulation of the press. As I said, *Sputnik* had been conceived in the Thaw but born after the cold had set in. By 1969, almost nothing was left of the Khrushchev legacy. All pine trees were routinely transformed into telegraph poles, and journalists found themselves wearing mental straitjackets. I had joined *Sputnik* because it promised something new, something different. I left it because the promise did not come true.

The third reason had to do with love.

I had just begun to work for *Sputnik* when my marriage to Valentina broke up. I felt miserable and badly needed someone to talk to. As fate would have it, there was another person working for *Sputnik* whose life, like my own, was falling apart and who needed a listener as much as I did. Her name was Kathrin.

Once, while still working for *Soviet Life,* I had walked out of my office to stretch my legs. As I stood by the door, I saw a woman walking down the hall in my direction. She was accompanied by several other people, but that was all I registered. I couldn't even tell you whether they were men or women. But today, over twenty years later, I can describe in detail that woman—her hair a glossy, glimmering mane of honey-colored curls; her eyes deep set and cornflower blue; her mouth perfectly etched, generous and sensual. I recall her dress—a tight, chic job with long sleeves buttoned at the wrists, a blotchy mixture of greens, browns, and blues that set off her hair wonderfully and matched her green and brown suede pumps. I must have gaped because, as she swept by like some empress with her retinue, I heard giggles.

Her image stayed with me, it lurked just below the surface of my sorrows. Then, on one of my first days at *Sputnik,* I saw her again. Much to my surprise and delight, I discovered that she worked there.

Many things drew us together. When our being together became obvious (we made hardly any effort to keep it a secret), it also became obvious that one of us would have to leave *Sputnik.* As managing editor, I had to OK everything that went into the magazine, including pieces edited by Kathrin. There was a serious issue of ethics involved.

Those were the three main reasons for my leaving *Sputnik,* a decision I found all the more easy to make because I had been made an attractive offer. During my last year with *Sputnik,* I had done some writing for the North American Service of Radio Moscow, the Soviet equivalent of the Voice of America's Russian-language Service. As the result, the editor had invited me to join the staff as a commentator. All I was expected to do, he said, was to write—as much and as often as I wanted, but specifically on domestic topics. I would write in English, read my own copy on the air, be responsible only to myself. I couldn't have asked for more. Novosty and the Radio Committee, as it was then called, had a gentleman's agreement not to steal each other's people, so I handed in my resignation, stating I had decided to become a freelancer. By the time Novosty found out I had gone over to radio, it was too late to interfere—although some people tried. I remember the head of the North American Service inviting me into his office and telling me that my "friends" in the Novosty personnel department had called to warn him how "dangerous," "disloyal," "untrustworthy," and "pro-western" I was. This happened after the crackdown on *Sputnik,* and for some people, the idea that I had escaped, that my head was still planted solidly on my neck, was unbearable.

The North American Service of Radio Moscow was a strange place. It consisted of four divisions: management, writers, translators, and news readers (announcers). The first two were comprised of "real" Soviets, people who were born, grew up, and were educated in the Soviet Union. To them, English was a foreign language. Some knew it extremely well, others very poorly, but very few of the writers ever wrote their copy in English, so the management people (deputy department and department heads, deputy editor in chief and editor) usually signed the Russian original (without that signature no story could be broadcast), which then went to division three for translation and then on to division four, the news readers. There was a smattering of "real" Soviets in these last two, but most of them were regarded as not really being kosher; these were people whose parents had emigrated from Russia before or soon after the revolution and who had returned in the thirties with their children to build socialism. Because of their background, these children had, with some rare exceptions, never completely mastered the Russian language; most of them had left the United States at an early age, had not acquired even a high school, let alone university, education. Hence, their English, while certainly better than that of the "real" Soviets, left much to be desired.

I found myself in a strange situation. I was absolutely fluent and had no accent in Russian; I was a commentator. Thus, I qualified as a member of division two. But I was just as fluent and accentless in English; what's more, I read my own copy on the air, which put me in division four. Traditionally, "real" Soviets looked down on the "immigrants" for their being apolitical. The "immigrants" looked down on the "real" Soviets for their not having a thorough knowledge of the country they wrote for or its language. This gave me certain advantages, but it also created a bit of hostility—as envy always does.

The "immigrants" begrudged me my establishment status as a writer, thereby pushing me into the "real" Soviets camp, who, in turn refused to fully accept me as "real" for all the reasons I have enumerated. Naturally, there were exceptions to this rule.

Writing for the North American Service turned out to be an amazingly instructive and satisfying experience, especially after the editor in chief called me in one day to propose something that would lift my journalistic career into a new orbit.

G.S., as I shall call him, was and remains one of the most interesting, gifted, and complex personalities I have ever encountered. He was fifty or thereabouts when we met, but he looked older. It would have been impossible to recognize him as the strikingly handsome young man in the photo of himself as a university student that he once showed me. The only things that remained were the sardonic expression, the mocking laugh in the greenish eyes, the slightly crooked smile. G.S. had a brilliant and unpredictable mind and an insatiable appetite for reading. I pride myself on being well-read, but he beat me hands down. I can only compare him to a human sponge: he absorbed everything he ever read and never forgot anything.

G.S. could charm a bird off a tree with his combination of wit, gracefulness, and devilish humor. He could also be totally repulsive. He was incredibly adept at reading others and ascertaining the chinks in their armor. He loved to see people squirm and somehow reminded me of a slightly mad entomologist who, having impaled a caterpillar on his needle, watches it desperately writhe in pain. G.S. was a profoundly cynical man, and I think he regarded any other outlook, any positive concept, as a challenge, as something to destroy.

He was quick to pick me out for what was indeed a unique offer. Would I like to do a daily three-minute talk, seven days a week? While this might not seem seismic to American readers, they must keep in mind at least two important considerations. The first relates to the past traditional policy of Soviet television and radio to play down personalities. The main figure on both television and radio was the news reader/announcer, a person who, by definition, could have no opinion. The public might prefer one announcer to another, but they had absolutely no reason to respect him or her for advocating a certain point of view. Journalists were regarded as pipelines, conduits for the official view. The less individuality they had, the better. I recall Sergei Lapin, chairman of Gosteleradio for many years, saying to an overly ambitious young reporter, "Who gives a shit what *you* think? Who are *you* to think, in the first place?" The idea was to keep the journalist in his place.

The second consideration was financial. Soviet journalists were (and, in the main, still are) paid according to one of the most bizarre systems I have ever encountered. They get a minimum wage, the size of which depends on their journalistic rank (junior editor, editor, senior editor, reporter, commentator, whatever). In addition, they get paid for everything they write. However, most are not allowed to earn more than 100 percent of their wage through writing. For instance, if one's wage is two hundred roubles a month, that person may earn a maximum of another two hundred roubles by writing. This is called his ceiling. For some the ceiling is 50 percent, for some it is 75, and only the very top journalists have no ceiling at all—for them the sky's the limit. But in addition to this ceiling, there is another esoteric practice, the so-called ratio.

One of the points Lenin made when he wrote about the function of the press (which was often) concerned the role of what he called worker-correspondents, ordinary folk who, though not professional journalists, regularly contributed to what appeared in newspapers. Lenin felt they would be more honest and would regard their activity as less of an ego trip than the journalist whose profession, let's not forget, has been and still often is referred to as the world's second oldest. This is not the place to debate Lenin on that subject, although I tend to think he may not have been completely wrong. But, as has almost unfailingly been the case, his suggestion was distorted to the point of becoming a parody of itself. A ratio was imposed on newspapers and magazines, on radio, and, when it appeared, on television: no less than 60 percent of all articles had to be written by authors who were not employed by the given publication or station. In certain cases, it was as high as 70 percent. Thus, if a journalist wrote four stories for his paper in a given month, he was forced to furnish another six written by outsiders. Only then would he be paid for his own four. Far from opening the newspaper columns and the airwaves to ordinary citizens, the sixty-forty ratio, as it has come to be called, has led to a situation where the professional journalist will accept a story that has no business being anywhere but in the wastepaper basket, do a complete rewrite on it, and thank the "author" in the process, because if he does not fulfill the ratio, his ceiling will be lowered—in some cases all the way down to the floor.

So what G.S. proposed was revolutionary: he was making me a star with my daily talk, and he was freeing me of any ceiling or ratio, for it was understood that a daily commentary precluded any other activity.

Naturally, I jumped at the offer. "Only please remember," he said, with that slightly crooked smile, "from this day on you do not have the right not to feel well, to be ill, to miss a day for any reason . . . except death."

"Vladimir Pozner's Daily Talk" went on the air on October 7, 1973. It went off the air on August 31, 1986.

Professionally, I think those thirteen years were the most important in my life. I learned to write, to express my thoughts in a way others could share. I experienced the unparalleled high of feedback: letters came to me from different parts of the United States, written by people I had never met, letters expressing gratitude, friendship, hope that someday we could all live together as human beings should, letters inviting me to break bread with their authors should I ever visit their city, letters that made my heart beat faster, that brought a lump into my throat, that gave me a sense of being needed, of doing a service. Yes, I got some hate mail, but wasn't that also a source of pride?

I was the *only* journalist in the Soviet Union, let alone the North American Service, who did a daily commentary. Bit by bit, my name began to be recognized. This could not but lead to envy. One of my colleagues called my talk "The Daily Drizzle." I laughed as hard as anyone else, never realizing the kind of hatred envy could engender. I later found out.

By and large, I delighted in what I did. I had been given carte blanche by G.S. I could write about anything I wanted—and that's exactly what I did. I chose subjects that I could write about honestly, subjects that would not lead me into confrontation with my boss or with my conscience. It was during those years, that I came to the conclusion that the journalist must be true to him or herself. It was also then that I fully faced the dilemma of being both a party member and a journalist and formulated my personal answer to it.

If I feel that the Party has taken an erroneous position, then that is what I must write. If writing that is not possible (as has been the case in the past), then I have no option but to be silent on that matter. But under no circumstances can I support what I deem to be wrong. As a member of the Party, I have a duty to inform it of my intentions. If our differences are irreconcilable, the Party is free to expel me, just as I am free to resign. But party-apparatus bureaucrats should not have the right or even the ability to intervene at a journalist's place of work by calling the editor and demanding that action be taken against that journalist—as they have done consistently in the past and continue to do today.

Working for Radio Moscow, I enjoyed a degree of freedom very few Soviet journalists had. The reason is so implausible as to sound perverse. Nevertheless, it is true. Because I wrote my commentary in English, only two people read it (the department head and the editor in chief) and OK'd it for the air. The shortwave broadcast to America began at 2 A.M. Moscow time and ended at 7 A.M. Because of that, nobody, or almost nobody, in the Soviet Union ever listened to me. Those who did were shortwave ham-radio operators, certainly not members of the bureaucracy whose job it was to keep an eye and ear open for anything subversive. In short, I and people working at the North American Service who wrote their stories in a foreign language were not monitored anywhere near as strictly as those who addressed the Soviet public. In a way, this illustrates the absurdity of the whole system: the most official source of information (the Foreign Service of Soviet television and radio) was actually far less official than almost any other Soviet source of information, simply because no one in the Soviet Union listened to it!

But that freedom by default, as I would call it, does not compare with what journalists enjoy today. Glasnost has freed us completely . . . almost. Limits still exist, even though I would call them more psychological than actual. Journalists still tend to look to party leadership to define the limits of the acceptable. A phone call from some party functionary can still kill a story. But then, as any journalist in the world will tell you (privately, at least), stories get killed all the time.

As long as the media is fulfilling its social responsibility, there will be controversial programming. Someone will have to decide what gets aired. The question is who? Management? Yes, but to whom does management answer? In the West, to parent companies and advertisers whose raison d'être is making money. If airing a controversial show is going to hurt ratings or offend a segment of the buying public, that show will not get on. That is probably the main reason why so much of American TV programming is a political and social desert, why market-controlled television fails almost completely to stimulate the kind of open political dialogue envisioned by the First Amendment. Money talks.

What about Soviet television? Traditionally, its managers answered to the party apparatus—and, as of this writing, the situation has not really changed. Strictly speaking, the chairman of the USSR State Committee for Television and Radio is a member of the government nominated to his post by the prime minister and confirmed (or rejected, as the case may be) by the Supreme Soviet. The government foots the bill for television and, as we all know, whoever pays the bill calls the tune. Some will demand that you follow that tune exactly as written, others will allow you to do some improvisation, but let's not kid ourselves: nobody allows you to play a *different* song.

Ultimately, the media should be accountable only to the public. That is possible only when and if the journalist is led by a strong sense of personal dedication to the fundamental purpose of journalism: the informing and the education of the public. But such dedication doesn't reside in a vacuum. In America, one has, on the plus side, the supportive strength of the First Amendment, examples from Tom Paine to I. F. Stone (both of whom suffered for their dedication to independent, searching journalism, to telling the truth as they saw it). One also has multiple journalistic outlets. On the minus side, there is the ever-increasing commercialization of the information media, the bottom-line pressure of circulation and ratings. Supposedly, the market assures the communication of controversial ideas and offers genuine choice. To whomever actually believes such soothing bedtime storie, I suggest they undertake the following experiment: switch on the evening news, turn your back to the set, and go click-click-click from network to network; discount the fact that you can distinguish between the *voices* of Tom Brokaw, Peter Jennings, and Dan Rather; and I defy you to tell me which of the three networks you are listening to. Not only are the news items the same, they are presented in virtually the same order and they are treated identically. The choices offered by the networks are the same as those offered by, say, *Time* magazine, *Newsweek,* and *U.S. News and World Report.* It's a choice of style, of personalities, but not of substance. That is the rule for mainstream media in the United States. Will that ever change? Can it?

Our problem in the Soviet Union is to replace party/state control of media with institutionalized diversity. If we succeed, we will provide our audience with substantive choices and, I hope, simultaneously increase journalism's accountability to the public. The structure to accomplish that has been around for a long time—in theory. The unions, at a national, republic, and local level, have their own newspapers and magazines. So do such professional organizations as the writers, filmmakers, scientists, farmers, and environmentalists. There are women's publications, youth publications, and so on and so on. Supposedly, they have reflected the interests of their constituency. In fact, they have followed the party line. This is beginning to change—and there could be no harder proof of that than the colossal increase in the circulation of virtually all newspapers and magazines that have, indeed, come to reflect the interests of their readers. But while this is true, it is no less true that we have no legal guarantees of our political independence.

As a television journalist, I have nothing in principle against government finance/control—provided that there is no government monopoly. In other words, besides government-controlled television, there must exist another network. Ideally (but also realistically), it should be controlled by the people. Technically, this is easily accomplished: send a coded signal via satellite that can be received by any TV set in the country but that requires a decoder to be enjoyed; rent the decoder for a modest sum (say, fifty roubles) on an annual basis. If people like your programming, they will come back the next year. If not, you're out of business. This is certainly no foolproof guarantee of high-quality, honest television. The desire to attract the viewer can very well lead to exactly the same kind of product one often finds on commercial television. There must be a very fine balance between the audience calling the tune and a *responsible* management making *responsible* decisions. Like it or not, this brings up the question about who makes the decisions. While there is no ideal answer, I believe it is possible to achieve a meaningful relationship between the viewer and the television management and journalists he or she supports.

I'm not Pollyannaish about the prospects of success, but it's clear to me that the Soviet media is moving away from its traditional source of control and toward public accountability. Major issues are being looked at for their systematic implications, a seminal change and one that is profoundly different from the U.S. media.

For example, ethnic violence in different areas of the Soviet Union was initially reported as straight news in the Soviet press. But today, the Soviet media pursue the much deeper question about *why* these things are happening, what their sources are. Without examining these questions, the problem cannot be dealt with effectively. The reality of the ethnic tensions has led to an ongoing public debate as to why these problems were covered up in the past, and what we as a multi-ethnic society must do to face the issue. What should our policy be formed in terms of language, school, curriculum, political representation? Such discussion doesn't guarantee action, to be sure, but without it, how can one seriously hope for broad-based understanding of the issue and participation in the decision-making process?

In the States, the press tends to define its role as communicating news, not as being a social catalyst. Yesterday's news is just that. So a racially tense mayoral election is soon forgotten, although the conditions that spawned it remain. There is no follow-up, no sustained, press-generated pressure for dialogue and change. Every year or so, the American government issues a report on poverty. In 1988, it showed that *one-half* of black children live below the poverty line. This was reported. End of story. Where is the national, press-stimulated debate on alternative solutions to this problem? Fundamentally, what is it about the economic structure that results in such a phenomenon? What changes, if any, might eliminate it? Given America's historical commitment to equality of opportunity, does this pose basic moral questions for the society? These issues, as a rule, aren't confronted by the media. That being the case, they aren't confronted by the society as a whole.

Why is this?

Part of the answer lies in the "just the facts" definition of journalism—but that is the one-fifth of the iceberg everyone can see. The other part is a product of who owns the media. If society defines news and information as a commodity, as a product ones sells—like gas, cars, or hair spray—certain things follow. One is that businesses act in their own interests, and stimulating broad public dialogue on social issues will not find support in corporate boardrooms precisely because such a dialogue might lead to conclusions they define as being against their interests. Contrary to what most Americans say (and believe), the U.S. mass media does not reflect a free marketplace of ideas but rather a marketplace for free-market ideas. Even more contrary to what most Americans are certain of is that they rank among the least, not most, informed of all nations.

The American establishment has succeeded in convincing most Americans that since they have access to whatever source of information they might wish to quench their thirst from, they indeed *are* the best-informed people on earth. The net result of that supreme propaganda con game is that most Americans simply *are not thirsty.* They are perfectly happy to survive on a diet of soda pop supplied by mainstream media.

A large number of Soviets, on the other hand, who realized early on that they were poorly informed and who indeed had no access to alternative sources of information, made it their business to tune in to foreign shortwave radio broadcasts, to look for information wherever it was available. As a result, they are today, by and large, a far better informed public than their American counterparts.

When I look at the mass media, East and West, I find myself asking more questions than I have answers to. For instance, can the media in a one-party state be structured to create genuine political independence and diversity of opinion? For the past four years, the trend has been both positive and dramatic. Some claim that it has become irreversible. I do not agree. To begin with, in my opinion, nothing is irreversible except time. Even the most democratic government bolstered by the finest system of checks and balances, does not make democratic rule irreversible: a fascist could be elected democratically to power. But in the Soviet Union, where central authority has existed for centuries and centuries along with the psychology that supports it, democracy is still in its infancy; the newly opened windows and doors can still be closed without too much fuss.

In the West, particularly in the United States, diversity is being undermined by the dynamics of corporate economics, which includes both mergers and the rapid development of a consumerist society oriented toward instant gratification. It is almost as though while the Soviet media is painfully learning the complexities of being responsible to the citizenry, the U.S. media is hell-bent on unlearning those same lessons. Information is regarded as a commodity. It has to be sexy, gift-wrapped, flashy, it has to *sell*—even if it really doesn't serve to inform at all. The concept of journalism as a vital watchdog, a politically diverse and critical social catalyst, the basis of an informed citizenry is very much part of the American outlook, but today it seems much more theoretical than a part of daily practice—at least to me.

Media coverage of the 1988 presidential elections was farcical. The once proud watchdog of politics was reduced to accepting spoon-fed sound bites. None of the major issues facing America received national airing. If the press is incapable of encouraging a meaningful presidential campaign, what does that say about its ability to stimulate sustained public dialogue on issues of substance?

In Lord Acton's adage concerning power's tending to corrupt and absolute power's tending to corrupt absolutely, one might substitute the word *wealth* for *power*. The Soviet media has been corrupt and absolutely corrupt because of the Party's power, which gradually became absolute. Today there seems to be an indication that this is changing. Power is gradually being assumed by those who were supposed to have it in the first place: the people elected to office by their constituencies. There is hope that the media will no longer serve the interests of just one entity, that of party/government, but the diverse interests of many groups, organizations, associations, and, yes, parties and will be guided by a sense of responsibility toward the citizenry. I speak as someone who has an inside view of that media, which, I believe, gives me the right to make such judgments.

I cannot do the same for the U.S. media, because I am on the outside looking in. But I must express my feeling that, as I look in, I see neither telegraph poles nor pine trees. What I do see is a dense jungle that seems to have forgotten that it was originally planted to feed the people with the fruit of information. It even seems to me that it has become cannibalistic and now feeds on the people by offering them whatever it takes to make them pay.

However, as I said, I am an outsider looking in. My vision may be impaired.

6

+>-<+>-

The Dragon, the Lizards,
and the Time of the Toad

Nikita Khrushchev was ousted from office in October 1964. It came as a total surprise—not only to me, but to just about everybody. Most people didn't know what to make of it. Was it good? Or was it bad? A plausible argument could be made for either opinion.

Americans find it hard to believe and even harder to understand that Khrushchev wasn't a popular leader in his own country. The intelligentsia was, beyond a question of a doubt, his staunchest supporter. Even though he was responsible for initiating the first dissident witch-hunts, even though he coarsely and publicly attacked the country's best painters and sculptors at the Manezh exhibit, even though he insulted the entire intellectual community at a famous reception on Lenin Hills, the country's cultural elite never forgot Khrushchev's historic anti-Stalin speech at the Twentieth Party Congress. Nor did they ever forget his crucially important stance on the rehabilitation of the millions of innocent people, both living and dead, victimized by the Stalin regime. But the vast majority of those whom we commonly refer to as "the people" had a very different opinion.

Many, if not most, of them found it difficult to accept the idea of Stalin's having been a criminal. More exactly, they would have accepted the view, even applauded it, had it not meant that *they* had been mistaken in bowing and scraping to Stalin. Agreeing with Khrushchev meant sharing the responsibility for allowing Stalin to do what he did. Khrushchev was willing to acknowledge that responsibility. Most people were not. They couldn't argue with the facts Khrushchev presented, but they didn't have to like what he told them—and they didn't.

But there was another factor in this equation, a factor far more powerful and yet far less tangible than anything Khrushchev could have said or done. It was, I believe, that he was too much of a muzhik—that is, too much of a peasant. He did not have anything like the intellect or the erudition of Lenin, nor did he have the dignified bearing of Stalin. He did not stand out; he was too common. Because of that, the majority of the people had no respect for him.

There are many amazing parallels between Russians and Americans, but none more striking than their attitude toward royalty. Both countries got rid of their crowned oppressors, yet both seem to be positively infatuated with kings, queens, and royal families.

It could, I believe, also be stated that in both America and the Soviet Union intellectuals are not very popular; but in election contests with so-called common people, they usually come out on top. Is this not because those same common people don't believe one of their own is suited for the job?

Khrushchev was not dignified. When he pounded his shoe on that UN table, when he publicly invoked "Kuzkin's mother" (the rough equivalent of promising to kick some ass), he was acting like a common man, like Joe Blow. And I happen to think that this was precisely what most Soviets resented. They wanted their leader to have more class.

But there were other reasons for not liking Khrushchev, reasons shared by both the common and not-so-common people of the Soviet Union. Khrushchev's name became omnipresent, as did his pictures. Documentary films were made about him. The whores of the second-oldest profession were quick to extol his wisdom, his statesmanship—and Khrushchev was quick to believe them. On another plane, Khrushchev's love affair with corn turned into a calamity for the Soviet farmer, who found himself ordered to plant this "magical crop" regardless of whether or not the conditions were good for it.

A blustering loudmouth, an uncouth, illiterate fool, a man who had neither dignity nor poise, the laughingstock of the world who, by the same token, turned his country into something to be laughed at—thus was Khrushchev conceived of by the majority. As such, his ouster could easily be interpreted as being good.

But for all of his shortcomings, Khrushchev had a few feathers in his green fedora. He had de-Stalinized the country. He had nipped Beria's attempt to seize power in the bud. He had unleashed the great potential of his country's genius, which had burst out in the form of Sputnik, Yuri Gagarin, and the TU-104. He had demonstrated compassion for the downtrodden of the gulag, he had personally intervened to have Solzhe-nitsyn's *One Day in the Life of Ivan Denisovich* published in *Novy Mir* maga-zine. He had chased away the clouds and brought in the sun that gave us the Thaw. Might not his ouster bring the cold back?

Those were just some of the questions that were being asked and discussed in October 1964.

It is sobering to look back on those times and to recall that no one predicted Khrushchev's downfall. No one had the foresight, the under-standing to realize beyond an iota of doubt that Khrushchev had to go, that there was no way he could remain. It was either him or the apparatus. The two were incompatible, and in those days no one could destroy the apparatus, not even Stalin, the man who created it.

Stalin needed a machine of subservient men and women who had voluntarily sacrificed their right to think in exchange for a belief in some-thing called communism. Most of these people knew as much about com-munism, as a philosophy and a theory, as Christian fundamentalists know about Christianity. They *believed* in this idea and, especially, in its high priest. The party apparatus was faceless and emotionless, capable of regis-tering even the smallest blip of individuality and dissent with the sensitiv-ity of a super-radar installation.

Stalin, the evil genius, created this Frankenstein's monster. It was utterly predictable, completely under his command. The machine ran on fear, the most perfect of all energy sources, the source that fuels itself. I think Stalin, that genius of evil, realized that the only way to keep the fuel from burning out was to keep changing the machine's parts. But what he could not foresee was that even mass-produced, identical spare parts are not limitless and that a machine created to search out and destroy whatever does not fit would one day turn on its creator. Stalin most definitely did not fit. As such, the apparatus had to see him as a threat to its existence. It would have destroyed Stalin and, considering how little is known about the details of his death, it is not totally absurd to consider that as more than a theoretical possibility.

Khrushchev didn't fit, either. What's more, he didn't inspire fear. Far from being the machine's creator, he was one of the parts shaped by the machine—or rather misshaped. Thus, the apparatus rejected him and selected its own ideal creation to replace him. That creation was Leonid Ilyich Brezhnev.

Allow me to digress.

In 1943, when the Soviet Union and the Allies were locked in battle with the Axis, Yevgeny Shwarz, a Soviet playwright of brilliant talent and scintillating wit, finished one of his least appreciated and most profound plays. It is called *The Dragon*.

Like nearly all of Shwarz's plays, *The Dragon* is an allegory set in fairy-tale form.

One day, a knight by the name of Lancelot comes riding into a strange kingdom. He immediately falls in love with a fair damsel from whom he learns that the kingdom is prosperous. What's more, its citizens are prosperous and healthy. Neither their minds nor their bodies are contaminated by the microbes of dissenting thought and physical disease, for many years ago the Dragon, the kingdom's ruler, destroyed the carriers of the former (the gypsies) and purified the habitat of the latter (the lakes and rivers) with the flames of his nostrils. All is well in this kingdom . . . except for a few minor things, one being that every year the Dragon selects the most beautiful maiden to be his wife. He takes her away, and she is never seen again. But even so, gossip has it that what he does to her is despicable beyond imagination. As fate would have it, the damsel Lancelot meets and falls in love with is the Dragon's bride-to-be.

Lancelot cannot believe his ears. He asks the maiden, do you not rebel? Do you not fight? Is there no one to protect you from that monster? The answer is no. It is hopeless. The Dragon is invincible. Naturally, Lancelot challenges the Dragon to do battle, and the Dragon accepts. Just before the fight, the two meet in the town square. The following conversation is, as far as I am concerned, one that addresses the nature of totalitarianism with greater depth, insight, and understanding than all the endless "scientific" Jell-O it has been my obligation to read.

DRAGON: How's your health?

LANCELOT: It couldn't be better, thank you.

DRAGON: What's that little basin on the ground there?

LANCELOT: My weapons.

DRAGON: My subjects gave you those?

LANCELOT: They did, yes.

DRAGON: What scamps. I'll bet you're upset.

LANCELOT: Not really.

DRAGON: Liar. I have cold blood, but even I would be upset. Are you scared?

LANCELOT: No.

DRAGON: Lies, lies. My people are very scary. You won't find their likes anywhere else. They are my work. I shaped them.

LANCELOT: Still, they are human beings.

DRAGON: Externally only.

LANCELOT: No.

DRAGON: If you could see their souls—ah, how you would shudder.

LANCELOT: No.

DRAGON: You would run away. Instead of dying for a bunch of cripples. I crippled them personally, my friend. You could not ask for a better job of crippling. You know, the human soul is like a cat, it's hard to kill. Chop a body in two and you've killed it. Tear a soul in two, it'll just become more obedient. Oh no, you won't find such souls as these anywhere. Only here, in my city. Armless souls, legless souls, deaf and mute souls, beware-me souls, police-dog souls, cursed souls. Do you know why the mayor pretends to be a tormented soul? So as to hide that he has no soul at all. Empty souls, venal souls, rascally souls, dead souls. It really is too bad they are invisible.

LANCELOT: That is your luck.

DRAGON: How so?

LANCELOT: If people could see with their own eyes what has become of their souls, they would sooner die than be your slaves. Who would feed you then?

DRAGON: Who knows, you may be right. Well, shall we begin?

They fight, and Lancelot wins. In the process, though, he is grievously wounded. The rumor has it that he is dead. But the people are free . . . or are they? The Dragon is gone, only to promptly be replaced by the two men who formerly did his bidding and carried out his cruelest orders, the mayor and his son Heinrich. The Dragon was exactly that—a monster, a heartless predator, an overpowering and seemingly invicible potentate who ruled supreme for three hundred years. The Dragon was feared and respected. When he came flying into town, breathing sulphur and flames, when the day turned into night at his coming, when claps of thunder announced his presence, even his enemies couldn't deny his stature. Only a dragon could have warped the souls of an entire nation. But once that had been achieved, even a lizard could take advantage of it—and that is what the mayor and Heinrich were, lizards. Mean, conniving, treacherous, petty, cowardly, corrupt—and therefore, in a certain sense, even more dangerous than the Dragon himself.

I will never understand how Shwarz got away with writing that play. Perhaps it has something to do with when it was written (Stalin had other things on his mind in 1943) and when Shwarz died—1948, just before Stalin began to put his postwar terror machine into high gear. So at least I have a theory. But I do not have even that to explain how he was able to predict what would happen after Stalin's death: that the Dragon would be replaced by a lizard.

Certainly none of us expected that, none of those in the journalistic community. I recall being quite critical of Khrushchev, especially in his last years in office. Another pet beef among journalists concerned Khrushchev's son-in-law, Alexei Adzhubei. Because of his family connection, Adzhubei's career had been meteoric. In a matter of a few years, he had gone from reporter for *Komsomolskaya Pravda*, the national Young Communist League daily, to editor-in-chief of *Izvestia*, the second most prestigious newspaper in the Soviet Union. He combined that post with scores of others, including that of unofficial minister of foreign affairs. Adzhubei was received by the pope and by heads of state, including John Fitzgerald Kennedy. Of course, there was a lot of envy around. Under Adzhubei, *Izvestia* became a truly interesting newspaper, but the common view was, "Hell, if I were married like Adzhubei, I could do as well, if not better." While it is certainly true that Adzhubei felt far more secure to act independently as editor because of who his father-in-law was, it is no less true that he was a man of imagination and talent. To this day, journalists who worked under him look back on those years as a golden age. They praise him for being fiercely protective of and unfailingly loyal to his staff. When Khrushchev was ousted, Adzhubei immediately lost his job. *Izvestia* soon became the boring newspaper it had been before, once again prompting the old joke about there being no truth in *Pravda* (*pravda* in Russian means "truth") and no news in *Izvestia* (which in Russian means "news").

But even though Khrushchev's excesses and Adzhubei's conduct, reminiscent of that of a crown prince, brushed many people the wrong way, I distinctly recall being apprehensive after the events of October 1964. No matter what his faults, Khrushchev was an honest man who was trying to do what he sincerely believed to be right. His heart was in the right place, and I felt that. There was something about Brezhnev that worried me. It didn't take much time for those worries to be confirmed.

The year 1967 marked the fiftieth anniversary of the socialist revolution, an event that warranted a special issue of *Soviet Life*. As managing editor, I proposed that we do our special issue on the city where the revolution was born, the city founded by Peter the Great, which he christened St. Petersburg, the city of the ten days that shook the world, the city that chose to be called Leningrad in honor of the man who led the revolution. Also, it was the city where my father was born and with which I therefore had a special relationship. Through a celebration of the city we would celebrate the revolution's fiftieth birthday, but do it in a way that would not insult the reader, would not come across as a piece of propaganda. The idea was accepted.

We—a group of writers and photographers—worked on the special issue for six months. It was one of the most exciting and rewarding experiences I ever had as a journalist. In Leningrad, I met some incredible people, two of whom I have never forgotten. Both are no longer with us, and both have the right to aspire to immortality.

Maria Vladimirovna Stepanova checked visitors' handbags and attaché cases before allowing them to enter the Hermitage Museum's Gold Treasure Room. Handing your bag to her, you would hardly pause to look at this tiny, frail old woman. The fact that she would answer you in any of five languages you might speak (French, English, German, Italian, Spanish), also did not register—after all, they were usually brief answers to such questions as "Where is the bathroom?" and "May I keep my umbrella?" The visitors would have been amazed had they known to whom they were speaking.

Maria Vladimirovna was born in the family of a Russian nobleman. Her father became the youngest admiral in the Russian Imperial Navy; he was one of Czar Nicholas II's closest friends. Maria was seven years old when her father died a hero's death in the Battle of Tsushima. As a gesture of gratitude for his service to the country, Czar Nicholas took little Maria into the royal family. She spent her childhood growing up in the Winter Palace, amid the splendor of the Hermitage, the balls and concerts, the unparalleled luxury of Russia's wealthiest family.

Soon after the beginning of World War I, Maria became a nurse. Along with many other young ladies of aristocratic upbringing, she served at the front lines, personally witnessing the horrors of war: surgery conducted without anesthetics, soldiers used as cannon fodder, filth, misery, and death. The revolution of November 7, 1917, brought an end to the war. Maria returned to Petrograd, as the city had been renamed by patriots who Russianized the German original, and went to work in a hospital as a nurse. She lived in a tiny attic apartment. One evening, loud banging on the door brought her to her feet. "They have come for me," she thought, knowing well about the Red Terror that had been declared as a retaliatory response to the White Terror of the counterrevolution. "Someone has recognized me and reported me," she thought to herself, "someone who saw me in the Winter Palace." She unlocked the door and saw her worst fears confirmed. A man in a leather jacket with a Mauser pistol on his belt and flanked by two armed sailors stared grimly at her. "Maria Vladimirovna Stepanova?" he asked. She nodded. "Come with me," he ordered. "Should I take my things?" Maria faltered. "Don't bother," he answered curtly, "you won't need them." Did that mean she would be shot? Maria wondered as she followed the man in the leather jacket down the seven flights of stairs, the two sailors bringing up the rear. A car was waiting at the entrance, a rarity in those times. "Get in," she was told. She sat in the back, between the two sailors, while the man with the Mauser sat up front. It was pitch dark outside, so Maria couldn't see where they were going. Soon the car stopped. "Get out," came the command. She did—and froze. She was standing in front of Smolny Institute, once one of the city's most famous educational centers, a privileged school for the daughters of the aristocracy, but now the headquarters of the Bolsheviks. Why had she been brought here, of all places?

"Follow me," said the gruff voice, and she moved forward, past the guards at the entrance, into the building, up to the second floor, past another set of guards, down an endless corridor, and into an anteroom buzzing with activity. "Wait here," said the leather jacket as he disappeared behind a closed door. Even if she had had the desire to run, the two sailors standing silently next to her ruled that out. The door opened and the gruff voice called out, "Come in!"

Maria Vladimirovna never told me whom she met in that room, who had discovered her existence and ransacked the city for her. She was difficult to interview, stubborn about not wanting to talk about personal matters. But I am a stubborn interviewer. I push and pull and cajole and usually get what I need. But when she flatly said, "No, I will not tell you who that was because I promised never to tell anyone," I knew that was it. She did, however, tell me what the discussion was about. "We know who you are," the man had told her, "we know you are an honest person, and we are asking for your help. The Hermitage Museum is a national treasure, it must become a national shrine for the people to visit. But we have no one who knows the Hermitage and the Winter Palace as you do. So we are asking you to move into the palace, to live there, and to make sure nothing is destroyed or damaged. Or stolen."

Maria agreed. She returned to the palace she had grown up in, a palace that was now dark, empty, a palace through which the cold wind came blowing from the Neva River, making the chandeliers sway and the cut-glass pendants clink and tingle, hauntingly reminding her of the splendid nights of gala balls and masquerades, of the dashing young men in their tight-fitting uniforms and the beautiful young ladies in the low-cut dresses, a time so recent and a time so ancient, a time gone forever.

Gradually, life came back to normal. Maria continued to work and live in the Hermitage. The world outside was turbulent, a mixture of triumph and tragedy. But its sound and fury passed through the Hermitage walls as a whisper. Years passed. Then, in the dawn hours of June 22, 1941, Hitler's Wehrmacht came crashing into the Soviet Union. Before anyone realized it, the Germans were at the gates of Leningrad. Would the city fall? If so, its fate had been sealed, for Hitler had publicly declared his intention of razing the cradle of Bolshevism to the ground, wiping it off the face of the earth.

The director of the Hermitage called Maria in for a private talk. There was only one other person present—a representative of the KGB. "Maria Vladimirovna," said the director, "I am going to ask you to do something so important, so secret that I must warn you in advance: give your consent or refuse before I tell you what it is, for once you know, you will be committed."

Maria nodded.

"Leningrad may fall," the director continued. "If it does, the Germans will destroy everything and steal what they don't destroy. That is why we are evacuating the entire Hermitage collection of paintings and art. But there is something else—the Gold Treasures, the unique works of ancient Greeks, of Scythian artisans. They are priceless. I want you to supervise their packing. Then, once the crates are ready, you will see them loaded onto trucks and you will have them taken to a destination that only the three of us know. Once you get there, you will have the crates buried—those who do the job will have been told they hold secret KGB documents. Nobody will want to risk stealing those. You alone will be responsible. Those treasures will be yours until we defeat Hitler and can bring them back to our beloved city."

Maria nodded.

For four long years, she lived in a tiny village somewhere in the far north (she refused to tell me its name). Along with the other villagers, she suffered from hunger, from the cold, from poverty. She had millions and millions worth of gold, gems, and other treasures at her disposal. Nobody would have noticed the loss of one little diamond out of several thousand. But when I asked her if that thought had ever crossed her mind, she gave me a look of such revulsion that I felt like someone who had been caught doing something utterly shameful and indecent—such as peeing on the casket during a funeral.

Came the day when the Gold Treasures returned to the Hermitage. And from that day until her death, Maria Vladimirovna Stepanova watched over them, checking the handbags and attaché cases of countless visitors. A little, old, frail lady who could answer you in any of five languages you might choose to speak. A little old lady you would hardly look at twice.

My other "immortal" was a very different kind of person. Anna Ivanovna Zelenova was a powerhouse of energy who moved with the speed and determination of a light tank. The beret perched jauntily on the side of her head, pulled down over her left ear, was the first thing one saw when she rounded a corner or came out of a room—invariably, it would be a head-down charge. And woe to whomever or whatever got in her way.

Everything about Anna Ivanovna was no-nonsense, down-to-earth business. She wore no makeup, her light brown hair was always drawn back and tied in a bun. She wore flat walking shoes and dressed in baggy suits. I repeat, everything about her was no-nonsense—except her eyes. Magnified by her thick glasses, they looked out at you with an expression of wonder, of surprise, of constant discovery, blue as forget-me-nots. She smoked Byelomor *papirosi,* cigarettes with a built-in cardboard holder, strong and smelly enough to make a normal person choke. She was a wonderful listener. She would sit there, her head cocked slightly, the smoking *papirosa* clenched between her teeth and sticking out of the corner of her mouth at a rakish angle, the beret perched atop her head like a wacky halo, her blue, blue eyes full of wonder. But she was an even better storyteller, and she had the most amazing stories to tell.

She was graduated from Leningrad University a few years before the war as an art major. She was offered the job of curator of Pavlovsk Palace, one of the loveliest among the many surrounding Leningrad. She took it, and when the Germans attacked and began to close in, she found herself alone in trying to save the palace. The troops were busy fighting, the local organizations had, by and large, panicked. Anna Ivanovna realized that the town of Pavlovsk would fall. She had no idea how the occupants would treat the palace, but she was not about to risk its future. Having only three trucks at her disposal, she meticulously went about collecting one original of everything in the palace: one armchair of each set, one sofa, one set of plates from each of the dozens of luxurious china dinner services, one fork, one knife, one spoon, one strip of wallpaper from each of the palace rooms, one piece of inlaid wood from each floor; every one of these and countless other items were inscribed in her personal notebook, photographed, packed, and loaded onto the trucks. Whether or not Noah actually did save the animal kingdom when he had a pair of each species come aboard his ark is debatable. But that Anna Ivanovna saved Pavlovsk Palace is undeniable. She was the last civilian to leave the town, her three trucks retreating along with the last Red Army tank. And she was the first civilian to return when a column of Soviet tanks came roaring into Pavlovsk hard on the Nazis' heels. I can see her sitting on the turret, *papirosa* clenched between her teeth, head down, beret pulled over her left ear, an image no less inspiring than Delacroix's famous *Marianne.*

She told me what the Germans had done to her beloved palace, she told me in a flat, emotionless voice betrayed only by the pain in her eyes.

"They chopped down all the trees in the palace park, oak trees, maples, and birches planted two hundred years before. They urinated and defecated in the palace rooms. They scribbled obscene words on the walls. They chopped up priceless furniture and burned it in the stoves. They destroyed everything they could lay their hands on, they tore up the floors, knocked down the walls, broke the priceless mirrors. The master race conducted itself worse than the Huns."

One day, you, my reader, will visit the Soviet Union. Of course, you will go to Leningrad. One of the tours includes a visit to Pavlovsk. Don't miss it. And when your breath is taken away by the refined beauty of this unique monument, when you stand speechless in front of its countless masterpieces, remember that when the Germans retreated in the winter of 1944, the palace lay in ruins. Had it not been for the foresight of Anna Ivanovna, it could never have been restored down to the last minute detail. Each of the one original items she had taken away served as a model for the restorers, the craftsmen, the artists who set about re-creating Pavlovsk. It was a work of love; the townspeople of Pavlovsk donated time, energy, and money, and people came from all over the country to contribute. There it stands today, proud and beautiful, and I can see Anna Ivanovna's eyes dancing with joy and total wonder as she looks out from wherever she is on this monument to her memory.

I recently came across an article in the *International Herald Tribune* (October 6, 1989) headed "Rebirth of Russia's Neoclassical Grandeur." It was about the beauty of restored Pavlovsk. I read it with immense pleasure, happy to see that Anna Ivanovna was finally receiving international recognition. But nowhere was her name or role mentioned. And the concluding paragraph read:

> That Pavlovsk should have been so splendidly restored is, of course, a great achievement, and one for which tourists have reason to be grateful. At the same time, and even though the Soviet Union now enjoys a much larger measure of freedom, all the marble, gold and silk strike a strange note in a country where, despite *perestroika,* bleakness and shabbiness are still the rule; it is impossible not to wonder whether this splendid restoration was not, in the end, a gilded substitute for artistic freedom.

What can I say?

For how many more years are western journalists and publications going to keep on insisting that any positive writing about the Soviet Union must be balanced by a negative statement—preferably at the end of the story.

Maria Vladimirovna and Anna Ivanovna. They were just two of the people in our story of Leningrad. That special issue of *Soviet Life* became a mosaic of human fates interwoven and forming the grand design that indeed was the story of the city of Peter and the city of Lenin, the cradle of three revolutions.

I was very proud of what we had put together, but the management of Novosty didn't like it. "What about the role of the Party?" I was asked. "Why have you focused on so many bad things, sad things, why isn't it all more upbeat?" The special issue came out—it was far too late to replace it—but entire sections were deleted, such as the story of why Leningrad starved during the German siege (to a large degree, faulty planning on the part of the party organization and the military was to blame).

During the McCarthy years in America, one of the Hollywood Ten, Dalton Trumbo, wrote a wonderful pamphlet called *The Time of the Toad.* It seems that the ancient Romans had a recipe for truly bad times: eat a live toad. No matter how obnoxious the situation might be, it could not be more disgusting than eating a toad. Eat a live toad, and you can stand anything, that was the idea. McCarthyism was America's Time of the Toad. For us, it was the Brezhnev years.

What happened to that special edition of *Soviet Life* was a precursor of things to come. It was like the first little sigh of a cold wind that sends a chill down your spine and then disappears, the soon-forgotten warning of the coming of winter. Other signs were quick to follow.

The Taganka Theater, directed by Yuri Lubimov, found itself under growing, stifling pressure from state censorship. Bits and parts of plays were cut, entire plays were prohibited, virtually every new production was a life-and-death battle between the director Yuri Lubimov's Taganka Theater and the bureaucratic apparatus, which, in this particular case, was represented by the Ministry of Culture. As I have pointed out, the apparatus's environment was uniformity. Anything that stuck out had to be cut down to size—and the Taganka Theater became a case in point. Ultimately, it was the impossibility of being anything but uniform that forced Lubimov to emigrate—along with many other Soviet artists, performers, writers, scientists, and so on.

But that word—*forced*—must be used carefully.

In the spring of 1987, I was a member of a small group of Soviet film people who had been invited to Hollywood by their U.S. counterparts. The delegation was headed by Elem Klimov, then secretary of the Union of Soviet Cinematographers and a prominent director in his own right. We were wined and dined and, at one such dinner, I remember Andrei Konchalovsky's being publicly snubbed by Klimov (Konchalovsky was a Soviet film director who was living in the West). When I later asked Klimov what that had all been about, he said, "Look, Andrei took the easy way out. When we were fighting to make honest pictures, when we were getting bashed by the bureaucrats, when we were almost starving because of the bastards who would not allow us to work, he married a French girl and got out. And he stayed out. Thanks to his father's influence, he preserved his Soviet citizenship and remained in good standing with the authorities. He chickened out when times were bad, and now, when things are changing, he wants to look good, he wants to be seen as one of those who fought for the change. I'll be damned if I'll be the one who helps him!''

Konchalovsky's stepfather, Sergei Mikhalkov, a writer of sorts, an opportunist par excellence, a man despised by every Soviet intellectual I know, a person handsomely rewarded by the Establishment for his absolute lack of any principle except the principle of serving the powers that be, enjoyed great power and influence during the Brezhnev years. There is little doubt that he protected Andrei, although I would have to believe he was motivated more by self-preservation (after all, if Andrei got into trouble, his stepfather could be held responsible) than by fatherly love.

But the point Klimov made stands as a kind of dividing line between many Soviet intellectuals—those who voluntarily left and those who stayed. Today, the latter look down on the former. Indeed, the emigrants took the easy way out. Instead of fighting inside their country, instead of standing up for what they believed in and taking the consequences, they fled. To make matters worse, they allowed themselves to be used (deliberately or not, that is irrelevant) by the other side, by people and organizations who in reality did not and do not give a tinker's damn about Russia's fate, about what may happen to the people of this country. Those who defected, those who married out were held up for all to see as the living proof of the Soviet Union's being an evil empire. They became pawns in a political game and, as such, did far more harm to their country than good.

None of these thoughts apply to those who were physically thrown out, told to leave, whose Soviet citizenship was suddenly and unlawfully revoked while they were abroad. While the politics of Solzhenitsyn or Brodsky, Rostropovich or Neizvestny, Lubimov or Galich may be questioned, their courage and integrity may not.

All of this brings me to the case of Andrei Dmitrievich Sakharov, a case I must discuss in the context of what at first seems to be an unrelated event: Czechoslovakia in 1968.

As the events in Czechoslovakia developed throughout the spring of '68, I felt a mixture of hope and dread. I had always believed that socialism could in principle do what no other system had achieved: create an environment that truly corresponded to humanity's age-old dreams of happiness, a society that wasn't predicated on the contradiction between the aspirations of the one and of the many. Now I thought I saw signs of that socialism developing in Prague, which was the basis of my hopes. On the other hand, I *knew* that the Soviet leadership could not permit that to happen. How did I know? I just did, that's all. But I knew it deep inside, my bones and blood knew it. My mind refused to acknowledge it. And so I argued that we would never invade Czechoslovakia. It was like an incantation, something one repeats again and again with the hope that, if repeated often enough, it will come true. But while I denied the possibility of an invasion, scoffed at the very idea, my inner self was preparing for the inevitable. And when the announcement came—I will never forget that sunny Moscow morning—I was ready. Ready to find a rationale to explain (and thereby defend) the invasion.

If you support a country that is based (at least in theory) on principles you share and that aspires (at least in its declarations) to create a system you are committed to, then you are prone to justify its actions. While this is, I believe, a universal truth, it acquired a special meaning for me in relation to Czechoslovakia.

Western propaganda was having a field day with the Prague Spring. Dubcek was the West's darling and "socialism with a human face" was the slogan of the day. But socialism with a human face was exactly what the West feared (and still fears) most. If socialism demonstrated its ability to guarantee security for one and all, plus all the democratic freedoms the West takes so much pride in, plus economic efficiency, plus a good quality of life for *all* people, would that not be seen as a mortal threat by the princes of capitalism and their minions? Generations of Americans grew up with the certainty that the car was an American invention (which it was not, the Germans have that distinction) and that American cars were peerless (which they were at one time), but when they finally realized that the Japanese had begun making better, more reliable, more attractive, and cheaper cars than Ford, Chrysler, and General Motors, Americans began to buy Japanese cars. That is human nature. Similarly, should Americans, or any other people, conclude that some other system offers a better life than their own, they will "buy" that other system.

Socialism with a human face could very well emerge as such a system.

Much of the western support for what Mr. Dubcek was trying to do was genuine, even though misled: the majority of people "knew" he was trying to do something good, even though they could not have explained what that was. In the same way, they "knew" that communism was bad, although they could not explain what communism proposed to do. The policymakers, however, never cared about Dubcek. There is reason to believe that they were giving him the highest possible profile on the assumption that he would fail, that the Soviet Union would intervene.

It is my belief that the power-behind-the-power in the capitalist world, such as the members of the Trilateral Commission, cannot afford to admit the existence of human socialism, for it pulls the rug out from under them, it brings their entire ideological structure tumbling down around their ears. In a way, their refusal to even harbor the thought of human socialism is as dogmatic as the most dogmatic Marxism. It reminds me of a wonderful story by Philip Roth called "The Conversion of the Jews" in which Rabbi Binder, who preaches that God can do anything, has no answer to Ozzie Freedman's question: if God can do anything, why couldn't He let a woman have a baby without having intercourse? Rabbi Binder is thus caught in a bind. If God could not do something so simple as to have a woman conceive without being laid, as Ozzie's friend Itzie succinctly put it, then God is clearly not capable of doing anything. On the other hand, if God could have a woman conceive without intercourse, then Jesus Christ could have been God's son—and what does that mean for Judaism?

I was sickened by the news of the Soviet invasion of Czechoslovakia—and no statements about its being a Warsaw Treaty Organization decision made any difference. What a great day for anti-Sovietism, what a great day for anticommunism!

What a dark, desperate, dismal day for people like myself, people who believed in an ideal.

Thus the dilemma: do I speak out, risks be damned? Do I attack my government and country for this undefendable act of tyranny? And do I play right into the hands of my adversaries who will, most surely, praise me for my integrity and pat me on the back while I squirm at their touch? The answer to that is yes. Be true to yourself no matter what. No matter who tries to use you, who tries to capitalize on your words or actions. Lincoln said it best of all: "I do the very best I know how—the very best I can; and I mean to keep doing so until the end. If the end brings me out all right, what is said against me won't amount to anything. If the end brings me out wrong, ten angels swearing I was right would make no difference."

But I was not prepared to act that way in the summer of 1968. The dilemma was too much for me, just as it was and has been for countless people who supported the Bolshevik revolution, supported the ideas and ideals of socialism and the ultimate goal of creating a communist society, who supported the Soviet Union, and who, because of those reasons, could not and cannot bring themselves to admit any faults with that country. Mind you, these are, by and large, courageous people, people who have suffered for their beliefs without flinching, people who can serve as models of dedication, profoundly honest people—which is why they have suffered on the rack of that dilemma. For them, the "to be or not to be" issue was and remains "How can I openly criticize the Soviet Union if that strengthens the hand of its greatest detractors?" And another thought, a much less noble one is "What will happen to me if I speak out?" Not "will something happen?" because there was no doubt about that, but "how bad will it be?"

And so, I rationalized. I argued that what had begun to happen in Czechoslovakia at a certain point no longer corresponded to what the people really wanted, no longer pursued the goal of a human socialism, but, in fact, was aimed at destroying socialism in Czechoslovakia. I argued that the people had never been given a chance to express their views, that the mass media did not represent the people's interests, that Dubcek and company had sold out to the West, had thrown open the border with West Germany. I argued that the West wanted to bring down the Czech government and have a pro-western government established in its place and that, considering the role Czechoslovakia had played as one of the detonators of World War II, considering its key geographical location in the very heart of Europe, the Soviet Union and its allies could not but regard this as a threat to their security. I felt then *and still feel* that those arguments were, in the main, valid. If I had stated them and added only one final line—that nevertheless, there is no justification for invading Czechoslovakia, there is no justification for Soviet tanks to be in the streets of Prague, we will live to recognize that fact and regret the decision—had I added that one line, I would have had nothing to reproach myself for today.

But I did not.

There were people who acted differently, who listened only to their consciences. To me, the most outstanding example is Sakharov.

I condemned Sakharov for appealing to the West. And when he was exiled to the city of Gorky, I made a case for that decision. What, I asked, do you do with a prominent citizen who allows himself to be used against his own country? Is it not true that *any* government will react to what it conceives to be a threat? That reaction may be more or less sophisticated, but when a system considers itself threatened by a person or an organization, that person or organization will have to suffer the consequences. Wasn't Joe Hill framed and shot because in his day union organizers were perceived as a threat to those in power? Weren't Sacco and Vanzetti fried on false charges because in their day Bolshevism was considered to be a real threat in America? Wasn't that what the infamous Palmer Raids were all about? Weren't Paul Robeson, the Black Panthers, Malcolm X, and Martin Luther King all regarded as threats to the powers that be and dealt with, each in his own way? So, I asked, what's the big deal? They exiled Sakharov to Gorky, which is like exiling someone to Detroit.

Was I right? Yes—concerning systems taking retaliatory action against those who fight them and seem dangerous. No—not if I truly supported the principles of socialism. In my heart of hearts, I knew it was wrong to exile anyone anywhere for speaking his or her mind. I knew it was wrong to send people to jail, to labor camps, to psychiatric wards for having committed the crime of anti-Soviet propaganda. But I could not bring myself to admit it openly. And so I adopted what I would call a very formal stance: Here is the law. You may like it or dislike it, but it is the law. If you break it, you must expect to be punished. Is there a law about anti-Soviet propaganda? Yes there is. Have these people broken that law? Yes they have. Has this been proven beyond reasonable doubt? Yes it has. So?

Ah, the beauty and the immorality of formal logic.

All you have to do is make one undeniably logical statement: "don't laws exist to be obeyed?" Once the answer you get is yes, you are home free. The one question I did not raise was whether the law is just. Wouldn't it be wonderful if there were one unequivocal answer to that seemingly simple question? But what justifies a law? If the majority of citizens support it, does that make it just? If so, then the law banning anti-Soviet propaganda was absolutely legitimate.

Let us not forget what the Soviet Union went through in its relatively short history, what the people suffered. Let us not underrate the fierce pride of a nation that sees itself as having triumphed against all odds. A nation with a siege mentality, in part inspired by a dragonlike ruler who then used it to his interests, in part a reflection of reality, of having been attacked by foes and surrounded by enemies. Let no one doubt the overwhelming support the people would give to even the most Draconian law aimed at anyone who slandered the Soviet Union.

But majority opinion is not necessarily just.

It takes enormous courage to fight your own people for their own good, to accept being pilloried by those whose freedom and rights you are defending. Andrei Sakharov is one of the few who belong to that category of fighters.

The laws were wrong, and what was done to those who broke those laws was wrong. And I hid behind the comfort of my logical constructions until I realized I could no longer do it. I could no longer live with myself. Once I admitted I had been wrong, I had to act. Sooner or later, the part of your mind that you have shut down, the doors you have closed, they open up. It happens to most people—and there are a very few who never close down at all. Even Sakharov did when he worked on the H-bomb. How does that self-reckoning take place? I don't believe there exists one universal answer to that question, but I have never heard anyone answer it better than Daniel Ellsberg, the man who stole the Pentagon papers. I was doing a television special on civil disobedience—this was in 1987—and Mr. Ellsberg was one of those involved in the discussion. At one point, I asked him if he remembered the precise moment when he decided to risk not only his career, but what could have been his liberty, even his life, by stealing those top-secret papers. And he told me how he had been in West Germany and had met with Martin Niemöller, a German pastor who had been the commander of a U-boat in World War I. The story he told Mr. Ellsberg, who told it to me, went as follows: "They came first for the Communists, and I didn't speak up because I wasn't a Communist. Then they came for the Jews, and I didn't speak up because I wasn't a Jew. Then they came for the Catholics, and I didn't speak up because I wasn't a Catholic. Then they came for me, and by that time there was no one left to speak up."

How long can you pretend that when they come for the communists, that is not your concern? Nor when they come for the Jews? And the Catholics? How long can you pretend that the victims of injustice are not your business? How long can you look the other way when people are put in jail or in psychiatric wards for their opinions? How long can you spout off about freedom and liberty and democracy while sipping a cool drink on the terrace of your five-million-dollar apartment on Fifth Avenue and Central Park, while people live in the streets in abject poverty, live in the ghettos like animals in cages? How long?

It is a question of how long you can look the other way, lie to yourself, justify your own fear of standing up and being counted, of bucking the current, of taking a risk.

I may have noted before that Yevgeny Yevtushenko was never my favorite poet or person, but he had four wonderful opening lines in one of his early poems about Galileo that have a direct bearing on all of this. Here they are in my translation (don't shoot the pianist, he is doing the best he can):

Believe me, Galileo's neighbor
Knew just as well, through thought and labor,
That round and round the earth does spin.
But what about his kith and kin?

That is the sixty-four-thousand-dollar question.

What happens to the people you are responsible for, the people you love, the people who are going to suffer because you chose to rock the boat? That is not an exclusively Soviet question. It applies everywhere. In China, in the United States, it exists wherever there is a human society that has certain values, traditions, and habits. The less secure a society, the more prone it is to crushing dissent. Also, it will take much quicker and more radical action against a dissenter it considers dangerous. But even the most secure society will, in the long run, take action against even a relatively obscure dissenter. Society has countless ways of retaliating. It can be brutal and unsophisticated, putting you in jail, in a camp, in front of a firing squad. Or it can be refined and have you fired or ostracized. It can get to you through your wife, through your children, by making *them* suffer for what *you* said or did. And so, when all is said and done, you really have only two options. One is to back off. You will almost never admit you made a conscious decision to look the other way, to disregard whatever it was that originally prompted you to declare war on your society. You will look for and, of course, find the "reasons" for backing off. But if you are honest, then some day you will have to admit that you did it because you were scared, you were weak, because you could not deal with the fear of what was going to happen to your family, to you. And I have had that fear in me. Let he or she condemn it who had the courage to choose the other way.

I happen to believe it is not a question of choice. You go for the other option purely and simply because you *cannot do otherwise.*

It has to do with Iosif Gordon's Mirror Test. You wake up one morning, you go to the bathroom, and while you are brushing your teeth, or shaving, or whatever, you see this face in the mirror—and you want to puke. God, is that me?

It does not happen to everyone. But when and if it does, then you have no option.

However, it is a gradual process. It happens only over a long period of time and only as the result of questions that keep coming back at you no matter how actively you try to push them away or dodge them. Over

the years, as I defended a philosophy I believed in, an ideal I was committed to, I had to ask myself must that lead to the justification of things that
I know are wrong? Must I refrain from criticizing my society because "the
other side" may exploit that criticism, may use me for a purpose diametri-
cally opposed to everything I believe in? If I refuse to see anything wrong
with my society for fear of betraying its ideals, am I not betraying myself?

As things got worse and worse under Brezhnev, these questions grew
in my mind. They loomed ever larger as my role as international inter-
preter/spokesman for things Soviet grew, thanks to my appearances on
U.S. television. The first such appearance occurred, I believe, in 1979 or
1980, when the Moscow ABC bureau chief, Anne Garrels, suggested to
her bosses the revolutionary idea of using a Soviet for discussions about
the Soviet Union or Soviet-American relations. Thus I appeared on
"Nightline."

Those first "Nightline" interviews made many Americans sit up and
rub their eyes. Was this a Russian? If so, how come he spoke like an
American? Not only spoke, but psychologically was on the same wave-
length? I soon became a bit of a celebrity. Quite a few people liked
me. Quite a few didn't. Some nearly had a fit about me—like George
Will, who in his column attacked Ted Koppel for referring to me as a
"colleague."

My situation was weird. At home, I was unknown, while in America
more and more people became familiar with my name. That I was allowed
to go on U.S. television via satellite from Moscow but was not permitted
to address a Soviet television audience reveals management's attitude
toward me. One the one hand, it saw me as an asset. Ever since G.S. had
launched my radio career by introducing my "Daily Talk" in October
1973, he had conducted a one-man PR campaign in my support. Journalists of Radio Moscow's Foreign Service have jokingly christened their
place of work "The Tomb of the Unknown Soldier"; it is a fitting definition, since they have no domestic audience at all, while the foreign audience is, to put it kindly, not large. Those who worked (and work) for
Radio Moscow were and are unknown. That is, until they move on either
to the Domestic service or to television, where they almost always become
extremely popular. I have already pointed out that it was actually easier
for a journalist to express his or her point of view while addressing a
foreign audience. The reporters and commentators who worked for the
Foreign Service were, as a rule, better informed, had a broader outlook,
and had a higher degree of individuality than their counterparts of the
Domestic Service.

Thanks to G.S., I became one of the few Foreign Service journalists whose name did not draw a blank stare when heard by our top management. But G.S. did much more than wage a PR campaign. He decided to unlock the door to travel abroad, the door that had been forced open briefly in 1969 by the KGB's Victor Alexandrovich when I went to Dresden to help bring my sick father home, the door that had then once again slammed shut. This was no simple task. But neither was G.S. a simple man. He went directly to the chairman of Gosteleradio, Sergei Lapin. I don't know what he said (he never told me), but Lapin agreed to help me. And so, in the spring of 1977, I was informed that I would be sent on a business trip to the United States. I was delirious with joy. A few days later, I was asked to participate in one of the most popular radio shows in the UK, "The Jimmy Young Show." It was, I believe, the first major western commercial radio program to come to Moscow for a series of live broadcasts, which included in-studio interviews conducted by Jimmy Young with different Soviets, both ordinary and well-known, as well as live phone calls from listeners in Great Britain. The event was, to borrow a British idiom, a smashing success. This was also my first appearance on a foreign show, and it was then that I, for the first time as I recall, openly criticized certain features of life in the Soviet Union. It was nothing earthshaking, to be sure, but it was, nevertheless, a complete departure from the usual. I was congratulated by both my friends at work and the Brits. Naturally, I was walking on air—not only because I felt I had done well on the Jimmy Young test, but because I knew my papers were being put through the proper channels for my trip to the United States.

On the eve of his departure from Moscow, Jimmy Young had a reception for all the Soviets who had participated in his show. And it was there, during that reception, that I learned that my visa had been denied. I wouldn't be going to America.

How can I describe my disappointment? For years and years I hadn't allowed myself to think about traveling. I had stuck that subject away into the deepest closet and told myself to forget about it—because thinking was too painful. Then, thanks to G.S., a glimmer of hope had appeared and, as time passed, the glimmer became a bright light. I allowed myself to dream of how it would be to set foot on the streets of New York City, how I would exult at roaming my old haunts. All at once, the dream was shattered.

Of all my years in the Soviet Union, with the exception of 1957, the hardest was 1977. In a way, I lost hope. I nearly gave up. I almost got down on my knees and prayed. Had that happened, I have no idea where

I would be and even who I would be today. I say this because of the way I feel about God. I should begin by saying, I have no room in my heart for the Church. I will grudgingly admit that the Church has demonstrated incredible staying power, but that is as far as I will go. My feelings about the existence of some supreme power are more ambiguous. There have been times when I have envied those who believe in God. There have been times of intense pain, of loneliness, of insecurity, of fear when I have been tempted to get down on my knees and pray (praying and getting down on one's knees are, to me, synonymous). But I have never succumbed to that temptation for fear that I would thereby commit an act of self-betrayal, that I would rise a different man. Perhaps a better one, perhaps not, but different. I would lose me.

In 1977, I nearly lost control. I drank too much, I got drunk, and when I was drunk I said things I didn't remember the next day. I told people I would emigrate, that I hated the place, that I felt anything but Soviet. I know those were difficult months for my wife. I know she suffered. What can I say, except that I am and always will be sorry?

I think part of what happened to me was also a reaction to my father's death in 1975.

Ours had always been a difficult relationship. It had become worse in 1957, when my father's reaction to my stated desire to return to America had been a threat to report me to the authorities and have me thrown in jail. Later, in the early sixties, I internally disowned my father—although neither he nor my mother ever knew about it. As I may have mentioned, my father was a very attractive and charming man. Women fell for him, and he was only too pleased to catch them. In 1961, or thereabouts, I began to hear rumors that he was having an affair with a woman half his age. The daughter of a famous Soviet film director, she was attractive in a foxy sort of way, quick-witted, and somewhat bossy (for reasons I will never understand, my father liked bossy women). Those rumors upset me, and I recall asking Iosif and Nina what to do. Iosif, who was my father's closest friend, must have spoken to him about our discussion, because a few days later my father asked me to come over for a talk. I will never forget it.

"I know people love to wag their tongues, and I realize you are no different from the rest of them," he said, "but how could you possibly partake in a discussion about your father, about his honesty? How could you doubt my love for your mother? How could you believe, entertain the thought, that I would think of causing her pain? How could you?"

Indeed, how could I? I begged his forgiveness, I felt rotten, dirty, despicable.

But there was something inside that refused to be convinced, a little voice that kept saying, "He's lying, he's lying." Back then, I had been communicating with an American girl whom I had met in 1957 during the World Youth Festival. I had asked her to write via General Delivery, just as she had asked me to do. A week or so after the discussion with my father, I went to the Central Post Office, in downtown Moscow, to check on whether there was any mail for me. I walked up to the General Delivery window and handed the girl my passport. She skimmed through the *P* file, took a letter, stuck it into my passport, and shoved it back at me. I picked up the passport and letter, turned, and began to walk away. I looked at the envelope. It was addressed to V. A., instead of V. V., Pozner. And it came from a resort on the Black Sea, where, as I knew, the lady of the rumors was vacationing. Without a second thought, I ripped open the envelope and began to read the letter.

I knew I had no right to do that, to read a letter that was not addressed to me. I knew and I didn't give a damn. *I had to read that letter,* I had to know the truth no matter what. And the truth was that my father had lied to me. My father was having an affair with this woman.

I have rarely wanted to kill. But this was one such time. Not because my father was sleeping with another woman—I was adult enough to realize that such things were more often the rule than the exception. But that he had lied to me and made me feel so terribly guilty, had made me feel I had somehow betrayed him—ah, that I could not forgive. I hated him for that.

A week later I returned to the Central Post Office, this time with the hope of intercepting a second letter. Bingo, I hit the jackpot! Again, the girl paid no attention to the difference in our patronymics and handed me what I had come for. Again, I read it, the rage boiling over in my heart. And I swore I would make my father pay for this—for what he had done to me, to my mother. I swore that some day I would slam the two letters down in front of him, cross my arms, and ask, "Now what do you say?"

It never happened.

All kinds of events interfered. My own breakup with Valentina, my new job at *Sputnik,* my falling in love with Kathrin, and, certainly more than anything else, the terrible and and final defeat suffered by my father.

During the Thaw of the early sixties, he had begun to elaborate a plan that, had it been allowed to develop, would have not only changed the face of the Soviet film industry but, quite possibly, would have affected the very foundations of the Soviet economic structure. The idea was quite simple: introduce economic measures to stimulate the production of quality, box-office-hit films. Simple as the concept sounds, it represented an unorthodox approach to movie-making, both East and West. In the West, where money is the ultimate goal, box-office considerations take precedence over such things as art, content, and quality. In the Soviet Union, the moviemaker doesn't depend on whether or not his product sells. The film writer is payed an advance for the scenario and, once it has been accepted, he has very little financial interest in the success of the film. What the director and a host of other people involved in the production will earn depends on the rating their film receives from a special commission, which judges the movie on the basis of its artistic and ideological merits and awards what is called a category (top category, first category, second category, third category). The higher the category, the better the pay. The number of people who actually see the movie is irrelevant.

My father proposed the following: pay the writer and the director a certain minimum fee. Once the movie is completed, have your commission give it a rating. Then bring it out, but don't pay anyone anything until you have figures to show how well the film is doing. Base final earnings on a combination of artistic and ideological merit and box-office appeal. Thus, if the film is a top category and box-office hit, everyone involved in the production makes a lot of money; a top category that flopped at the box office pays less but the money will reflect appreciation for artistic skill and innovation. Finally, a low category film that's a big crowd-pleaser gets even less, to discourage artists from producing kitsch.

Such an approach would not be accepted in the United States, or, for that matter, in any capitalist country. As long as something sells, who cares whether or not it has an educational value, whether it has a positive or negative influence on teenagers, and so on? My father believed that in a socialist society, things were different, that in a socialist society economic incentives could serve to stimulate quality products—film being just one example. I firmly believe he was right—in theory. But insofar as the Soviet Union of those times was concerned, he was absolutely wrong.

Along with the writer Konstantin Simonov and the director Grigori Chukhrai, my father developed a proposal for the creation of a new independent entity called the Experimental Creative Film Studio. It took two or three years for a decision to be reached, but in 1963, the studio was born and my father was appointed as its head. But in those times, when the concept of economic incentives (more for good work, less for poor work) flew in the face of everything the bureaucracy stood for, when the idea of an organization's being economically solvent and independent of the government was interpreted (correctly, I must admit) as a threat to the system, the studio had to be high on the bureaucracy's hit list. The fact that it survived for as long as it did, nearly five years, and produced several fine pictures bears testimony to how vibrant it really was.

The decision to close the studio came in early 1968. It was a blow from which my father never recovered. He handed in his resignation on October 24, 1968, the day of his sixtieth birthday. In the spring of 1969, he suffered a nearly fatal heart attack.

The time for me to confront him with those two letters had passed. What's more, thanks to Kathrin, my father and I had become friends. It took her love, her passion, her intelligence to make my father understand how wrong he had been in trying to force me to accept his judgment on everything. I know that he was immensely proud of me, but he could not bring himself to admit that he had been wrong and was sorry until Kathrin made him understand that he would be a far happier person if he did.

Those last five years must have been very hard for him. Not that he ever complained. He would sooner have died than admit to weakness or regrets. It is simply something I sense. He hated his heart condition. All of his life, my father had been trim, quick on his feet, graceful. As one person put it, he never walked—he flew. He had always been healthy and strong; he had never had as much as a cold. Now he was ill, and psychologically he could not cope with that situation. He refused to exercise, even to go out for a walk, try as my mother would to get him to go outdoors. He became flabby, even grew a bit of a potbelly.

But I think his physical discomfort was nothing compared to his mental suffering. He had gambled his whole life, as well as that of his wife and children, on going to the Soviet Union because, as he believed, it was a just society. He had seen his career ultimately destroyed, his hopes dashed. He knew my mother was unhappy, for she had never felt at home in Russia—she was too French for that. Although he was proud of me, he never saw me rise to the top of my profession. The one joy he did experience was when Paul, my brother, brilliantly presented his thesis on ancient Vietnamese culture (at least we have one scholar in the family!). My father did not live to see and experience glasnost and perestroika (I can imagine how delighted, how triumphant he would have been!). Although he doggedly held on to his faith in the revolution that had so captivated him as a child, he must have had moments of the darkest despair.

The last time I saw him was in July 1975, when Kathrin, Paul, and I saw him and my mother off to Paris. I remember he looked thin, frail, and his color was not good—there was a tinge of yellow in his face. Ten days later, my mother called to tell me that he was dying. He had been diagnosed as having galloping leukemia. They would arrive, she said, by plane on the following day. From that point on, I remember being two people. One did whatever had to be done—made phone calls, arrangements, and whatnot—but that wasn't really me. I was the one who sat there, frozen, alone, cut off from it all.

Paul and I went to the airport. I had no car in those days, so Victor Alexandrovich, my father's faithful KGB friend, had sent a car and driver to take us. The driver was a young man of about thirty. For some reason, I remember that he looked exactly like an Irish cop: red hair, blue eyes, white skin, white teeth, and a superb build. The car was a Zhiguli, a Soviet Fiat. It had standard plates and looked like any other car, but it had a souped up motor—and the driver would have been one of the top contenders at Le Mans. We roared along the ring road at nearly 180 kilometers an hour (about 110 mph). Every now and then, the driver would turn on his siren, at the sound of which every car in front of us would pull over, letting us pass.

I remember Paul couldn't get enough of it. He *loved* this exhibition of power, of right of way. He gloated as we sped along—and I never forgot, and it still hurts to think about how he behaved.

When we reached the airport, we were met by an Aeroflot official who told me they had just received a message from the pilot of the Paris-Moscow flight that someone had died on board. I knew who had died.

My father passed away at thirty thousand feet above the face of the earth. Not in the Soviet Union, not in France. He died nowhere, he died in between, he died, it might be said, symbolically. And every time I think of him, of his death, which is often, I feel a deep pain. Because of how shabbily life treated him. Because I miss him. Because, much as I did not want to admit it, I had always loved him.

I still have those two letters I picked up at General Delivery. The woman who wrote them is still around. She's become a relatively prominent film critic. Maybe I'll send them to her. With a nice little note. Why not?

So when I went a bit crazy in 1977, once again knowing that I was not trusted, that I was a second-class citizen, I think that a bit of the craziness had to do with my father's death.

The chairman of Gosteleradio, who had made a few phone calls on my behalf, reacted to the denial of my visa as a personal affront. It had nothing to do with his liking me or having a high opinion of my work. It had to do with status and prestige. He was, after all, the chairman of a very important organization, a member of the all-powerful Central Committee of the Soviet Communist party. He also was a personal friend of Leonid Brezhnev. When he wanted something, he expected to get it, and no piddling KGB flunky was going to turn down a personal request from Mr. Lapin.

As a result of his resolve, I was sent on a short trip to Finland in 1978. The business at hand—television exchanges of folk music—had nothing to do with my work. It was just a pretext to move me up the next rung of the travel ladder. Finally, in 1979, I had my first real trip abroad—to Canada. I was invited to Toronto to participate in a television panel discussion show called "What Is Truth?" produced by a man named Ralph Kirchen. Like Jimmy Young, Mr. Kirchen had brought his show to Moscow (I think it was in early 1979), taped a series of programs, and taken them back to Canada where, as he informed us, they had done extremely well. As a follow-up, he invited several of the Moscow participants, myself included, to tape a series of shows in Toronto.

I quickly established a friendly relationship with Ralph and his charming wife, Norma. He seemed to be genuinely interested in developing relations with the Soviet Union at a time when that was anything but popular. He returned to Moscow on several occasions. Gradually, I became his "favorite" Soviet. He had me over again in 1979 and twice the following year, both to participate in his show and to tape a couple of pilots for a series tentatively titled "World Power Politics." These included debates with such dignitaries as Admiral (retired) Elmo Zumwalt and the former U.S. ambassador to Moscow, Malcolm Toon.

In April 1980 Ralph brought me to London, where he had signed an agreement with the BBC to put on a two-part debate between myself and the former *Washington Post* bureau chief in Moscow, Bob Kaiser. The debates ("East vs. West: War or Peace?" and "East vs. West: Whose Way Is Best?") were, as I recall, interesting enough, but not nearly as interesting as the conversation I had with Ralph on the evening before we parted. We were discussing the debates, when suddenly, out of the blue, Ralph told me that not long before coming to London, he had been visited by the Royal Canadian Mounted Police. What did they want? I asked. Ralph shot a side glance at me and said, "They wanted to know whether I thought you might be tempted to defect." I distinctly recall the strange feeling I had that Ralph was not so much telling me what the RCMP had asked as he was relaying their question. "What did you say?" I stalled. Ralph laughed and said, "I told them to get the fuck out of my office." I nodded. "You did the right thing," I said.

Earlier I noted that the top management of Gosteleradio regarded me as an asset. Now, I believe, the reader can understand why. There were very few journalists, if any, who could do the job I was doing, who not only were absolutely fluent in English, but who were also profoundly committed to the ideas and the ideals of socialism, who were effective in combating the anti-Soviet/anticommunist bias that had become second nature to most people in the West. But the very reason for my effectiveness, or credibility (basically the same thing), was my willingness to admit shortcomings, to furnish a personal viewpoint, to be critical of certain things in the Soviet Union. But it was one thing to allow me to state my views to a foreign audience, and something altogether different to permit me to do the same at home. What was acceptable for a foreign broadcast was out of the question for domestic consumption. But since I was what one might call a known quantity, since there was hardly any doubt among the management concerning my tendency to speak out, regardless of the audience, there was a good reason to keep me off Soviet television. That was the other consideration.

The more prominent I became on western television, especially in the United States, the surer I felt of myself and the greater my tendency to stray from the straight and narrow path of orthodox propaganda. Then, in the fall of 1981, I slipped on the razor's edge.

I had become somewhat blasé about being interviewed by the western press, so when a request came in from *People* magazine, I took it in stride. The interviewer worked for one of the two U.S. wire services in Moscow but was also a stringer for *People.* Hence, he had no byline in the magazine. Nor, I suppose, did his contract permit him to do that kind of work—which is why I do not give his name. The interview was nothing out of the ordinary, the usual handful of predictable questions, one of which invariably was, "Can you disagree with the government?" Today, publicly disagreeing with the government in the Soviet Union has become a national pastime, but in those times you had to be extremely courageous to criticize any government policy. So the question was tricky. If you said no, that was the end of your credibility insofar as any western audience was concerned. The usual way to handle that question was to bob and weave, use the yes-but approach, do a couple of verbal headstands, turn a few cartwheels. But I was sick of that, so I said, "Yes, I can." The next question was obvious: "Would you care to provide an example?"

At that point, I had the strange sensation of a chess player who sees the trap his opponent is setting for him but does nothing to stop it; on the contrary, he moves exactly as his opponent wishes him to.

"Sure I'll furnish an example," I said. "Take capital punishment. The government supports it, I don't, and I've said so publicly." The *People* stringer looked at me and smiled. "Mr. Pozner, what about a foreign-policy example? For instance, Afghanistan? Do you agree with the government policy there?"

"Check," a voice inside me said, and I answered, "Mate!" And plunged ahead: "From a popularity standpoint, the decision was not a wise one. We have lost a lot of international support, probably will lose more. Of course, I don't think popularity was a consideration in the decision."

This, you will agree, was not a big blast. It was more like a BB gun. That part of the interview never appeared in *People*. But it did in the wire-service story the gentleman filed the next day—a story that nearly cost me my job.

A young man with whom I had had a couple of run-ins picked the story off the teletype and gave it to a man who, for personal reasons, wished to destroy me. (I prefer not to give his name, be it only because I am not, as the reader might otherwise conclude, settling a score. I am demonstrating how even something as innocuous as what I said could be terribly dangerous.) He in turn took it to Enver Mamedov, who was at that time the first deputy chairman of the board of Gosteleradio.

In a matter of hours, the news had spread. Pozner was in disgrace, Pozner was going to lose his job. Many colleagues began to look the other way when they saw me coming down the hall. But most of them did the opposite: they made a point of showing me their support—acts of courage I have never forgotten and for which I will always be grateful. Meanwhile, the machinery had been set in motion. A party meeting was convoked to discuss my transgression. It was quite an experience. The man who headed the entire Foreign Service was eloquent in describing my bourgeois upbringing, my lack of class principles. He called for my expulsion from the

Party, a measure that would automatically have led to my being fired. A variety of views were expressed, some being a repetition of Yevstafyev's (he was the boss, so it was wise to follow his lead), others calling for clemency. There were a few isolated voices that qualified the whole affair as a sham. But they were quickly silenced. The final decision was to give me an official party reprimand and to take me off the air for several months. I later learned that some people had gone to Chairman Lapin and advised him to fire me. Lapin's comment was, "Firing Pozner is no big deal. But who will do his work?"

The party reprimand and the whole incident had other repercussions, one being that my next trip to Canada, scheduled for October 1981, was called off and my right to travel was, once again, revoked. When I phoned Ralph in Toronto to tell him I wouldn't be coming, his reaction surprised me. It was as though his very life depended on my visit. He was almost hysterical. That was the last time I ever spoke to him. Ralph Kirchen disappeared. I sent him several postcards but never got an answer. Later, whenever I'd meet someone from Toronto, I would ask them if they knew Ralph Kirchen or had ever seen a show called "What Is Truth?" They raised their eyebrows and shook their heads. Then one day, I heard from one of the people who had been on the panel of the show, a Canadian writer by the name of Doug Hall. He wrote to tell me that he had watched my career spiral, had seen me many times on "Nightline," and was happy for me. He also informed me that Ralph Kirchen had turned out to be an embezzler, that he had been forced to sell his house and all his belongings, and that he was now driving a taxi in Toronto and paying back his debts. I couldn't believe my eyes. Ralph a crook?

Was there a tie-in between my right to travel being withdrawn and Ralph's downfall? For some reason, I believe there was. Perhaps he failed to carry out a mission he had been entrusted with and so lost support.

The wire-service interview, which nearly wrecked my life, had opened with the following lead (this is not a verbatim quote, but it is extremely close): "Leonid Brezhnev may run the Soviet Union, but for millions of Americans Vladimir Pozner is the Kremlin's voice." As I was later informed, that intro actually did me more harm than my comments about Afghanistan. Strangely enough, when it was all over, when my nose had been rubbed in the dirt, when I had been made to understand how defenseless I was, I suddenly experienced a sense of relief. That, I believe, was the first signal of my coming internal liberation.

A few months later, when I was allowed back on the air, I was interviewed on "This Week with David Brinkley." There were two people on before me, one of whom was an American businessman whose name I don't remember. The other was Arkady Shevchenko, the ranking Soviet diplomat who had been recruited by the CIA and had defected. This was not my first encounter with Shevchenko; we had faced off during a "Nightline" show focusing on Yuri Andropov's becoming general secretary of the Soviet Union.

I recall being seated facing the camera in a Moscow studio listening to the intro on my earpiece when Ted Koppel came on and announced the participants. One was a former Hungarian journalist who had known Andropov in his capacity as ambassador to Budapest, the other was the former CIA director Admiral Stansfield Turner, and the third was Shevchenko—news that nearly knocked me out of my seat. One of our unwritten laws, religiously observed, stated that no Soviet citizen could have any contact, much less a conversation, with a traitor. That included everybody and anybody who had chosen to leave the Soviet Union and who disagreed with its policies—hardly acts of treason by even the strictest standards. Shevchenko, however, qualified to a T. One of the Soviet Union's ranking diplomats, a protégé of Andrei Gromyko, under secretary general of the UN, he had agreed to work for the CIA. When things began to get hot, he defected.

What was I supposed to do? As I sat there, my mind racing, Ted asked me to share my feelings about Andropov, the man. I said that I had never met him, had no personal opinion, and could only furnish the main points of his curriculum vitae. Next came Admiral Turner, Andropov's U.S. counterpart when he was chairman of the KGB. Turner was to the point, unemotional, fair. He clearly was no Andropov fan, but he was not out to do a hatchet job—as opposed to Shevchenko, who proceeded to earn his keep by painting the ugliest picture he could. Then Ted asked me whether I agreed with what the two preceding gentlemen had said.

My guardian angel saved me once again.

My answer was that, while I was ready to talk to any *American*, including Admiral Turner, I flatly refused to have anything to do with traitors. But this man, I continued, had not only betrayed his country. He had betrayed his wife and his two children. This, I said, is something I know firsthand, because it just so happens that my son goes to the same school as that man's daughter. When Shevchenko defected, I said, his wife, who was in Moscow at that time, committed suicide. He is responsible for the death of his wife, for leaving a son and a daughter parentless.

No, I won't have anything to do with him, I concluded. I wouldn't even talk about the weather with him.

When I concluded my statement, there was a pause—one of the few I have ever encountered on U.S. commercial television. Then Ted said something to the effect that if I refused to speak to Mr. Shevchenko, no one could force me to, a point with which I most heartily concurred. From that point on, Shevchenko was silent.

I was later sent a tape of the show and saw Shevchenko's acute discomfort when I spoke about his family. Had he thought that I had such knowledge, I'm sure he would have refused to go on the show—as I would have done, had I known he would be one of the participants. But thanks to the fact that I took him out and didn't exchange a single word with him, I didn't break the unwritten rule about communicating with traitors. (Let me say that while luck and quick thinking saved me, I take no pride in having dealt that way with Shevchenko. I would have preferred to debate with him. No one should have the right to force you into a situation where you cannot speak to someone else; no one should have the right to make such decisions for you.)

Now, on the Brinkley show, Shevchenko was back. However, because of the way that show is structured—none of the guests speak to one another, they are interviewed separately and independently—I wasn't worried at all. That was on a Sunday.

On Monday morning, I received a call from the head of the International Affairs Department of Gosteleradio. His message was brief. Prepare for the worst. Lapin wants to see you tomorrow, first thing in the morning. Someone told him you spoke to Shevchenko.

I don't even recall trying to explain. I hung up and went back to sleep. I woke up in a wonderful mood, realizing I didn't care, feeling my internal liberty, knowing that if I was fired (almost a certainty), it was not the end of the world by any means. The hell with them, I thought.

On the following morning, at nine sharp, Lapin's secretary called to tell me that the chairman was expecting me. When I entered his office on the fourth floor of Gosteleradio's downtown headquarters, I saw he had company. The group included his first deputy Mamedov, another deputy by the name of Henrikas Juskiavicus, and the head of the International Affairs Department. I approached, said good morning, and sat down facing Lapin acros the desk. What followed is indelibly imprinted on my mind.

Sergei Lapin had many talents, not the least of which was acting. He looked at me with an expression of digust bordering on loathing and asked, "How could you agree to talk to that scoundrel?" I answered that I had not exchanged a word with him, at which Lapin's face assumed the expression of a man who has just stepped on a toad—no, into a foul sewer. "But you participated in the same program with him!" he stated. I nodded. But, I explained, I had had the last word, I had been able to say what I wanted to several million Americans, and I was sure I had done the right thing. Lapin leaned back in his armchair. Now his face expressed haughty disdain. "So you believe you did the right thing? Well, let me tell you, we believe differently. In fact, we happen to believe you are not qualified to do the kind of work we have entrusted you with. What do you think of that?" I looked him straight in the eye and asked, "May I leave now? I presume I am free?" That was unexpected. Lapin glanced around at his silent audience, spread his arms, and said, "You see how he reacts to criticism? You see how much he dislikes hearing anything but praise?" At that moment, I experienced a feeling of bliss, because I knew I was going to tell the old bastard off. "Not at all," I calmly answered. "On the contrary. I have worked here for close to fifteen years and have yet to hear a kind word from you or any of your people. I'm used to being criticized, that's not new at all." The head of the International Affairs Department had been tugging at my sleeve, trying to make me shut up. He was petrified. Lapin was somewhat taken aback. "You must understand," he said in a somewhat petulant tone, "your work is like that of a mine searcher. You cannot afford to make a mistake." "I beg your pardon," I said, really beginning to enjoy the conversation, "but I came here to work as a journalist, not as a sapper. But since you've chosen that example, let me use it. The soldier who looks for mines knows that if, heaven forbid, he should step on one, his buddies will do everything they can to save him. We, who work here for you, know that if we should have the mischance to step on a mine, your people will do everything they can to finish us off." Deathly silence followed. Then Juskiavicus looked up at the ceiling in a contemplative way with full knowledge there would be no consequence and said, "I wonder how they will punish Shevchenko for having participated in the same program as Pozner?"

Lapin was anything but stupid. The absurdity of the situation was obvious. No less obvious was the fact that I would not be cowed. He nodded and said gruffly, "You may go now. We will think about what to do." I got up, smiled, said "Have a good day," and left.

Two days later, I was informed that the Soviet ambassador in Washington, Anatoly Dobrynin, had sent a glowing report of my performance on the Brinkley show to the Foreign Office. The news certainly gave me some satisfaction, but it was secondary to the satisfaction and joy I experienced upon walking out of Lapin's office. It was pure jubilation. The dragon that had sat coiled in my heart, which every now and then had sent waves of fear pulsing through my veins, that dragon was dead.

But the Dragon was, and still is, very much alive.

It lives on in the armless, the legless, the soulless souls it created.

It sucks on its pipe, strokes its mustache, bares its yellowish teeth in a smile of glee, and looks on with tiger eyes as the nation, like a present-day Laocoön, struggles to break free.

7

⊰◆⊱

Breakthrough

When I arrived in the Soviet Union, the majority of the people believed in the system. Stalinist terror notwithstanding, they believed in Stalin. On May Day, when millions of Soviets marched in celebration of the International Day of Workers' Solidarity, they believed in what they were marching for—in Red Square in the heart of Moscow and in thousands of village squares across the country.

The first blow to that belief was dealt by Khrushchev and his de-Stalinization campaign. Khrushchev thought that by hitting the Stalin legend with a sledgehammer, he could destroy the legacy. As in many other cases, he was wrong, his understanding limited by his cultural and educational limitations. It could be argued that Khrushchev's head-on assault on Stalin may have destroyed as many ideals and created as much cynicism as it did good as a kind of shock therapy for the nation.

The first years of the Khrushchevian Thaw were also marked by a wave of enthusiasm, a point I noted earlier. The one does not contradict the other. The dialectics of life are far more complex than most of us, both in the media and outside of it, usually care to acknowledge. The depiction of Stalin as a power-hungry despot, a mass murderer, an evil genius was as profoundly shocking to some as proof that God never existed would be to a devout believer. But, and at the same time, the current of fresh air generated by that denunciation touched the nation's parched lungs and was so good that it created a sense of euphoria and exultation. On the one hand, profound despair, disillusionment; on the other, an even greater belief than before.

Some say Khrushchev's real motives for de-Stalinization had nothing to do with the goals of liberalization and democracy, neither of which had any appeal for a man who was, part and parcel, a product of the Stalinist system. Rather, they say, it had to do with the struggle for power with such dangerous contenders as Beria and Malenkov, both of whom were seen as being much closer to Stalin (along with Molotov and Kaganovich) than Khrushchev. But, they continue, Khrushchev could not conduct his anti-Stalinist policies to their logical conclusion without admitting that he, too, had blood on his hands. Khrushchev had occupied top party posts at the worst of times: Moscow (1935–1938) and the Ukraine (1938–1947). He had signed many death warrants of as many completely innocent people. He had to trim the sail of de-Stalinization before its waves reached his own boat. Hence the contradictory nature of his reforms.

While all this may be true (and certainly is, in part), the rehabilitation of the unjustly repressed, the redressing of wrongs, regardless of their ultimate goals (which, in my opinion, pursued nothing more than justice), had a salutary effect on the country. But as Khrushchev consolidated his power, as he first permitted and then encouraged the birth of his own cult, public opinion became less optimistic, more critical, more doubtful.

In a strange way, Khrushchev reminds me of Napoleon. Had the emperor, the leader of the French revolutionary (!) armies, given the people of Russia their freedom, had he abolished serfdom, he would have won the campaign of 1812. Quite possibly, czarism would have ended a century before it was overthrown. Who knows what the consequences might have been, not only for Russia, but for the world? But the fact of the matter is, quite simply, that Napoleon *could not do that.* Not because he lacked the authority, but because it was psychologically beyond his grasp. Napoleon was a military genius, and the military mind has its limitations. Because of those limitations, Napoleon was brought down in Russia, and not the least reason for his defeat was the guerrilla warfare waged on him by the people, by the peasants, by the serfs he could have so easily won over. Can it be said, therefore, that Napoleon could have, at least theoretically, won his Russian campaign? No, it cannot, for as I noted earlier, the mentality of Le Petit Caporal excluded even the theoretical possibility of his acting like an abolitionist.

Had Khrushchev gone all the way, had he allowed real democratic expression, had he intervened on behalf of Krasnopevtsev and other Moscow University students, sentenced to ten years of labor camp and exile for running an underground press and calling for the creation of a second party, had he refused to put Siniavsky and Daniel on trial for what they had written, had he refused to declare open season on dissidents, had Khrushchev done all these things, the chances are that he would have won, that he would have broken the apparatus's stranglehold on Soviet society at a time when the apparatus was scrambling to regroup. But to expect any of those things is to miss the essential point that Khrushchev could no more act that way than a cat can be expected to bark. And so he lost popular support and, ultimately, his power.

Insofar as hope and belief are concerned, one is tempted to call the Brezhnev years the *coup de grâce.* But far from putting society out of its pain, far from acting with the immediacy of a bullet in the brain, those were years of a kind of mental gangrene. Society saw its fingers and toes rot and drop off, smelled its own putrescence, tasted its corruption, heard the discordance of its double-talk, and laughed.

It laughed at the spectacle of Brezhnev's pinning four gold stars of Hero of the Soviet Union and one of Hero of Socialist Labor to his chest. It laughed at the spectacle of the entire Brezhnev clan wheeling and dealing and black-marketing in gold, diamonds, hard currency, and whatever else was available. It laughed at the spectacle of a nondescript officer by the name of Churbanov marrying Brezhnev's daughter and in no time at all receiving the rank of general and being appointed first deputy minister of the interior. It laughed at the spectacle of Nikolai Scholokov, the country's top law-and-order enforcer, pocketing the valuables taken from thieves and gangsters, forcing helpless old women to sell their family antiques to his scavengers for less than nothing. It laughed at the spectacle of Brezhnev's crony, Rashidov, top party man of Uzbekistan, linking arms with the local mafia and acquiring mind-boggling wealth at the expense of women and children forced to labor for nothing in the cotton fields. It laughed at the spectacle of bribery at all levels, of everything having a price, even government decorations. Society watched all this and much more, and its laughter was reminiscent of Gogol's famous "laughter through tears."

Some people threw themselves out of windows and under cars, others drank themselves to death, and others joined the free-for-all, stuffing their pockets, their bellies, their mouths with everything they could grab or bite off.

But others refused to die. Or give up.

For two decades, up to 1985, thinking people debated whether it was possible for things to change. The writing seemed to be on the wall,

Brezhnev and the party apparatus seemed to be entrenched for good in the seat of power, the humanistic ideals of socialism, which had galvanized the nation through periods of terrible hardship, seemed to have degenerated into obscene slogans. There seemed to be no sense in fighting for change, be it within the Party or without, for those who fought were either ignored or punished. The consensus (both in the Soviet Union and abroad) was that fundamental changes were beyond hope. Yet there were those who kept saying that the status quo could not continue, that it was the dark before the dawn.

I was one who held that view, in part because it seemed logical. No society remains static, there must be an up once you have gone down, and, as far as I was concerned, we had hit absolute rock bottom. But more than logic, *I had to believe* change would come. I held on to that faith like a drowning man at sea holds on to a spar.

Many of my closest friends told me I was crazy. "You are a naive idealist," one said. "You don't understand this country, the Russian people. Nothing will ever change, except for the worse. You are out of your fucking mind."

They had every reason to feel that way.

Leonid Brezhnev's death on November 10, 1982, came as no surprise. The faltering old man who seemed not to know where he was, whose speech impediment at times made his pronouncements incomprehensible, had become the laughingstock of the nation. He was the target of countless jokes, each a stinging comment on his failing mental capacities:

PERSONAL SECRETARY TO BREZHNEV: Leonid Ilyich, you're wearing different shoes, one brown, one black. I'm afraid you will have to return home and change them.

BREZHNEV (after a few minutes' thought): What good will that do? The pair at home also has one brown and one black.

Or:

BREZHNEV TO HIS SPEECHWRITER: I have to give a speech tomorrow about peaceful coexistence. But make it short. Fifteen minutes, maximum.

On the following day, the speechwriter asks Brezhnev: Well, Leonid Ilyich, how was the speech? Did they like it?

BREZHNEV: They liked it, yes, but why did you make it so long? I asked for fifteen minutes, you gave me one hour.

SPEECHWRITER: Do you mean you read all four copies?

I repeat, Brezhnev's death came as no surprise. But the emergence of Yuri Andropov as general secretary most certainly did.

For reasons I have yet fully to comprehend, his appointment was interpreted by many as being positive, as a reason for optimism. Yet this was the same man who for fifteen years had headed the KGB and had been responsible for the pitiless stamping out of dissent. One of his first acts as general secretary was to have vigilante-type groups of citizens patrol movie theaters, food and department stores, and even public baths in search of people shirking their work. The desire to put a stop to the country's disastrous lack of discipline is understandable, but the method chosen to achieve that aim was, in my opinion, reprehensible. Amazingly enough, it enjoyed majority support, and to this day, Andropov is remembered with fondness.

No less amazing, the West also did a bit of cheerleading in Andropov's honor. Supposedly he had a fine collection of LPs; rumor had it that he enjoyed jazz; the word was that he loved good whiskey; unimpeachable sources had it that he spoke English. Don't ask me why, but according to the "logic" of Soviet watchers, all of this was deemed to bode good.

The upbeat Soviet reaction to Andropov's appointment may have two explanations. First, in a time of almost total corruption, he was perceived as being honest. His modesty, his reticence, the absence of any rumors concerning the escapades of his children and relatives, all of this created in people's minds an image refreshingly different from Brezhnev and his clique. Second, Russians have traditionally opted for strong leadership, especially in times of stress. There is a commonly shared belief that results are best achieved by bashing whoever needs to be bashed, preferably with something heavy. The former chairman of the KGB was made to order for that purpose.

I, for one, have nothing good to say about Yuri Vladimirovich Andropov. I witnessed hardly any positive changes in domestic policy during the fifteen months of his tenure. In foreign policy, he was responsible for threatening to break off talks with the United States should that country begin to deploy Pershing II and cruise missiles in Europe, and then for carrying out that threat and thus playing into the hands of hawks such as Richard Perle. The first Pershing was deployed, the Soviet Union left the negotiating table in Geneva, and from that point on, the Pentagon was free to deploy to its heart's content.

Andropov died on February 9, 1984. Again, his death came as no surprise, since his illness had been an open secret for months. But the election of Konstantin Chernenko to the post of general secretary was a different matter. I don't know a single person in the Soviet Union who took that news seriously. Nobody who watched the ceremony of Andropov's funeral in Red Square, which was televised nationwide, will ever forget the tragicomical spectacle of Chernenko struggling to raise his right hand to the brim of his green fedora in a futile attempt to salute the body of his deceased comrade. I recall experiencing physical pain as the hand slowly, as if pulling an enormous weight, rose past his shoulder, inched by his neck, finally stopped at ear level, hung there trembling for five or ten seconds, and then dropped to his side, exhausted. There were several of us in the office that morning, and we all looked at one another. One of us remarked, "That man hasn't got long to live, for sure."

Anyone who knew anything about anything realized that Chernenko was a compromise figure. The question was who was next? The three front runners, the names that figured most prominently in discussions, were Gorbachev, Grishin, and Romanov.

Gorbachev had been elected to the Politburo in the fall of 1980. He was relatively unknown outside of party circles. Nevertheless, the word was that Gorbachev was the liberal in that troika. The other two were far more familiar figures.

Victor Grishin combined his Politburo function with that of first secretary of the Moscow City Party Organization, an extremely powerful and prestigious post. He was, it could be argued, the epitome of the apparatchik: faceless, formless, colorless. I have never heard anyone say anything about Grishin that spoke about the man's character. He functioned as part of the machine, he knew the rules. He was, as the Russians say, neither meat nor fish. Which is not to say that he didn't look out for his interests. A telling comment on Grishin's mentality is provided by the marriage of his son, a story relatively few people know. It begins with one of the Soviet Union's most evil characters, Lavrenty Beria. Beria was a pervert (it was probably one of his more attractive features) who, as I mentioned earlier, had squads of men patrolling the streets of Moscow with an eye out for beautiful women to be picked up and brought to him for his pleasure. He had them, enjoyed them, and allowed them to leave, keeping as a memento only their brassieres. However, there was one exception. A sixteen-year-old girl had once caught Beria's eye, so much so that he had gone to speak to her parents about his intentions. Although Beria was married, he took this girl when she was seventeen and treated her as a second wife. She lived with him and bore him a daughter. Many years later, long after Beria had been condemned to death and shot, Grishin's son met and fell in love with Beria's illegitimate daughter. They started going out. One day he proposed to her, but her mother was adamant. "Stay away from the high and mighty," she told her daughter. "I suffered enough to know." She refused to speak to the young man. When he phoned, she would bang down the receiver, and when he knocked at the door, she would open it, take one look, and slam it in his face. Then, one day, Grishin paid the mother a visit. "Why are you against my son's marrying your daughter?" he asked. "Do you consider this to be a mismatch? Is it because the son of Grishin is not good enough to marry the daughter of Beria?" He wasn't joking. Nor was he trying to be ironic. He was absolutely serious, for as a product of the apparatus, he continued to look with awe upon those who lived and worked with the Dragon.

I know this story as a fact—it was told to me by the girl's mother. Her name and that of her daughter are of no interest, except for gossip, which is why I have not divulged them. The interesting—riveting, to me—part of the story is in the dynastic marriage and Grishin's attitude.

The third contender, Grigory Romanov, was universally feared and disliked. Formerly head of the Leningrad Regional Organization, Romanov had made a name for himself as a ruthless, dictatorial, power-mongering functionary. His arrogance was such that, as the story went, he allowed only a select few into his office at the Smolny party headquarters. Usually, he conducted all discussion sitting alone in his office facing a TV camera, while those he addressed sat in another room and watched a television screen. Supposedly, for his daughter's wedding, he had had one of the sets of imperial china taken from the Hermitage museum and brought to the banquet hall for the family feast. This rumor was never corroborated, but, considering Romanov's disregard for one and all, it could well be true. Of the three men, he was unquestionably the hard-liner. His election as general secretary would almost certainly have led to a return to a modernized, but no less horrid, version of Stalinism.

Konstantin Chernenko passed away on March 10, 1985. On the

following day, a plenary session of the Central Committee elected Mikhail Gorbachev as its general secretary. Prior to that, however, the Politburo had made its selection and undoubtedly announced it to the Central Committee session as the Politburo's recommendation. We know that Gorbachev was recommended. What we do not know is who voted for him and who did not.

There is reason to believe that the sixty-two-year-old Romanov, realizing that he didn't have sufficient backing to win, threw his support to Grishin, nine years his senior. If that is so, his plan was clear: with a man like Grishin in power, it would have been relatively easy for Romanov to have his main opponent, Gorbachev, pushed out of the Politburo. Once that was achieved, Romanov could sooner or later count on taking Grishin's position—probably sooner, considering Grishin's age.

The Politburo vote was close, but even that statement is based on hearsay. What we do know, however, is that of the ten men who constituted the Politburo then (Aliyev, Gorbachev, Grishin, Gromyko, Kunayev, Romanov, Shcherbitsky, Solomentsev, Tikhonov, and Vorotnikov), seven were later retired: Romanov (July 1985), Tikhonov (October 1985), Grishin (February 1986), Kunayev (January 1987), Aliyev (October 1987), Solomentsev (October 1988), and Shcherbitsky (September, 1989).

Gromyko, whose active support for Gorbachev played a crucial role in the Central Committee's vote, remained a member of the Politburo until his death in 1989.

The number of senior party officials who died between 1981, the year of the Twenty-sixth Party Congress, and 1985, the year when Gorbachev became general secretary, was so high as to prompt Moscow wags to come up with the following joke.

QUESTION: What is the most popular sport among party officials?

ANSWER: Drag racing on caissons.

I remember the sense of excitement created by Gorbachev's election, a feeling in the air, a quickening of the country's pulse. There was absolutely nothing in his official biography that reflected a commitment to radical change, there was no evidence to support the great expectations his election brought to life. But the people knew—as they almost always do. Animals know about the coming hurricane or earthquake, they sense it long before we do. Could it be that we, political animals, have that same sixth sense for approaching social change?

Gorbachev's first speech was different than anything the Soviet people had heard since the time of Lenin. He began by saying what everyone knew, but no official had been willing to admit: the economy was grossly inefficient and in need of fundamental restructuring; labor productivity was extremely low; energy waste was staggering; the production of consumer goods and foodstuffs was well below world standards in both quality and quantity. Radical measures were needed, he said, "to raise the country to a qualitatively new stage of social and economic progress." But Gorbachev went further, tying economic reform to political change: "We have a clear understanding that this task cannot be accomplished without attaining a new level in developing socialist democracy." He added, "Publicity is an inalienable part of socialist democracy and a standard of all public life. Extensive, timely, and frank information is evidence of trust in the people, respect for their intelligence and feelings and of their ability to understand events."

To a nation that had lived through decades of strict censorship and information control, that brief sentence, that first call for what would become known throughout the world as glasnost, held the promise of radical transformation.

But we had all heard speeches before, albeit not so radical, speeches full of the most wonderful ideas and promises, speeches that had affected our lives as much as the Pop! of a bottle of champagne. Was this speech more of the same? We soon discovered that it was not; we soon realized that the appearance of Gorbachev signaled a breakthrough for the country. And in the process, each of us experienced his or her own personal breakthrough.

Not surprisingly, my breakthrough was a media event. Just as the crackdown on *Sputnik* magazine ushered in for me the stifling stagnation of the Brezhnev years, so did "Leningrad-Seattle: A Citizens' Summit" symbolize, in my opinion, the beginning of glasnost. "A Citizens' Summit" was what has come to be called a spacebridge—something the history of which is worth recounting.

When Ronald Reagan was campaigning for the presidency in 1980, there were people, both in the United States and in the Soviet Union, who did not take his anti-Soviet confrontational rhetoric seriously. Their view was that liberal presidential candidates become more conservative when they enter the Oval Office, and vice-versa. While that may be the general rule, it has exceptions—and Ronald Reagan was one of them. I had absolutely no illusions about the future of Soviet-American relations should Mr. Reagan defeat President Carter; when he did, I predicted a serious worsening of relations on the "Nightline" program of November 5, 1980. As time showed, I was right on target.

From the day President Reagan assumed office, the relationship began to worsen—that is to say, it went from bad to terrible. But the blame rests not only or exclusively with Ronald Reagan. When the Soviet leadership decided to use military forces in Afghanistan, it clearly signaled its own desire to worsen the state of relations with the West, in particular the United States. As of this writing, we still do not know exactly how that decision was made, which individuals were responsible for having done their country and people one of the worst disservices in their history. In the absence of such information, I would like propose what I believe to be a plausible theory.

By the end of 1979, two things had become crystal clear. First, that the United States Congress would not ratify the SALT II Treaty signed by Jimmy Carter and Leonid Brezhnev. Second, in response to the numerical superiority of Soviet SS-20s, NATO had decided to deploy the Pershing II and cruise missiles in Europe, international opposition notwithstanding. Both of these decisions were major defeats for Soviet foreign policy, especially for the architects of détente. There is legitimate reason to believe that the more hawkish elements of the Establishment saw this as their chance. In that connection, I think of the man who ran the North American Service of Radio Moscow when I began to work there, Nikolai Karev. He opposed détente from the day it began with the spring 1972 visit of President Nixon to Moscow. He wrote letters of protest to the Central Committee stating that there was only one way to deal with "imperialist America"—and that was from a position of strength (replace "imperialist America" with "totalitarian Russia" and see if it reminds you of anything or anybody). Karev had been swiftly removed from his office and replaced by a much more liberal and open-minded person. But the Karevs hadn't disappeared by the end of the seventies, and the events of that period played into their hands. I can imagine them saying to Brezhnev, "See? Didn't we always tell you détente wouldn't work? That you can't trust the Americans? That the only thing they respect is power? So let's show them some muscle!" Afghanistan was the ideal place to do that. It had a common frontier with the Soviet Union, it was considered a military nonentity, and it was a good testing ground for Soviet modern weapons and military tactics and strategy.

My theory may be wrong, although when all the facts are known, as they undoubtedly will be, I think they will support me. But be that as it may, the U.S.-Soviet relationship deteriorated at a catastrophic rate. By the end of 1981, virtually all contact had been interrupted. Beside the absence of official exchanges, the number of American tourists visiting the Soviet Union dropped drastically, while the number of Soviets visiting the United States, which had always been close to zero, stayed that way. It was in this void that the concept of the spacebridge was born. Several people can claim to have invented the idea: Jim Hickman, Rick Lukens, Joseph Goldin, Pavel Korchagin, and Sergei Skvortsov. The concept was simple enough: use TV satellite technology and wide-screen televisions to bring two large groups of people together. That concept crystallized in Moscow in the summer of 1981 during discussions between the five gentlemen just mentioned. The Americans, Hickman and Lukens, had come as one of the very first pioneers of citizen diplomacy. In their meetings with their Soviet counterparts, they mentioned the U.S. Festival, a rock concert with a message that was to take place in San Bernardino, California, in September. The festival, they said, would be an open-air affair attracting as many as a quarter of a million people daily. The rock concert would take place on a stage but would also be shown on a gigantic screen for the benefit of those seated too far away to see the action. It was at that point that someone asked why we couldn't beam a signal from Moscow and pick it up on that screen in San Bernardino.

On September 15, 1981, at 8 P.M. Pacific time and at 7 A.M. of the following morning Moscow time, nearly three hundred thousand people in San Bernardino sent a wall of roaring delight thundering down the valley as they welcomed the image of several hundred Soviets that had just flashed on their screen. Meanwhile, in a faraway Moscow studio, a cry of delight and disbelief went up at the sight of the giant Californian crowd on the studio screen. There was an exchange of songs, and that was all. It was the world's first spacebridge.

Some saw it as a piece of hi-tech razzle-dazzle. But others immediately realized its potential for bringing Soviets and Americans together at a crucial time in their history, a time when their governments were not on speaking terms. This understanding led to a series of spacebridges, the majority of which I hosted. These included "Moscow-California" (with the second U.S. Festival, held a year after the first); the "Peace Child" spacebridge, honoring the memory of Samantha Smith; the "Remembering War" spacebridge, which brought Soviet and American veterans of World War II together on the occasion of the fortieth anniversary of the linkup on the Elbe River in April 1945; a spacebridge called "Children and Film" during which youngsters in Moscow and San Diego looked at one another's movies and shared impressions. All of these, plus a few I have not mentioned, were edited down to air size (sixty to ninety minutes) and shown at prime time on National Channel 1 in the Soviet Union. They were given far less prominence in the United States. Interestingly, they were soon forgotten in both countries. The reason for that, I believe, was their artificial nature.

As I noted, the relationship between the two countries had reached an all-time low. The majority of Americans feared and disliked the Soviet Union, while their Soviet counterparts had serious doubts about U.S. intentions. One would, however, never have reached that conclusion by watching those first spacebridges. For a variety of reasons, not the least of which was the consideration that things were bad enough without making them worse, both U.S. and Soviet participants were selected with a view to their desire for better relations with the other side. They weren't interested in being confrontational, they weren't interested in scoring points. They were looking for new avenues of communication.

All of this was fine and gave people a good feeling; yet they could not help but realize how little these exchanges corresponded to the real state of affairs. These TV specials were, in a way, wishful thinking; because of that, they didn't leave a deep imprint on people's minds. That was the history of the spacebridge exchange when Gosteleradio and Seattle's KING-5 TV agreed to do a radically different kind of spacebridge. It would feature an audience of two hundred ordinary Americans in Seattle and the same number of ordinary Soviet citizens in Leningrad—hence the name, "A Citizens' Summit." I was to be the Soviet moderator. My American counterpart would be Phil Donahue. I had suggested his name early on, not that I had ever met Phil personally; I simply felt that if anyone was qualified to do a people's summit, he was the man.

Today, when doing things with the Soviet Union is chic, it is fun to sip a gin and tonic and reminisce about the difficulties of those times—especially when the reminiscer wasn't personally involved. Let us not forget that Phil Donahue was the *first* American television celebrity to risk his standing by "doing something with the Russkies." My American counterparts on all the previous spacebridges had not been television personalities; they might have been regarded as pinkos for participating, but they took far less of a risk than Phil.

Many of his colleagues in the television business, to say nothing of the Kremlinologists he consulted, told him point-blank that he was a fool, that he would be used by the Russians, that he would never be allowed to say what he wanted. He was made to understand that he, Phil Donahue, should stick to doing talk shows and stay away from politics, where the Russians would eat him alive.

That Phil refused to be intimidated speaks to his credit. That he was apprehensive speaks to his common sense.

Phil had insisted upon his team's coming to Leningrad to select the Soviet studio audience. If this were not allowed, he said, if the American side could not unequivocally state that it had personally picked the Soviet participants, American viewers would immediately think that the Soviet audience had been handpicked by the KGB. I saw his point but felt it would take a bit of doing to make our management accept it. As things turned out, my apprehensions were unfounded: in the winter of 1985, a group of Donahue researchers came to Leningrad to select the studio audience. Several of us were there to meet them. They wanted an audience that represented a cross section of Leningrad: industrial workers, shipbuilders, longshoremen, nurses, teachers, students, doctors, and so on. Obviously, these people couldn't be selected by simply stopping them at random in the city streets. No less obviously, the American group couldn't hope to get into a factory or a hospital without our help (just as we, when we traveled to Boston to select the U.S. audience for our second spacebridge, couldn't have had access to many organizations and people without the active support of our American hosts). In Leningrad, we worked together in what I would regard as near-perfect harmony. At the end of the day, we would gather in one of the rooms of the beautiful Astoria Hotel and go through the list of names of would-be participants we had selected. The Donahue people always had the last word about cutting whomever they wished from the list; the Soviets only gave advice. In slightly over one week, we had our audience. With the spacebridge about one month away, we parted company.

I planned to return to Leningrad a day before the event, but a frantic call from one of my colleagues in the advance group forced me to change my plans. The Leningrad Regional Party Committee, he said, had decided to round up the spacebridge studio audience for a briefing—something I could not possibly allow. As soon as I received that news, I hopped on a plane. Forty minutes later, I landed in the Leningrad airport. One hour later, I was closeted with a couple of my Moscow buddies. What were we to do? The management of Leningrad television would just as soon disobey the regional party committee as they would commit hara-kiri. Let's not forget, Gorbachev had been in office a mere eight months, the Party's hold on society had not even begun to weaken, and its authority was still absolute. Nobody was going to risk the party committee's wrath. I made an appointment with the head of the ideological department, Galina I. Barinova.

The Leningrad Regional Party Committee headquarters are located in Smolny Institute, a historical site I mentioned earlier. It is heavily guarded, as are virtually all party buildings (whom are they afraid of?), with security officers sprinkled all over the premises.

Party functionaries, like birds of a feather, immediately recognize one another. They share certain features. These are usually not immediately discernible, especially to those whose contacts with these people have been limited. But the features and markings, while more or less subtle, are no less evident to the experienced eye than a tiger's stripes. Among other things, these include manner of dress—(conservative in style and color, similar in appearance to what the top party leadership is wearing); manner of speech (somewhat gruff, deliberately not refined, "people talk"); and manner of shaking hands (your hand is firmly seized and jerked up and out). There are a host of other details, all of which, when taken together, allow party functionaries to recognize one another on sight.

Galina Barinova didn't fit the image. Tall, slim, distinguished, dressed with taste, still quite attractive, she reminded me more of a corporate businesswomen than of anything else. After greeting me (the handshake was firm but without any pulling or jerking) and inviting me to sit down across the desk from her, she asked, "What can we do to allay your worries?" I told her what I had heard about the decision to brief the audience. I also told her that I was absolutely opposed to it. "Why?" she asked. I explained that, in principle, briefing an audience that had never had any contact with Americans might even be a good idea. But in this specific case, it was out of the question because, and I made this quite clear, if word ever got back to the American side, they would interpret it as an attempt to brainwash, put pressure on, intimidate, and coach the Soviet participants. And that, I said, would be the kiss of death for all future spacebridges. "Really?" she said. "And how will they ever find out?" I must admit that the question and the degree of cynicism it indicated floored me. But I staggered to my feet at the count of eight and came back with a few punches of my own. There is, I pointed out, a U.S. consulate in Leningrad. Its people will be watching the event and reporting everything back to their Moscow embassy. What's more, I said, once you bring that audience of over two hundred people together for the briefing, some of them are going to tell their friends and relatives about it. The news is bound to get out.

Barinova smiled—perfect lips, expertly painted a dark red, parted just enough to show two rows of perfectly white teeth—pressed a button on the intercom on a small table loaded with phones to her left. A voice came on: "Yes, Galina Ivanovna?" "Get Pyotr Petrovich here. Immediately." She looked over at me. "Pyotr Petrovich works for the bureau," she said, using the commonly accepted euphemism for the KGB. "He'll be right over." And indeed he was. The Leningrad KGB headquarters is located on Liteynaya Street, quite a distance from the Smolny Institute. Of course, the bureau may have had an office in the party building. But the fact remains that Pyotr Petrovich materialized out of nowhere in no time flat. It was my distinct feeling that he whizzed into Barinova's office, but whizzed in silently, sideways, deferentially, braked sharply one hairsbreadth away from Barinova's desk, and stood there, head slightly bent and inclined, as if to say, "I am at your service."

"Meet Vladimir Vladimirovich Pozner," Barinova said, "and be seated." We shook hands—a brief touch-and-let-go—and Pyotr Petrovich allowed his knees to bend just enough for his backside to meet the edge of the chair Barinova had pointed at. Thus he sat, or rather perched, reminding me of a somewhat aging, somewhat balding parrot with faded blue eyes.

"Pyotr Petrovich," Barinova began, "do you have any information about our American friends? Are they showing any particular interest in the Leningrad-Seattle linkup?" He looked back at her unblinkingly, pursed his lips, frowned slightly, then shook his head and said, "No, Galina Ivanovna, all is calm." She nodded. "So there is nothing to worry about, Pyotr Petrovich?" Again, he looked into her eyes, pursed his lips, then decidedly shook his head. "All is calm," he repeated. "Thank you, Pyotr Petrovich, you may go now." Peter the Parrot, as I had come to call him, jumped off his perch, nodded to us, and whirred out of the room. "Well?" Barinova asked me softly.

I knew I had lost. But I had one last card to play. "Galina Ivanovna," I said, "if you insist on briefing the participants, there is nothing I can do about it. But if anything happens, it is your responsibility. I want it on the record that I warned you about the possible consequences. It is now out of my hands."

Until very recently, one of the many advantages of being a party official was the chance to give orders without taking responsibility. If things went well, the party official got the credit. If they didn't, the other people got the axe. So when I refused to accept responsibility for what might happen because of the party committee's decision, I was putting Barinova in a position party functionaries at her level avoided at all costs.

"There is no need to be so categorical," she said with a smile that would have made Peter the Parrot chirp. "We are not bureaucrats." She stood up, grasped my left arm above the elbow, and said, "Come along, so-and-so is expecting us," (she used a name and patronymic I have since forgotten, but the person she was alluding to was the number-two man of the entire Leningrad party organization, the secretary for ideology). We left her office, walked down one of Smolny's endless corridors—something I have done since then on several occasions, each time thinking of Sergei Kirov, the Leningrad party boss who was shot in the back of the head by a hired killer as he walked toward his office, an assassination that was Stalin's pretext for unleashing the wave of terror that wiped out all opposition, along with the Soviet Union's finest people.

The second secretary's office was gigantic—it could easily have seated our future spacebridge audience. The man who greeted me was in his mid-fifties. All I remember is that he wore glasses, had a well-modulated baritone, and did a lot of flapping with his arms. He gave me the traditional jerk-up handshake and said, "If you do not advise us to brief the participants, we won't. It's as simple as that. You know best. We trust you. Implicitly. Good luck."

I must have had a very stupid look on my face, because Barinova began to laugh. It was only then that I realized how well they had been prepared. They had been ready to cancel the briefing even before I came. All they wanted to do was hear my reasoning. The whole bit about inviting Peter the Parrot was pure theater (even though Peter may not have known it); they had been testing me. And as soon as I told Barinova it was their responsibility, they passed the ball right back to me and ran. If anyone was to be dumped for a loss, it would be me.

Came the day of the spacebridge. I was in total control—like the patient who has just been told he has terminal cancer. He knows he is going to die, so why make a fuss? Especially considering how little time he has left. Three . . . two . . . one . . . and we were off! I think everyone on the Soviet side, myself included, was stunned by what happened during the actual bridge. The American audience came out swinging and hammered the Soviet Union on a whole range of issues—emigration, anti-Semitism, human rights, dissidents, freedom of speech, Sakharov, Afghanistan, KAL Flight 007, Solzhenitsyn. Nothing remotely like this had ever been on Soviet television, let alone expressed by Americans on Soviet television! Imagine, if you will, a television special featuring a rigorous critique of the American way of life by a Soviet audience, the show being broadcast throughout the United States during prime time on all three networks. The Soviets would be hitting away on racial discrimination, economic inequality, drugs, crime, police violence, the homeless. Dramatic as that might seem, it was in fact far more so for Soviets who had never heard their country criticized publicly.

As moderator, I was smack in the middle of a truly wild situation. I was operating simultaneously on several planes. First, it was my responsibility to help the two sides communicate. Second, I had to keep evaluating my behavior and try to determine how I should react to Phil, who was coming on like Rambo—should I slug it out toe to toe, or should I refuse to be drawn into a confrontational exchange? Third, I was thinking about the people standing on the sidelines—the television executives plus Galina Barinova and company from Smolny Institute. What were they thinking? Fourth, and last, I was wondering whether this spacebridge would actually ever get on the air and, if it did, how much would be cut? I think it's fair to say that my situation was far more complex than Phil's, and the nature of my audience did not make things any easier.

Our participants had almost all been selected by Marilyn O'Reilly, who had worked for the Donahue show for many years in Chicago and New York. She was an expert in her area. But in addition to being an expert, this Irish-American from the Windy City, the mother of seven (six boys and a girl), was absolutely charming. Without speaking a word of Russian, she managed to establish a human rapport with every Soviet she spoke to. They loved her. Loraine Landelius, another Donahue staffer, came across as kind, warm, and sensitive. Those were the first Americans most of the Soviets had ever met, and they automatically concluded that all Americans were like Marilyn and Loraine. They came to the studio with that understanding. Some had even brought little bouquets of flowers to wave at their American "friends." They had sat on their chairs smiling, waiting for this hands-across-the-ocean spectacular to begin, and they had been clobbered. The Soviets became very defensive. They refused to open up. While some of the Americans volunteered harsh criticism of shortcomings in their own country, the Soviets refused to follow that example. Try as I might, I could not get them to be human.

Glasnost was in its infancy, and most people still preferred to play it safe. They knew all too well what had happened to those whose only "crime" had been to criticize what they perceived to be shortcomings of Soviet society. They had been accused of spreading anti-Soviet propaganda and put away for it. And mind you, they had not done this *on television,* for God's sake. Since there was no one else to turn to, I spoke out, doing my best, whenever appropriate, to point out Soviet failures as well as successes. I realized the risks, but I had made my decision long before the spacebridge. What's more, I had no choice—*someone* from the Soviet Union had to admit at least part of the truth.

As the Soviet side stonewalled, the Americans got angrier. The barrage of criticism threatened to blow the show out of the water as far as its ever getting on the air was concerned.

When it was over, I was exhausted. My wife, Kathrin, and a close Leningrad friend of mine had been seated on the sidelines. Now, when I looked over at them, I read consternation in their eyes. My colleagues from Moscow, Sergei and Pavel, seemed to think that everything had been fine. But they were young and, I felt, didn't really understand the political implications of what had happened. The Leningrad party officials were shell-shocked. I remember Barinova's not-so-confident smile and parting words, "Very interesting, very interesting indeed," and I also recall my own reaction: the bastards are waiting for a reaction from higher up. I was emotionally drained, completely deflated. More than anything else, I wanted to forget the whole thing.

Unfortunately, that was out of the question. We had to do our edit— and we had promised not to cut the nitty-gritty, not to edit out whatever might be displeasing to Soviet ears. Our honor was at stake here, and our careers. At the end of the spacebridge, Phil had spoken about the great respect Americans have for the Soviet people. But, he concluded, how can such a great, talented, wonderful people permit themselves to be ruled by a group of faceless octogenarians? How the hell were we going to get *that* on Soviet television?

Perhaps I should point out that we had a gentleman's agreement with Phil to keep both edits, American and Soviet, as similar as possible. However, because one was done in Moscow and the other in New York, plus the fact that the American version couldn't be more than forty-six minutes long (the constraints of Donahue's show), while the Soviet version was planned for ninety minutes of airtime, the edits had to be very different. That was a fact both parties accepted. But we were mutually suspicious of each other; any cut was almost automatically perceived as being motivated by political considerations. Looking back on those final edits, I feel both sides preserved their integrity and honesty.

Our airdate was in February 1986, just two days before the opening of the Twenty-seventh Party Congress. Since this was no average show, the chairman of Gosteleradio had asked for a preliminary screening. That is an evening I have never forgotten.

The spacebridge team, plus the head of Gosteleradio's International Department, came trooping into the chairman's office. He was accompanied by two of his deputies and a gentleman from the Central Committee of the Party who was responsible for overseeing television's activities. The chairman, Alexander N. Aksionov, had just recently replaced Lapin, and most people didn't know what to make of him. He was, in many ways, the archetypal party functionary. He had occupied a series of posts, ranging from commander of a guerrilla warfare unit in Byelorussia during the Nazi occupation, to Byelorussia's minister of the interior, to Soviet ambassador to Poland. He was, as I later discovered, a good man: basically kind, fair, scrupulously honest. But he was also terribly limited in his outlook, a man, I would say, with tunnel vision. Describing the communists of revolutionary times, the poet Nikolai Tikhonov wrote, "If nails were made of such people, there would be no stronger nails in the world." The description suited Aksionov perfectly. Strong, unbending, direct, with a faith in the Party that bordered on the religious and a certainty that the party worker (like himself) could do any job.

That concept has a history of its own. As the Party gradually usurped the Councils (Soviets), as the Party apparatus superseded the government in every and all areas, the party worker came to be regarded as tinker and baker and candlestick maker—he could do any job, he was qualified by virtue of being a professional party functionary. When such an individual lost his party job for whatever transgression or because of whatever intrigue, he would be appointed to a post that, alas, usually called for expertise and professional training (more often than not, an ambassadorship). There was a time when party workers did indeed represent the country's intellectual elite, but Stalin's gigantic lawnmower cut off their heads, leaving only the conformists and the nondescript alive. The system through which party functionaries were chosen was self-regulating; it weeded out anyone with individuality, with a differing viewpoint, with any significant degree of self-respect. This could not but lead to a situation when the party functionary, as a rule, was not fit for *any* job except so-called party work. The net result of appointing party bosses to other important posts has been catastrophic—a fact that my country has yet to publicly acknowledge.

A. N. Aksionov spent three and a half years as chairman of Gosteleradio and demonstrated a total lack of understanding, of any ability to provide it with leadership. He achieved nothing and has already been forgotten.

But on that evening, I knew nothing about the man who would either kill the program or allow it to live. I was seeing him in the flesh for the first time, and what I saw did not particularly impress me: the typical three-piece black wool suit of the party functionary, thick glasses, a round, nondescript face, a small, tight mouth, a buttonlike nose, dark hair brushed back from a somewhat narrow forehead.

Aksionov gave each of us a bone-crushing handshake, invited us to sit down, and pushed the screening button. Throughout the next hour and a half, I kept watching him, hoping for some sign of what to expect. But the poker face never changed. No smiles, no frowns. Nothing. Later I realized he wanted to keep his deputies in the dark. No sooner was the screening over than he turned to one of them and asked for his opinion. This was the man who headed the Foreign Service Division of Gosteleradio. He was also the man who had called for my expulsion from the Party for daring to question the wisdom of the Soviet government's decision to go into Afghanistan. He was, in my opinion, the perfect conformist, a man who could, depending on the circumstances, defend or attack the same point of view or action with equal conviction. I could almost read his mind as he prepared to answer the chairman. The boss had given no indication of his assessment, but it stood to reason he couldn't possibly support such a show. Everything about it sent danger signals flashing through the bureaucratic mind and, since glasnost was still in embryonic form, there existed no precedents to serve as guidelines. The odds were against the spacebridge, and Yevstafyev went with the odds.

"First," he said, "the material needs serious editing. But even then, it does not rate being shown nationwide. So, number two, I would suggest limiting it to Leningrad alone—and even then, I can't say I fully recommend it. Finally, this is not the time to put it on the air, not on the eve of such a major event as the Party Congress," he concluded.

I had been watching the chairman's face all the while, and again, not a muscle had twitched. Trying to guess his thoughts was like trying to read the mind of a stone statue.

"Thank you," Aksionov said and nodded at the other deputy, who headed radio's Domestic Service. This man was notorious for being afraid of everything, especially of making a decision that might, in any way, displease someone higher up. His reaction to the spacebridge was predictable. It could not, should not, be aired. What's more, what was all that talk about Jews and refuseniks and dissidents supposed to mean?

By the time he finished speaking, I began to feel sick. It wasn't because I feared loosing my job—I had gotten over that quite a while earlier. It was the idea of the show's not getting on the air and what the American reaction to that would be. To say nothing of how I would look in Phil's eyes.

That is why I began pinching myself, when the next man to speak, Grigory Oganov of the Central Committee, literally said the following: "This is what television is really all about. I think it is an outstanding program, one that heralds a new era in Soviet television."

I was still in a state of mild shock when Aksionov said, "Now that everyone has spoken, allow me to share a few ideas with you. To begin with, I wish to congratulate all of you who worked on this program. You have done a highly commendable job. Furthermore, it is not simply an outstanding piece of work, but I regard it as the best possible gift we could present to the Twenty-seventh Party Congress, which, as you all know, opens the day after tomorrow. Soviet television can be proud of what you have done, and you deserve the highest marks for your achievement."

It was one of those moments in life that we all dream about but know will never happen. And suddenly it does. It was then that I fully understood what it means to walk on air. This was a total triumph, there was nothing I could compare it to. I wanted to climb the walls, make obscene gestures at the two deputies, yell like a banshee. Instead, I shook hands all around, floated out of the office—and then, the antidrinking campaign be damned, we all went out and got roaring drunk!

To this day, I do not know why Aksionov said what he said. Somehow, I cannot believe he was expressing his personal view. Somehow I have to think that he had a sneak preview of the spacebridge in some very important person's company, or that a cassette was sent to that very important person in advance. Having witnessed Aksionov's reluctance to support anything out of the ordinary, his refusal to back his own people when he got bad vibes from the Central Committee apparatus, his negative attitude toward more outspoken journalists, it seems almost impossible that he would have risked taking the responsibility of putting such a radically different program on the air. My guess is that he had been briefed.

"Leningrad-Seattle: A Citizens' Summit" was telecast on prime-time national Soviet television—not once, but twice. It was seen by at least one hundred and eighty million people and was a sensation. Overnight, I became a celebrity. By a fluke of circumstance, I was the first Soviet to be seen by the nation in an unrehearsed discussion with ordinary, everyday Americans. The fact that I had spoken the truth, been willing to admit problems and failings that all Soviets knew existed, the fact that I had, at the same time, stood up for my country on issues of principle struck a chord across the country. For decades, people had been given no choice but canned, predictable programs where awkward truths were discreetly ignored. Gorbachev had called for openness, for honesty. This space-bridge was a spectacular demonstration of the new approach. It involved both straight talk and Americans and, as such, it challenged both internal and cold-war bugaboos that we had lived with for decades.

The public response was overwhelming. Letters to the editor swamped newspapers across the country. Gosteleradio alone received over seventy thousand letters. One of the majority views was predictable: "Finally, we are talking to Americans without a middleman, finally we are in direct contact. How wonderful!" The second was, at least for me, completely unexpected. It expressed a devastating critique of the Soviet audience: "Comrade Pozner, how did you ever assemble so many idiots in one studio? Why were our people so uptight? Why did they lie? Why wouldn't they admit things like the Americans did? If you had had the sense to invite me, rest assured, you would not have regretted it." That view, expressed both much more and much less politely, came to remind me of the famous saying "I have met the enemy and he is us." Without realizing it and, perhaps, for the first time, we as a nation had looked at ourselves on television and experienced shame.

Today, a mere five years later, Soviets express their views on television more vehemently, more openly, and with a far more critical view of their government, leaders, and system than most Americans. That is, of course, the result of glasnost, of perestroika, of the truly revolutionary changes that have occurred in this country. But I would like to believe that the first impulse in that direction came from the Leningrad-Seattle space-bridge, from the painful blow it dealt to the national pride. It was, in my opinion, a spectacularly successful example of television shock therapy. One that Americans are also badly in need of but have never gotten.

It must be said that from the outset, U.S. commercial television was reluctant to support the spacebridge idea. The networks stayed away from it initially. Even when Roone Arledge, president of ABC News, demonstrated the courage, imagination, and originality of thought to put on a series of spacebridges linking the U.S. Congress with the USSR Supreme Soviet ("Capital to Capital"), it was aired *after* "Nightline," and only the hardiest of news junkies stayed awake to see it.

Supposedly, spacebridges are not sexy, they will not win their time period, and their ratings will leave much to be desired. That is the conventional wisdom American television officials of different rank and standing have shared with me. But that begs several questions. How do they know? On the basis of what facts do they make this judgment?

The Leningrad-Seattle spacebridge was offered to all the different stations that air Phil Donahue's show. Most of them backed off *without even a preview.* The viewer's "freedom of choice" was fully honored. However, the lucky minority that did get to see the spacebridge reacted with just as much enthusiasm as their Soviet counterparts. I received several hundred letters from the United States, and it could be said that the average American's view both coincided with and differed from that of the average Soviet. Much like their Soviet counterparts, the Americans applauded the opportunity to address one another directly via satellite, to talk on a people-to-people basis rather than on a government-to-government level. Also, like the Soviets, they were very self-critical. Americans found themselves to be aggressive, arrogant, pushy, chauvinistic. They lauded the Soviets for being more restrained, for being more knowledgeable. As for the difference, it had to do with Soviets really not being very surprised, at least physically, by the American audience, whereas Americans were clearly not expecting to see what they saw. This was best expressed by a woman from Philadelphia who wrote, "I always knew Russian women have children, just like we do. But it took that kind of exchange, I had to see them as living people, up there on the screen, for those children to register, to come alive. It changed my whole perspective about who the Russians are."

Another woman, this one from Kansas City, marveled, "I was stunned to see that the Russian women were attractive, well dressed, wore makeup, had nice hairstyles. I thought they all wore babushkas and were ugly."

That lady had probably formed her image of the typical Russian woman on the basis of the Wendy's hamburger ad of the "fashion show" in Moscow, where the number-one model is a huge fat woman who stomps around in boots, wears a military suit, no makeup whatsoever, steel-rimmed specs, and so on. The ad is stupid, it is an insult to Russian women (we can live with that), it is an insult to Americans' intelligence (can they live with that?), and it does, stupidity notwithstanding, enhance the stereotype of the Soviet Union one finds in American cartoons, movies, TV serials, comics, and so on.

Could it possibly be that one of the reasons why spacebridges have been rejected is precisely because they destroy that stereotype?

The "Citizens' Summit" aired, as I mentioned, two days before the opening of the Twenty-seventh Party Congress, an event that attracted universal attention. It was, after all, the first post-Brezhnev Congress; what's more, the changes that had taken place in the Soviet Union between March 1985, when Gorbachev was elected general secretary, and February 1986, the month of the Congress, were revolutionary. What other breakthroughs would the Twenty-seventh Congress make? That question brought more foreign correspondents to Moscow than any other political event in the country's history. I was still ABC's "favorite commie," so I wasn't too surprised when that network made me a very interesting proposal: to be interviewed live from Washington, D.C., by David Brinkley immediately after President Reagan's national address on the defense budget. Naturally, I accepted.

The interview with David Brinkley became a cause célèbre. However, some preliminary remarks are needed for the story to be properly appreciated.

A month or so earlier, Ronald Reagan's key advisers had concluded that congressional opposition was building against yet another increase in the military budget, which had doubled over the past six years. The previous November, Reagan had met for the first time with Mikhail Gorbachev in Geneva. This meeting resulted in a perceptible reduction in U.S.-Soviet tension. And the president's men had seen a private poll that showed that three-quarters of Americans believed that the United States was militarily stronger than the Soviet Union. The president's advisers decided that only Ronald Reagan could turn the tide; he would take his case for more arms directly to the American people. The President's speech was scheduled for February 26 at 8 P.M., EST.

Because of the eight-hour time difference between Moscow and Washington, I had to be in the studio no later than 3:30 A.M., Moscow time, the following morning. The president spoke for little more than twenty minutes. He did his best to rally the nation, painting a portrait of a world made dangerous by the Soviet Union's military might and godless ideology. He had charts and graphs depicting ongoing expansion of the "giant Red Army" and displayed a map of the globe, dramatically illustrating the spread of communism in Africa, Asia, and Latin America in the seventies. "The record of Soviet behavior," he said gravely, "the long history of Soviet brutality toward those who are weaker, reminds us that the only guarantee of peace and freedom is our military strength and our national will. The people of Afghanistan and Poland, of Czechoslovakia and Cuba, and so many other captive nations, they understand this."

Following the president's speech, which ran several minutes shorter than expected, Speaker of the House Jim Wright gave the Democratic party's view. He spoke for slightly over twelve minutes. Then Brinkley, in his laconic style, summarized what the politicians had said, then briefly interviewed ABC's White House and congressional correspondents about how the speech would play on Capitol Hill. That concluded, he swiveled in his chair and told his American audience, "And now we'll go to Moscow to hear what Soviet political commentator Vladimir Pozner has to say about all this."

I expected to have roughly two minutes of airtime, so I gave a brief summary of what I felt were the flaws in the president's analysis and stated that, in my opinion, his speech had not been very honest. Mr. Brinkley wanted to know what hadn't been very honest.

I had been hoping he would ask.

President Reagan spoke about SDI, I said, or Star Wars. And he accused the Soviet Union of having begun developing a strategic defense initiative of its own thirteen years ago, ten years *before* President Reagan announced his Star Wars program. Now that means that for ten years, the Soviet Union had worked on a space-based anti–ballistic missile system, a system that presented a mortal threat to the United States, a system specifically prohibited by the ABM Treaty of 1972. And for ten years *there was not a single voice in the American military or government raised in protest.* What's more, when the president himself announced SDI in March 1983, he made no allusion whatsoever to this being a response to Soviet Star Wars activities. I asked the American people if they believed that could be possible. Did they believe we could develop an SDI of our own without the United States noticing it when the U.S. military is capable of counting every tactical nuclear weapon that we have?

It was, I must say, a rather devastating argument. But to make things worse, David Brinkley kept coming back for more. Our conversation lasted for nearly eight minutes, after which Mr. Brinkley said, "Thank you very much," swiveled back to his audience, and signed off.

After which all hell broke loose.

Informed of what had happened, Reagan was furious, bitterly asking a group of senators "why in hell is the media so eager to help the Russians?" End of act one.

Act two. The president's chief of staff, Donald Regan, had press director Patrick Buchanan view a tape of my interview. Buchanan then wrote a scorching letter to ABC News president Roóne Arledge that labeled me as a "trained propagandist" and asked, "Would you have felt it an expression of fair and balanced journalism if in the 1930s, Mr. Churchill's calls for rearmament of his country were immediately followed by the BBC's granting an unrebutted commentary to some functionary of the Third Reich?"

Act three. An incensed Representative Robert Dornan (R-Calif.), speaking on the House floor, referred to me as "a disloyal, betraying little Jew." He soon regretted this, because he was attacked by B'nai B'rith et al. for making anti-Semitic remarks. Good old Bob immediately took a trip to Jerusalem and the Wailing Wall; there, he did some wailing himself, had the scene videotaped, and did a little speech on how much he loved the Jews and that the only reason for his unfortunate remark was that he was terribly upset and angry and that his time was almost up. He had not meant to say "Jew," he had meant to say "turncoat." Oh yeah? When was the last time anyone heard anybody call someone a "little turncoat"? Come on, Bob, admit it was a slip of the tongue—a Freudian slip.

Act four. An ABC News executive came out saying that Pozner should not have been allowed to go on so long and without rebuttal, but Americans have the right to hear the other side's view.

Act five. The next morning, the incident was front-page news across the country. *USA Today*'s headline ran, "Reagan Scores ABC: Airing of Soviet Commentator's Rebuttal." The *Washington Post* gave the story a more presidential air: "Reagan Says Media Erred: Soviet Got Air Time to Answer President." For a week, columnists and commentators weighed in on the issue. Even the *Wall Street Journal* joined in with an editorial entitled "Vladimir Who?"

Act six and last. ABC officially apologized to the White House.

That was in March 1986. Since then, I have been on some ABC News programs, but not as often as before. I say this without rancor, because I fully understand ABC's predicament. But what I fail to understand is why Americans were never told that ABC had no intention of putting me on unrebutted? That Peter Jennings was supposed to be in the studio with me but couldn't be there because he was ill with the flu? That Pierre Salinger, who was supposed to substitute for Peter, never made it to the studio? Americans were made to believe that somehow this Pozner, this Kremlin mouthpiece, this betraying little . . . turncoat had somehow held the ABC camera, microphone, studio, satellite transmission, and David Brinkley hostage and forced nearly eight minutes of his fascist views.

But let us return to the Leningrad-Seattle spacebridge.

In the Soviet public's eye, I had emerged full-blown as television's personification of glasnost. Most people didn't know that for years I had been able to address only western audiences—American, French, British, Canadian—because my views had been considered too controversial for Soviet consumption. The Soviet reaction to me was overwhelmingly positive. But there was also a negative backlash, best expressed in the letter of a certain Bochevarov from Leningrad. The letter, printed in *Izvestia*, was also sent to the KGB and the Central Committee of the Communist Party. It accused me of being pro-American, an enemy of the people, disloyal—in short, Bochevarov represented (and represents) the Bob Dornans of the Soviet Union. The letter in *Izvestia* stimulated an avalanche of letters supporting me, which I must admit was nice. But there was a surprise in store for me.

Izvestia's Alexander Bovin, one of the Soviet Union's leading foreign-policy experts, had written a short comment on Bochevarov's letter. It was to the point, critical, but somewhat restrained. A short time later, Bovin received a letter from Roy Medvedev, then one of the more well-known Soviet dissidents, today a member of the Soviet Parliament, who wrote to tell him about Bochevarov. The man, according to Medvedev, was an active member of the chauvinistic and anti-Semitic organization Pamyat. Bochevarov had tried to recruit Medvedev several years before and had, in the process, acquainted the dissident historian with Pamyat's goals, such as the restoration of czarism in Russia, the purification of the Russian nation, the expulsion of all infidels (meaning, mainly, Jews), and the like. Medvedev felt that, considering who Bochevarov represented, Bovin could have written something more forceful.

That was the first time I was attacked by Pamyat, although since then, I am proud to say, I have become one of that organization's prime targets.

In August of 1986, the years of keeping me off the air were suddenly over and I was given the title of political observer, the top journalistic rank in this country. I had, it might be said, arrived.

The changes in the Soviet Union since Gorbachev's arrival have been more than dramatic. In the economy, a crucial area, we have seen the once omnipotent bureaucracy retreat step by step, its authority being transferred to the factories and the farms. We have seen the bureaucracy consolidate and take a measure of control and then witnessed people-power in the nationwide coal-miners' strikes that broke the bureaucracy's hold. Pay is being based more and more on quality of performance; unprofitable enterprises are being allowed to go bankrupt. From a rigid system of price controls, we are moving inexorably toward an economy with major free-market elements. The rouble is on its way to becoming a convertible currency. But the change has not been restricted to economics. The political system too is being overhauled—perhaps even more drastically than the economic.

In 1985, when Gorbachev began speaking about democratization, very few people understood what he meant. The year 1987 saw the first experiments with multicandidate elections at the management level in factories, certain institutions of higher learning, and so on. But to many, this looked more like play than the real thing. By early 1988, though the word *pluralism* was not yet in vogue, we were already witnessing the emergence of organizations and interest groups substantially independent not only of the Party, but of any other official authority as well. They were quickly christened "nonformal organizations," although "nonestablishment" would be a more exact description. They weren't political parties, but they had platforms, and they spoke out actively on a variety of topics, from the environment to art. The 1989 elections to the Supreme Soviet demonstrated their power, not only in the Baltic republics, where the candidates of such nonestablishment organizations as the Popular Front and Sajudis were swept into office, but in many other regions of the country as well.

The groundwork for those elections were laid at the Nineteenth All-Union Party Conference in June 1988. It was there that party delegates adopted such goals as having a truly independent judiciary and a full-time powerful legislature, complemented by a powerful executive branch. It was also there that Mikhail Gorbachev scored one of his major triumphs when he proposed that, in principle, the local party leadership run for office in local, as well as national, elections. His reasoning seemed perfectly sound, especially to the people he was addressing. After all, did not real power in the country belong to the Party? And since that was the case, why not make the de facto situation a de jure reality by having party and government leadership merge? Most party officials applauded the idea. Most liberals were concerned. They harshly accused Gorbachev (not publicly, of course) of selling out to the conservatives. Instead of loosening party control, instead of letting the Soviets (the Councils) exercise government power, as had originally been their purpose, he was turning the Soviets lock, stock, and barrel over to the Party.

There were a few of us, however, whose views differed. Gorbachev had added one caveat to his proposal: should a party leader not be elected, then he would have to give up his party position. Gorbachev's reasoning was foolproof. How can one be a leader without popular support? But the possibility of losing an election never crossed the party bureaucrat's mind, first, because they never lost and second, because none of them believed "real" elections would ever be allowed. A minority of the intellectual community interpreted Gorbachev's proposal as being a brilliant strategy to legitimately get rid of the more conservative party elements. And we were right.

No less than thirty-eight regional party first secretaries got the boot during the elections. These men, dukes and princes in their fiefdoms, were dealt a numbing blow. But in addition, the people, the electorate, suddenly realized they could make a difference, that the ballot as it now existed gave them real power. And that has made it a new ball game.

The party functionaries are extremely unhappy—and have said as much to Gorbachev. His answer has, essentially, been "vous l'avez voulu, Georges Dandin, vous l'avez voulu"—that is what you all voted for at the Party Conference. And so they did. Meanwhile, the nation is rubbing its hands and licking its chops as it looks forward to the elections to local government where, beyond a question of a doubt, most party officials who risk running for office are going to get creamed (along with the present-day local government authorities).

There is a passage in one of Kipling's less well known books, *Stalky and Co.,* where one M'Turk describes a certain kind of Japanese wrestler: "These wrestler-chaps have got some sort of trick that lets the other chap do all the work. Then they give a little wriggle, and he upsets himself. It's called *shibbuwichee* or *tokonoma* or somethin'." Well, I would call Mikhail Gorbachev a master of *shibbuwichee.* Time and time again, he has let the conservative opposition do all the work, then has given a little wriggle and they have upset themselves.

The decisions of the Party Conference are just one example, a rare example when at least some people were able to read the *shibbuwicher*'s mind and guess what the wriggle would be. Usually, that is not and has not been the case.

I remember Mark Taimanov, an International Grand Master and, at one time, a contender for the world chess crown, talking about losing his match with Bobby Fischer by the implausible score of six to zero. For those of you whose knowledge of chess is limited, I should make it clear that Grand Masters never lose matches by a score of whatever to nothing, especially considering that a draw counts for half a point and more games are drawn during a match than are won or lost. So when Taimanov fell to Fischer six-zip, it was a sensation that rocked the chess world. It was, in fact, such an unbelievable affront that the Soviet Chess Federation stripped Taimanov of his title as Grand Master of the USSR. Later, when several other Grand Masters were blitzed by Fischer, the Soviet Chess Federation realized its mistake, but refused to acknowledge it. To this day, Mark Taimanov retains the rank of International Grand Master but has not had his Soviet ranking restored.

Describing his famous defeat at the hands of the future world champion, Taimanov said, "When Grand Masters play, they see the logic of their opponent's moves. One's moves may be so powerful that the other may not be able to stop him, but the plan behind the moves will be clear. Not so with Fischer. His moves did not make sense—at least to all the rest of us they didn't. We were playing chess, Fischer was playing something else, call it what you will. Naturally, there would come a time when we finally would understand what those moves had been about. But by then it was too late. We were dead."

Gorbachev is that kind of a political player. No one understands his moves. Not until it is too late. And that is why, in my opinion, he was able to rise through the echelons of power, through the Young Communist League, through the party ranks, up and up, all the way to the Politburo, and even be elected to the post of general secretary. If anyone had been able to read his mind before that, Gorbachev would be dead.

That statement hardly answers the question skeptics have kept asking: "If Gorbachev was and is determined to push through radical reforms, how come he was appointed to the Politburo at the height of Brezhnev's rule?"

There is still no conclusive answer to that question or to the others that flow from it. Still, certain things are clear.

Contrary to western thinking, a reformist element had existed in the

Soviet Communist party ever since the Khrushchev years and probably before. Certainly, it was fragmented and its influence hard to see. But it was there, composed of people who profoundly believed in socialism's potential, people who had decided to work for change from within. Their decision had mixed results. By observing party discipline, by not talking out of school, they greatly limited their visibility; in many ways, they seemed ineffective—nothing appeared to change. Still, they achieved some results in stimulating local economic experiments, in sustaining at least some measure of political dialogue within the Party, but most critically, they remained in positions of potential influence.

It is one of the striking ironies of Soviet history that, during the Brezhnev years, there were two groups pushing for radical reform: the hidden, reformist communists and the very visible, vocal dissidents. If one had claimed at that time that there was significant common ground between them, people would have said he was crazy, and both groups would have agreed. I feel that even today many, if not most, would ridicule the idea. Yet I maintain that it is true. Certainly, a faction of the dissidents were completely anti-socialist. Solzhenitsyn, for example, believes socialism and communism to be unmitigated evils and has always advocated the restoration of a theocratic, Russian-nationalist authoritarian state. But others, like Sakharov, were seriously advocating human rights and calling for an end to the abuses of our own constitution.

In my opinion, it fulfilled the needs and desires of cold warriors, East and West, to lump all dissidents together as being anti-Soviet. The West lionized them as heroes in the anticommunist battle for freedom. Moscow attacked them all as traitors who were selling their country to the imperialists for a paltry thirty pieces of silver.

Watching all this were the reformist communists, Mikhail Gorbachev among them. During most of the Brezhnev years, he and almost all those now closest to him had extensive experience *away from Moscow.* Although they too enjoyed the special privileges of the party elite in the form of special stores and hospitals, limos and dachas, these people saw firsthand the hard realities and spiraling problems of Soviet life. By the mid-seventies, economic problems were apparent even to the Moscow hierarchy, and some experimentation in industry and agriculture was authorized. The reform-minded party types had ample opportunity to ponder the results—to see the connection between local control, profit sharing, worker participation, initiative, and high morale on the one hand and bureaucracy, apathy, and corruption on the other. These were good, honest men and women who traced the chain of cause and effect back to the source, who came to understand that a healthy, vigorous economy is the product of physically and spiritually healthy human beings.

The old guard, interested in improving economic productivity, brought some of the innovative managers to Moscow so that their techniques could be applied on a broader scale. Clearly, this would not have happened if the central bureaucratic authorities had felt it represented a threat to their power. Being second-rate thinkers and pseudo-Marxists, they failed to see the integral connection between economic and political reform. They thought they were bringing in a few plumbers to fix the leaks. What they got was a demolition crew and reconstruction team.

What is the correlation between the evolution of history and the emergence of the key individual, the right man doing the right thing at the right time? I don't pretend to know the answer, but I do know such people emerge. From the bastion of nonthinking, double-talking conservatism came Mikhail Gorbachev.

Gorbachev's policies have been as upsetting to the American establishment's view on the Soviet Union as it has to the Stalinist view. Both are terribly unhappy with perestroika, and both predict Gorbachev will fail. Thus, in the United States, Kremlinologists such as Marshall Goldman have continued to predict that Gorbachev has a year, maximum, a year and a half left in office. Other "experts," such as Zbigniew Brzezinski, predict the initial disintegration of the Soviet Union and its consequent consolidation under a Russian chauvinist strongman. The predictions vary, but the bottom line is the same: socialism will not work, the Soviet Union cannot be "good." That refusal to admit the possibility of positive change does not speak as much about hardened intellectual arteries as it reflects an almost panicky fear of having one's entire life's work proven to be garbage. For decades, this type of Kremlinologist has preached a certain sermon to the American government and people. Now the preacher is faced with the disastrous threat of being defrocked.

In the Soviet Union, a great many people lived their lives and based their activities on a blind belief in Stalin, in the Party, in the superiority of the Soviet system. Step by step, all three of those beliefs have been, or are in the process of being, destroyed. Stalin turned out to be a mass murderer, a man whose preoccupation with personal power far outweighed his allegience to the revolution and Lenin's heritage. The Party became the most reactionary force in the country, corrupt, a vehicle for careerism, an organization offering its own elite rewards and privileges that contradicted every ideal of the revolution. As for the system, the great advantages it had proposed—such as free education for all people from preschool to graduate studies, free medical care for one and all, no matter how complex, guaranteed gainful employment for one and all—all of these promises had become warped, almost caricatures of themselves.

"Have I lived my life in vain? Has everything I believed in been a lie?" Those are just some of the questions people asked and continue to ask themselves. And the Stalinists refuse to admit anything was ever wrong. They look back with yearning on a simple time when life was black and white, when they felt secure in their almost one-dimensional ideological outlook—very much like the Kremlinologists in the United States. And so they too predict and hope Gorbachev will fail. But these enemies of perestroika are right about one central reality—perestroika faces enormous difficulties.

One has to do with this country's historical absence of democratic tradition. When King John was forced to issue the Magna Carta in 1215, a document that is one of the roots of American democracy, Russia was being overrun by the Tartars—not the most democratically inclined people in the world—and she remained under that yoke for three centuries. By the time Russia finally won her independence, she found herself a backward country. She had experienced no renaissance, no flowering of the arts, no development of the artisan and the merchant. Politically, culturally, and economically, Russia was already retarded. One of the ways by which her rulers attempted to achieve economic parity was through the introduction of serfdom—no, they did not import slaves like some countries did, they turned their own people into slaves—another great act of democracy. By the end of the fifteenth century, serfdom had become legal at the state level. It was abolished only some three hundred years later, in 1861. Three hundred years of Tartar rule, plus three hundred years of serfdom and czarist autocracy. Could this not but affect the national psyche?

But even after 1861, czarist rule continued. And while certain elements of bourgeois democracy began to creep into the social fabric, they were hardly of a scope to radically change outlooks. After the Romanovs were finally overthrown in February 1917 and before the Bolsheviks came to power in November of that same year, democracy had its first chance—but a chance badly hindered by World War I, which had sent millions of Russian peasants as cannon fodder to the front lines, millions who wanted out.

Had the socialist revolution not led to a civil war, had the West not supported the czarist White armies, had there been no western intervention on Soviet soil, had the revolution been allowed to progress without bloodshed, it is not farfetched to suppose that a new kind of democracy, socialist democracy, would have developed in the Soviet Union. But the fact of the matter is that none of this occurred. The do-or-die situation of the civil war was anything but conducive to democracy. On the contrary, it demanded a dictatorial leadership, which, though anything but czarist in essence, employed authoritarian methods reminiscent of what people had always been used to. Russia's experiment with democracy was finished, basically, by mid-1918. It was resumed sixty-seven years later. Stalin was the cause of democracy's strangulation, but Stalin was also the result of a lack of democratic tradition. A Stalin would not have been supported by a democratically educated nation. The lack of such a tradition, of such an education, remains a major obstacle to perestroika.

Another is opposition.

Opposition of a passive nature on the part of those who simply cannot deal emotionally with the change, those whose outlooks and life-styles are seemingly threatened, those who don't want to know how bad things are, who would prefer to live in the comfort of their former ignorance.

Opposition of a more active nature on the part of those who have lost the faith, who no longer give a damn, who are looking out only for their own interests, and who, therefore, refuse to make any effort if they are not immediately compensated for it.

And active opposition on the part of those who are losing power. They are a mix—party functionaries at different levels, both in the big cities and in rural areas; government bureaucrats, from the highest to the most lowly, in the countless ministries, enterprises, plants, and organizations; ranking and petty officials in the local, republican, and national legislatures, in the trade unions, in the nooks and crannies of this gigantic country that they have milked as if it were some gigantic udder. They don't want to let go. And they fight back. They insert paragraphs and qualifications into laws that render them inefficient; they drag their feet on urgent decisions; they spread rumors to increase instability. They pour oil onto burning fires.

Just one example. When the tension between Abkhazians and Georgians was at the breaking point but still under control, a decision was made to close down Sukhumi State University and to transform it into a branch of Tbilisi State University. Sukhumi is the capital of Abkhazia; Tbilisi is the capital of Georgia. That decision could not but detonate violence—as indeed it did. In my opinion, the timing and the character of that decision speak for themselves. It was a calculated attempt to hurt Gorbachev at a crucial moment in the development of perestroika, the time of the First Congress of People's Deputies and the First Session of the Supreme Soviet.

Finally, there is the all-important problem of the Soviet economy. Will perestroika succeed in radically reforming the economy quickly enough to give the people the satisfaction of seeing an improvement in the quality of their lives?

One of Mikhail Gorbachev's closest advisers, Alexander Yakovlev, described the process of perestroika as "a breakthrough into the unknown."

The unknown? That's a frightening concept to people who have forgotten—or never knew—how to think for themselves.

The key difficulty today, the central task of perestroika, lies in the revival of belief in the ideal based on the reality of each person's existence. That is hard to do for those who have been hurt, for those who have been disillusioned, for those who have grown up with a belief in authority and a fear of questioning it. A friend of mine recently said, by way of making a point, "Do you know why Moses not only led his people into the desert but kept them there for sixty years? Because they had all been slaves, and he did not want anyone with even a vestige of the slave mentality to go to the Promised Land. He had to wait until all of them died, until a new generation of people who had never experienced slavery was born. Only then could he bring them to the Promised Land. And, mind you, he himself was not allowed to enter it."

The analogy is a good one: before we can really hope to move ahead, the generations that lived under Stalin and under Brezhnev will have to pass away. I think there may be some truth to that. People who have been contaminated by the fear and by the cynicism of those two societies are ill fit to function under perestroika. It would be wonderful if we could all live in some desert until a new, healthy generation replaced us all. But we can't. We don't have the time. We must move ahead, even with the ball and chain of that other mentality dragging at our legs and making our progress that much more difficult.

But only a liar or a blind man can deny the progress of the past four years.

For as long as I can remember my political views, I believed that socialism had the realistic potential to provide a more fair, just, and open society than any other system that preceded it. I came to that conclusion for many reasons—my father's views, my own reading, my personal experiences. But during the thirty-seven years of my life in the Soviet Union, I came clearly to understand the way in which socialism had been led down a crooked, tortuous lane away from the road originally mapped by some of humanity's most profound minds. This distortion occurred because of a combination of circumstances—some objective (such as the absence of a democratic heritage), some subjective. I witnessed the results of a distorted socialism and saw it being further distorted, almost like a physical violation. In a way, it reminded me of what the Chinese used to do to a female child's feet, binding them tight to keep them small and delicate. A foot doesn't naturally grow that way. This practice caused terrible pain, but the children survived—as cripples, tottering around on tiny feet like some kind of penguin. You can do that to a human being. You can produce any kind of monster, a hunchback if you wish, just as they did in the Middle Ages. You can do it even better with the human soul— remember the Dragon? And that is precisely what Stalin, and those around him, did to socialism.

I came to think that the ultimate test would be whether socialism had the strength to survive and rebound. I had lived through the first attempt, the Khrushchev years. And while it had been bitterly disappointing in many ways, it had provided a glimmer, a hope of what was possible. And even when the rollback came under Brezhnev, when ground was lost that had been so painfully gained, when, in a certain sense, the distortion of socialism became even worse than under Stalin, even then I continued to believe that there would come a time of change. I could not have predicted when it would happen. Society's watch ticks to a different beat than those of human beings. I realized that it might well take fifty years, that I would probably never see it happen. But I believed it would come. And then, with Gorbachev, it began to happen. I suppose it had to—either that, or the entire society would go down the tubes.

Which reminds me of a curious analogy.

When the Wall Street stock market crashed in 1929 and the Great Depression set in, many predicted capitalism was on its way out. Their forecasts seemed well based. The entire capitalist world was going to pieces. Millions and millions of people were jobless, homeless, hungry, hopeless. Productivity was down, profits tumbled. In the United States alone no less than one hundred thousand Americans applied to leave for Soviet Russia.

Many people, myself included, believe capitalism in America was saved by a man of great vision and courage. His name was Franklin Delano Roosevelt. Had it not been for his New Deal, for the laws he pushed through Congress, for such emergency organizations as the National Recovery Administration, for such long-term organizations as the Tennessee Valley Authority, had it not been for his foresight in furnishing Americans with the Social Security Act of 1935, it is quite possible that the American people would have opted for another system. Roosevelt saved capitalism by injecting a healthy dose of socialistic programs to correct the excesses of "free market" capitalism. It was he who propelled the federal government into such things as the regulation of stocks and the banking system. To this day many of America's high and mighty hate Roosevelt because he forced them to share just a little more of the mind-boggling wealth and put just a little more responsibility for the nation's well-being where it should be—with the federal government.

In a way, Mikhail Gorbachev is our Roosevelt. He is in the process of saving socialism in this country. And he is doing it by injecting some of the things developed in capitalist societies: parliamentary and institutional pluralism, law-based society founded on respect for individual rights, an economic marketplace, a degree of private enterprise and private ownership. And because he is also making sure that the power goes back to where it was always supposed to be, to the people, to the Soviets, there are many who hate him.

It took a war, a tremendous economic shot in the arm, for American capitalism to recover fully. We will have to make our comeback without a war. That's for sure. It will be tough going. But we are on our way.

When the Leningrad-Seattle spacebridge went on the air, I knew I had been right in my expectations. It was a personal triumph of faith. Over the years I had said to myself, hang tough, don't sell out. Many people did. Some conformed, others emigrated. I don't blame them. At worst, I feel sorry for them because they broke. I knew that, should I break, the game would be all over for me. You can glue a broken glass, a china cup. But not a human being. Like Humpty Dumpty, when we break, all the King's horses and all the King's men cannot put us back together again.

During those years, I often though of Mikhail Bulgakov, a writer who never saw his masterpice, *The Master and Margarita,* published in his own country, who could not dream of becoming famous and beloved, whose first works were attacked, slandered, ridiculed, whose later works were banned, who asked to be let out of a country that did not need him—and was refused, who was finally *allowed* to work as a technician for the

Moscow Art Theater, who died unknown to the nation he had suffered for. And yet who triumphed. Hail, Mikhail Bulgakov! Hail the countless others, famous and not, who never sold out!

How exhilarating to see truth break through, to see the tide turn. Yes, there are heavy seas ahead; yes, we still have to sail a long way before we reach our destination. But we are on our way.

And not only the Soviet Union. For nearly half a century, we have all lived in a hostile, bipolar world. In part, that reality was generated by Stalin; in part, by the dictatorial structures and mindset he left behind; in part, by the West stoking those fires. Now, in the Soviet Union, we are building something new, and we are demolishing that legacy in the process. Can the cold war survive without us? I think not.

For all of us, it's a new ball game.

It's breakthrough time.

8

◄◆►

Homecoming

On May 14, 1986, after an absence of thirty-eight years, I returned to America, the country of my childhood and early teens. The trip had been put together by a group of local television stations in New York, Chicago, Boston, Washington, San Francisco, and Seattle.

During the entire ten hours between Moscow's Sheremetyevo-Two International Airport and Kennedy International Airport in New York City, including the one-hour stopover at Gander, Newfoundland, where Soviet passenger jets stop to refuel (it's cheaper there), I kept trying to get used to the idea that this was really happening. It seemed unreal. How many times had I dreamed of this? How many times had I seen myself walking down the streets of New York, ringing a school friend's doorbell, exulting at the expression of amazed delight on his face as he suddenly recognized me—"he" being Steve McGhee, or Bobby Hollander, or Artie Muschenheim, or Harry Montague? How many times had I woken up, my face wet with tears, because my dream had turned into a nightmare of never being able to go back?

One day, I was listening to one of my favorite albums, *A Tribute to Woody Guthrie,* a live concert of Woody's songs performed by Pete Seeger, Arlo Guthrie, Bob Dylan, Joan Baez, and other greats and not-so-greats. I sat there immersed in the music I loved so dearly, and then, as if from far away and from a great depth, came Odetta's voice singing "This land is your land," and suddenly I found myself weeping, unable to control myself, like a child, gasping for breath, waves of sadness pouring over me, America pulling at my heart and soul. I couldn't stop, I couldn't even drink the glass of water that Kathrin brought me. I could only cling to her as my last refuge, my only solace.

That was before I began to travel. That was before a small part of my dream came true when Kathrin and I were able to go together and spend a month in France, where we were invited by my aunt Toto. She and her husband, Roger, met us at the Gare de l'Est. Roger was my "Oncle Cheval," thus called because he would sit me on his back and ride me down to the bomb shelter during the German air raids of 1940. Now, in 1980, they took us to their apartment on boulevard Victor, in the fifteenth arrondissement, the apartment I had spent so much time in when I was a five-year-old French kid. My mother and father lived in the same building, I think it was a floor higher or lower, I don't remember exactly, but I preferred my aunt and uncle's place because of Prosper, the king of all poodles.

Dog lovers are funny people. They tell the most preposterous stories about their four-legged friends, thus providing ammunition for such jokes as, "Now I'm not one to tell you lies about my dog's intelligence, no sir! I wouldn't dream of telling you he beats me at chess. Absolutely not, as a matter of fact, I always beat him." I don't know whether Prosper played chess. But that he was far brighter than many people I have met, had a greater sense of humor, and was infinitely more refined and tactful. That is something I can vouch for.

Prosper was big even for a standard poodle. He was black and white, the wearer of the finest Afro I have ever seen, the real, natural thing. Prosper would never have allowed anyone to trim, cut, or otherwise tease his hair. His favorite game was hide-and-seek. He would bring you his ball and cock his eye at you expectantly. You were supposed to say, "Prosper, go stand in the corner and no peeking." Prosper would dutifully go stand in the corner, head to the wall, while you hid his ball. Ever so slowly, he would turn his head and look over his shoulder, fully expecting you to say sternly, "Prosper! No cheating!" This was part of the ritual and had to happen two or three times before Prosper was told he could now look for his ball. That was his supreme moment. He would come walking out of the corner with a questioning look on his face, as if to say, "Confound it, where could you possibly have hidden my ball this time?" You were supposed to say "warm," "hot," or "cold," depending on how close Prosper came to the ball. Invariably, he took the worst possible direction. Your calls of "Cold! Cold!" would bring him up short. He would turn around, look at you with an expression of infinite sadness in his eyes, then shrug, like the true Frenchman that he was, and walk off in another, totally wrong direction. Of course, he knew *exactly* where the ball was. His sense of smell was infallible, but his desire to play was unconquerable.

During the first summer of the German occupation, I lived in a rural town with my aunt and Russian émigré friends of hers, most of whom I have completely forgotten. But I remember Prosper. Every morning he used to take me fishing. There wasn't much food to spare, so Prosper fed himself. He would wade into the shallow water of the local stream and, like some black-and-white grizzly, duck under the water and surface with a fish between his teeth. Or he would take a mighty slap with his paw and send a fish jumping and twisting onto the riverbank.

Proper died at the ripe old age of twenty-one, long after I had left France, but long before I returned. I think about him often, and I was thinking of him again as we entered the apartment of my French childhood and I found myself staring out of the bay window and looking at the building of the ministère de l'Air. Time suddenly became compressed—it collapsed, it folded, and there I stood, five years old, looking out of exactly the same window at exactly the same building, fully expecting to hear my mother say, "Vovka, viens boir ton lait," and being therefore startled to hear my aunt's voice—the low, somewhat hoarse, almost masculine voice of a seventy-year-old, two-pack-a-day smoker—say, "Vova, come have a shot of whiskey, I think you need it."

But going back to France was only part of the dream. Twice it had nearly all come together. The first time was in 1983, when Jim Dabakis, a local broadcaster from Salt Lake City, set up a national speaking tour for me. It was scheduled for October. With that in mind, Kathrin and I had decided to take our annual vacation in September. It was then, while we were enjoying the wonderful weather of one of Bulgaria's nicest Black Sea resorts, that a Soviet fighter shot down KAL Flight 007. Not surprisingly, my trip was cancelled. Not by the State Department as some rumors had it. Nor was I physically taken off the plane by the KGB, as some other rumors had it. Simply, the Soviet authorities came to the conclusion that, conditions being what they were, I would be in physical danger if I went to the United States at that time.

When we returned to Moscow, I argued that now was precisely the time to go—now, when things were really difficult, when there was a need for an alternative viewpoint. All to no avail.

In 1985, another public-speaking tour was set up for me, and again, I was vacationing with Kathrin and a close friend, this time not far from

Leningrad, when I learned that my trip to America had been canceled. Why? Once more, the motive supposedly was concern for my safety. I am not saying that concern was without grounds. But I feel there was some force out there in far left field that didn't want to be responsible for me, for what I might say in America. There were, I believe, some officials who were afraid that I might defect—and then someone would be held responsible for having OK'd my trip.

So when I stepped off that plane in May 1986, when I lined up at immigration, when I picked up my luggage and breezed through customs, when I walked out and saw a man holding up a sign that said POZNER, when he took my bags and escorted me to the stretch limo that Multimedia, Phil Donahue's company, had sent for me, and when the car slid smoothly forward, leaving Kennedy behind, I was in a state of shock.

Let us leave me sitting in that limo, straining my eyes for the first hint of the Manhattan skyline, and discuss a matter of relatively minor importance, yet one that I cannot resist.

Americans come to the Soviet Union expecting trouble, looking for problems. After all, it is Commie Land, ain't it? It is the Evil Empire, right? Maybe it's gotten better, but Gorbachev has not yet publicly admitted he'd rather be dead than Red, has he? Americans come in looking for anything that will corroborate their worst fears. Seek and you will find . . . and find they do, almost immediately, in the person of the Soviet immigration border guards. These uniformed young men sit in glassed-in compartments. They take your passport, read it carefully, check the visa no less carefully, and take a couple of long hard looks at your picture in the passport and at you. They usually do not talk to you (most of them are eighteen-year-old kids who speak no other language than their own and who realize you probably are not fluent in Russian), nor, as a rule, do they smile. They are on duty and take their work seriously. If they were anything but Russian, Americans would hardly pay any attention. But they are Russians, so: "Gosh, the way they stare at you gives me the willies!" "Boy, what an oppressive feeling," "Why don't they ever smile? Is it because they aren't allowed to?"

I wish those same Americans had to deal with the U.S. Immigration Service. Incidentally, Soviet citizens, returning to their country, have to go through the same border guards as do foreigners. American citizens do not go through U.S. Immigration. If they did, they would be in for some unpleasant surprises. Those people don't smile. They ask you questions *in English,* and if you don't know the language, that's your problem.

Either find an interpreter or get out of line and wait until someone finally takes pity on you. U.S. Immigration officials—I speak only of my experience—are often impolite. When you visit the Soviet Union, you are required to fill in a form for customs. The United States demands that you fill in two forms, one for customs and one for immigration. The latter includes a question about where you will be staying. Chances are, you don't know the name of the hotel that has been booked for you by the people who are meeting you at the gate. Don't try to explain that to the immigration official. He or she won't even listen, they will wave you away. Imagine the conclusions one could draw by generalizing and putting the United States in the context of its immigration service.

In the distance, I saw New York. And my heart stopped. Supposedly, that's impossible. Doctors will tell you that cardiac arrest means death. As a human physiology major, I'll corroborate that statement. But there are exceptions to that rule, and I am one. Because my heart stopped, and I am still alive.

A couple of years after my first return trip to New York, Phil Donahue took me for a ride on his yacht, the *Mugsy*. We sailed out of Westport, Connecticut, and down Long Island Sound. The weather turned foul, the wind got stronger, and the rain started coming down, harder and harder. By the time we entered the East River and passed Rikers Island, it had become dark. On we went, pelted by the rain, buffeted by the wind and the water, past Roosevelt Island and under the Queensboro Bridge, past the myriad lights of the UN Building, under the Williamsburg Bridge, the Manhattan Bridge, and that old favorite of mine, the Brooklyn Bridge, the waves getting bigger, the *Mugsy* pitching as the East River opened into Upper New York Bay, Phil steering a course straight toward the Lady, both of us in slickers, the wind howling, and the two of us howling right back. And then Phil put the ship on autopilot and took me downstairs and inside, fumbled around with some switches and whatever, and then, in super-duper, hi-fi stereo I heard "America . . . America . . . God shed His grace on thee . . ." The *Mugsy* seemed to take a bow in front of the Statue of Liberty, then veered right and headed back toward Manhattan. As the island's diamond-tipped nether end drew closer, Phil pushed a button and Liza Minelli began belting out "New York, New York" as only she can do it.

Phil was, as he later admitted half-jokingly, trying to get me to defect. If not that, at least make me break down and cry. Well, nice try, Phil, but after seeing the New York skyline come jutting up to meet me after thirty-eight years, I could take any emotional stress with a smile.

The limo stopped at the Drake Hotel at Fifty-sixth and Park and, because I spent my first few days there, the Drake is and always will be my favorite hotel. I vaguely remember checking in, being escorted to my room, being shown how the TV set worked, how to use the air-conditioning, how to open the mini bar. I remember tipping the bellman, shutting the door behind him, hurriedly changing, splashing some water on my face, and going out for a walk. Out on Fifty-sixth, I turned right, crossed Madison, hit Fifth, turned left, and began walking downtown. There were throngs of people all around, a sea of faces and voices, but I was alone, I was walking in a shell of silence, I was invisible to one and all. I was trying to understand what was happening to me, what was going on inside. It was something strange, something I couldn't quite grasp, something . . . And then, suddenly, I knew, the truth tied a knot of pain in my stomach, a knot of fear, for what I had discovered was that I felt as though I had never left.

Time and time again I had told myself, "Don't expect too much. Remember Thomas Wolfe? You can't go home again. It'll be a foreign place, that will hurt, but things change in forty years, things change." Yes, New York had changed, but it was still my New York. I loved the streets, I loved the smells, I loved the hustle and the bustle, I loved it then, when I was a kid, though I didn't know it, didn't think of it, I loved it dearly, the bad of it and the good of it. Now, so many years later, I still loved it, my town, my Big Apple.

I stared at people walking by, I wanted to cry out, "Hey, you, all of you, look, it's me, I'm back, hey, you motherfuckers, wake up, check it out, you thought I was gone, never coming back, well, think again you bastards. I love you!"

Only nobody looked. Nobody batted an eyelid. C'mon, kid, this is Noo Yawk, who gives a shit about you or anybody else?

But they sure were looking on the following day, when I was a guest on Phil Donahue's show. His predominantly female audience gave me a hand when I told Phil I loved New York, but they weren't going to be conned by a Russian commie—a rather nervous one, as I recall. Earlier, I related how I had tap danced and made a fool of myself with the question of my being, or not being, a Jew. I recall another no less interesting exchange on this show. A woman in the audience asked me, "Mr. Pozner, do you believe in God?" My answer was succinct and direct: "No, I am an atheist," a response that was greeted by the entire audience of over two hundred people with what sounded like a gasp of horror and disbelief, almost as if I had said that I eat babies for breakfast. Later, an American friend advised me never to admit to being an atheist. "Rather," he said, "tell them you are an agnostic. It sounds great, most people here don't have the slightest idea what it means, in fact, they'll think it's some kind of religion." He was right. It is not easy to be an atheist in America.

When Americans consider it opportune to point an accusing finger at the Soviet Union and enumerate its shortcomings and transgressions (which is often), high on their list one invariably finds "lack of religious freedom." I won't argue the point, not because it is true (the degree of religious freedom in the Soviet Union today is far greater than most Americans imagine), but because I feel Americans should think twice before they surrender to that most American of traits: innocent, but nonetheless insulting, arrogance, the conviction that somehow, for some reason, they are better than others, special, that the American way is not only the best, but (just between you and me) the only really acceptable form of behavior. Americans should, I believe, ask themselves, why is it that in all American courts of law, one is asked to to tell the truth, the whole truth, and nothing but the truth on the Holy Bible? Why? Is the American concept of justice based on the assumption that Christians are honest, that other religious denominations are somehow more prone to lie, and that atheists cannot be trusted?

Why is it that when the president of the United States is sworn into office, he takes his oath on the Bible? What is the chance of an American's being elected president, if he (forget about she—an American female atheist will become president of the United States when the shrimp whistles) openly admits to being an atheist? Is it easy for an American family and its children to be known atheists—and I don't mean just in the Bible Belt? No, they won't be persecuted by the United States government, but what about being persecuted by the community? What about their kids getting hassled or even beaten up because they don't believe in Our Lord Jesus Christ? Doesn't freedom of conscience also mean freedom *not* to worship? Shouldn't the atheist have exactly the the same rights and opportunities as the believer?

Of course, I didn't get to say all that on Phil Donahue's show. But I stimulated enough interest to be invited back for a second show on the following day.

Those first two days were also my first in-the-flesh meetings with Phil. I very much enjoyed his fairness, sharp questioning, good logic, the way he quickly spotted holes in my arguments and went for them but always gave me a chance to answer. But I enjoyed him even more off the air. We have become friends, and so what I say is colored by that feeling. Yet I say it without hesitation of being accused of bias. In Russia, we use the word *friend* sparingly, unlike Americans who will introduce you as "my friend" after you've had three drinks together. Before becoming friends, the Russians say, you have to consume a *pood* of salt together. A *pood* is an old Russian measure of weight equal to sixteen kilograms. That's about thirty-five pounds—imagine how well you get to know a person by the time you have shared that much salt together! A friend is someone you know as well as yourself. A friend is someone you can always count on, no matter what the circumstances, someone who will always support you, someone you trust implicitly. So when I speak of Phil as a friend, I'm saying a lot.

I have seen Phil at his best—during the two spacebridges we did together and during the profoundly moving show he did with children who had cancer. I have time and time again marveled at his insight, his intelligence, his honesty. And that is why I am so troubled by the kind of programs he feels he must do to compete with Oprah Winfrey and Geraldo Rivera,

New York City had changed in the thirty-eight years of my absence. It had become even wealthier. You could smell the sweet, rotting aroma of money. Once upon a time, the Empire State Building was New York's symbol; now it was Trump Tower. But New York had also become poorer. I was stunned by the bag ladies, by the number of people living in the streets. I had heard and read about it, I had watched the television documentaries, but seeing it firsthand was something else. Back in the forties, in a much less affluent America, there were no bag ladies. Nobody lived in the street. Yes, they had flop houses. New York had its Bowery. But people didn't live in cardboard boxes. There was Harlem but no South Bronx, no neighborhoods that looked like moonscapes, no houses blackened by flames, windows either gaping or sealed with sheet metal. There was no crack. Junkies were a rarity.

There were other differences as well, little things such as the people speeding around on bicycles. The only bike riders back then were kids. You bought a bike to deliver newspapers. You didn't hop on a ten-speed and go tearing around in the New York traffic; you would have been crazy to do that. Now the traffic was much worse, but you had these people with leather helmets weaving in and out, blowing whistles, a special breed of kamikazes.

Those were some of my first impressions on days one and two of my visit, but they registered later, they sifted through the storm of emotions that swept me up and carried me, dizzy and gasping, until I had the time to settle down—and they with me.

After the first Donahue show, I returned to my school, City and Country. There was a film crew from WGBH in Boston following me around (they would prepare a one-hour profile called "Your Not So Average Russian, or the Pozner File," which I will discuss shortly), and even they were amazed when I gave them a tour of the school. I had forgotten nothing. I showed them where the principal's office had been, where the shops were. Coming back to my childhood was not easy, but I held up pretty well until the new principal gave me a couple of xeroxes of *Yardbird,* the old school paper. The May 1, 1946, issue (vol. 1, no. 5, Three Cents) offered, among many other items, this poem:

> *The Voice*
> *There was a man*
> *With a big mustache*
> *And a very wooly beard,*
> *And where ever he went*
> *He was sure to be heard*
> *For his voice was so very terribly*
> *Loud . . . that it beat the thunder*
> *In the cloud.*
> *It made your ears deaf,*
> *Your fingers numb,*
> *And made you feel as if you were*
> *Dumb.*
> *One day there was a drought,*
> *And the man got awfully, terribly*
> *Hoarse. His voice died out*
> *And every body laughed and cried,*
> *They were so happy, they nearly*
> *Died.*
>
> *Vladimir Posner*

There was something about reading that poem that was much more powerful than looking at a picture of yourself when you were twelve years old. I had seen many such pictures; I knew exactly how I looked when I was twelve. But I had completely forgotten how I spoke, what I thought. So in a mystical way I was meeting myself, a twelve-year-old kid who was shaking my hand and smiling into my eyes, so happy, so confident, his whole life ahead of him, and I felt like hugging him tightly and telling him not to worry, that everything would be OK.

Then I turned around, and there stood Artie Muschenheim and Steve McGhee, and that's when I started to come apart at the seams. Both brought back a flood of memories, especially Steve, the school's top athlete and best student, the tallest kid in our last-year class. Even as a thirteen-year-old, Steve had been remarkably contained, hardly ever raising his voice, fighting only when challenged, and always winning, always a little aloof, combining his school studies with cello lessons—something that always awed us. Now Steve stood there, several inches shorter than me, almost completely bald, but with the same very steady green eyes, the slow, warm smile. "How are you, Vlady?" he said, using my old school name. I had trouble answering.

Meanwhile, the WGBH crew was shooting away, and at one point the director, Steve Atlas, asked Steve and Artie if, as kids, they ever had concerns about "this commie, Pozner." And they laughed at the craziness of the question, and I laughed, too. It was one of those moments in life when you cut to the center, through all the baggage we hang on ourselves over time. From the reporter's experience, the political values his life had taught him, it was a serious question; for the three of us, it was absurd. We could have told him about what we had shared, about spending evenings together in Bobby Hollander's penthouse apartment when his parents were out, drooling over the art photography album that Bobby was not supposed to touch, discussing the technique of French kissing, and taking turns with Bobby's binoculars watching a couple in the building opposite his do a strange sexual dance—she, dressed in panties and bra, shaking a pair of maracas, while he, fully dressed, pranced around her. They would appear in the bright rectangle of the lighted window, then disappear behind the left or right frame, and appear again until, suddenly, the light went out. We could have told him those, and many more, stories, but what was the point? That was not what the man wanted to know. He wanted an answer to a question that we didn't have to run through intellectually, comparing the relative importance of political ideas and human relationships. The answer was clear and instant—we were *buddies*. I have often thought of that moment and of its meaning.

I have also often thought of the WGBH final product, the thirty-minute "Pozner File." It was structured so that three experts could analyze my views and thoughts. You remember my story about Galina I. Barinova, the head of the Leningrad Regional Party Committee's ideology department, who wanted to brief the Soviet participants of the Leningrad-Seattle spacebridge? Had she had her way, we would have been accused of brainwashing our audience, a crime that, I'm sure we would have been told, bespoke our distrust of our own people. With that in mind, I ask you to take a look at the following assessments made, on camera, for "The Pozner File" by Arnold Zenker, described as a former television personality and one of the most successful media coaches in the country; Alex Beam, former Moscow correspondent for *Business Week;* and Marshall Goldman, head of Harvard's Russian Research Center.

ZENKER: Everything about Vladimir Pozner is made for that medium (television) . . . If you do what I do for a living, it's like being a violinist and watching Isaac Stern. You say, "Isn't that interesting, doesn't he do that well?" How does he carry that across? Little nuances, he makes what I call "gives," gives that don't cost him very much . . .

BEAM (commenting on my reaction to being asked if I was Jewish): Obviously, he handled the Jewish question very badly. In a sense, that's because of his training, which belies his pose as a spontaneous Soviet Joe . . .

NARRATOR (commenting on my being invited twice in a row on the Donahue show): Phil Donahue figures prominently in the Pozner strategy. His program gives Pozner a direct line to a vast block of middle America . . .

GOLDMAN: When we watch Pozner on television, what we have to keep in mind is that he has a line that he is trying to peddle. You just have to . . . Do you want to buy a car from that man? You have to keep asking yourself, "Am I prepared to take the warranty that he's presenting?" And for the most part, there are, you know, the horn may be working, but the tires may be flat. And you have to look at everything he says in that context.

Is there really all that much difference between Barinova and those gentlemen, between what the Leningrad Party Committee was trying to do and what WGBH actually did? Quite frankly, I don't think so.

Barinova and her organization are probably more honest in their intentions; they frankly admit that people have to be briefed. None of those quoted above, or WGBH, would ever come out and say the same.

To me, the message is clear. The ideological captains of the American media don't trust their people's ability to "correctly" make up their own minds any more than Soviet ideological commissars trust theirs.

I have been analyzed inside out. It has been an amazing experience that reflects the insecurity of those who have spent their lives breeding anti-Soviet stereotypes. They demonstrate a kind of paranoia that, expressed in the simplest terms (which they never do), boils down to this: if Americans see me as an ordinary human being, an honest *Soviet,* they will begin to question not only the stereotypes they have been taught but, even more dangerous, the cold war, the militaristic, anticommunist policies they have come to accept as necessary.

For years, Soviet spokesmen have appeared on American television. But they were not a source of concern because they fit the image. It was the accent, or the face, the manner of argument, whatever. And so, because they were so typically "Russian," their effectiveness in getting Americans to listen to what they were saying was extremely limited. Once they were seen as "Russian," they could say anything in the world, it didn't matter, because Russians were bad guys by definition. The only good Russians were the ones who defected—and the audience was carefully instructed on that matter before any such person appeared on the screen: "And now, here is that great fighter for human rights in the Soviet Union, a man who was warmly received yesterday by President Reagan, Anatoly Shcharansky."

The "bad Russky" image was the result of decades of ideological effort. From the 1918 cartoon of the Bolshevik beastly barbarian mentioned earlier to Ivan Drago, the image was burned into countless American minds, reinforced by rigid, dour Soviet spokesmen, and took on an additional and crucially important dimension. When a "Russian" spoke, the public knew they were listening to the bad guys, the liars, the evil ones. The medium was the message.

But Vladimir Pozner did not, does not fit the image. This guy is a Russian? Now that is really scary—to the right wing, especially. Even to some liberals. When I debated a Harvard scholar by the name of Daniel Yergin (that was in Toronto, in 1979), he insisted a little American flag be set in front of him on the table, while a small Soviet flag be put where I sat. Such was his fear that the audience might not realize who was who.

Since I don't fit the image, people sit up and *begin to listen.* It is not because they automatically trust me, far from it, but this Russian who sounds like an American makes them remove the ideological plugs from their ears. And that is what upsets the George Wills and Marshall Goldmans of the world. Because once people start listening, they just may come to the conclusion, seven decades of anti-Soviet propaganda notwithstanding, that at least some of what I say makes sense. That thought makes the ultraconservatives shudder. The only way to counter it is by explaining my presence in America as being part of a devious Soviet plot. Never mind that I was not allowed to travel to America until 1986, never mind that I was kept off Soviet television until that same year, never mind that there is no way I could ever have gotten on American television had it not been American television's initiative, never mind any and all logic.

During my first visit to America in nearly forty years, as I traveled around the country, I kept running into that mentality, that fear of admitting that I was legitimate, a human being with a point of view. It happened with Reed Irvine, the gentleman who heads Accuracy in Media, who became so flustered that, after calling me a liar on the air during a Koppel special, he had to admit he had "forgotten" what I had lied about. I saw how fear bred hatred and how hatred increased fear. I saw how Americans are manipulated just as much (but far more expertly) by a "free" press and a "democratic" government as Soviets have been by their "controlled" press and "totalitarian" government. I saw this, but it gave me no pleasure. I had not the slightest desire to say, "Hey, they are just as bad as we are!" All I experienced was sadness.

During the first days of my trip, I was buffeted by the storms of my emotions. It took me a while to trim my sails and regain balance. And when I did, the feeling of euphoria, of the dream come true gave way to the painful realization that I had not come home again, that home was neither here nor there, that home was inside me, in the people I loved, in my wife and my children. I grasped the truth that the America of my dreams was, finally, as different from reality as the Soviet Union of my teenage illusions.

I remember the sorrow of that knowledge rising up in me as I stood half a mile from the Golden Gate Bridge. It was on May 27, 1986, exactly one year to the day after my mother died here in San Francisco.

During the ten years after my father's death, she had gradually lost interest in life. She went out, of course, visited friends, she even traveled.

But her only real joy was to be with Paul, who continued to live in the same apartment with her, with me, and with her granddaughter Kathrin. In 1982, or thereabouts, she was diagnosed as having an aneurysm of the aorta. The doctors said surgery was possible, but her heart might fail. When I asked her whether she wanted to have the operation, she said no, she would live as long as her body allowed her to and go when the time came. The time came when she was visiting our friends, Dulce and Michael Murphy, in San Francisco. She died in Dulce's arms quickly and painlessly, the only good thing that can be said about an aneurysm's bursting.

I remember the phone call that woke me up in Moscow on the morning of May 28th—Kathrin's birthday—and Dulce's voice telling me the news.

Isn't it amazing that death shocks us? Birth doesn't, yet death is as natural as birth. I know my mother is dead. I acknowledge the fact. But I refuse to accept it as normal.

Two weeks after mother's death, I received a letter from a man who had been in love with her, who had, I think, loved her all his life. I had known him when we were living in America, I had seen him again when we were living in Berlin. He had always seemed to be a gentle, kind, and intelligent person. But he was (and still is) much more than that—as his letter made me realize. I don't think anyone could ever have described her as well as he did. I certainly cannot. So I have chosen to take the easy way out and to have you part with her as I did—by reading the letter. I omit only what is addressed directly to me and does not involve her.

"I knew your mother for about fifty years and said good-bye to her several times with the thought that we would never see each other again: in New York in the late thirties, when she went back to Paris with your father; in 1948, when she left the United States (she was in bad shape that time, disturbed by the pressures and dangers of the times and of the choices that had been forced on her); in Berlin in 1952; in Paris during one of the visits she made there with your father; in Florence, where I went to see her after your father's death (she was visiting Lola together with Toto); and finally, in Rome a few years ago, when I put her on the train for Paris after a visit she had made with me. So—over that almost-a-lifetime—I saw her changing, growing older and weaker (the blows were many: there were more violent upheavals in her life than she was equipped to handle) and more frail. It is a wonder to me that she lasted as long as she did. It wouldn't have been a surprise if she had given up sooner.

"In the thirties ('36–'37?), she was gay and full of life, courageously making her way on her own—a bachelor girl with a little boy (your father was in Paris and they had not yet decided to make a life together). She had a zest for life and the courage to explore and enjoy it. She was sexy (children find it hard to think of their mother as having once been sexy) and I had an adolescent crush on her. That romantic feeling I had about her (nothing ever came of it) colored my thoughts about her ever after. Even when I saw her the last time, frail and frightened, there was still a trace of that aura about her. It came to life in an occasional remark, a laugh, a flashing gleam in her eyes. Life had been hard on her, very hard, but it hadn't quite crushed the spark that attracted me so long.

"But the hard times didn't come until long after our first meeting. She had some good years in Paris, and then back in the USA during the war and immediately afterwards. There was a struggle to make a living when she and your father got to the USA (my family helped them get there, when they escaped to Spain from German-occupied France), but they managed without much difficulty (your mother was strong and resourceful then). Then there were years when the money rolled in: Paul was born into relative luxury in a house just off Fifth Avenue and had a nanny to look after him, and your mother bloomed. She was in her element, and her element was French-American bourgeois well-being and culture—a world of stylish clothes, the latest novels and art shows, entertaining friends and business connections at dinner or in restaurants, a summer house at the beach filled with relatives and young children (the biggest crises were an over-cooked roast or a child's sore throat). The big dramas were occasional family quarrels. Your father's sisters never quite accepted your mother. They rather looked down their noses at her because she didn't have their strength or education and because she didn't have a career that would bring credit to *them.*

"That lack of appreciation (love?) wounded her. I think there was in your mother's childhood experiences something that left her vulnerable and fearful. Your aunts' criticism of her she resented, but somehow she felt it was deserved. She was *not* as tough and as brilliantly capable as they were. There was, as a result, a crack in your mother's defenses—a crack that was to widen with the blows that were to come.

"Then, as they say in America (as they used to say) the 'shit hit the fan.' The Cold War began. Your father was a Soviet citizen and the US government cracked down on him: phone tapping, surveillance, blacklisting, and finally expulsion (just how this last came about I don't remember.

The message of the authorities was clear, however). Your mother wasn't made for this kind of warfare. She didn't have the political understanding or conviction that would have helped her stand up to this persecution. At bottom, she felt that she was being unfairly, unjustly punished for something she hadn't done. She couldn't fight back. She didn't know how. Nor did she have anything to fight with. Whatever self-confidence she had once had was eroded by the bullying, sarcastic treatment to which she was frequently subjected by her husband and his sisters. Her nerves began to feel the strain and to show signs of giving way.

"I saw them in New York about this time (by then I was based on the West Coast) and tried to set up an educational film business with your father (his former partner and the movie company he had worked with for years were frightened of having anything to do with him). That didn't work out. But occasionally I baby-sat with your mother when your father went out on business. That was the first time I saw the fear that was to become chronic: a fear that probably had its origins in early childhood; perhaps she had been at some time abandoned.

"When New York became impossible, they (your mother and father) decided to go back to France. Now a new catastrophe struck. Your father was denied entrance. He was a Red! And the USA had blackened his name with the French authorities.

"If your mother was to return to France, it would have to be without her husband. A choice was in the air. On the one hand was a French citizenship of which she couldn't be deprived: a bourgeois, comfortable way of life, but without her husband, the struggle to work and on her own raise the children (there was no thought of her *not* raising the children). On the other hand was the unknown, war-devastated Soviet Union: material hardship, language (she didn't have a word of Russian), complete dependence and helplessness (she couldn't work because of the language barrier), separation forever from her sisters and friends (so it seemed in those dark cold war days). The choice was too difficult. She cracked somewhere deep down, but she made a decision. (I should say here that she never discussed this with me. I'm guessing as to what took place.) The family (probably the welfare of the children played the most important role in determining her decision) came first. So she went along with her husband and the children to the Strange Dark Continent.

"She got no warm reception from the Russians. On the contrary. The pressures built up. Job (your father found it extremely difficult to get work in his field at the level for which he was trained); housing problems (the police told them to get out of Moscow); lack of friends and family; the problems of the children's adjusting to a totally different society and different standard of living. Somewhere in these months, perhaps after the move to Berlin (yet another language, another adjustment, another isolation) your mother had a nervous breakdown that required hospitalization.

"But there was a strong, resilient core in her. I take my hat off to her. She pulled herself together and buckled down. The problems of raising the children, of getting enough of the right kind of food and clothes . . . these difficulties helped involve her in living: otherwise she might have drifted off and out of this world.

"It was shortly after this that we saw each other in Berlin . . .

"Your mother had a steel front tooth, the sight of which shocked me. She was vain of her beauty. It was what she thought to be her most valuable asset. To have a naked steel chunk in the front of her mouth must have been a terrible blow. It symbolized the brutal changes to which she had been subjected. Adversity hadn't changed her, though. She was still oriented toward clothes and beautiful objects and good food: so were all the other people in the [Soviet] compound, to my surprise. Your mother was amused and condescending about the taste levels of her neighbors: the insatiable survivors of the Great War, avidly collecting dishes, furniture, artificial flowers, pianos! Your mother didn't join the hunt. It was beneath her. She remembered only too vividly the styles of New York and Paris. Later, I think, she tried weakly, but without enthusiasm, to imitate the others. She had to learn not to stand out as being too different. It was camouflage to help her survive. Her heart really belonged elsewhere, however. Paris . . . New York . . . Washington.

"Next meeting. Paris. Your father was with her, so it must have been about twelve years ago. She cooked a lovely lunch. I stopped off to see them in Paris on a flight from London to Rome, and both your father and mother talked and talked, telling me about what had happened in the years between our last meeting, which had been in Berlin, in 1951. There were difficult times. Very difficult. Your father was bitter. He had a right to be, having given up a good, prosperous way of life for his ideals; and then, in the end, he felt he had been very shabbily treated. Betrayed. Your mother, who had never had any roots in or hopes for your father's homeland, had no such feelings. She had expected shabby treatment, and had been pleasantly surprised that things were no worse than they were. Perhaps her struggles to get along as a young girl in Paris and in the USA on her own in the Thirties had prepared her for the daily grind of worry about job, housing, food supplies, nice clothes. She seemed to have enjoyed the contest with the System—a contest in which she had done better than most. She no longer compared her standard of living with that which she would have had in America or Paris, but with that of the people around her in Moscow. And by those standards she was more than Keeping Up. And her work gave her satisfaction, too. Most meaningful of all, however, was her satisfaction in her sons' achievements. I believe it was the security she derived from that that provided the core of her identity. And it was that hard-won identity that impressed me. She came with me when I went back to the air terminal late that afternoon—she wanted to see me off. Again we didn't know if we would meet again, but it had been wonderful to make contact after more than twenty years of not having seen or even written to each other, and her making the trip with me was an act of friendship and an expression of the meaningfulness of our meeting.

"After that we saw each other twice: after your father's death, in Florence; and in Rome, when she stayed with me. By then, without your father's presence and support (she needed him because, as I said before, because there was a crack in her ego, a hole in her self-confidence), she was frightened of the world and I felt that by travel and seeing old friends, she was trying to fill the hole—to reassure herself that she had a meaningful existence. It was a battle against old age, ill health, and loss of the identity that marriage and family life had given her. And the battle went on. She was incredibly brave, I think.

"And she had, at times, remarkable insight about herself. She wrote to me, in replying to the letter of condolence she had received from me after your father's death, something like this: 'A friend once said of me that my life was like that of a goldfish in a bowl. I have never forgotten that remark.' And I have never forgotten it either.

"Why am I writing this long letter? . . . Well, I can't put flowers on her grave, wherever it is. This is a bouquet for her that I am sending to you. I think she would have approved. In any case, I hope what I have written will add to your understanding of your parents and, thus, in the long run, add to your understanding of yourself."

There are some minor mistakes. Not all the dates are correct. My father was not expelled from America, although circumstances forced him to leave. Nor did the letter shed any additional light on what I already knew about my parents. But it is one of the finest, most insightful, most loving portraits of my mother. If it were a painting, I would hang it on my study wall. As a letter, I keep it on my desk within easy reach.

Thinking about my mother when I was in San Francisco, I couldn't help wondering how *she* had found America when she revisited it after so many years, what *her* reaction had been to this country where she had lived from 1934 to 1939, and then again, from 1940 to 1948. What were *her* impressions?

My own opinion is based on my upbringing in America—the things I saw and lived firsthand—and on many years of study and thought. I believe it is impossible to understand the changes in the United States (as well as what went on in the Soviet Union) without recognizing the magnitude of the cold war's impact.

If any single event changed and then shaped the course of my life, that event was the cold war. It forced my parents to leave America. It did not allow them to return to France. It precipitated my father's acceptance to work for the Soviet government in East Germany and then move to the USSR. Had there been no cold war, my life would have taken a completely different direction and I would be a very different person.

Similarly, the United States and the Soviet Union—in fact, all countries—were shaped by cold war policies.

I do not propose to talk about who is to blame for the cold war. I will only say that I do not subscribe to the black/white mythologies of the time, still pervasive in some circles, that either a "global imperialist conspiracy" or a "world communist conspiracy" was the cause. The issue I am raising has to do with the consequences of the hostile, bipolar world that emerged.

No nation can wage war without a tremendous effect on its national psyche. War means enemies, a life-and-death struggle, a hardness of mindset quite different from normal times. To the extent they exist in a given society, democratic freedoms, dissent, the questioning of government policy are necessarily circumscribed in the struggle for national survival.

The cold war was aptly named. It contained all of these elements. But unlike any hot war of modern times, it lasted *forty years.*

In the Soviet Union we have only recently begun to understand the profoundly negative impacts that four decades of cold war pressures have had on our society. This "war" in many ways brought out the worst tendencies of Soviet society, playing into the hands of its most repressive, paranoic elements, stunting the development of the humanistic, democratic principles socialist and communist philosophy are based on. It stifled any and all open questioning of where we were headed as a country. Questions, criticism, and doubt were tantamount to "supporting the enemy." And, given the hard political realities of a bipolar world, there was a modicum of truth in the charge. Our economy, our media, our education, even our most basic social values—all were warped by the perpetual political warfare with the West. In foreign policy, our declared commitment to social justice and international law was likewise affected. In Eastern Europe, in Afghanistan, and elsewhere, cold war realities and psychology led the Soviet Union into what might be qualified as a quasi-colonial mind-set, where small nations were viewed as pawns in a super-power chess game. In many respects, at home and abroad, the results have been disastrous. And it is no coincidence that our coming to grips with these disasters—and the psychology that spawned them—was tied to re-thinking the cold war.

I believe that the cold war has affected the United States virtually the same way; and with very little rewriting, the above paragraph would fit very well. But being a far richer, more powerful country, America has been able to absorb more harm without feeling it, and it has yet to confront the full spectrum of what the cold war has done to its quality of life, its humanitarian traditions and democratic values.

Were it not for the cold war, would there have been a McCarthy era, with its still-visible scars prescribing the limits of the "acceptable political debate"? Would 35,000 Americans have died in Korea and 50,000 in Vietnam, along with two million Vietnamese? Would such vicious dicta-tors as Marcos, Franco, Somoza, and Pinochet have received American support? I think not.

In 1948, when I was still living in New York, President Truman signed a bill into law, the preamble of which stated that it was the right of every American to live in decent housing. Four decades later, the realization of that commitment to a basic human right seems to be reced-ing. Lyndon Johnson's War on Poverty was nothing more or less than a casualty of the cold war. The deprivation of urban ghettos, the erosion of the public education system, the spiraling epidemic of drug addiction are known to all Americans. Would any Americans strongly disagree with the view that these affronts to the American sense of decency would not exist in their present form, would not be tolerated, were it not for decades of cold war military spending and an outlook that accepted as truth that the struggle with world communism was more vital than the basic needs of American society?

I do not think that a fair assessment can escape the conclusion that both the United States and the Soviet Union paid a terrible price—eth-ically as well as economically—for the cold war.

*   *   *

I must say I found a disquieting similarity between the kind of leadership we had in the Soviet Union before Gorbachev and the kind I found in Reagan's America. The same aggressiveness, the same arrogance, the same ignorance. That both systems have been able to survive, regardless of the quality of their leadership, is a left-handed compliment to their vitality.

It may be said that we see and hear only what we want to see and hear, that we phase out whatever contradicts our ideological mindsets. American right-wingers visiting the Soviet Union find evidence everywhere of people suffering from totalitarian oppression. American left-wingers come across only evidence of the opposite nature. Soviets who visit the United States with the thought of emigrating see only a land of wealth and opportunity for all, while others see nothing but the homeless. We all have our biases. I certainly have mine. So when I say that I didn't come to America with the secret hope that my political beliefs would be supported by what I found, I realize the suspect nature of that statement. Nevertheless, it is true. The sight of poverty amid American wealth, of abject misery amid scandalous affluence, didn't make me rub my hands with glee.

My homecoming was bittersweet.

The sweetness was in being there. In revisiting my childhood. In standing in front of 24 East Tenth Street, looking at the first- and second-floor windows, and in my mind's eye going back forty years and seeing us all—my mother and father, my dog Jouk, my infant brother Paul, my beloved Julia—living a life that seemed so distant as almost to never have been. The sweetness was in hearing "Noo Yawk," asking for and eating a frank with the works, jogging in Central Park and stopping to listen to two violinists playing Vivaldi's double concerto; the sweetness was in going out to Yankee Stadium and watching a ball game, in sitting on the steps of St. Pat's, in crossing over and watching those exhibitionists skate in Rockefeller Plaza. There was plenty of sweetness, more than I could tell you, enough to fill the heart. The unlikely sweetness of the Fulton Fish Market, which stank but smelled better to me than Opium, Poison, or Chanel No. 5, the Fulton Fish Market with its gulls, and spars, and warehouses, and fish restaurants, and cobblestones, and a million and a half other things that don't mean anything to anyone except someone who was a twelve-year-old kid and who used to come down here when it really was a market and take pictures with his first Kodak camera and pretend that here is where all the pirates docked their ships, here is where the buccaneers and the privateers sailed from, here is where all adventure began, with the tangy ocean smell hard in your nostrils, and here is where it all ended when you sailed back into port after circling the world.

I didn't come looking for the sweet. It was there, waiting for me. As was the bitter.

The cops patrolling Washington Square on the lookout for dope peddlers. Kids lining up in the doorways of crack houses in the Village. The stench of urine heavy in the air, and people sleeping on benches and on the sidewalks in Tompkins Square. Bitterness in the faces of a forgotten America, an America written off by corporate capitalism's ethic.

Sitting in the lounge and waiting for the early morning express that would whisk me from New York to D.C., I watched as one man, obviously under the influence of wine or drugs, giggled and laughed madly, pointing his finger here, there, and nowhere at some spectacle only he could see, inviting everyone else to join the fun. Finally, after a few more laughs, he took off his coat, rolled it up, pillowlike, and laid his head on it. He was instantly asleep, his face—very Hispanic with its white skin and black mustache and pointed beard—now calm, no longer contorted, and so displaying the fine features of what had once been a strikingly handsome head. He lay there on the bench, his torso almost at right angles to his legs, which hung down and rested on the floor. Then another man approached, a black man dressed in what clearly were secondhand clothes. Tall and lanky, he too was drunk or drugged. He gesticulated wildly, spreading his arms wide and bowing, moving in a series of shrinking circles that finally brought him up to the sleeping man. He sat down next to him and gave him a tentative shove with one finger. Getting no reaction, he pushed a little harder. Again, nothing. He then gave the coat a tug. And another one. The man's head slipped down onto the bench. The black man got up, spread his arms, and took a bow, as if to say, "See what I've done?" He then picked up the coat, rolled it up even tighter, stuck it under his arm, and, with a sly grin on his face, sidled out of the lounge. The beggar stealing from the poor man.

There must have been at least fifty people who saw that scene. They watched it out of the corners of their eyes, holding their magazines, morning papers, pocket books in front of their faces. They never said a word. It didn't concern them. Those two men came from a different and dangerous world, a world that, somehow, was not quite American as far as they were concerned.

For some reason, the scene made me think of the Nebraska farmer who had visited my home in Moscow some years ago with a group of

American high-school students he had latched on to after losing his own group in the Kremlin. We had been discussing problems of Soviet agriculture when he shared the following story. "I'm a farmer," he said, "and every year I burn some of my crops, some of my harvest. What we call the excess. I do that because the government pays me not to produce more than a certain amount. I know there are hungry people in my own country who could use that produce. I'd be glad to give it to them. What's the sense of planting and weeding and harvesting if you're going to destroy part of your own labor? But I can't give it away. If I do, the government will cut me off. If I produce too much, prices will go down. That'll hurt me, hurt the economy—at least, that's what they say. So I destroy food that hungry people need. If that's what America is about, I sure wish it would find a way to change."

Bitter thoughts.

When I boarded the Aeroflot plane that was to take me back to Moscow, I was elated at my own desire to return . . . home! To my family, to the place that I loved, to the land that fate had put me in. Yes, I was elated, for I had feared that the reality of my dream—returning to America— would make me captive. It hadn't. Now, when the great jet picked up speed, lifted off, and began its long climb, now, when I saw New York below me, when, once again, the city of my love made my heart beat faster, I knew mine would always be a bittersweet parting and arrival, regardless of my destination.

I had come to terms with being part of two societies, two countries, both of which I love, both of which I work for.

I could finally write the book I had wanted to and unsuccessfully tried to write for so many years.

9

Parting with Illusions

I thought this last chapter would be a review of arguments: "Ladies and gentlemen of the jury, I believe system A to be better/worse than system B, and here is why." I would then present the statistics, the facts, the statements to prove my case.

I thought I would examine the raucous chorus that has been demanding that we interpret perestroika and all the events that have accompanied it as the demise of Marxism and Leninism, as the death of communism.

I thought I would call people's attention to the so-called choice between prosperity and social justice, the illusory belief that social security and justice are bad for economic growth, the proposition that to be fairer means being poorer, that there must be a trade-off between economic equity and economic efficiency. I thought I would show such "profound wisdom" for what it really is: a smoke screen, camouflage for greed.

I also thought I would ask a question. If you are presented with a blueprint but decide to ignore it, or even do the opposite of what it calls for, should you blame its author if your building collapses? With that in mind, I would also ask is socialism to blame if those who claimed to have built it refused to follow the precepts of its architect, creating a gargoyle instead?

These were some of the things I thought this last chapter would be about.

I was wrong. For this book is not about which is the better system. Rather, it concerns one human being's search for truth, one person's preoccupation with the global human condition, one man's belief that, as

Sweet Charity once sang, "There's gotta be something better than this!"

On the closing day of the First Congress of People's Deputies in June 1989, I, along with the entire Soviet nation, along, perhaps, with a billion or more people around the world, watched what was in effect the grand finale of what had been a tragedy/drama/comedy of Shakespearian proportions. An old man, but not as old as he looked, stood resolutely at the lectern demanding that he be allowed to address the assembly—some two thousand citizens who, like himself, had been elected to the country's supreme legislative body. He had asked for fifteen minutes, a request greeted with catcalls, cries of "Nyet! Nyet!" from what distinctly seemed like the majority.

The man was Andrei Sakharov.

He spoke. And since what he had to say was predictably critical of what the First Congress had achieved and not achieved, since, as always, his wording was blunt and undiplomatic, the aggressive majority, as the more conservative part of the assembly has come to be called, began to clap. This action has given birth to a new expression, "to clap down," that is, to drown a speaker's words in rhythmic applause that hinders him from speaking and functions as a contradiction in terms: applause *against* what is being said. Speaker after speaker had been clapped down by that aggressive majority. Now their goal was to force Sakharov to step down.

That tactic had worked in most cases. But this was something else. The clappers were dealing with a man who had faced the party apparatus and the state machine and who had refused to flinch, a man who had willingly given up more than any of the clappers had ever dreamed of having.

For several years, my wife and I have rented a small summer cottage in Zhukovka, a village situated some twenty-five kilometers from Moscow. It is, however, not only a village. It might be said that Zhukovka is really much more of a rural resort for many of the country's high and mighty, past and present, than it is a village. In addition to just plain Zhukovka, the place name one sees as one drives past this scenic spot on the Rubliovo-Uspensky highway, there exists Zhukovka-One, Zhukovka-Two, and Zhukovka-Three, enclaves hidden behind high fences where the privileged elite are rented country homes at unbelievably low prices. In addition to these state-owned facilities, there are private homes, or rather mansions. A ten-minute walk from our cottage will bring you to an alley lined by homes belonging to the Brezhnev family, to the cellist Rostropovich (who allowed Solzhenitsyn to live there and write). There also stand the brick buildings that Stalin presented as gifts to the scientists who had contributed to the creation of the Soviet Union's nuclear arsenal. Sakharov was among them, a scientist who had been awarded the country's most coveted title, Hero of Socialist Labor, awarded not once, not twice, but a staggering three times. Not surprisingly, he too had been given a mansion for his labors. It stood and stands as a symbol to the kind of extreme privileges he enjoyed and relinquished, as a testimony to what he gave up because of his principles.

This was not a man who could be clapped down.

And as we all watched, riveted to our television sets, we saw him facing the hostile majority, raising his voice above the tumult, waving his arms as if to push back the wall of sound coming at him from the hall, saying what he had come to say, demanding that the delegates, the country, the whole world listen.

It was a scene I will never forget. A scene full of symbolism and addressing many issues.

It addressed the issue of the human capacity to prevail. No matter what. In spite of the most adverse circumstances.

It addressed the issues of integrity and honesty. You can bury them under layers of dirt, you can pour concrete over them, you can lower them into the deepest mine shafts, freeze them in polar ice, you can burn them in ovens and gas them. They remain unconquerable.

It addressed, most directly, the issue of what is happening in the Soviet Union.

Simón Bolívar, as he was dying, is reported to have said, "Those who serve the revolution plow the sea." The power of the imagery takes my breath away. What could possibly be more futile than to plow the sea? Is revolution really nothing but foam, a swell that subsides and merges with the vast expanses of the sea of history?

We have very little to go on in our search for the answer to that crucial question, for modern history has given us only a handful of revolutions. France, Russia, China, Cuba . . .

What about America, you ask? The events of 1776 were no revolution, for the American people did not rise up in fury against *their own* rulers, their own government, which is what revolutions are all about. The American people rose up against a tyrant, they rose up for their independence from a *foreign* potentate. Theirs, in present-day terms, was a war of liberation, a thought that prompts me to wonder whether today's United States of America would support George Washington and his Continental

Army? I tend to believe it wouldn't, that it would side with Great Britain, just as it has consistently supported the most conservative regimes in their battles against their own people. But I have strayed from my subject.

Revolution is, at best, an unhappy event. It is an act of desperation, the final option. People don't rise up in anger, don't risk their well-being and lives until they have been pushed to the limits of their endurance. Revolutions upset the old institutions, turn societies inside out. They split nations, turning father against son, brother against brother. But they do this in the name of the most noble of all goals: the ultimate happiness of humankind, for that is the undeniable driving force of all revolutions. They are led by dreamers who are motivated by love and compassion for others. These men never start out as power-hungry dictators, yet that is often how they end. In that sense, it could be argued that all revolutions ultimately fail. And, in the short term, that view is not absurd.

Robespierre, the purest spirit of the French revolution of 1789, a man who called for the abolition of capital punishment, wound up wallowing in the blood of the Terror he had begun. The revolution itself, born with the words "Liberté, égalité, fraternité" on its lips, produced from its womb none other than Napoleon, an emperor, a man who set out to conquer the world. When Napoleon was finally disposed of, he was replaced by another Bourbon king. Was that what the people of France had fought and died for? Was that what the revolution had been about? Of course not. And so, in the short term, it is true that the revolution failed. But in the long term, it triumphed. In the long term, it led to the creation of the French Republic, it fired the world's imagination, it stimulated thoughts and dreams. It took time and more uprisings (as failed revolutions are usually called). But the promise of 1789 was indeed realized— about a century later. The revolution set something into motion, something that would not, could not travel a straight path, something with a secret momentum of its own that, initially, seemed fatally flawed but that finally prevailed.

The Russian revolution of November 1917 proposed to go much further than liberty, equality, and brotherhood. It proposed to create a society where there would be no haves and have-nots, where the ruled would be the rulers, where greed would have no place because wealth would no longer be a goal or have a social value. The men who led the revolution had the best intentions in the world. Granted, perhaps not all of them did. Granted, each of them had their limits. But to depict them, one and all, as a group of scheming fanatics who forced their views down the throat of an entire nation—what a simplistic view of history. And what a pessimistic one, for it bespeaks the belief that you can indeed fool most of the people most of the time—and the majority of the Soviet nation supported both the revolution and, later, Stalin. Why? one might ask. How could a majority of the people back this ogre, this demon, for so many years? Those are good questions, and they demand good answers.

If Stalin had been the person of today's political cartoon, he could never have been an entire nation's idol. There *must* have been something more, something else. I could formulate what it was in my own words, but I prefer to cede the floor to one of the Soviet Union's harshest critics— Alexander Zinoviev. A brilliantly erudite scholar and philosopher, a man whose peasant roots enrich his sophisticated analysis of his country with earthy common sense and a zesty, biting humor, Zinoviev became an overnight celebrity when his book, *Yawning Heights,* was published in the West in 1976. Because of it, he was fired and stripped of his academic titles and rank. In 1978, he was told he had the choice of either leaving the USSR or being incarcerated and exiled. With a wife and a daughter to support, it was an offer he couldn't refuse. Expelled from his own country, he was then stripped of his Soviet citizenship. He now lives in West Germany.

I furnish these data to underscore Zinoviev's impeccable credentials as an anti-Stalinist. In August 1989, he was interviewed by the *Moscow News,* one of print media's most pro-perestroika publications, and asked why he had, in certain remarks quoted in the western press, seemingly justified part of what Stalin had done. Here is his answer:

"I became an anti-Stalinist when I was sixteen. *Now,* of course, every-one is an anti-Stalinist. But I, adhering to the rule that the dead cannot be my enemies, changed the orientation of my critique of reality. I began to study the Stalin period as a scientist. And came to the conclusion that, no matter what, it was a great period. It was horrible, tragic. Countless crimes were committed during that time. But the period as a whole was not criminal. If one approaches history from the criterium of morality and law, then it must all be conceived as a crime. I do not justify the horrors of the Stalin period. I only defend its objective assessment. And I despise those who today make their fortunes criticizing a past that neither threatens them, nor can defend itself. As they say, even a donkey can kick a dead lion. About collectivization. I know what a kolkhoz is, I worked in one. My mother was a kolkhoz member for sixteen years, she went through all the horrors of collectivization. But to her dying day she kept a picture of

Stalin in her copy of the New Testament. Why? Thanks to collective farms her children were able to leave the village and partake of contemporary urban life. One son became a professor, another the director of a large industrial plant, the third a colonel in the army, the remaining three all became engineers. The same kind of story applies to millions of other Russian families. The collective farms, while a tragedy, nevertheless freed millions of people from the trammels of private property and from the stupidity of village existence."

One may argue that, had there been no Stalin, that peasant woman and her six sons would have had a better life. Perhaps that is true. In fact, it is almost certainly true. But it means less than nothing to that individual woman who was, like over 70 percent of the population, illiterate, condemned to live as a beast of burden and to see her six sons do the same, yet whose entire existence was transformed by Stalin's collectivization. No wonder she saw him as a saint, someone who had performed a miracle, who could do no wrong.

And what about her six sons? Well, one became an outspoken and outstanding critic of the Soviet system, but he is hardly typical. What is typical is what happened to him, his brothers, and so many others. And that is what makes the issue so complex, so much harder to grasp, so impossible to write off as an aberration. In the past, Americans took justifiable pride in a system where "anyone" could become president, "anyone" reflecting not only the revolutionary view that all men are created equal, but also the period when the United States was in a phase of active development, industrial expansion. In the Soviet Union, virtually all the leaders of the nation are the sons and daughters of those who tilled the land and mined the coal—and their rise to power primarily began under Stalin.

According to Euclidean geometry, the shortest distance between any two points is a straight line. But that axiomatic truth does not apply to Lobachevsky's geometry, which opened a new era in our understanding of space. History is far more multidimensional than any geometrician ever imagined. What kind of a line connects the Second Congress of Soviets, addressed by Lenin on the day after the Bolshevik revolution, November 8, 1917, with the First Congress of People's Deputies, addressed by Sakharov on June 9, 1989? The line zigs and zags, but it has a logic, incomprehensible as it may seem.

It makes no sense to judge a historic period on the basis of "what if?" What if Stalin had died of the flu when he was five years old? What if Lenin hadn't been so badly wounded by a would-be assassin in 1918 and hadn't died so early? What if? As the Russians say, "If it were all ifs and maybes, mushrooms would grow in your mouth, and it would be not a mouth, but a vegetable garden."

The illusion that revolution is the shortest path from what your society is to what it should be is precisely that: an illusion. The destructive force of a revolution is initially more powerful than its creative potential. Revolution denies due process, and the price of that denial is high. In a way, it is like the difference between dynamiting an old house or methodically tearing it down. The first seems clearly to be the faster way. One big, spectacular Bang! and the whole thing comes tumbling down. But it also goes flying off in different directions, shattering a window here, dropping bricks on some hapless heads there, spreading a cloud of dust all over— and when that dust finally settles, we find that we cannot even begin to build the new, wonderful edifice of our dreams because of the mass of debris that must be removed, debris of such scope as we could not have imagined and for the removal of which we do not have the tools. And so we cart it away on makeshift stretchers, in wheelbarrows, we pass the broken bricks and chunks of masonry from hand to hand. And simultaneously, amid this chaos, we build. But what we build is nothing like what we had hoped for, nothing like the pictures we had drawn, for we had no idea of the conditions under which we would work. Our building is completed by trial and error, two floors up, one down, a slow, tortuous process.

What about evolution, the orderly method? It starts out being much slower. You put up a protective fence, you work behind an opaque plastic curtain. It seems to take ages. But then, one day, down comes the curtain, down comes the fence, and, oh wonder of wonders, the new building stands there looking exactly as it was supposed to look. And though it took much longer to tear the old one down, nobody got hurt in the process. What's more, the new building went up much faster.

But to believe that description is yet another illusion, for even the most cursory look at human development will show that evolution has been a process of endless painful struggle. Nothing has been achieved without enormous sacrifices, without pain. Evolution is not orderly.

Revolution is a kind of war, tough to make much sense out of from the trenches: all you see is the savagery and the bloodshed. But savagery and bloodshed are part of evolution as well. Revolution compresses centuries into decades, as was the case in Russia, and the tragedy of that process was evident precisely because it happened so quickly.

We are far more shocked by what occurred on Tiananmen Square than by the slow destruction of many more lives in the ghetto. Why? Because of the former's visibility, its drama. The ghetto creates an illusion of being less inhuman.

Revolution and evolution. The first is probably a product of the second. A product we might prefer to do without at times, but that is beside the point.

Parting with illusions is a painful process, for those illusions are drugs to our thought processes. They change our perception of reality—sometimes only slightly, like marijuana and cocaine, sometimes profoundly, like heroin and LSD. We become addicted to illusions, for they give pleasure. But when reality forces its way in, we discover that we are no longer capable of dealing with it. Like crack, illusions can kill.

Parting with illusions is painful because there is no medication, no rehabilitation center. You do it on your own, and you do it cold turkey. And because of the pain involved, some of us never do it. The pain is caused by doubting what seemed undeniable, by questioning what seemed sacred, by contemplating the possibility of being wrong.

Hard as it is for the individual, it is even harder for societies. And even more vital. A society based on illusions poses a terrible threat to all of its individual members, for it must in the end fall.

Sometimes, our daily existence so powerfully endorses our illusions that only the keenest minds are able to look down the road and around history's corner.

Imagine asking an Egyptian in the days of the pharaohs to question slavery's eternal character. Slavery had already existed for some three and a half thousand years, thirty-five centuries. How could anyone doubt what seemed to be the natural order of life? Or you could ask someone who lived during the ten centuries of feudalism whether he doubted that the monarch was anointed by God himself. You would have been considered mad to even think such a thought.

Like nature, human society has its laws and its flaws.

The Middle Ages were in many ways far more oppressive and left humanity a far poorer heritage than slave-owning Athens. But without the Middle Ages, there could have been no Renaissance.

Over the ages, humankind has evolved, and over the ages there has been a common dream of happiness. Whether it be the Hebraic Garden of Eden or the Avestan Yima's garden, whether it be the Sumerian Dilmun or Tep Zepi of Egypt, the Hellenic Golden Age or the Krita Yuga described in the *Mahabharata*, east and west, north and south, from the most primitive to the most sophisticated cultures, we all share the dream of a paradise, of a place where we all shall live happily ever after.

The spectacle of Andrei Sakharov standing his ground and speaking his mind gave me hope that, perhaps, out of the darkness, out of the pain, out of the turmoil and terror, out of the cruelty, but also out of the passion, out of the dreams, out of the heroism and the sacrifices, perhaps we are now witnessing the birth of something that will help us rediscover what humanity lost so many centuries ago but has never forgotten.

I could very well be wrong.

Regardless, I am confident that humankind will create a human world.

I have no illusions about being there to enjoy it.

I no longer harbor illusions about any one society's having a lock on the truth, having all the answers.

I no longer believe revolutions are shortcuts to a brighter future, even though revolutions cannot be denied.

I do not believe either property or ideology to be sacred, and to those who would destroy even a single human being in defense of either, I say, a plague on your house!

I believe, like Molière's Don Juan, that two and two make four, that four and four make eight, that man does not live by bread alone, but neither can man live without bread. I believe that creation is happiness, that self-expression is creation, that we create through work, and that work creates us.

The words quest and question are derived from a common root, they are bound together in our human destiny. We question our condition and thus continue our quest for the golden light that seems to shine beyond the horizon. That will never stop, and that is, finally, my only certainty.

In the words of Oliver Wendell Holmes, "Certainty is generally illusion, and repose is not the destiny of man."

Index

Index